SIXTH EDITION

AMERICA'S Musical LANDSCAPE

JEAN FERRIS

Emeritus Professor of Music
Arizona State University

McGraw Hill

Connect
Learn
Succeed™

Connect
Learn
Succeed™

Published by McGraw-Hill, an imprint of The McGraw-Hill Companies, Inc., 1221 Avenue of the Americas, New York, NY 10020.

This book is printed on acid-free paper.

1 2 3 4 5 6 7 8 9 0 DOC/DOC 0 9

ISBN: 978-0-07-340140-9
MHID: 0-07-340140-4

Vice President, Editor in Chief: *Michael Ryan*
Publisher: *Christopher J. Freitag*
Development Editor: *Marley Magaziner*
Executive Marketing Manager: *Pamela Cooper*
Senior Production Editor: *Karol Jurado*
Production Service: *Melanie Field, Strawberry Field Publishing*
Manuscript Editor: *Jennifer Gordon*
Design Managers: *Margarite Reynolds, Allister Fein*
Cover Designer: *Kay Lieberherr*
Photo Research: *Poyee Oster*
Senior Production Supervisor: *Louis Swaim*
Media Project Manager: *Thomas Brierly*
Composition: *10/12 Times by Macmillan Publishing Solutions*
Printing: *PMS 273U, 45# New Era Matte Plus, RR Donnelley & Sons*

Cover image: *Famous Rock, Grand Canyon,* 2000 (oil on canvas).
Howard Ganz. © Howard Ganz/The Bridgeman Art Library/Getty Images

Library of Congress Cataloging-in-Publication Data

Ferris, Jean.
    America's musical landscape / Jean Ferris. — 6th ed.
        p. cm.
    1. Music—United States—History and criticism.   2. Music appreciation.   I. Title.
    ML200.F47 2010
    780.973—dc22

                                                                    2009023138

The Internet addresses listed in the text were accurate at the time of publication. The inclusion of a Web site does not indicate an endorsement by the author or McGraw-Hill, and McGraw-Hill does not guarantee the accuracy of the information presented at these sites.

www.mhhe.com

With gratitude to my publisher, to all the editors whose expert, creative, and friendly efforts made this text possible, and to Sony's Tom Laskey, whose outstanding CDs bring the music to our ears.

About the Author

Twenty years after completing a bachelor of music degree in music history and literature at the University of Michigan, I received an MA, also in music history, at Arizona State University, where I then taught music history and appreciation for the next twenty years. *Music: The Art of Listening* and *America's Musical Landscape* evolved for use in my classes, and I am delighted that other instructors have found them useful, too.

My interest in travel and in world cultures began early, encouraged by attending high school in Manila, Philippines, and later by living for nearly a year in Japan with my husband and our four children. I still travel extensively, and when home stay busy playing the piano, cooking, practicing yoga, reading, doing needlework, and of course writing. And there's always time to enjoy our twelve grandchildren!

Contents

3

Religious Music in the Colonial, Revolutionary, and Federal Periods   43

4

Secular Music in the Colonial, Revolutionary, and Federal Periods   59

PART 2
The Tumultuous Nineteenth Century   68

5

Religious Music in the Early Nineteenth Century   75

6
Popular Music of the Civil War Era   85

7
Concert Music   104

PART 3
The Growth of Vernacular Traditions   124

8
The Rise of Popular Culture   127

9
The Jazz Age   148

10
Jazz 1930–1960   165

11
Country Music   186

18
Music for Films   320

19
American Opera   337

PART 6
Tradition and Innovation
in Concert Music   352

20
Experimental Music:
Revolution   356

21
Early Twentieth-Century Mainstream Concert Music: Evolution   373

22
The Avant-Garde, Continued   387

23
The Recent Mainstream   399

Online Listening Examples

(Listening guides for the Online Listening Examples are at the Online Learning Center. The music may be available at YouTube or other sites, or in most cases may be purchased very reasonably from iTunes.)

Barber, Samuel: "Knoxville: Summer of 1915"

Beach, Amy Marcy Cheney: "The Year's at the Spring"

Braxton, Anthony: *92 + (30, 32, 139) + (108c, 108d) for Creative Orchestra*

Cage, John: *Aria* and *Fontana Mix*

Copland, Aaron: Variations on "Simple Gifts" from *Appalachian Spring Suite*

Cowell, Henry: "The Tides of Mananaun"

El cutilio

Gershwin, George: Concerto in F

Gershwin, George: *Rhapsody in Blue*

Gillespie, Dizzy: "Shaw 'Nuff"

Gottschalk, Louis Moreau: "Bamboula"

Ives, Charles: *The Unanswered Question*

"Jarabe tapatío" ("The Mexican Hat Dance")

Joplin, Scott: "A Real Slow Drag" from *Treemonisha*

MacDowell, Edward: "To a Wild Rose" from *Woodland Sketches*

Menotti, Gian-Carlo: "To This We've Come" from *The Consul*

Monroe, Bill: "It's Mighty Dark to Travel"

Reich, Steve: *Drumming*

Rodgers, Jimmie: "Daddy and Home"

Still, William Grant: *Afro-American Symphony*, first movement

Williams, Hank: "Your Cheatin' Heart"

Wills, Bob: "New San Antonio Rose"

Preface

The survey course for which this text is designed affords the same broad coverage of musics—classical and popular, secular and religious, vocal and instrumental—as does the traditional music appreciation course predominantly featuring European examples. Here we tackle the happy task of introducing basic musical terms and concepts using selected examples of outstanding American music.

As suggested in the title of the text, I have often related music to other arts, finding such comparisons to have pedagogical as well as aesthetic value for nonmusicians perhaps more familiar with visual and literary than with aural experience. Asher B. Durand's stunning landscape painting *Kindred Spirits* (p. 72), an eloquent portrayal of the nature poet William Cullen Bryant and the Hudson River School painter Thomas Cole sharing reverent admiration for their country's natural splendors, in fact inspired this text, which seeks to capture some of that painting's expression of the interdependence uniting American art and artists.

The musical landscape we explore stretches from the Pacific to the Atlantic coast between Canada and Mexico, and Hawaii—the areas comprising today's United States. Though influences abound from above and below the northern and southern borders, and though each of the many cultures of North, Central, and South America and Mexico has a rich American musical landscape of its own, time constrains most American music courses to cover only some of the music, of only certain regions, within the United States. Regret for what we cannot cover must encourage us to extend our exploration as soon and as far as possible throughout all of the Americas.

New to the Sixth Edition

- The proportion of *vernacular* to classical coverage has again been expanded.
- Less attention to early concert music allows more to *recent classical music, pop, rock, hip-hop,* and *jazz.*
- The discussions of *hip-hop* and of *modern music business* are more in depth.
- Several *new Listening Examples* add variety and appeal to the listening experience, and most of the *returning listening guides have been rewritten* to offer more detail than in previous editions.

- The *content has been reorganized,* according to helpful suggestions from reviewers using the text.
- The text-specific Online Learning Center at **www.mhhe.com/ferrisaml6** offers further supplemental material, including Online Listening Examples and Suggestions for Further Listening/Viewing/Reading, as well as multiple-choice and true/false quizzes, projects, and links to useful websites. While the websites may change from time to time, students will be well advised to form the habit of creatively checking the Internet as they study each chapter. Simply entering as keywords the name of a composer, a piece, or an instrument, for example, reveals information to further students' experience and understanding of every topic.

Special Features

- Prelude: Introduces basic technical information concerning texture, form, and notation. Students may browse through the Prelude at the beginning of a term and return to it readily to refresh their understanding as the concepts recur throughout the course. While instructors will differ in the emphasis they place on the Prelude, it's as essential a part of the text, and the course, as the prelude of a well-written music composition is to that work.
- Part Openers: As in the last edition, relevant social and cultural information appears before each section in Part Openers, available to those who find them valuable, but unobtrusive for those who choose to leave them out. The Part Openers are not intended as material to be absorbed for test purposes, but as enriching and thought-provoking information related to the music covered in that section. They set the context in which music was conceived and first experienced, and broaden students' perspective of music's place in the cultural environment.
- Part Summaries: These present terms and names with which students should have become familiar, much as they might appear in a concert program or a newspaper review.
- Effective Learning Tools: Terms to Review, Key Figures, Online Listening Examples, Suggestions for Further Listening, and Listening Examples provide students with extensive support to master the material and enhance their knowledge of American music. Critical Thinking questions prompt further inquiry by students.

Recordings

The three CDs accompanying the text offer students generous opportunity to apply their developing listening skills to representative selections of music. Restrictions imposed by recording companies often determine what we may and may not include; it is especially difficult to acquire permission to use current or even recent popular music. Of course students and/or instructors may wish to supplement class listening experiences with relevant examples from their personal collections; and the Internet offers innumerable opportunities to hear complete pieces or excerpts via computer. Listening guides for pieces listed as Online Listening Examples are included at the Online Learning Center, should instructors choose to assign or to play in class some of this music. Besides these options, two relatively new resources greatly expand the listening opportunities available to students today: YouTube, which offers viewing as well as listening experiences; and Apple's iTunes Store, where music from a generous collection can be downloaded for a modest fee.

Support for Instructors

For the instructor, we offer the following resources at the Online Learning Center:

- Instructor's manual
- Test Bank
- PowerPoint slides
- Online Listening Examples

I continue to be indebted to colleagues and friends whose expert advice assists me in improving this text and bringing it up-to-date. Particularly, I wish to thank my friend and outstanding jazz musician Dan Pinson for lending his expert ear to some of the jazz interpretations in this edition.

My editors for this project have all been particularly patient, helpful, supportive, and in every way magnificent. I must express profound gratitude especially to Marley Magaziner, development editor, who contributed enormously to the improvements in this edition; to Jennifer Gordon, copyeditor extraordinaire, whose sharp eyes and keen mind caught and corrected untold numbers of potential missteps; and to Melanie Field, whose skill and good nature in ushering us through the production process were simply phenomenal. Thank you all so much!

I am most grateful as well to the following prepublication reviewers, who shared valuable suggestions for improving the text based on their experiences using it: Kay Crouch, Caldwell Community College; Donat Lamothe, Assumption College; Robert Romanski, University of South Florida; Beth Smith, Virginia Highlands Community College; and David Thompson, Marian College of Fond du Lac.

Jean Ferris

Introduction

ost Americans today would find it difficult, perhaps impossible, to experience a day without music, so pervasive is the sound of music in our everyday lives. Music enhances many of our social, religious, and work-related experiences. Music sets rhythms for us to dance or exercise to, keeps us company at work or play, enhances our concentration and our emotional response when we are viewing a film or a musical, accompanies some religious services, helps us go to sleep at night, and makes it easier to wake up in the morning and to prepare for another day filled with the sounds we individually enjoy.

From the wide field of *popular* musics, we generally develop preferences for certain kinds, or styles, over others. That is, from the incredibly rich menu of sounds available today we might choose most often to hear rap, jazz, rock, country, pop—or something else. Some of us enjoy instrumental music; others prefer song. Our tastes change over long periods of time, and our preferences may differ from one moment to another, depending on our mood or circumstance at a given time.

The great world of *classical* music, as it is often called, also encompasses a tremendous range of sounds. Unfortunately, none of the terms generally used to distinguish between the music we call popular and the music we call classical is truly descriptive of the differences we recognize between them. We can agree that music that serves no functional purpose, but simply expresses an abstract concept a composer thought worth sharing—music that requires intense concentration and sometimes a measure of learning and experience on the part of the listener—differs from music that exists primarily as a means of entertainment. It is difficult, however, to describe differences between these two kinds of music without implying unintended and inappropriate judgments of value. Commonly we speak of music that requires extensive training on the part of composers and performers, and that may assume some guided experience on the part of the listener, as *classical, art, concert,* or *serious* music; but none of those terms properly distinguishes between this music and much of the music played by DJs on popular radio sites. No one is more *serious* about music than outstanding singer-songwriters in the popular fields. Many great American songs have survived beyond their days of initial popularity to become *classics* in their own right. *Concerts* are among the most important venues for experiencing so-called popular music of many kinds. And *art* suggests simply a creative means of expression, with no inherent requirement that it be simple or complex or even good. Further confusing the issue, many so-called classical pieces have become so familiar and well-loved that today they are performed in concerts we refer to as *pops.*

The terms italicized above, however, have become inherent parts of the language of music. You will hear and read them in formal and informal discussions of music, and we will use them in this text, although with sensitivity to the unintended connotations they have acquired. Words, after all, serve only to broaden our ideas about music and our knowledge of its history. No words can substitute for the glorious experience of hearing, and understanding, the great and beautiful musics of the United States.

The more we understand about musical forms and the elements that constitute the building materials of music, the better we are prepared to enjoy music of all kinds. Recognition of the historical context in which music was conceived, and an awareness of the relationships between music and the other arts of a given period, will enhance our understanding and our pleasure. It is my personal wish that your delight in listening to all kinds of music will increase immeasurably as you discover the many and varied aspects of America's musical landscape.

PRELUDE
Basic Properties of Musical Sound

Music, an art of organized sounds, is virtually limitless in variety and in the power to enchant and challenge our ears. However, because it never holds still, and we can neither see nor touch it, understanding music can be an elusive thing, and the world's greatest music may prove challenging to the unprepared listener.

The more we understand the qualities of music, the elements of which it is constructed, the historical-social setting in which a given piece evolved, the intent of the composer, and the contributions of the performer or performers, the greater will be our intellectual, emotional, and aesthetic rewards for listening to any kind of music. One can readily develop a sense of musical form, making it easier to enjoy a piece of some length. And while it is unnecessary to be able to read music in order to enjoy listening to it, some knowledge of how music is notated may be of interest even to the casual listener. The purpose of our Prelude, then, is to explain some basic concepts that may serve as a helpful introduction to your music experience, and to which you may refer for review throughout your course of study.

The Elements of Music

Musicians generally recognize four **elements of music**—rhythm, melody, harmony, and timbre—as the fundamental materials of which music is composed. As we listen to music, any one of the elements—a memorable tune, a driving rhythm, the unusual sound of an exotic musical instrument—may attract our attention; but more often we respond to the combination of two or more of the elements of music without methodically analyzing the name and proportions of each.

Understanding these building blocks of music enhances our listening and provides a vocabulary with which to discuss a piece in some detail. Further, listening with *awareness* of what we hear greatly increases our capacity to enjoy all kinds of music.

Rhythm Because music consists of arrangements of long and short sounds and silences, **rhythm,** having to do with time relationships in music, is the most basic of the elements. The system of music notation used in the Western world indicates the rhythm of music by giving the *proportional* length of each

1

TABLE 1	Rhythmic Notation			

This table assumes that the quarter note equals 1 beat. Any other note value may equal 1 beat instead, the number of beats per other note values changing proportionately.

Notated Symbol	Name	Rest	Number of Beats per Note	Number of Notes Equal to 4 Beats
𝅝	Whole note	–	4	1
𝅗𝅥	Half note	–	2	2
♩	Quarter note	𝄽	1	4
♪	Eighth note	𝄾	½	8
𝅘𝅥𝅯	Sixteenth note	𝄿	¼	16

sound and silence; that is, written music dictates the duration of each sound or silence only in relation to other sounds and silences in the piece.

Rhythmic values are expressed in the familiar terminology of fractions (Table 1): the value of a *half note,* for example, is equal to half the value of a *whole note.* But the specific duration of a half note depends upon the **tempo,** or rate of speed, at which the music is performed. *Tempo,* which means "time," is one of many Italian words adopted into a virtually universal music language during the sixteenth and seventeenth centuries, when Italians dominated music in the Western world. Foreign musicians studying in Italy absorbed the techniques and much of the terminology of their Italian masters, which they shared with their own students and patrons upon returning to their homelands. Since then, many Italian music terms have been used all over the world, remaining in common use today.

Music listeners quickly become familiar with the most common Italian words for tempos, shown in Table 2, which regularly appear in printed concert programs and often also in newspaper reviews of concerts and recordings.

Meter Just as language is formed of irregularly occurring accented and unaccented syllables, musical sounds, too, may occur without specific rhythmic organization. If, however, musical sounds are arranged in rhythmic patterns, similar to those of poetry as opposed to prose, we say the music is metered.

Meter organizes rhythm into units called *measures,* each containing a particular number of pulses, or beats. The common meters are *duple* (two beats per measure), *triple* (three beats per measure), and *quadruple* (four beats per measure). In Western practice—that is, in music based on European traditions of the seventeenth through the nineteenth centuries—the first beat of each measure is normally accented, or stressed; and if there are four or more beats per measure, there is at least one secondary accent as well.

TABLE 2	Common Tempo Indications
Largo	Slow; "broad"
Adagio	Slow; "at ease"
Andante	Moderately slow; "walking" tempo
Moderato	Moderate
Allegro	Fast; cheerful
Presto	Very fast
Vivace	Lively
Molto	Very (allegro molto = very fast)
Non troppo	Not too much (allegro non troppo = not too fast)
Con brio	With spirit

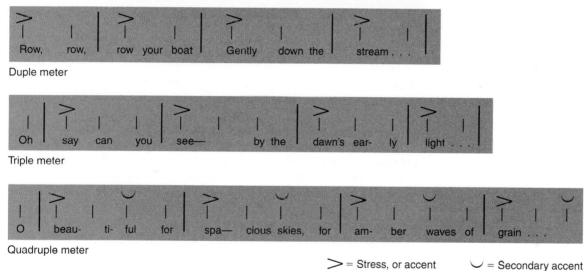

Duple meter

Triple meter

Quadruple meter

$>$ = Stress, or accent $\smile$ = Secondary accent

FIGURE 1

Common meters, showing accents.

For example, in quadruple meter (Figure 1), the secondary accent falls on the third beat.

Melody

Musical sounds, called *tones,* are caused by something vibrating at a particular frequency, or rate of speed. Tones are said to be relatively high or low in *pitch,* depending upon the rate of vibration of the medium producing the sound: The faster a string on a violin or the column of air in a trumpet vibrates, the higher the level of pitch. Much as a sentence is a meaningful succession of words, a **melody** is a meaningful succession of tones of various levels of pitch. (The words *tone* and *note* may be used interchangeably, *tone* suggesting the sound as it is heard and *note* its written representation.)

FIGURE 2

A piano keyboard, indicating intervals of a second, a third, and an octave.

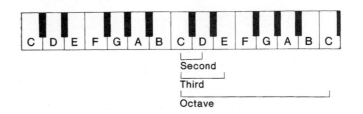

Tones have letter names, A through G. The *interval,* or distance, between tones is named according to the number of tones it includes; for example, from A to B is a *second,* from A to C, a *third,* and so on (Figure 2). The most basic interval is the *eighth,* called an **octave,** the two tones of which share the same letter name and sound nearly alike. The higher tone of the octave vibrates at exactly twice the rate of the lower tone, the simple relationship of their frequencies (the ratio 2:1) causing minimal tension between them.

All keys on a keyboard that bear the same letter name *look* the same as well, because they occupy the same position relative to other keys. For example, if we start at the left of the keyboard and move up, we see that the last white key before the third of the three black keys is always an A (Figure 2), D is always the white note between the two black notes, and so on.

Scales. Melodies are based on **scales:** stepwise rising or descending patterns of pitches within the range of an octave. By the seventeenth century, two particular seven-note patterns—the *major* and *minor* scales—had been accepted as those that best served European composers of concert music, and they continue to prevail in Western music today.

The major and minor scales each include two *half steps* (the closest distance between two keys on a keyboard) and five *whole steps* (the equivalent of two half steps). The white notes of the octave from C to C on the keyboard correspond to the pattern of the major scale, while the white notes of the octave from A to A correspond to the pattern of the minor scale.

Music based on the major scale sounds very different from music that is minor, because of the different order in which the half and whole steps occur (Figure 3). If you can play a keyboard instrument, you might play the first three notes of "Doe, a Deer" from *The Sound of Music,* beginning on C. These are the first three notes of the major scale. Now *lower* the third tone by a half step, or begin playing on A and use all white keys, and you will hear how the melody would begin if it were based on a minor scale.

We will discuss scales other than the major or minor as they apply to music covered later in this text.

Further Characteristics of Melody. Melodies of course have rhythm, the tones of a melody occurring in some order of long sounds, short sounds, or both. If a melody, such as a children's song or folk song, is particularly singable and memorable and seems complete in itself, we call it a *tune.* A different kind

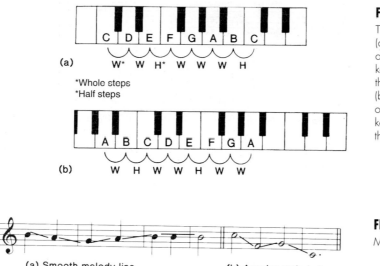

FIGURE 3

The major and minor scales. (a) The white notes of the octave from C to C on the keyboard correspond to the pattern of the major scale. (b) The white notes of the octave from A to A on the keyboard correspond to the pattern of the minor scale.

FIGURE 4

Melodic contours.

of melody is a brief, fragmentary melodic idea or *motive,* recurring throughout a piece, particularly in instrumental music. Probably the most famous motive in Western music is the four-note "knocking" pattern (short-short-short-long) that begins Beethoven's Symphony No. 5, identified at least as readily by its rhythm as by its melodic characteristics.

Because we may draw a line up or down from one note of a melody to the next, we think of a melody as *linear* and identify its contour as angular (with large leaps between the tones), smooth (with the tones closely connected), or some combination of angular and smooth. Figure 4 compares, for example, the smooth contour of "Merrily We Roll Along" with the angular shape of "Westminster Chimes." Other familiar tunes that might further clarify this distinction are "America" ("My Country, 'Tis of Thee") (smooth) and "The Star Spangled Banner" (sharply angular in contour).

Harmony

The melodies of European and American music generally are accompanied by simultaneous combinations of tones called **harmony,** defined as the sounding of two or more different tones at once in a logical or meaningful (not necessarily beautiful) manner. The system of harmony that has governed Western music for nearly 400 years, based upon the major and minor scales (the tonal scales), is called *tonality* or the *tonal system.*

Purposeful combinations of three or more different tones constitute **chords,** which enrich the sounds of Western music and please Western ears much as linear perspective adds depth and pleases the eyes of lovers of Western art. Indeed, chordal harmony, like linear perspective, is a peculiarly Western concept; both the aural and the visual concepts evolved during the Western Renaissance, and neither has become characteristic of non-Western arts. While the notes of a

I   ii   iii   IV   V   vi   vii°   I

melody are written in succession, or in linear fashion, the tones of a chord are notated vertically, above and beneath each other.

Tonal Harmony. The first tone of a major or minor scale, called the **tonic,** represents a kind of home base, from which a piece of music in the Western tradition is likely to begin and on which it is even more likely to end. The tonic names the **key** of a composition; for example, we say a piece is in the key of A major, meaning that the tonic note is A and most of the tones are those of the major scale. For another example, a piece based on the D minor scale is said to be in the key of D minor.

Each of the tones in a major or minor scale bears a specific relationship, relatively distant or close, to the tonic. The fifth step of the scale, called the *dominant,* is the tone most closely related to tonic. It is heard frequently during a piece, and it seems to bear almost a gravitational pull back to tonic, or home base. The second-closest tone to tonic is the fourth step above (or the fifth below) tonic, called the *subdominant.*

The most basic chord in the tonal system, consisting of three alternate tones (or a third piled on top of a third), is called a **triad** (Figure 5). Triads may be built on any tone of the major or minor scale and bear the same relationship to tonic and to each other as the tones upon which they are built. Thus the strongest relationship is between the tonic triad (often represented by the Roman numeral I) and the triad built upon the fifth note of the scale, or the dominant (V). The next-closest chord to tonic is the triad built upon the fourth, or sub-dominant, step of the scale, which provides a somewhat weaker drive toward tonic.

The I, IV, and V chords, then, provide the cornerstones of tonal harmony. Many simple melodies are effectively accompanied by just these three closely related chords.

Timbre The quality or **timbre** (tam′-breh) of a musical sound depends on characteristics of the medium producing it. Thus musical instruments have distinctive timbres according to their size, the material of which they are made, and the manner in which they are played. For example, the timbre or "color" of the sound produced by a violin differs from that of a flute, and the sound produced by plucking the string of a violin is unlike the sound made when the same string is bowed.

Pitch also affects the timbre of musical sound: Notice how the high tones of a piano differ in timbre as well as pitch from the very low tones of the instrument, and how men's and women's voices are distinguished in terms of timbre as well as the range of their pitches.

TABLE 3 Dynamic Levels		
Levels of Volume		
Italian Term	*Abbreviation*	*English Meaning*
Pianissimo	pp	Very soft
Piano	p	Soft
Mezzopiano	mp	Moderately soft
Mezzoforte	mf	Moderately loud
Forte	f	Loud
Fortissimo	ff	Very loud

Another factor affecting the timbre of a voice or instrument is the loudness or softness of the sound, called its **dynamic level.** Composers often vary the dynamic level within a piece for many reasons: to achieve emotional effects, to illustrate events described in the text of a song, or to achieve extramusical effects in descriptive instrumental music. The Italian words *piano* and *forte,* respectively meaning "soft" and "loud," are among the commonly used dynamic terms included with their abbreviations in Table 3.

Form

When describing a work of art, we might first mention its **genre**—that is, the kind or category of music to which it belongs, such as orchestral, choral, or folk. We also often consider the manner in which it is organized—its **form.** There are many approaches to formal design, based upon principles of *repetition* and *contrast,* with repetition lending a work unity, symmetry, and balance, and contrast providing the variety necessary to sustain interest. A play, for example, may have one or several acts, a novel a number of chapters, a poem one or several strophes or stanzas. Similarly, an instrumental musical composition may have one or several sections, or *movements.*

Songs, too, are organized according to textual or musical properties. The most common song form, called *strophic,* has two or more verses, each set to the same music.

Music Notation

Although one may well enjoy listening to and even performing music without learning to read music notation, some conception of how music is written may be of interest. For centuries, Western music has been written on a *staff* of five lines and four spaces (Figure 6). Musical pitches and rhythms are written as *notes,* and notated silences are called *rests.* The staff forms a kind of "ladder," with each line and each space representing a particular pitch. A sign called a

FIGURE 6

Pitches notated in the treble (high) and bass (low) clefs. Certain tones, including "middle C," may be notated in either the bass or the treble clef.

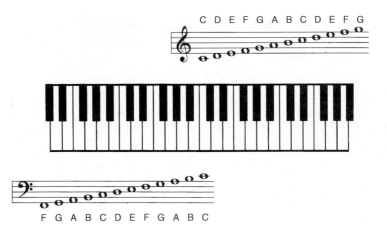

clef, placed at the beginning of the staff, indicates that a particular line represents a specific pitch, thus fixing the relative position of all the other pitches on the staff.

Understanding just these basic concepts of how music is written allows us, without really "reading" music, to follow the ascending and descending patterns of tones written on a page and have an approximate idea of how the music would sound.

Elements of an American Sound

Because America's early settlers came from many different cultures, it took time for music to acquire a characteristic American sound; but surprisingly soon music, like the English language, changed its accent in the New World. The manner in which the elements of music are selected and combined, the choice of timbres, various means of musical expression such as changes in dynamic level and in tempo, and the purpose for which music is intended are among the nearly indefinable qualities that determine a particular composition's characteristic sound, or **style.**

In music, as in fashion, *style* refers to a manner or mode of expression, and again as in fashion, style in music is affected by the time and the culture that produce it. For example, American rhythms may be more flexible than those characteristic of European music; and although the delay or anticipation of accented beats called *syncopation* occurs in music worldwide, its bold and consistent use gives much American classical as well as popular music a distinctive flavor. The long, irregular melodies of pieces such as Samuel Barber's *Adagio for Strings* (Listening Example 74) are sometimes thought to reflect the informality, personal freedom, and lack of physical and cultural boundaries associated with the ideal American life. Jazz musicians, by using traditional instruments in new and unusual ways, caused Americans to alter the timbres of symphonic as well as popular musics, as we hear for example in William Grant Still's *Afro-American Symphony* (Listening Example 75).

Thus, although much American music is stylistically indistinguishable from music by European composers of the same period, perhaps you will sense in some American pieces a certain audacity, a generous expansiveness, a peculiar irregularity, or some other scarcely definable attribute that simply "sounds American."

How to Improve Your Listening Skills

Attendance at live performances as well as repeated and concentrated study of the text's listening examples are essential to furthering your understanding and enjoyment of music, for no written or spoken words can substitute for the impact music makes on our minds and hearts. It is not difficult to develop skills to enhance your listening comprehension and pleasure—not just for now but for the rest of your life.

First, approach each listening experience with expectations of enjoyment. Next, try to memorize music as you hear it so that it will quickly become familiar, and so that you will develop an awareness of a composition's form even as you listen to it for the first time. Remember to apply the knowledge gleaned from your class discussions and from this text to the music you are hearing. By listening actively, even *creatively,* you will participate in the successful collaboration of composer, performer, and listener that makes possible the magnificent experience of enjoying great music.

Listening Example 1 offers the opportunity to apply your developing listening skills to the well-known African American folk ballad "John Henry." We will discuss folk ballads in more detail in Chapter 2; meanwhile, notice that the song tells a story, in many verses, all set to the same music (**strophic form**).

Virgil Thomson (1896–1989)
"The way to write American music is simple. All you have to do is be an American and then write any kind of music you wish."

Listening Example 1

"John Henry"

In the late nineteenth century, the story of a former slave who had become a "steel-driving man" passed from person to person—both black and white—through many regions of the country. The text of the song would be adapted to local and timely conditions. Thought to have originally been associated with the 1870–1872 construction of the largest tunnel built up to that time, other versions have John Henry hand-driving his steel drill to lay railroad track. In each case, the legendary hero pits his strength against the newly invented steam drill, winning the contest but losing his life in the effort. Each time you listen to this song, try to hear something that escaped your notice before, "stretching your ears" to capture all that the performance offers.

CD 1
Track 1
2:55

—Continued

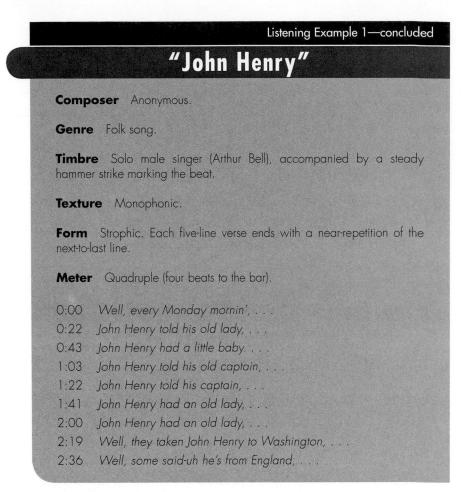

"John Henry"

Composer   Anonymous.

Genre   Folk song.

Timbre   Solo male singer (Arthur Bell), accompanied by a steady hammer strike marking the beat.

Texture   Monophonic.

Form   Strophic. Each five-line verse ends with a near-repetition of the next-to-last line.

Meter   Quadruple (four beats to the bar).

0:00   *Well, every Monday mornin', . . .*
0:22   *John Henry told his old lady, . . .*
0:43   *John Henry had a little baby. . . .*
1:03   *John Henry told his old captain, . . .*
1:22   *John Henry told his captain, . . .*
1:41   *John Henry had an old lady, . . .*
2:00   *John Henry had an old lady, . . .*
2:19   *Well, they taken John Henry to Washington, . . .*
2:36   *Well, some said-uh he's from England, . . .*

Terms to Review

elements of music	scale	timbre
rhythm	harmony	dynamic level
tempo	chord	genre
meter	tonic	form
melody	key	style
octave	triad	strophic form

Critical Thinking

What roles does music currently play in your life?

What do you think music contributes to a visual experience, such as watching a film or television?

Has music ever enhanced your ability to remember something—an advertised product, for example? If so, how?

Music in Early North America

The Early Years: Historical and Cultural Perspective

Scholars believe that human experience has always included music, although music's sound and its place in society have differed widely from one time and one culture to another. Even today some people differentiate between "music" and "noise"—often disagreeing, however, on which is which—whereas others deny the distinction. Some consider sounds of nature, such as birdcalls or thunder, a kind of music; others do not. For some people, music is art, and for others it is simply an integral part of their everyday experience. Speakers of some languages have no word for music at all, although music is fully integrated into their daily experience. But always, it seems, patterns of sound—one possible concept of what we mean by music—have found a meaningful place in human society.

The Beginnings of Music in America

Although today's American music is rooted in the artistic styles and experiences of European and African cultures, long before the first white settlers or black slaves touched the North American shores the people living here were making music of their own. Even though we have no firsthand knowledge of the music of the early North American Indians, Native American music traditions have evolved so slowly over vast periods of time that we may imagine their early music concepts bore a close relationship to those of today.

Native Americans Scholars generally believe that the people destined to be called North American Indians or Native Americans began coming to this continent from Asia between 18,000 and 40,000 years ago, crossing the land bridge then existing where the Bering Strait is today, and spreading south from Canada and Alaska into Mexico and Central and South America, and eastward to the Atlantic Ocean and the Gulf of Mexico. New archaeological evidence suggests, however, that the New World may have been colonized on numerous different occasions, beginning thousands of years earlier than previously thought and by people arriving from several different regions of Europe. It is possible, for example, that the people who established an ancient campsite 45 miles south of Richmond, Virginia, recently dated at around 18,000 years old, came by sea across the Atlantic rather than by land from Asia. Still, although fascinating research continues as new discoveries occur, it appears likely that *most* of the people who first arrived on the North American continent came from Siberia by crossing the Bering Sea land bridge.

Whatever their distant heritage, all early American Indian cultures shared a close dependence upon and affinity with the natural world. However, over vast periods of time they developed a very broad linguistic and cultural diversity. Thus when Christopher Columbus arrived in the region of the Bahamas, late in the fifteenth century, well over 300 American Indian cultures with several hundred languages inhabited what is now the United States. Today we generally recognize eight geographic areas, within each of which many tribes share cultural characteristics similar to each other's but distinct from those of Native Americans inhabiting other cultural regions (see Table on p. 14).

Today's descendants of the early Native Americans retain a strong reverence for and a sense of oneness with nature, expressed in their music as in all their arts—although the term *arts* here gives us pause, because traditional American Indian dry (sand) painting, weaving, pottery, basketry, and music all had spiritual and utilitarian significance without which they would have been meaningless. For example, magnificent buckskin shield covers, designed according to divine instruction, protect the wearer as much by the sacred design etched, incised, or painted on them as by the heavy material of which they are made. The Western separation of sacred and secular concepts has little meaning among Native Americans, for whom religion, art, music, and poetry are the inseparable threads—the warp and woof—of life and culture.

Fight scene painted on a Sioux shield cover. The central mounted warrior shows the manner in which shields were held.

Plains		East	
Northern	*Southern*	*Northeastern*	*Southeastern*
Arapaho	Comanche	Iroquois nations	Cherokee
Blackfoot	Kiowa		Creek
Cheyenne	Western Cherokee	Wabanaki	Seminole
Crow			Shawnee
Dakota (Sioux)			

Great Lakes	Southwest/ Southern California	Athapaskan
Menomini	Hopi/Zuni/Other "mesa" pueblos	Apache
Ojibwa (Chippewa)	Maricopa	Navajo
Winnebago	O'odham (Papago)	
	Pima	
	Rio Grande Pueblos (from three language families)	
	Yavapai	
	Yuma	

Great Basin/Northern California	Northwest Coast	Eskimo/Inuit and Athapaskans
Paiute	Bella Coola	Eskimos of Alaska, Canada, and Greenland
Pomo	Kwakiutl	Northern Athapaskans (Slave, Kulchin, Dogrib)
Shoshoni	Nootka	
Ute	Salish	
	Tlingit	

Our brief survey can only generalize about important concepts generally shared by members of different Native American cultures, especially up until the early years of the twentieth century, before which time their cultural expression remained quite consistent. During the last century, acculturation brought about significant changes in Indian music, the changes varying from one region to another; yet many basic tenets of Native American culture retain their ancient values today.

European Emigrants

During the sixteenth century, Europeans began to arrive and settle on the North American continent in large numbers, bringing with them their various musical customs. Missionaries, adventurers, explorers, and settlers traversed the land stretching from Florida to the northern California coast. Maps and pictures drawn by these intrepid travelers, vividly depicting American Indians as they appeared to the newcomers, and the great natural beauty of the newly discovered land, encouraged other Europeans to join them in the vast New World. Soon French Catholics and French Protestants (Huguenots) in the Southeast, and Spanish Catholics and Sir Francis Drake's Protestant Englishmen in the Southwest, were persuading American Indians to join them in singing Christian songs as part of their effort to convert them to Christianity.

The Pilgrims and Puritans arriving in New England early in the seventeenth century were Protestants, whose protests against the Roman Catholic church included some concerning the performance of religious music. That century also brought English Quakers (members of the Society of Friends) as well as German-speaking Protestants, such as the Mennonites and Moravians.

All these brave settlers left behind them a rich and varied cultural experience. Roman Catholics had enjoyed generous support for their arts, including music, from royalty and the church. The Protestant New England settlers, sharing simple tastes, generally avoided the extravagant characteristics of the music style (*Baroque*) then prevalent in Europe, but many of them loved art and music and made both a significant part of their life. The lyrical folk songs and rollicking dance tunes of various European cultures also traveled with the settlers to become a part of their new experience in their adopted homeland.

Puritan Society

The more we learn about the Puritans, the more we realize how inappropriate is the stereotype of them as plain and wholly serious, for Puritan society included sophisticated men and women of keen wit and high intellect. Some brought with them their personal libraries, but the small ships carrying them to America had scarce room for such luxuries, and before long the colonists began to produce their own new literature, largely consisting of didactic religious tracts but also including memoirs, essays, and poetry.

The New World's first poet, Anne Bradstreet (1612–1672), busy wife of a colonial governor and the mother of eight, composed a significant body of poetry despite her own serious illness and the rigors of colonial life. Though she declared her peers believed "my hand a needle better fits" (than a poet's pen), she was admired then as now for her learned and well-crafted poems. Here is an example:

I am obnoxious to each carping tongue,
Who sayes, my hand a needle better fits,
A Poets Pen, all scorne, I should thus wrong;
For such despighte they cast on female wits:
If what i doe prove well, it wo'nt advance,
They'l say its stolen, or else, it was by chance.

Although the practical early New Englanders had little use for art for art's sake and specifically excluded art from their churches, still their daily experience was rich in artistic expression. For example, the graveyards adjacent to their plainly furnished houses of worship often contained elaborately carved and decorated headstones. They furnished their homes with many functional articles of beauty, covering tables and beds with fine needlework to provide protection from cold New England drafts, while beautifully carved furniture, hand-painted dishes, and toys elaborately constructed for the delight of children lessened the severity of New England colonial life.

Anne Bradstreet (1612–1672).

Gravestone in a colonial churchyard.

Elizabeth Davis, *Mrs. Hezekia Beardsley,* c. 1785–1790.

Although landscape painting held little attraction for early New Englanders more inclined to tame than to admire natural wonders, portraits served the practical purpose of preserving a likeness and so were highly valued. Most portrait painters were amateur artists who earned their living as farmers, as shopkeepers, or in some other trade, and who thought of themselves simply as craftspeople producing commodities of practical worth. The rather flat or linear quality of American folk art lends it a pleasing flavor distinct from the professional products of their European contemporaries. Ironically, these early artists often painted their subjects dressed in elaborate finery, suggesting an attraction to worldly goods surprising in the staid Puritan society. But how astonished these modest people would be to know the aesthetic and monetary value their work has acquired today.

The African Experience in Early America
Even before the Pilgrims' arrival at Plymouth Rock in 1620, Africans were being forcibly brought to, and made to work in, the New World. At first African slaves constituted a minuscule portion of society in New York or New England, and even in southern colonies; but after 1700 the importation of slaves greatly increased. By the time of the American Revolution, there were slaves in large numbers in the South, where their forced services made possible the great plantations that produced the coffee, tobacco, sugar, rice, and (much later) cotton on which the southern economy relied.

During the eighteenth century, a surge of humanitarian feeling gave rise to strong movements against the continuing slave trade, which finally was prohibited in the United States twenty years after the ratification of the Constitution. However, the strong protests of Quakers and other religious groups notwithstanding, antislavery sentiment had little effect in this country until well into the nineteenth century. In New England, slavery proved unprofitable and disappeared, but in the South the invention of the cotton gin in 1793 made slavery an even more integral part of the plantation system than before.

Forbidden to practice their familiar African religious rituals and to sing songs, dance, and play musical instruments in their accustomed ways, the brutally uprooted Africans and their American-born progeny, starved for religion, attempted to adapt traditional African musical expression to worship of the white people's Christian god. Their early efforts mostly met with ridicule, because their white owners regarded them as "beasts" unfit to receive religious instruction of any kind; but here as in their fatherland, the slaves integrated music and faith into their daily lives.

Revolution, in Classical Style

Eighteenth-century Americans of European descent reflected a strong European influence, enhanced by increased opportunities for travel and communication from one continent to the other. European artists of this time had adopted the *classical* ideals of ancient Greek sculptors and architects, who strove for perfection of form, balanced designs, and relatively restrained emotional expression. Artists on both sides of the Atlantic, in fact, from about 1750 until 1825 applied order, balance, and emotional restraint to their work, rendering the Age of Reason in social and political affairs the Age of Classicism in the arts. To distinguish eighteenth-century visual works of art rendered in this cool, reasoned manner from their ancient classical models, we call them *neoclassical* in style; but too little ancient music remains to cause confusion in terms, and the eighteenth century is known as the Classical period of music.

Paradoxically, the Age of Reason spawned several violent revolutionary movements, and Americans joined a number of European nations in firmly rejecting rule by absolute authority and establishing a republican form of government. Enlightened intellectuals—hardly impassioned fanatics—led the American Revolution, the classical influence evident, for example, in the cool, reasoned language of the Declaration of Independence, which begins "When in the course of human events it becomes necessary for one people to dissolve the political bonds which have connected them with another . . ." America's founders, led by Thomas Jefferson and influenced by

Classical influence is reflected in the orderly layout of streets and the prevalence of Greco-Roman architectural style in Washington, D.C.

outstanding French neoclassical architects, designed Washington, D.C., to be an orderly city of wide and regular streets with many grassy parks and shady trees. The simple lines and classical columns of Washington's state buildings, although not constructed until the early years of the nineteenth century, clearly represent the ideals of the Classical period during which they were planned.

Painting in Eighteenth-Century America

Although American artists during this century had more training and sophistication than the folk artists of the settlers' period, their finest works retained an innocence, honesty, and decorative sense distinguishing them from the more elegant European works of the same era. John Singleton Copley (1738–1815), America's greatest colonial artist, was largely self-taught. He developed a highly personal style rooted in the American tradition and governed by classical order and reserve. Becoming increasingly, though reluctantly, involved in events relating to the impending American Revolution, Copley sailed for Europe in 1774, intending to return to America when peace

17

John Singleton Copley, *Mrs. Thomas Boylston*, 1766.

Charles Willson Peale,
The Staircase Group, 1795.

John Singleton Copley, *Watson and the Shark*, 1778. Oil on canvas, 72½ in. × 90¼ in. (184 cm × 229.5 cm). Although largely self-taught, Copley effectively captured the seething action and dramatic interplay of emotions between the desperate characters in his masterful painting.

was attained, but in fact he spent the rest of his life abroad.

In Europe, Copley studied with the famous American expatriate Benjamin West (1738–1820), who encouraged him to paint historical and heroic subjects. Although the subsequent paintings were more elegant and polished than Copley's early American portraits, they were correspondingly less distinctive and interesting. One of Copley's later paintings, *Watson and the Shark* (1778) is of great interest, however, for in it Copley produced a warm and sympathetic portrayal of an African American man attempting to assist a white man—Watson—desperately floundering in the water. The would-be rescuer has thrown a rope, which Watson has missed, as the shark looms menacingly nearby. (Notice how the African American's outstretched arm, mirroring that of Watson, contributes to the symmetry and the drama of this strong painting.) Such a subtle and sympathetic rendering of relations between African Americans and whites was unusual in that time, and Copley's painting is in every way a masterpiece.

Charles Willson Peale (1741–1827) also studied for a time in Europe with Benjamin West, returning to America to become the leading artist in Philadelphia for many years. Peale revealed the classical thirst for knowledge in his boundless curiosity about a broad range of subjects, implementing his ideas (in the practical, classical way) by establishing the first American museum of natural history, in Philadelphia in 1802.

Peale, who fought in the American Revolution, painted fine, lifelike portraits of the leaders of the young nation. His painting *The Staircase Group,* reflecting the eighteenth-century interest in scientific measurement and optical effects, is so realistic a portrayal of Peale's sons standing on a staircase that George Washington is said to have bowed to the boys as he passed by the painting one day.

Today we recognize the dominant effects of many cultures on the evolution of American music, but the traditions and practices of all the early inhabitants— those native to the land, the early European arrivals, and the people brought by force from their African homeland—have deeply colored the complex landscape of American music. From at least the early seventeenth century, the music heard in the widely separated inhabited regions of the continent reflected highly disparate values and sounds. Nevertheless, Indian, African, and European musics had some things in common: all were more likely to be performed by amateurs than by professionals, in intimate (inside or outside) domestic or worship settings than in a concert hall, and often (although not always) with spiritual connotation. The distinctions we draw now between sacred and secular music and between high and low art—and the difficulties we experience in finding appropriate terminology to distinguish one kind of art from another—had little meaning in the early American experience. ♪

North American Indian Music

ong before European settlers arrived in the New World, North American Indians were practicing their own vital music traditions, essential and integral to their most basic daily experience. Because their music always occurred in association with other activities—dance, religious ritual, prayer, work, recreation—their languages included no word for music itself; yet for American Indians then as today, life without music was unthinkable.

Songs

Never an independent concept but always a part of dance, celebration, games, work, or prayer, Native American music essentially consists of songs imbued with strong powers to accomplish a given end, such as success in fishing, healing, gambling, or winning a bride. American Indians think of their songs not as *composed,* but as *received,* often in a dream or vision—gifts of power from the spirit world. The owner of a song may sell it or may grant someone else the right to sing it, usually in exchange for a gift; or a song may be included among the items in one's will.

Songs, which are highly valued in American Indian cultures, have been preserved through the ages not by notation but by a rich and vital oral tradition—handed down, that is, from one generation to the next through performance and memorization, stressing the necessity for completely accurate rendition. Navajos, who think of their songs as enriching experiences, sometimes count their wealth in terms of the number of songs they know. And because a basket weaver, for example, sings not only to ease the drudgery of work but more importantly to make a basket pleasing to supernatural spirits, the song must be performed and listened to with propriety.

Native American music certainly does *not* all sound the same to the discriminating ear: The songs of some tribes, for example, are low-pitched, sounding practiced or controlled, whereas songs of others lie very high in the voice, pulsing vibrantly with emotion and energy. Even within a given tribe, songs for gambling, war dances, lullabies, and healing ceremonies vary widely in their sounds.

FIGURE 1.1

The pleasing repetition of geometric patterns in this lovely Navajo blanket unifies the design much as melodic repetition unifies a Native American song.

Although there are as many kinds of Native American songs as there are Native American cultures, some characteristics do apply to all or most. Melodic phrases generally begin on a relatively high pitch and descend without wide leaps, approximating the inflection typical of a spoken phrase. A song often consists simply of many repetitions of one or more phrases or partial phrases, much as designs on baskets, blankets, and other Native American art often consist of repeated geometrical patterns (Figure 1.1). Such aural and visual repetition has a nearly hypnotic effect, enhancing a work's spirituality and artistic coherence, while also suggesting the ideal balance of nature for which the Native American constantly strives.

Songs are usually sung by a solo voice or by men and women singing together in **unison** (all singing the same notes at the same time). Although men's voices lie an octave lower than women's, and although **call-and-response**—a solo voice alternating with a group—sometimes leads to an overlap between the leader's and the other singers' tones, there is never harmony in the Western sense. Slightly different versions of the same melody performed simultaneously, however, produce variety in the musical *texture*.

Texture
Much as we describe the texture of a piece of fabric according to the way in which its threads are interwoven, so we describe the **texture** of music in terms of its "threads," or melodic lines. The combination of lines of music may or may not achieve harmony.

Music consisting only of one line of melody, such as a Native American song or flute piece, we call **monophonic** in texture, the prefix *mono* indicating the sounding of one line of music. No matter the number of voices or instruments performing the same melody in unison, the texture of the music remains monophonic, and there are no harmonic combinations of sound.

Native American group singing, however, often involves an overlap between voices singing slightly different versions of the same melody. This musical texture, called **heterophonic,** is often heard in musics outside the Western tradition. Here, too, there is no intention to produce harmony, but simply to enrich or enhance, or to perform in the most natural and comfortable way, the melodic line. Figure 1.2 is a visual representation of monophonic texture (*monophony*) and heterophony.

FIGURE 1.2

Musical textures, monophony
and heterophony.

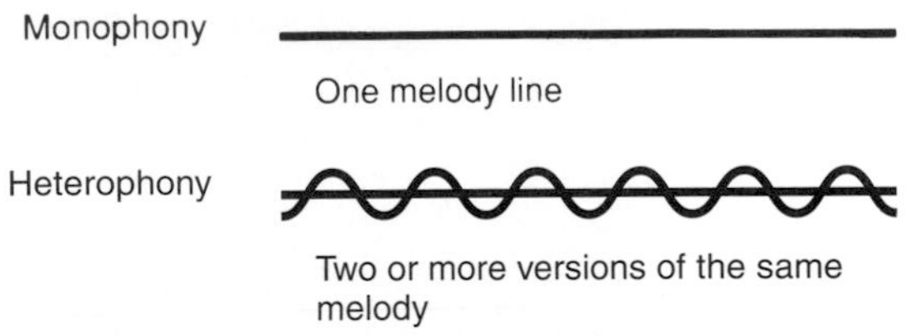

Monophony   ─────────────────
                  One melody line

Heterophony   〜〜〜〜〜〜〜〜
                  Two or more versions of the same
                  melody

Texts   Song texts may be in a native language or, recently, in English. Some texts are simply a series of consonant-vowel clusters or **vocables**—neutral syllables, such as *hey, yeh,* or *neh,* which may in fact convey meaning in themselves. For example, as part of the Navajo Night Way curing ceremony, teams of young men compete in the singing of *Yeibichai (Yeh-be-chy)* songs while masked dancers, personifying the sacred spirits of their grandfathers (*Yei-bi-chai* means "spirits-their-grandfathers"), bring supernatural healing power to help the sick. Every one of the hundreds of Yeibichai songs, consisting entirely of vocables, contains the call of the *Yei: Hi ye, hi ye, ho-ho ho ho,* immediately identifying the song as belonging to this tradition. You will clearly hear the distinctive call in Listening Example 2, an excerpt from a Yeibichai chant song. Notice here the

---

Listening Example 2

Yeibichai Chant Song (excerpt)

On the ninth (last) night of the Night Way ceremony, Yeibichai appears, accompanied by masked dancers shaking their gourd rattles, and by the unearthly call of the gods.

**CD 1
Track 2
0:57**

Genre   Religious dance.

Timbre   Male voices, singing in unison, accompanied by the shaking of gourd rattles. The falsetto tones heard here are particularly characteristic of this and of some other Native American songs as well.

Melody   Repeated high-pitched tones interspersed with even higher cries of indeterminate pitch, producing a rather florid melodic line featuring dramatic upward leaps.

Texture   Monophonic.

Form   Strophic. A long phrase is repeated many times, with minimal variation.

Rhythm   A steady pulse marked by rattle shakes (two to the beat).

Text   Vocables punctuated with the distinctive call of the Yei.

alternation between singing in the normal range of the voice and singing in the extremely high **falsetto** tones, lying above the normal voice range.

Sioux Grass Dance

Perhaps easiest to identify of all Native American styles is the singing of the Plains Indians, whose regions stretch from the foothills of the Rocky Mountains east to the Mississippi River and beyond, and from the Gulf of Mexico north into Canada. High in pitch, tense in quality, and harsh in tone, this sound is entirely distinct from that of European-based American music (Listening Example 3). No less is it distinct, however, from the music of other Native American cultures, and from other kinds of music (simple lullabies or intimate songs, for example) of the Plains Indians themselves.

Usually referred to today as a grass dance, because of the grass braids the dancers wear at their waists, this is the stirring war dance music heard, or

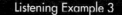

Listening Example 3

Sioux Grass Dance (excerpt)

CD 1
Track 3
0:55

To perform this stunning dance, two teams of costumed dancers enter the area, each dancer carrying a tomahawk or another weapon. Facing each other, the teams dance in place, brandishing their weapons in a threatening manner. Next, forming a circle, they move around clockwise, crouching, leaping, and yelping dramatically. Individually, the dancers simulate the motions of battle, alternately forming and breaking the original formations.

Genre Dance.

Timbre Men and women singing (approximately) in unison. Notice the tense quality of the voices and the high, falsetto tones. Some phrases are introduced by a leader's call. The insistent beat of drums and delicate shaking of rattles accompany the singers, while the yells of observers as well as participants add to the drama and excitement of the dance.

Melody Each phrase begins high in pitch and descends, much as a spoken phrase often ends lower than it began. The melody descends by narrow intervals, the only large leaps occurring from the end of one phrase to the beginning of the next.

Texture Heterophony.

Form Strophic. Each verse or stanza (or strophe) consists of a descending phrase.

Rhythm A steady, duple pulse, marked by the drums and rattles.

FIGURE 1.3
Stirring music performed in the emotional Plains Indian style enhances the drama of the traditional war dance.

imitated, in countless western movies. The strong pulsations, the very high pitches sung in falsetto range, and the tense quality of the voices enhance the emotional intensity of this exciting music, as do the elaborate costumes and dramatic steps of the dancers (Figure 1.3).

Sound Instruments

Although little music is performed by instruments alone, sound instruments, as they are called, often support or "hold up" a song. Navajo flutes, the primary melody-playing Native American instrument, are usually made of cedar wood and may be elaborately carved and decorated (Figure 1.4). Traditionally the flute was sometimes used as a courting instrument, played by a young man who trusted the wind to carry his flute-song to the woman he loved, and who hoped the sounds of his flute, by their beauty and perhaps by magic as well, would persuade her to become his bride. The Navajo flute, rarely heard during the first three quarters of the twentieth century except among families and occasionally at large intertribal gatherings called **powwows,** is frequently heard today at tribal fairs, powwows, and concerts of traditional music. It has no standard dimensions because its finger holes and air column are based on finger measurements and are therefore never the same. Each flute has its own sound and pitch. The flute reper-toire now includes newly composed courting songs as well as Western-influenced classical pieces composed especially for this unique instrument. (You may hear and see Navajo flute players perform on YouTube.)

Far more common and widespread are percussion instruments, especially container rattles of several kinds: A rattle element, such as pebbles, sacred corn, or beans, placed into a gourd or pot or into a container made of hide or bark, is shaken in time to the rhythm of a song or swung in a circular motion

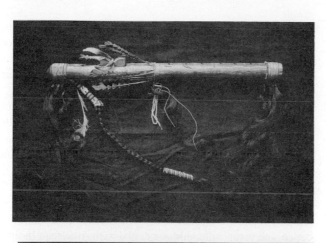

FIGURE 1.4

Decorated flute of the Northern Plains Indians. This Kiowa Indian flute with a carved wind cap is decorated with painting, feathers, and braided hair.

FIGURE 1.5

Two Northwest Coast carved wooden rattles from the Tlingit culture, carved with double birds' heads. These date from the late nineteenth century and come from the area around Sitka, Alaska.

to produce a continuous sound (Figure 1.5). For certain sacred ceremonies, the shaking of deer hooves or shells suspended from a stick (a suspension rattle) produces quite a different sort of rattling effect.

Rasps, percussion instruments normally made from a long stick of wood into which notches have been carved, are rubbed with another stick or a piece of bone (such as the shoulder blade of a sheep) to make a rasping sound. To amplify the sound, the rasp may be placed on an inverted basket or on a piece of hide over an open hole in the ground.

Drums, carrying great importance in Indian culture, exist in profuse variety. Most are made of wood, with one or two heads of the skin of deer or some other animal. The Zuni, Navajo, and Apache, however, sometimes use less resonant pottery vessels or drum jars. Hollowed-out logs, or *log drums,* tall and thin or short and wide, common to the Plains area, have become the powwow drum of today.

Contemporary Indian Song

The late nineteenth century and the twentieth century witnessed many changes in North American Indian music, as some cultural traditions nearly succumbed to overwhelming influences from modern American life. Among the earliest changes in traditional Native American music practice, for example, was the development of pan-Indian song styles, which evolved as the introduction of the horse and later the automobile increased intertribal contact. Soon Native American peoples from many tribes, speaking various languages, were meeting at powwows to share their dances, songs, and ceremonies with one another and sometimes with a public audience.

The modern powwow is common not only on reservations but also in many cities across the United States. Some Native Americans follow the powwow circuit throughout the year, often traveling many miles to sing, dance, and rodeo. The use of either English or vocables is particularly convenient for singing powwow songs, which unite the people as Native Americans and also as members of a particular tribe, authenticating their ceremonies and helping keep the people in balance with nature. Powwow songs also allow visitors from other cultures not only to view but sometimes even to participate in the wide variety of music, dance, and visual splendor associated with American Indian culture.

Professional Musicians

A recent surge of interest among Native Americans concerning their own heritage, together with new appreciation among other Americans of the rich Indian cultures, has produced a wealth of research and of live and recorded performances of both traditional and new Native American music. Some Native Americans have adopted elements of contemporary popular or vernacular musics, modifying these to suit their needs and desires; and rock bands, country-western groups, and gospel quartets flourish on many reservations today.

Other Native American musicians have chosen an academic route, studying music at universities and conservatories and applying their native gifts and experience to composing and performing concert music within the Western music tradition. Among the most prominent of these is **Carlos Nakai** (b. 1946, Figure 1.6), a classically trained cornet and trumpet player who became fascinated with the haunting sounds of the Navajo-style flute and made an exhaustive study of the instrument, which he calls "a sound sculpture—a piece of art that also creates sound." Today Nakai collaborates with musicians in many fields, finding new expression for the Navajo flute in jazz ensembles, in piano-guitar combinations, and in the concert hall. He even uses electronic techniques, including the electronic synthesizer and digital delay, together with the cedar flute. (Carlos Nakai performances are available on YouTube.)

To many American listeners, Native American music sounds more "foreign" than the music of many distant cultures. However, Americans are becoming more aware of and sensitive to the values of a music born and nurtured in this land we all share. The end-of-chapter list includes only a few of today's many prolific and successful professional Native American musicians, but a search on the Internet for "Native American music" will yield innumerable examples of contemporary American Indian popular and concert musicians and their music, and you may follow the links that pique your interest or arouse your curiosity.

Louis Ballard, a prestigious composer, music educator, and music journalist of Cherokee, Quapaw, Scottish, French, and English heritage, once said in reference

FIGURE 1.6
R. Carlos Nakai (b. 1946)—Native American flutist, composer, and educator.

to the uniqueness of each Navajo flute, "Don't ever let 'different' be 'alien.'" His comment applies as well to our approach to the music of Native Americans, who freely share the arts by which all humankind receives the most gracious blessings.

Terms to Review

unison	monophony	falsetto
call-and-response	heterophony	powwow
texture	vocables	

Key Figures

Carlos Nakai
Louis Ballard
Other Figures in Classical Music
Edward Wapp
John Kim Bell
Brent Michael Davids

Other Figures in Popular Music
John Trudell
Black Lodge Singers
Burning Sky
December Wind
Sharon Burch

Joanne Shenandoah
XIT
Keith Secola
Karen Therese
Clan/destine

Critical Thinking

What specific characteristics of the Native American music you have heard distinguish it from the European or American classical or popular music with which you are familiar?

What influences in modern American life can you suggest that may have affected Native American music? What changes would such influences cause?

Early Folk Music

Folk music refers to simple songs and instrumental pieces whose origin has been lost or forgotten, or to music composed in an informal style traditional in certain cultures. Unpretentious, easy to remember and to perform, folk music appeals to inexperienced listeners and sophisticated musicians alike.

The folk music of the United States springs from many ethnic and cultural sources: English, Irish, Scottish, Welsh, German, and other European influences abound. Africa, too—particularly West Africa—introduced an immeasurable wealth of musical sounds and traditions to folk as well as to other musics in America. Much of the recent urban and country folk music we shall consider in Chapters 11 and 14 is deeply rooted in the traditional music introduced here.

Spanish Traditions

The Spanish founded St. Augustine, Florida, in 1565. It is the oldest continuously surviving European settlement in the United States, and Spanish music traditions remain strong in that area of the country. (A historian recently pointed out that not until 2055 will the flag of the United States have flown over St. Augustine as long as the Spanish flag did.) In regions of the Southwest as well, one still hears Spanish folk songs and dances and folk **hymns** (religious songs) reflecting their origins in seventeenth-century Spain or more recent Mexico. Missionary priests taught Indians to sing hymns, for example, and Spanish troops guarding forts near the Christian missions sang ballads and love songs at their work.

www.mhhe.com/ferrisaml6e

Vendors' songs, work songs, lullabies, and all manner of Spanish folk dances, or *bailes,* formed an ordinary part of the Spanish settlers' lives in the New World. Performed now as in years past to celebrate engagements, weddings, birthdays, and other happy social events, such rollicking *bailes* as *El cutilio* (an Online Listening Example) lighten the hearts of those who hear them—though few remember how to dance the intricate steps popular 150 years ago.

Alabados

Alabados One of the first kinds of religious music in California, Texas, and New Mexico was the **alabado,** a Spanish hymn, or religious song (*alabado sea* means "praised be"). Alabados became part of a thriving Spanish folk tradition that survives today in remote villages of the American Southwest. Long and invariably sad, alabados project the profound loneliness of the beautiful but remote regions inhabited by those who sing them.

Some alabados, probably introduced by Franciscan priests, are related musically to the chants of the Roman Catholic church; newer alabados use major and minor scales (see p. 4). Like chant, the religious texts are sung without measure, the rhythm conforming to that of the words. Alabados performed during religious processions are sung in unison, unaccompanied except perhaps by flute figures evocative, some say, of the tears of Mary, and a twirling rattle. Alternatively, alabados may be sung by a solo voice or by a lead singer, often a priest, alternating verses with group responses. The latter method offers missionary priests, for example, a prime opportunity to teach the stories of the Bible in song.

Many examples of alabados may be heard on YouTube.

Corridos

Corridos Storytelling songs or **ballads** with roots in both Mexico and parts of the southwestern and western United States, **corridos** relate the unofficial history of Mexican or Mexican American communities and their heroes. Powerful meditations on honor and bravery, corridos focus more on the stories they tell—of heroes, villains, romances, and historic events—than the music, which usually consists of a simple melody performed unaffectedly with sparse accompaniment. During the nineteenth-century Mexican war of independence and the twentieth-century Mexican revolution, corridos informed the people of newsworthy events. More recent corridos have celebrated famous leaders, including Martin Luther King, Jr., and César Chavez; delivered moral messages; related tales of everyday life and love, immigration, and the drug trade; and expressed nostalgia for Mexico.

Traditionally sung by a solo vocalist accompanied by a guitar, corridos have in modern times been performed, and made more complex, by popular music groups. (Los Tigres del Norte, a highly popular Mexican band, includes at least one or two corridos on each CD it produces.) Chordal accompaniment of a melody line results in the musical texture called *homophonic.*

Homophonic Texture.

Homophonic Texture. When a melody is accompanied by chords, we call the resulting texture **homophony,** or **homophonic texture.** The accompanying voices (instrumental or vocal) produce harmony, but are not primarily of melodic interest themselves. Hymns sung in unison by a church congregation are often accompanied by an organ or piano adding chordal harmony; a band provides harmonic accompaniment while the crowd sings "The Star Spangled Banner" at a football game; folk singers may accompany themselves by strumming chords on a musical instrument. All of these are examples of homophonic, or **chordal,** texture (Figure 2.1)

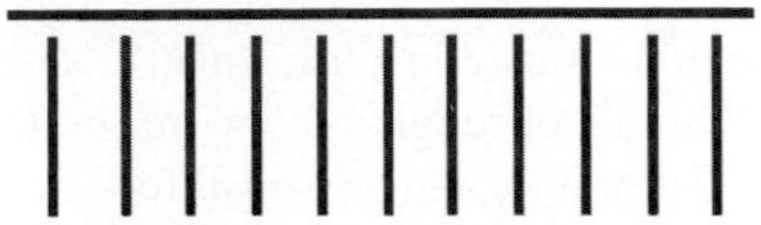

FIGURE 2.1

Homophonic texture: a melody accompanied by chords.

Listening Example 4

"El corrido de Gregorio Cortez"

CD 1
Track 4
2:44

The story, from the early 1900s, concerns a young Mexican falsely accused of horse stealing. When captured, in self-defense he shot and killed the arresting sheriff, who had fatally wounded the young man's brother.

(The lyrics and English translation may be found online by entering the song's title as key words. Brief instrumental interludes separating each verse make it easy to follow the words and music.)

Composer   Anonymous.

Genre   Corrido (norteño ballad).

Timbre   Male duet, singing in simple harmony, accompanied by accordion and guitar. The instruments play a brief introduction, interludes between the stanzas, and the ending.

Texture   Homophonic (chordal).

Form   Strophic. Versions vary from singer to singer, some having as many as twenty four-line stanzas, but recording on 78- or 45-rpm records forced singers to shorten the number of verses.

Meter   Triple. Notice the **oom**-pah-pah rhythm of a waltz.

Tempo   Fast.

The Texas-Mexican border performance style, called *norteño* in northern Mexico and Tex-Mex or tejano (*tay-ha'-no*) in Texas, often includes an accordion, as heard in "El corrido de Gregorio Cortez" (Listening Example 4).

British Traditions

The early English settlers who arrived in the New World around the turn of the seventeenth century brought few musical instruments with them; but in time, as violins and other, mostly stringed, instruments became available, the settlers and colonists played the fiddle tunes and dances familiar from their British childhood. Many traditional songs acquired new words and altered melodies, reflecting American dialects and New World experience as they were handed down from one generation to the next.

These folk music traditions survive today in rural and mountain areas, where the style of singing and playing instruments is remarkably close to that of seventeenth-century Britain. Simple lullabies, such as "The Mockingbird" ("Hush, little baby, don't say a word, Papa's gonna buy you a mockingbird"), delightfully silly and entertaining nonsense songs, various work songs, and singing games ("Did You Ever See a Lassie," "Go In and Out the Window") all belong to the American folk song repertoire.

Folk Ballads

British folk ballads, delivered from memory by a solo voice, with or without accompaniment, offer little background information about the stories they relate, presenting the essential elements and allowing the listener's imagination free rein to flesh out the details. Although the events described often are of a dramatic, even tragic, nature, these ballads present them in a simple, direct, nearly emotionless manner, time and place remaining pleasantly abstract.

British ballads were a major source of entertainment in early America (Figure 2.2). Sung by amateurs for their own or their families' and friends' pleasure, they often included a very large number of stanzas, so that the entertainment might last as long as possible. Having survived through oral tradition, their authors unknown or forgotten, they evolved as the product of many people over long periods of time, remaining subject to alteration today. Thus ballad

FIGURE 2.2

Early Americans gather to enjoy informal music and dance.

singers often add, alter, or delete stanzas as they perform, lending a song local or timely relevance, or simply expressing the irrepressible creativity of the balladeer.

Among the most popular subjects for ballads is the ill-fated love affair, such as the one described in the very famous "Barbara Allen" (Listening Example 5). A favorite song of President George Washington, this is one of a great number of folk ballads that have survived apparently intact since their British (in this case probably Scottish) origin. Some of these very old songs seem to have been better preserved in America, in fact, than in the land that introduced them, and they have long been adopted into the American folk repertoire.

Like many folk and other simple melodies, "Barbara Allen" is based on a five-note, or **pentatonic,** scale corresponding to the five black notes within an octave on a keyboard. (Any five notes may be selected to form a pentatonic scale, but the black-key pattern is the most commonly used.) You might try playing this and many other tunes, including "Merrily We Roll Along," "Oh! Susanna," and "Old Folks at Home," entirely or for the most part on the black keys of a keyboard instrument.

"Barbara Allen"

CD 1
Track 5
2:48

The seventeenth-century story is of young "Sweet William," who is dying for love of "hard-hearted Barbara Allen." She loves him, too, of course, and—remorseful for having repulsed his advances—soon joins him in death. A red rose and a green briar miraculously grow and join above the ill-fated lovers' adjacent graves. The words vary from one performance to another, the song having been handed down through centuries by oral tradition, but the story remains the same.

Composer   Anonymous. The ballad, sometimes called "Barb'ry Ellen" or another similar name, probably originated in Scotland in the early seventeenth century.

Genre   Folk ballad.

Timbre   Unaccompanied male singer (Pete Seeger).

Melody   The melody, like the words, exists in several versions. It is based upon a pentatonic scale that uses only the tones of the five black notes of a keyboard. Many children's songs and folk melodies are based upon this simple scale.

Texture   Monophonic.

—Continued

Listening Example 5—concluded

"Barbara Allen"

Form Strophic. As in most ballads, there are several four-line stanzas, varying in number according to the particular performance.

Rhythm There is a steady underlying pulse and a general sense of triple meter. The rhythm is refreshingly irregular, and the phrases are sometimes asymmetrical, adapted to suit the informal text.

0:00	*In Scarlett Town, where I was born, . . .*
0:19	*'Twas in the merry month of May . . .*
0:39	*He sent his servant unto her . . .*
1:02	*Well slowly, slowly got she up . . .*
1:24	*Then lightly tripped she down the stairs. . . .*
1:45	*Oh, Mother, Mother, go make my bed, . . .*
2:06	*They buried Barbara in the old churchyard; . . .*
2:26	*They grew and grew up the old church wall . . .*

Early American Folk Music

Early emigrants also reflected the influence of another kind of British folk tradition, the **broadside,** written and printed on a very large sheet suitable for public display, or sometimes printed in a newspaper (Figure 2.3). As early as the seventeenth century, Americans began to alter traditional ballads to fit their new experiences, setting original words to old tunes. For subjects, some broadsides took historical or topical events, such as mine disasters, famous murders, or train wrecks; some offered moral instruction or delivered impassioned political commentary. Much like the Internet today, broadsides offered an opportunity to state one's case anonymously, often in brutally satirical terms, free from censorship or retaliation.

The first stanza and chorus of a famous patriotic ballad of the Revolutionary period, "The Liberty Song," exemplify the inflammatory character of political broadsides. (Interestingly, the author of these fervent words, set to an English air called "Heart of Oak," had urged appeasement with England and staunchly opposed revolution.)

The Liberty Song

Come, join hand in hand,
Brave Americans all!
And rouse your bold hearts
At fair Liberty's call;

FIGURE 2.3

In 1768 *The Boston Chronicle* printed John Dickinson's inflammatory text, which he defiantly set to the tune of a popular English patriotic song.

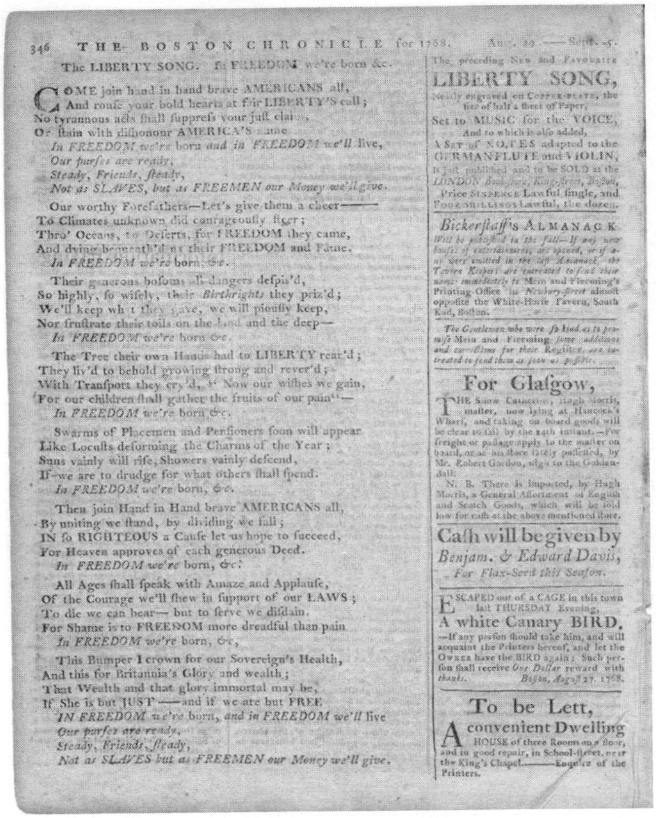

346 THE BOSTON CHRONICLE for 1768. Aug. 29 —— Sept. 5.

The LIBERTY SONG. In FREEDOM we're born &c.

COME join hand in hand brave AMERICANS all,
And rouſe your bold hearts at fair LIBERTY'S call;
No tyrannous acts ſhall ſuppreſs your juſt claim,
Or ſtain with diſhonour AMERICA'S name
In FREEDOM we're born *and in FREEDOM we'll* live,
Our purſes are ready,
Steady, Friends, ſteady,
Not as SLAVES, but as FREEMEN our Money we'll give.

Our worthy Foreſathers—Let's give them a cheer——
To Climates unknown did courageouſly ſteer;
Thro' Oceans, to Deſerts, for FREEDOM they came,
And dying bequeath'd us their FREEDOM and Fame.
In FREEDOM we're born, &c.

Their generous boſoms all dangers deſpis'd,
So highly, ſo wiſely, their *Birthrights* they priz'd;
We'll keep what they gave, we will piouſly keep,
Nor fruſtrate their toils on the land and the deep—
In FREEDOM we're born &c.

The Tree their own Hands had to LIBERTY rear'd;
They liv'd to behold growing ſtrong and rever'd;
With Tranſport they cry'd, "Now our wiſhes we gain,
For our children ſhall gather the fruits of our pain"—
In FREEDOM we're born &c.

Swarms of Placemen and Penſioners ſoon will appear
Like Locuſts deforming the Charms of the Year;
Suns vainly will riſe, Showers vainly deſcend,
If we are to drudge for what others ſhall ſpend.
In FREEDOM we're born, &c.

Then join Hand in Hand brave AMERICANS all,
By uniting we ſtand, by dividing we fall;
IN ſo RIGHTEOUS a Cauſe let us hope to ſucceed,
For Heaven approves of each generous Deed.
In FREEDOM we're born, &c.

All Ages ſhall ſpeak with Amaze and Applauſe,
Of the Courage we'll ſhew in ſupport of our LAWS;
To die we can bear— but to ſerve we diſdain.
For Shame is to FREEDOM more dreadful than pain
In FREEDOM we're born, &c,

This Bumper I crown for our Sovereign's Health,
And this for Britannia's Glory and wealth;
That Wealth and that glory immortal may be,
If She is but JUST——and if we are but FREE
IN FREEDOM we're born, *and in FREEDOM we'll* live
Our purſes are ready,
Steady, Friends, ſteady,
Not as SLAVES but as FREEMEN our Money we'll give.

The preceding NEW and FAVOURITE
LIBERTY SONG,
Neatly engraved on COPPER-PLATE, the ſize of half a ſheet of Paper,
Set to MUSIC for the VOICE,
And to which is alſo added,
A SET of NOTES adapted to the GERMAN FLUTE and VIOLIN,
Is juſt publiſhed and to be SOLD at the *LONDON Book-ſtore, King-ſtreet, Boſton*,
Price SIXPENCE Lawful ſingle, and FOUR SHILLINGS Lawful, the dozen.

Bickerſtaff's ALMANACK
Will be publiſhed in the fall—If any new houſes of entertainment, are opened, or if any were omitted in the laſt Almanack, the Tavern Keepers are entreated to ſend their names immediately to Mein and Fleeming's Printing-Office in *Newbury-ſtreet* almoſt oppoſite the White-Horſe Tavern, South End, Boſton.

The Gentlemen who were ſo kind as to promiſe Mein and Fleeming *ſome additions and corrections for their* Regiſter, *are entreated to ſend them as ſoon as poſſible.*

For Glaſgow,

THE Snow Catherine, Hugh Morris, maſter, now lying at Hancock's Wharf, and taking on board goods will be clear to ſail by the 24th inſtant.—For freight or paſſage apply to the maſter on board, or at his ſtore lately poſſeſſed, by Mr. Robert Gordon, ſign to the Golden-Ball.

N. B. There is imported, by Hugh Morris, a General Aſſortment of Engliſh and Scotch Goods, which will be ſold low for caſh at the above mentioned ſtore.

Caſh will be given by
Benjam. & Edward Davis,
For Flax-Seed this Seaſon.

ESCAPED out of a CAGE in this town laſt THURSDAY Evening,
A white Canary BIRD.
—If any perſon ſhould take him, and will acquaint the Printers hereof, and let the OWNER have the BIRD again: Such perſon ſhall receive *One Dollar* reward with *thanks*. *Boſton, Auguſt* 27. 1768.

To be Lett,

A convenient Dwelling HOUSE of three Rooms on a floor, and in good repair, in School-ſtreet, near the King's Chapel.——Enquire of the Printers.

No tyrannous acts shall
Suppress your just claim,
Or stain with dishonor
America's name.

(Chorus—*repeated between the stanzas of the song*)
In freedom we're born,
And in freedom we'll live!
Our purses are ready,
Steady, friends, steady;
Not as slaves, but as free men,
Our money we'll give.

—AMERICAN WORDS BY JOHN DICKINSON

Less objective, abstract, and timeless than ancient ballads, American broadsides proved less likely to survive beyond the period that introduced them; thus few of the American folk ballads we remember and enjoy today were written before the second half of the nineteenth century. But even before that time, each geographic area of America was producing songs and instrumental pieces expressing the typical local experience. Frontier people sang songs about freedom, equality, danger, and the beauty of nature in the wild. Ballads commemorated the opening of the Erie Canal (1825), the gold rush in California (1849), and other events of intense local concern. Slaves produced their own music, expressive of their particular loneliness and suffering. And songs of miners, farmers, railroad workers, and even outlaws also joined the American folk repertoire. Lullabies served every segment of the population, and play and party songs entertained adults as well as children. Performed in the same plain, direct manner as their British counterparts, American ballads reflect in their titles—such as "John Henry," "Billy the Kid," "The Erie Canal," "The John B. Sails," or "The Ballad of Casey Jones" (Listening Example 46, p. 192)— their uniquely American source and character.

Sailors' work songs or **chanteys** appeared as New Englanders became heavily involved in sea trade and traffic, and as sailors working on the rivers, too, developed songs about their trade. The origin of the hauntingly beautiful "Shenandoah" (Listening Example 6) is sketchy, but the song seems to have originated in the early nineteenth century in the areas of the Missouri and the Mississippi rivers and eventually to have made its way down the Mississippi to the open ocean, where deep-sea sailors adopted its rolling melody as their own. (Shenandoah was the name of an Indian chief living on the Missouri River.) It has remained one of America's favorite folk songs.

Listening Example 6

"Shenandoah"

From the 1820s, this lovely, plaintive ballad tells of a white (Canadian or American) trader who courted the daughter of Shenandoah, an American Indian chieftain, and carried her off in his canoe, only to abandon her later on the banks of the Missouri River. A favorite song of sailors—some of whom must have experienced similar conquests and subsequent remorse, and who loved to sing it while away on long, lonely voyages—the song is sometimes thought of as a chantey.

CD 1
Track 6
1:48

Composer Anonymous.

Genre Folk ballad (chantey).

Timbre Solo male singer (Pete Seeger), accompanied by very sparse strumming of a few supportive guitar tones and simple chords.

Melody Based on a pentatonic scale. (The occasional use of a note not belonging to the pentatonic scale does not change the pentatonic flavor of the melody.)

—Continued

"Shenandoah"

Texture Mostly monophonic, the guitar adding little in the way of harmony.

Form Strophic; verse-refrain.

Meter Quadruple (four beats per measure).

Tempo The slow, relaxed tempo and somewhat irregular accents, closely following the natural rhythm of the text, suggest the roll of waves and the easy sway of a ship.

0:00   *Oh Shenandoah, I love your daughter. . . .*
0:34   *Oh Shenandoah, I long to see you. . . .*
1:12   *For seven years I've been a rover. . . .*

African Traditions

Unlike the European settlers, who arrived in the New World of their own free will, Africans were forcibly brought to America in European slave ships, beginning early in the seventeenth century—about the time the Pilgrims arrived at Plymouth Rock. By 1700 slavery had become common throughout the thirteen colonies.

Many slaveholders harshly discouraged references to African gods and religions in any traditional song or dance. Especially British Protestants, who considered African music customs savage and heathen, did everything possible to eradicate their slaves' native religion and culture. Partly to this end, the first babies born to slaves in this country (unlike those in other areas of the New World, such as Haiti, Cuba, or Brazil) often were separated from their families to be raised on other plantations. There they learned African lore and language from older Africans, of course, but they also began to accrue experience with America and with English.

Slaves in New England worked much as slaves worked in the South but were treated with more leniency, often enjoying a measure of free time in which to entertain themselves and their masters by singing, dancing, and playing musical instruments. The admiration they excited by their music was not always to the slaves' advantage, however: Newspaper lists of slaves for sale and of runaways often referred to their outstanding musical abilities, adding to their desirability as commodities to be owned and abused.

As adults, the first generation of slaves born here began to develop their own music, rooted in African customs and sounds, but genuinely African *American,* expressing their new experience in a new sort of African American language.

Whereas the first slaves had sung in African dialects, work songs and other songs gradually came to be sung more in English, pronounced, however, with African rhythms. For a long time, some African words continued to be used, perhaps for the purpose of obscuring seditious meaning from white people. When even the blacks could no longer understand the African languages, meaningless but rhythmic syllables were used as well.

Field Hollers

Most of the slaves forced to work on the plantations in what is now the southeastern United States came from West Africa, where they had commonly integrated music with their daily work. Particular kinds of songs became associated with certain tasks, such as fishing, weaving, hunting, or tilling their farms. In America, the familiar fishing, weaving, and hunting songs lost relevance, but slaves, such as those pictured in Figure 2.4, poured all the anguish of their new, tragic experience into **field hollers**—loud, rhythmically flexible, emotionally expressive chants or cries sung by a solitary voice. Some field hollers had words ("Where *are* you-u-u . . .?") but most, as in Listening Examples 7 and 8, used neutral syllables easily heard over distances.

Ring Shouts

Another African tradition translated to an African American experience was the religious **shout,** or **ring shout,** performed at religious services or camp meetings. The "shouters" formed a ring and shuffled energetically to the singing of a spiritual (see pp. 77–81) or hymn. Though careful to hardly lift their feet from the floor (lifting the feet would constitute dancing, a forbidden entertainment at services), the shouters, accompanied by singers and sometimes singing themselves, gradually quickened their pace, as they became caught up in an ecstasy of religious fervor that often kept them moving until they fell from sheer exhaustion.

FIGURE 2.4

In a Cotton Field. Wood engraving, drawn by Horace Bradley, 1887.

Listening Example 7

Field Holler

With hollers such as this, people established wordless but heart-warming contact with fellow workers who, hearing the poignant cries, could respond with expressive hollers of their own.

CD 1
Track 7
1:15

Timbre   Solo male voice.

Melody   A simple, narrow, mournful phrase on three tones, repeated.

Rhythm   Free, flexible.

Text   Neutral syllables, easy to sing and to hear over distances.

Listening Example 8

Father's Field Call

This father's field call or holler illustrates the high falsetto range, lying above the normal, full, chest voice, which enhanced the ability to call over long distances.

CD 1
Track 8
0:22

Timbre   Solo male voice in the falsetto range.

Melody   Begins with an upward leap, succeeded by a naturally falling inflection. This call is reminiscent, in fact, of the familiar "Yoo-hoo."

Rhythm   Free, flexible.

Text   Wordless.

Work Songs   In Africa, another kind of song, the **work song,** accompanied such rhythmic tasks as rowing, hoeing, or chopping trees. Traditional work songs expressed joy and pride in hard work for one's family and land, and gratitude to the gods for their help.

In America, too, slaves made up, or **improvised,** work songs as they labored in pain and sorrow, adapting the words, however, to their tragic new condition. Work songs often accompanied American plantation slaves, setting the pace and synchronizing the movements of groups of forced laborers. The songs, strophic in form, were performed in the characteristic West African music practice known as call-and-response, in which the leading lines of each verse, sung by a single voice, alternate with a repeated phrase, or refrain, sung by the group.

Listening Example 9, "Hammer, Ring," recorded at a state penitentiary in Texas in 1934, indicates how work songs facilitate the movements and lighten the mood of laborers working under the most difficult and depressing conditions.

"Hammer, Ring" (excerpt)

CD 1
Track 9
2:36

Hammer songs accompanied men driving the spikes that fastened long steel rails to wooden railroad ties. From the dramatic Bible story of Noah and the ark, the leader of this hammer song, recorded in 1934, improvises simple lines of text, to which the men—swinging 10-pound hammers freely from the shoulder in a complete circle about the head—rhythmically respond, "Hammer, ring!" The relentless rhythm and driving energy of the piece support and reinforce the regular rhythm of the hammering men.

Notice occasional variations in the inflection of the melody line, which add emphasis or emotional intensity to the delivery. Notice, too, the occasional calls, cries, or shouts of the workers. While their response is generally sung in unison, occasional flights of creativity among individuals vary the texture of their singing.

Composer   The song was improvised by Jesse Bradley and a group at State Penitentiary, Huntsville, Texas.

Genre   Work song (hammer song).

Timbre   Male singing voices.

Melody   The melody largely consists of the tones of a minor triad: The verses use *one* and *three* of the triad, and the refrain sometimes adds *five*.

Texture   Monophonic/heterophonic.

Form   Strophic. Each verse consists of a line of text, repeated, with the refrain "Hammer, ring!" interspersed between lines. The leader sings each line; the hammering men sing the refrain (call-and-response). Occasionally the leader repeats the introductory verse.

Meter   Duple.

0:00   *Won't you ring, old hammer?* . . .
0:06   *Broke the handle on my hammer* . . .
0:13   *Got to hammerin' the Bible* . . .

Freedom Songs During the first half of the nineteenth century, a movement known as the Underground Railroad assisted slaves seeking escape to free states, Canada, or elsewhere. This network of abolitionists, religious groups, and other sympathizers provided fleeing individuals transportation, supplies, and safe houses along secret routes. Their dangerous work allowed a tragically small, yet significant, number of slaves to reach freedom. Songs such as "No More Auction Block for Me" (Listening Example 10) encouraged them on their perilous mission.

Musical Instruments In Africa, drums often accompanied work songs, sometimes providing two or three different underlying rhythmic patterns in a complexity difficult for Western ears even to hear. Using drums for communication

Listening Example 10

"No More Auction Block for Me"

This haunting freedom song from about 1800 expresses the determination of slaves to escape the humiliation of being sold at auction, the agony of separation from family, and the terrible physical punishment to which they were daily subjected. The melody, almost identical to a traditional West African song, inspired two twentieth-century anthems of the civil rights movement: "We Shall Overcome" and Bob Dylan's "Blowin' in the Wind," both of which can be heard on YouTube. Solemnly sung here by **Odetta** (Odetta Holmes, 1930–2008), the song evokes the anguish of the slaves and their determination to achieve freedom.

CD 1
Track 10
2:09

Composer Anonymous.

Genre Freedom song.

Timbre Contralto voice (Odetta), quietly accompanied by mixed chorus.

Texture Homophonic.

Form Strophic.

Meter Quadruple.

0:00   *No more auction block for me . . .*
0:31   *No more pint of salt for me . . .*
1:04   *No more driver's lash for me . . .*
1:35   *No more auction block for me . . .*

as well as for music, West Africans developed an extremely fine sense of changes in tone and timbre, together with truly remarkable rhythmic techniques.

Many slaves brought small drums and simple string instruments with them on the slave ships, where their captors sometimes compelled them to perform music to keep them occupied and while away the time; but slaveholders on southern plantations generally banned the use of African drums, fearing that the thrilling drumbeats might incite revolt. Slaves compensated for the loss of their drums by improvising percussive instruments from empty oil drums, metal washbasins, and whatever else might be available and by clapping, body-slapping, and stamping the rhythms of their songs and dances. Rattles or bits of shell or bone added to simple instruments further enhanced the driving beat.

West African gourd **banjos** (variously called *banjar, banza,* and other similar names) arrived in the American colonies by way of the slave trade in the late seventeenth century. Developed from ancient Arab prototypes, the African banjo typically had four strings, three long and one short, the short string providing a rhythmic and harmonic **drone** (a repeated tone of constant pitch). By stretching an animal skin across the open side of a hollowed-out gourd or calabash, slaves created their own primitive banjos, destined in more sophisticated form (such as the four-string banjo seen in Figure 2.5) to provide limitless entertainment for Americans and others of assorted ethnicity and culture.

FIGURE 2.5

A four-string banjo.

What of African Music Survives Today?

Today's African American musics are deeply rooted in African traditions that arrived in the New World with the first slaves. Call-and-response, for example, became a basic characteristic of African American vocal and instrumental music, as we shall see when we study blues, vocal and instrumental jazz, the religious folk songs called *spirituals,* and many other kinds of contemporary black music. Improvisation is inherent in the concept of jazz and colors much other music as well. Much African American music is still based on the "bent" or flexible tones of the *blues* scale (see p. 150), unheard in this country until the first West Africans arrived. Even more apparent is the emphasis in African American music on rhythm over melody, and the complexity of African rhythms compared with those of Western (European) music.

Terms to Review

folk music
hymn
alabado
ballad
corrido

homophony (homophonic or
    chordal texture)
pentatonic
broadside
chantey
field hollers

shout, ring shout
work songs
improvised
banjo
drone

Key Figure

Odetta

Critical Thinking

What opportunities do today's political, religious, or personal satirists have to avoid prosecution by those they attack? Compare the potential for free expression in rap lyrics, cartoons, television entertainment, movies, newspapers, books, and on the web, with that of the broadsides in colonial and revolutionary America.

In how many ways might you distinguish between African and African American music?

Religious Music in the Colonial, Revolutionary, and Federal Periods

A s early as the sixteenth century, inhabitants of the New World experienced a variety of native and imported musics. These included Roman Catholic music, with which French and Spanish visitors accompanied their own worship and which they taught to Indians in Florida and in parts of the Southwest as part of their effort to convert Native Americans to Roman Catholicism.

Music at the Spanish Missions

Music had an important part in the religious training of American Indians by zealous Spanish missionaries, who taught their more or less willing converts to sing the songs and prayers of the Christian church, usually set to very simple tunes. Soon American Indians were learning to sing in choirs, play in church orchestras, and even make simple European-style musical instruments. They learned traditional Spanish music, religious praise songs or hymns, and even the more difficult Gregorian chant, traditionally sung by trained soloists and choirs. At Christmastime, they participated in musical nativity plays called *Las posadas* (The Lodgings), commemorating the struggles of Mary to find a place in which to deliver the baby Jesus.

The Spanish missions remained active in California, where missionaries and their Native American students regularly performed Catholic church music until the Mexican government ordered the missions closed in 1833. A large number of musical instruments, as well as manuscripts of Mass settings and other church music of varying levels of complexity, have been found at some of the mission sites, many of which can still be visited.

While Catholic music remained important in regions of the country inhabited by Spanish, French, or Mexican people, the Protestant custom of singing psalms and hymns dominated the religious music experience in this country. These religious songs inspired and comforted urban and rural people in the North and South, but New England's practices exerted the strongest and longest-lasting influence on American music.

Psalm Tunes

In 1517, a German Catholic cleric, Martin Luther (1483–1546), instigated the Protestant Reformation by advocating reform of certain questionable practices by the Roman Catholic church of his day. The movement thus begun stimulated a number of independent-minded people in northern European countries to form their own Protestant sects, each adhering to particular tenets of religious and secular conduct, including the place of music in worship.

Unlike Catholics, whose formal religious music was sung in Latin, Protestants sang their hymns in their vernacular, or common, language. They also preferred simple, folklike tunes, which everyday people could sing, to the elaborate Gregorian chant or complex choir pieces sung by trained Catholic monks.

The Pilgrims and Puritans arriving in New England early in the seventeenth century were Protestants, whose protests against the Roman Catholic church included some concerning religious music. People who followed the strict teachings of the Swiss reformer John Calvin (1509–1564) believed that the *only* texts suitable for singing in a worship service were those of the **psalms,** 150 inspirational verses found in the Old Testament of the Bible. Thus Calvinists forbade the singing in church of hymns, which had freely written texts not necessarily based on passages from the Bible or from church liturgy.

Although poetic in style and expression, however, the psalms as they appear in the Bible are neither metered nor rhymed and therefore do not lend themselves readily to congregational singing. Thus Calvinists retranslated all the psalms into verses having a regular number of lines, with patterns of weak and accented beats, suitable for setting to music.

The Calvinists did not intend their **psalm tunes** to stir emotions or draw attention to the music itself, because they believed the only purpose for music in a church service was to enhance expression of a religious text. Therefore, because musical instruments cannot express words, harmony increases music's sensuous appeal, and neither instruments nor harmony will serve to clarify a text, the Calvinists consistently sang their psalm tunes in church **a cappella** (unaccompanied) and in unison. It is important for us to understand, however, that the separation between sacred and secular experience typical of the modern American experience did not apply in colonial America. Thus it was quite usual for Calvinists to sing psalm tunes austerely in church, but in harmony and with elaborate instrumental accompaniment in family and social gatherings at home.

The New Englanders' psalm singing became, in effect, a kind of folk tradition. Psalm tunes were of a folklike nature and generally were learned from oral experience. Strophic in form, most had four-line stanzas, as is common in much folk song, and the ornamentation and variation in the singing of psalm tunes were typical of the manner of singing songs in the folk tradition.

Psalters   The newly metered and rhymed psalm verses were printed in books called **psalters** for use in congregational singing. Some psalters contained

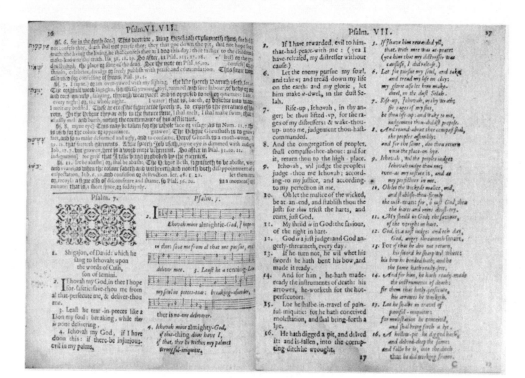

FIGURE 3.1

Pages from the *Ainsworth Psalter* (Amsterdam, 1612), showing a psalm tune and the manner in which each verse of the psalm has been retranslated into rhymed and metered verse.

notated melodies, whereas others printed no music but only the words of the psalm verses, which could be sung to widely familiar and well-remembered folk, popular, or hymn tunes (Figure 3.1).

The first collection of psalm tunes was printed in Switzerland in 1539, nearly a century before the Pilgrims and Puritans came to the New World. This early psalter included a setting of Psalm 100 (Listening Example 11), known today as "Old Hundred."

Many of the English settlers had enjoyed playing and listening to musical instruments in their homes, but few managed to bring any instruments with them to the New World. Furthermore, because travel between the continents was costly, time-consuming, and dangerous, the settlers soon lost touch with current music events abroad. The psalters they brought with them did not provide a separate tune for each of the 150 psalms, since all verses with the same metrical pattern could be sung to the same melody. The tunes they did include, however, were often so merry in mood and lively in tempo that skeptics referred to them as "Geneva jigs" (remembering the origins of Calvinism in Geneva, Switzerland). In a similar vein, Shakespeare, in *The Winter's Tale*, described a Puritan who "sings psalms to hornpipes." For some time the music experience for both Pilgrims and Puritans consisted of singing psalm tunes a cappella for worship in church and in harmony and accompanied for entertainment at home.

"Old Hundred" (excerpt)

Of all the beautiful psalm tunes, this one from about 1550 has become the best known. It is often sung by congregations in Protestant churches today, sometimes with a text beginning "From all that dwell below the skies" and sometimes as the Doxology ("Praise God, from Whom all blessings flow").

CD 1
Track 11
0:24

Composer   Louis Bourgeois (c. 1510–c. 1560).

Performers   Gregg Smith Singers.

Genre   Psalm tune.

Timbre   A cappella singing. The choir, or chorus, sings in four-part harmony (soprano, alto, tenor, bass), with the melody in the high, or soprano, female voices.

Texture   Homophonic.

Form   Strophic. (Only one stanza is heard on the CD.)

Rhythm   Although the melody has remained unchanged for centuries, the rhythm has been altered. Modern Protestants generally sing "Old Hundred"—so called because of the tune's association with Psalm 100—in the rhythm heard here, or in another equally regular rhythmic pattern, neither pattern having the rhythmic variety, interest, or vigor of the settings enjoyed by early congregations.

Meter   Quadruple. (We have considered meter as defining the number of beats per measure. In another sense, *meter* may refer to the pattern of syllables in a stanza of text. Thus each stanza of the text to "Old Hundred" has four lines, and each line has eight syllables, a pattern called *long meter*. Any text with this meter could be sung to any long-meter tune.)

In a surprisingly short time, the settlers developed an American taste and tongue, making the language of their old psalters seem stilted and old-fashioned. Thus only twenty years after landing at Plymouth Rock, in 1640, an American psalter titled *The Whole Booke of Psalms Faithfully Translated into English Metre,* but popularly known as the **Bay Psalm Book,** was printed in Cambridge, Massachusetts, the first book printed in the New World. No tunes were included in the first editions of the Bay Psalm Book, but each edition after 1690 included music (Figure 3.2).

FIGURE 3.2

Pages from a later edition of the Bay Psalm Book, the first book printed in the American colonies.

Other Protestant Music

While John Calvin proscribed all music but the singing of psalm tunes in church, Martin Luther encouraged the joyful singing of simple tunes and lighthearted texts in worship, even composing some hymns of his own. Thus while Calvinists confined their worship music to the unaccompanied singing of psalm tunes, American Lutherans sang hymns, many of which (including Luther's best-known hymn, with a sturdy tune and a strong text beginning "A mighty fortress is our God") appear in hymnals currently used by many Protestant sects.

The late seventeenth century and early eighteenth century brought further waves of emigrant Protestants, including members of the English Society of Friends, known as Quakers, and Shakers, a later offshoot from the Quaker sect (so called because of the trembling induced by their religious emotion during

"'Tis the Gift to Be Simple"

This well-known piece from about 1848 was composed as a dance song, the last two lines constituting instructions for dancers to perform as part of their worship expression.

CD 1
Track 12
1:09

Composer Joseph Brackett, Jr. (1797–1882).

Genre Dance song.

Timbre Women singing in unison, a cappella (unaccompanied).

Melody Notice that the melody, in a major key, moves mostly stepwise with few leaps, winding up and down, "bending" and "turning" in a manner eminently suited to the text.

Texture Monophonic.

Form Through composed. (In this performance, each half of the song is repeated.)

Meter Duple.

Text It is probable that the words (readily available online), while describing the motions of the worship dance, also had double meanings: One should "turn" away from evil, "bow" humbly before God, and "bend" like a willow to adversity and strife.

www.mhhe.com/ferrisaml6e

worship). A Shaker song, "'Tis the Gift to Be Simple" (Listening Example 12), with words and music by Joseph Brackett, Jr., has become a well-known tune with both sacred and secular associations. It was composed as a dance song, the last two lines constituting instructions for dancers to perform as part of their worship expression. The American composer Aaron Copland (see pp. 374–380) included a series of variations on the tune in his composition titled *Appalachian Spring,* which has become one of the most familiar passages of American orchestral music (see the Online Listening Examples). In 1963, a British songwriter, Sydney Carter, used Brackett's tune for his song "Lord of the Dance," which became widely popular. More recently, "Simple Gifts" was sung at two presidential inaugurations: Ronald Reagan's (1985) and Bill Clinton's (1993); and film composer John Williams included the melody in his original instrumental composition "Air and Simple Gifts," performed at the 2009 inauguration of President Barack Obama.

The form of the song is **through composed,** meaning that each line of text has its own music.

German-Speaking Protestant Sects Responding to William Penn's policy of religious toleration, a number of German-speaking Protestants fled persecution in their homelands and came to this country to settle first in Pennsylvania, and later in other regions. Here, free from persecution, they kept much of their European culture intact, their language and religious practices largely isolating them from the Protestant Anglo-American mainstream of the thirteen colonies.

The Mennonites (of whom the Amish were a later offshoot) first arrived in 1683, mostly from Germany. They brought their own hymnals and psalters, and during the last quarter of the eighteenth century, Mennonite schoolmasters also compiled tune books containing traditional texts and tunes. They decorated the title pages of their tune books with a Pennsylvania-German Mennonite folk art called *Fraktur* (meaning "broken"), a highly ornamental combination of calligraphy and script with flowers, figures, and geometric designs (Figure 3.3). However, the Mennonites preserved their lovely old hymn tunes largely by oral tradition, singing them today in versions differing widely from written sources such as student notebooks and hymnals.

Of the new immigrants, the German-speaking Moravians had by far the most significant effect upon music in America. The Moravians arrived in 1735 together with the famous Methodist missionaries and hymn writers John and Charles Wesley. Having been severely persecuted for their religious beliefs and

FIGURE 3.3

Fraktur. This beautifully illuminated manuscript of the thirty-fourth psalm, made by an anonymous artist in 1802, may have been intended to hang on the wall of a home.

practices in their homelands of Moravia and Bohemia, the Moravians wished to settle in America, where many intended to serve as Christian missionaries to African and Native Americans. Settling first in Georgia, the Moravians then moved north to found Bethlehem, Pennsylvania. They also established communities in Salem (Winston-Salem today), North Carolina, and other areas in what is today the eastern United States.

Music had been an important part of the Moravians' experience in Europe, and they continued to compose and perform beautiful music in their new land. Integrating hymn singing and other religious music into their daily lives, some Moravians also wrote secular songs and instrumental music, sophisticated and complex beyond those of other early Americans and revealing their strong German and Czech heritage.

The Great Awakening
Beginning in 1735, a series of strong religious revival movements known as the (first) Great Awakening swept the eastern seaboard. The movement began in New England cities, where many Puritans perceived a lessening of moral rectitude and an increase in intellectual, as opposed to spiritual, interests. People living on small farms and plantations in remote rural areas, consumed with scratching a meager living from hard and difficult land, had largely abandoned religious customs fostered by the close communication and churchly discipline of parish life.

But the Great Awakening spread like wildfire from North to South, stirring latent religious fervor and raising concern among urban and rural folk not only for their own redemption, but for that of black slaves and Indians as well. All this religious enthusiasm further stimulated the rise of psalm- and hymn-singing in America.

Early Efforts at Musical Reform

The Moravians' musical influence was strong but limited in scope, and most colonials had no opportunity to hear or to practice good music. Although each edition of the Bay Psalm Book printed after 1698 included several notated tunes, few people knew how to read music, and as the old tunes came to be remembered differently in various towns and villages, New Englanders began to disagree as to how they should be sung. In order to learn each tune as they thought it should be rendered, some congregations adopted the practice of **lining out,** in which a more or less musically literate leader sang one line of the psalm, which the congregation then repeated in unison, performing each successive line in this awkward manner.

Lining out satisfied very few. Some of the leaders, with voices untrained and sometimes unattractive as well, began the songs too high or too low, causing people in the congregation to squeak above or grumble below their comfortable singing ranges. In the effort to improve or enliven the effect, leaders and sometimes congregational members embellished the tunes at will, grossly distorting their original sound. Becoming accustomed to such altered (in a sense Americanized) versions of the old tunes, many people resisted all efforts to impose the regular style of singing the tunes as they were written.

The Singing School Movement As the advantages of being able to read music notation became apparent, certain better-educated ministers printed collections of tunes, prefaced by detailed instructions on how to read music notation, and set out to teach New Englanders to read the tunes printed in their psalters. Although the traditional system of music notation is quite easy to learn (you may want to refer to pp. 7–8 of the Prelude), some amateur teachers attempted to devise even simpler methods, including one based on the four syllables then commonly used to sing pitches (*fa, sol, la,* and *mi*) that placed on the staff the first *letter* of each syllable (*f, s, l,* or *m*) instead of the traditional note heads.

The efforts of the teaching ministers soon were supplemented, and eventually assumed, by talented amateur musicians, who became known as **singing school masters.** Some of these self-taught music amateurs, having previously earned their living as shopkeepers, merchants, or farmers, or in other practical trades, became itinerant teachers, traveling from town to town and holding informal singing schools in the local meetinghouse, church, or school for a limited period of perhaps two or three months. People welcomed the singing school masters to their towns, because singing schools became popular social as well as educational events. Interested men, women, and young people attended the singing lessons several times a week and, at the end of their instruction, gave a performance demonstrating their accomplishments to the town's proud public. Then the singing school master traveled on to another place.

The singing school movement, which began in Boston about 1720 and experienced its greatest activity throughout New England from 1760 to 1800, finally spread north into Canada and south through New York, New Jersey, Pennsylvania, and Maryland, and into the Carolinas. In fact, singing school masters offered widespread instruction and inspiration, especially in rural and remote areas, well into the nineteenth century. Necessarily hardy and independent individuals, the singing school masters devised their own teaching materials, compiled collections of familiar psalm tunes and other religious songs, and composed tunes of their own. Some wrote extensive introductions to their music primers, including information about the syllables to be sung and the elements of music. The first Americans to write music with a distinctively American (at least, non-European) sound, they are collectively referred to as members of the **First New England School** of composers.

A "school" of artists generally includes people living at about the same time, in the same geographic region, and sharing certain artistic goals and similarities of style. The First New England School composers, who lived in late-eighteenth-century New England, shared the goals of teaching people to read music and to sing. Most of the simple folklike songs they composed as teaching tools had religious texts and so were also suitable for congregational singing and for private entertainment at home. The best songs of these "Yankee pioneers" were as

rugged, naive, and honest as the sturdy tunesmiths who made them because, untouched by the influence of their sophisticated European contemporaries, they relied upon old, familiar techniques and their own honest taste. Colonial Americans, after all, had been out of touch with European music since the early seventeenth century, when tonality first became the harmonic system of the Western world, and the singing school masters had only a rudimentary comprehension of the tonal system. More significantly, they did not feel constrained to conform to *anyone's* rules. Sometimes they turned to pretonal techniques, basing some melodies on modes or on simple pentatonic scales.

William Billings (1746–1800)

William Billings, a tanner of hides who became famous as a singing school master and composer, was the first American to produce a book of tunes all of his own composition (Figure 3.4). Billings's *New England Psalm Singer* was printed (by Paul Revere) in 1770. Although Billings had attended singing school himself and continued to study music throughout his career, he considered "nature" the best teacher and confidently judged the quality of a piece according to how much he liked it. Well aware, for example, of the conventional relationships between consonant (at rest) and dissonant (tense or active) sounds, Billings and other composers of the First New England School often remained independent of such rules, making refreshingly unorthodox musical decisions to please their own ears. (Annoyed at criticism of his music by certain less adventurous listeners, Billings flaunted his unconventional ideas by writing a song titled "Jargon," with flagrantly outrageous harmonies sure to offend the sensibilities of delicate taste.) Considered by his contemporaries to be eccentric but talented above the ordinary, Billings had many admirers; but he failed to realize much profit on his tune books, because there was no effective copyright law in his day. Forced to work as a street cleaner late in life, this remarkable early American composer died a poor man.

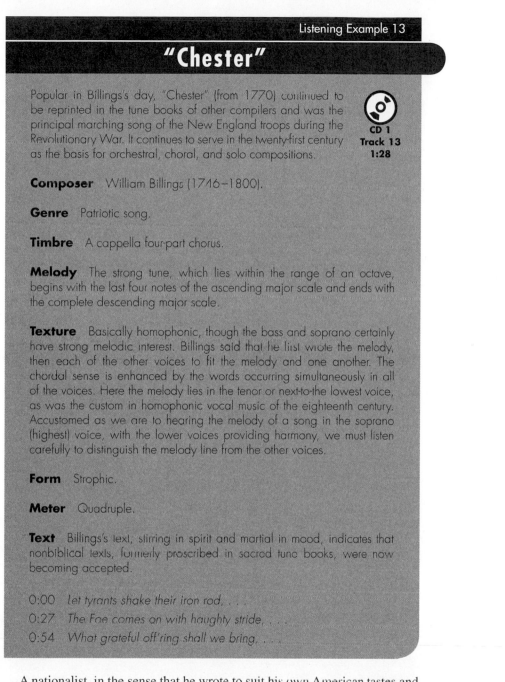

Listening Example 13

"Chester"

Popular in Billings's day, "Chester" (from 1770) continued to be reprinted in the tune books of other compilers and was the principal marching song of the New England troops during the Revolutionary War. It continues to serve in the twenty-first century as the basis for orchestral, choral, and solo compositions.

CD 1
Track 13
1:28

Composer   William Billings (1746–1800).

Genre   Patriotic song.

Timbre   A cappella four-part chorus.

Melody   The strong tune, which lies within the range of an octave, begins with the last four notes of the ascending major scale and ends with the complete descending major scale.

Texture   Basically homophonic, though the bass and soprano certainly have strong melodic interest. Billings said that he first wrote the melody, then each of the other voices to fit the melody and one another. The chordal sense is enhanced by the words occurring simultaneously in all of the voices. Here the melody lies in the tenor or next-to-the lowest voice, as was the custom in homophonic vocal music of the eighteenth century. Accustomed as we are to hearing the melody of a song in the soprano (highest) voice, with the lower voices providing harmony, we must listen carefully to distinguish the melody line from the other voices.

Form   Strophic.

Meter   Quadruple.

Text   Billings's text, stirring in spirit and martial in mood, indicates that nonbiblical texts, formerly proscribed in sacred tune books, were now becoming accepted.

0:00   *Let tyrants shake their iron rod, . . .*
0:27   *The Foe comes on with haughty stride, . . .*
0:54   *What grateful off'ring shall we bring, . . .*

A nationalist, in the sense that he wrote to suit his own American tastes and made no attempt to imitate European sounds, Billings produced a number of stirring patriotic songs, some of which describe specific events of the American Revolutionary War. "Chester" (Listening Example 13), a favorite of the Revolutionary period, is sometimes referred to as the first American popular song, because it was widely sung and played by bands and by solo instrumentalists for general pleasure and entertainment. "Chester" appeared with its first verse in the collection printed in 1770, but Billings added defiant topical stanzas after the war broke out.

Unlike most of the music we have studied so far, consisting of one line of melody without harmonic accompaniment, "Chester" was written and is usually performed in chordal, or homophonic, texture. In other words, Billings wrote not only the tune, but also its accompaniment. People had long enjoyed singing harmonized versions of their religious songs at home if not in church; and by the time of the First New England School, harmony was no longer excluded from music in the worship service.

In our Listening Example, "Chester" is sung a cappella, but it might have been accompanied by one or more instruments doubling the voice parts. The belief that church music must enhance—never detract from—worship had caused strong prejudice against the instrumental accompaniment of church music, since instruments could not express a text but simply added a sensuous dimension to the sound. But, as noted above, this prejudice began to lessen about the time of the First New England School, as some churches accepted accompaniment of congregational singing by organ or by string or wind instruments. The violin, associated with popular dancing and widely condemned as the "devil's fiddle," gained acceptance only slowly, but the bass viol, flute, clarinet, and bassoon increasingly accompanied singing or were even used to play short instrumental passages.

Canons

A **canon** is a melody that forms meaningful harmonies when performed with "staggered entrances"—that is, when successive voices begin the same melody at later times (Figure 3.5). Each voice continues to the end of the melody, simply dropping out at the end of the tune while any remaining voices continue until they drop out in turn. (Here "voice" refers to a line of music, whether sung or played by musical instruments.) Although the voices indeed form harmony when sung together, each line is *melodically* conceived—there is no chordal concept—and so we call this texture **polyphonic,** meaning two or more melodic lines are performed together. In the case of a canon, each melodic line is the same, but because they are performed starting at different times, they produce combinations of different tones (harmony).

"When Jesus Wept" (Listening Example 14), one of Billings's best-known and best-loved songs, is a circular canon, or **round,** which continues to make harmonic sense when repeated any number of times.

FIGURE 3.5

A canon. Each voice enters in turn, singing the same melody. The resulting combination of tones produces attractive harmonies.

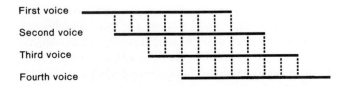

First voice

Second voice

Third voice

Fourth voice

Listening Example 14

"When Jesus Wept"

This haunting melody from the late eighteenth century, exquisite in its simplicity and beauty, expresses the essence of the poignant text. When performed "in canon"—that is, with each of four voices entering in turn, continuing to the end, and perhaps repeating the whole—it becomes a harmonic as well as a melodic treasure.

CD 1
Track 14
1:16

Composer William Billings (1746–1800).

Words Billings wrote the words as well as the music.

Genre Canon.

Timbre Here, mixed chorus (soprano, alto, tenor, bass). The canon may be performed by any combination of voices.

Melody The melody, in minor mode, is written so as to form meaningful harmonies when performed in canon, or with "staggered entrances."

Texture Monophonic when performed in unison; polyphonic when performed in canon.

Form A four-part circular canon, or round. There are four phrases, any two or more of which form harmony when performed together.

Meter Triple.

Text The ending is particularly effective, as the last voices sing the moving words in unison, the other voices having dropped out in turn.

When Jesus wept, the falling tear
In mercy flow'd beyond all bound.
When Jesus groan'd, a trembling fear
Seiz'd all the guilty world around.

Fuging Tunes Late in the eighteenth century, a new kind of song called a **fuging tune** became very popular, and by 1810, about 1,000 of these had been written. A fuging tune consists of two sections, which we will call **A** and **B** (Figure 3.6). The first section (**A**) is chordal, or homophonic, in texture, the

FIGURE 3.6

A fuging tune. Section A is homophonic in texture, as represented by the dotted vertical lines. Section B begins with staggered entrances (polyphonic texture) but ends with chords. Section B is repeated.

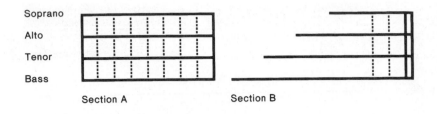

Section A   Section B

melody lying in one voice (usually the tenor) while the other three (soprano, alto, and bass) provide chordal harmony.

The second section of a fuging tune (**B**), which begins with staggered entrances, gives each voice melodic interest; thus the texture is polyphonic. But unlike a canon, in which each voice performs the *same* melody, entering and dropping out in turn, a fuging tune has four similar but *independent* lines of music, which finally end together on a chord. The second section is repeated, rendering the form of a fuging tune **ABB.**

Fuging tunes were fun to sing, offering everyone an interesting and varied part and challenging housewives, farmers, shopkeepers, tavern owners, young people—all those who enjoyed music—to put to use their hard-won singing school skills. "Sherburne" (Listening Example 15) by **Daniel Read** (1757–1836), another well-known member of the First New England School of composers, was an immensely popular fuging tune in late-eighteenth-century

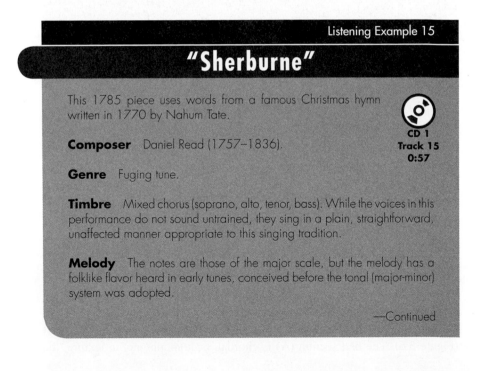

Listening Example 15

"Sherburne"

This 1785 piece uses words from a famous Christmas hymn written in 1770 by Nahum Tate.

CD 1
Track 15
0:57

Composer   Daniel Read (1757–1836).

Genre   Fuging tune.

Timbre   Mixed chorus (soprano, alto, tenor, bass). While the voices in this performance do not sound untrained, they sing in a plain, straightforward, unaffected manner appropriate to this singing tradition.

Melody   The notes are those of the major scale, but the melody has a folklike flavor heard in early tunes, conceived before the tonal (major-minor) system was adopted.

—Continued

"Sherburne"

Texture   Homophonic and polyphonic. The first section (**A**), consisting of the first two lines of text, is homophonic in texture (all four voices singing the same words at the same time imply chordal texture). The second section (**B,** the third and fourth lines) is mostly polyphonic: It begins with "staggered entrances," each melodic line imitative of, but not identical to, the others. (Here, different words in different voices enhance our ability to hear in a linear fashion, aware of each individual line of music.) The last few syllables are sounded simultaneously in all the voices, and the section ends on a chord.

Form   Fuging tune: **ABB**.

Meter   Duple. You may notice a pause, however, on the word *night.* Such irregularities are characteristic of this simple tradition.

Text

While Shepherds watched their flocks at night
All seated on the ground
The angel of the Lord came down,
And glory shone around.

America. A comb maker who also owned a general store and taught singing school, Read probably was the most popular composer of fuging tunes. "Sherburne" remained widely known until the Civil War period and still is sung in parts of the country today.

Besides Billings and Read, many singing school masters composed psalm tunes, hymns, canons, and fuging tunes for the edification and enjoyment of their pupils. Although these practical men conceived of their music as teaching material rather than art, we value it today as strong, beautiful, and genuinely American in character, much as we appreciate the work folk artists of the period produced, functional in purpose but beautiful in its own right. (Figure 3.7). Recent American composers have used the tunes of the First New England School composers and their contemporaries as inspiration and source material for music of our own period. (Notably, William Schuman, a Pulitzer Prize–winning composer with strong national interests, wrote a symphonic concert piece titled *New England Triptych* based on three of Billings's songs, including "When Jesus Wept" and "Chester." See Listening Example 78.)

FIGURE 3.7

The Sargent Family, American
School, 1800, canvas,
0.974 cm × 1.280 cm.
Folk artists, like the singing
school masters, accomplished
highly attractive art in their
efforts to provide a practical
service—here, to preserve
the likenesses of this young
American family.

Terms to Review

psalms

psalm tunes

a cappella

psalter

Bay Psalm Book

through composed

lining out

singing school masters

First New England School

canon

polyphony (polyphonic
    texture)

round

fuging tune

Key Figures

William Billings

Daniel Read

Critical Thinking

Why do you think twentieth-century American composers
such as Henry Cowell, William Schuman, and Otto
Luening found fuging tunes a fertile source of inspiration
for the composition of concert music?

In what ways might you describe the music of the singing
school masters as folk art?

Why do you think many eighteenth-century American
Protestants enjoyed singing fuging tunes more than psalm
tunes?

Why do you think some of the psalm tunes (including
"Old Hundred") remain so well-known and well-loved
today?

Secular Music in the Colonial, Revolutionary, and Federal Periods

P
ublic concerts began to be performed in some of the larger American cities beginning in the late 1720s—about the same time as in Europe. For most of the eighteenth century, however, Americans showed little interest in formal concert music, most remaining largely unaware of the outstanding composers of their time: the Austrians Wolfgang Amadeus Mozart (1756–1790) and Franz Joseph Haydn (1732–1809). Because even the best-educated American audience had very limited experience with serious music, early concerts consisted of simple and popular pieces—marches and dance tunes, for example, interspersed with folk and popular songs from the contemporary theater. Stirring "battle pieces"—imitating on harpsichord, organ, piano, or band and orchestral instruments the sounds of gunfire, marching troops, bugle calls, and other warlike effects—numbered among the most popular concert attractions.

Music in Everyday Experience

Home music, work music, music for entertainment, and music for dancing dominated American music throughout the Revolutionary and federal periods. In rural areas, combined work and social affairs such as barn raisings, maple sugaring, and corn husking often were accompanied by singing, fiddling, or other musical activities and followed by dancing. Music in New Orleans must have been particularly rich and varied, because African, Native American, Caribbean, French, and Spanish cultures all were part of life in that vibrant city. One artist depicted a prominent New Orleans family entertaining themselves and perhaps some friends with music (Figure 4.1).

Music publishing had become an important business by the latter part of the century, producing quantities of sheet music appropriate for the amateur performer that consisted mostly of simple vocal and piano pieces sometimes referred to as "household music." More and more Americans had musical instruments such as violins, guitars, oboes, and flutes in their homes. Popular keyboard instruments included small and often elaborately decorated *virginals* (Figure 4.2) as well as harpsichords and early pianos, called *fortepianos,* some of which were built in America. The fortepiano was smaller and more delicate

FIGURE 4.1

The Family of Doctor Montegut, José Francisco Xavier de Salazar y Mendoza, 1794–1800, oil on canvas, 59″ × 74″. Collection of the Louisiana State Museum, loan of Mr. Gustave Pitot.

FIGURE 4.2

Double spinet, or virginal, made by Ludovicus Growelus (Lodewijck Grauwels). Early virginals were oblong boxes small enough to be placed on a table, but late in the eighteenth century, the term was applied to various keyboard instruments.

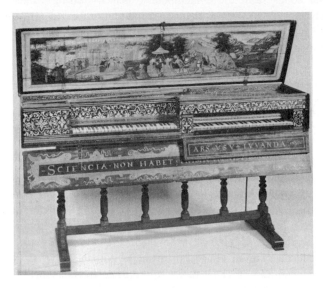

than the modern instrument, but as its name implies, it was able to produce varied dynamic levels according to the touch of the performer. Children and young women learned to sing and play simple pieces by taking lessons from immigrant professional musicians.

Servants, both African American and white, sometimes were chosen for their musical abilities and expected to contribute to music making in the home.

Talented African Americans sometimes supplied music for social dancing and played at dancing schools, in taverns, and for formal balls. The favored instrument to accompany dancing was the *fiddle:* Smaller and lighter than the modern violin and producing a louder and more vibrant sound than was considered appropriate for genteel listening, the eighteenth-century instrument was heard more often in the barnyard or ballroom than in the parlor.

Prestigious Musical Amateurs

Many talented and accomplished European emigrant musicians greatly enriched the American concert experience before and after the turn of the nineteenth century. Although Europeans continued to dominate professional music performances, however, American amateurs became increasingly active in various phases of musical activity. Many joined musical societies founded in a number of larger American cities, which presented instrumental or choral music—mostly written, however, by European composers. Professional foreign musicians often joined the members of amateur societies for their concerts, which lasted for as long as three or more hours.

The first performances in America of important European symphonic and choral works were given by amateur Moravian musicians, whose compositions and performances were of the highest quality, for they were amateurs only in the sense that they composed and performed music for the love of it (as the root of the word *amateur* implies) rather than for money. As news spread of the Moravians' outstanding concerts, people traveled long distances from other settlements to hear them. George Washington and Benjamin Franklin numbered among the Moravians' most fervent admirers.

Well-to-do patrons and musical amateurs such as the famous statesman **Thomas Jefferson** (1743–1826) supported the efforts of the musical societies by contributing generously of their time, money, and talent. Jefferson, a fine musician himself, participated enthusiastically in music activities, although he insisted that the arts were meaningful only as they bore relevance to everyday life. An accomplished architect who designed buildings to be beautiful as well as efficient, Jefferson apparently considered the musical arts an essential part of the human experience as well. He played the violin, as did Patrick Henry, who sometimes joined Jefferson in duets to entertain themselves, their friends, and (before the Revolution) illustrious representatives of the king's government in Williamsburg, Virginia. Most early Americans agreed with Jefferson that art—especially American art—must be practical to be worthwhile. John Adams considered even "practical" art a luxury inappropriate for the people of a young democracy, although he admired well-written sermons, political documents, or tracts.

Benjamin Franklin (1706–1790), who warned that Americans should not cultivate a taste for the arts before they were able to produce art, clearly considered Europeans superior in this regard. Conceding that poetry, painting, and music might be useful under certain circumstances, he complained that America had no musicians of the caliber of outstanding European performers,

FIGURE 4.3

Benjamin Franklin playing his glass harmonica.

and that even concerts performed by Europeans in America were inferior to the performances Franklin heard in England and on the continent.

Franklin wrote verses to set to tunes that he enjoyed, learned to play the guitar and the harp very well, and even invented a musical instrument called the **armonica** or **glass harmonica** (Figure 4.3), which became enormously popular in its day. This instrument consists of a series of hollow, hemispheric glass bowls or bells, each with a short neck. The glasses are mounted on a horizontal spindle, each fitted inside the next largest with a finger width of brim exposed on which to play. The performer keeps the spindle turning through a trough of water by working a pedal, while producing a delicate sound by rubbing the wet rims of the glasses with the fingers. The mysterious sounds of the glass harmonica were reputed to make women faint, soothe marital disputes, and even wake the dead! (Mozart frequently played the instrument at the Vienna home of the hypnotist Anton Mesmer, who used it to help induce trances in his patients.)

The first secular songs published in America were by Europeans, many from England, and were usually associated with the theater. But about the same time that the singing school masters were writing religious songs to use as teaching tools, other amateur American composers began to write music with neither a religious nor a practical purpose. **Francis Hopkinson** (1737–1791), an extraordinary American who became our first secretary of the navy and one of the signers of the Declaration of Independence, also was much concerned with the artistic dimension of American life. Hopkinson wrote several songs intended for concert or recital performance (amateur or professional), as opposed to folk or popular pieces. A zealous patriot in the political sense, Hopkinson nevertheless conceived his songs in conscientious imitation of the English songs of his day. Unlike the sturdily independent singing school masters, Hopkinson held the "cultivated" eighteenth-century American view that the colonists were inferior in the arts and best advised to emulate European styles, as he did in his song titled "My Days Have Been So Wondrous Free."

Although Hopkinson appears to have been the first American to attempt songs of this nature, soon other Americans also composed songs European in style, with texts, however, often based upon American subjects—several in honor of George Washington. Most early American art songs, unlike their more demanding European models, were suitable for performance by amateurs.

Early American Theater

Musical theater became popular in some areas during the 1730s, as growing numbers of European professional musicians became associated with both the theater and the concert hall. Although their songs and instrumental interludes were performed in concert halls as well as in the theater, theatrical performances made their works popular and afforded them a living.

These highly trained professional musicians provided performance and educational opportunities previously denied colonial Americans. Two early centers of music activity—Charleston (North Carolina) and Williamsburg (Virginia)—had active theaters well before the middle of the eighteenth century. Anglican religious influence prevailed in the South, and the English church authorities—unlike the Calvinists—had largely abandoned Oliver Cromwell's seventeenth-century scruples regarding theatrical performances.

In 1778, however, under wartime stress, the Continental Congress decreed that "frequenting Play Houses and theatrical entertainments has a fatal tendency to divert the minds of people from a due attention to the means necessary for the defence of their country and preservation of their liberties." Accordingly, Congress banned all theater performances. The lifting of the ban in 1789, and the passing a year later of the first national copyright act (which protected printed materials including music for fourteen years with the possibility of renewal for another fourteen) encouraged a wave of foreign, mostly British, musicians to come to America. They performed onstage and in orchestra pits, taught music to aspiring amateurs, and composed many pieces, including some of America's first popular songs.

Musical theater grew in popularity as interest in music and the theater moved north to New York and then to Philadelphia, which soon dominated the musical scene. There the enthusiasm of such influential patrons as George Washington, who justified his fondness for theater by declaring that it had the practical effect of elevating one's manners, overruled the Quakers' disapproval of theatrical performances. In fact, however, manners were hardly elevated at theatrical performances, where informality to the extent of rowdiness prevailed. Those sitting in the cheaper seats, called the gallery, yelled freely at the actors and musicians, demanding to hear their favorite songs and criticizing the performance in the frankest and rudest terms. They tossed bottles and fruit into the orchestra pit or onto the stage, and despite the presence of soldiers hired to keep order, pandemonium often reigned.

The American stage at this period offered a potpourri of entertainment. Performances, lasting four or five hours, usually included a main drama and also a shorter, lighter, often comic piece. Music was added even to nonmusical plays, with musical entertainment provided between the dramatic pieces and after the comedy. Sometimes a march played at the end led the audience out of the hall to attend a nearby dance.

Most of the plays performed in eighteenth-century America were English pieces adapted to suit American taste. Shorter and lighter than contemporary European works, they also included more comedy. A short musical play credited to Francis Hopkinson in 1781 may have been America's earliest original musical theater work, although Hopkinson probably just set new words to existing music. In any case, foreign professionals dominated the American popular music stage for a considerable period, significantly affecting the development of music in America.

Early Bands

In 1777, General George Washington issued an order requiring "every officer, for the credit of his corps," to provide military music to American troops. The first American military bands, established during the Revolutionary War, consisted only of drums and small flutes called *fifes*. The duties of these **fife and drum corps,** many of whose members were African Americans, extended far beyond lifting the spirits and quickening the steps of the amateur soldiers (Figure 4.4). They also announced the beginning and end of the day, called the troops to meals and other activities, and transmitted commands on the battlefield that could not otherwise be heard over the noise of musket fire.

Besides fife and drum corps, some military bands in the colonies began to develop, very gradually, along the lines of those in Europe. In 1792, the first laws were passed standardizing the formation of American military bands to resemble European models, which had long included a variety of woodwinds and brasses as well as percussion instruments in their ensembles. And in 1798, President John Adams signed into law the creation of the United States Marine Band, which included thirty-two drummers and fifers, a drum major, and a fife major. This early band soon acquired two horns, two clarinets, one bassoon, and a bass drum, in which form it played for the inauguration of Thomas Jefferson in 1801. Early brass instruments, however, lacking valves that allowed players to change pitches manually, were relatively difficult to play, and only after they were fitted with valves, about 1830, did brass instruments assume the significant melodic responsibilities in military and concert bands they hold today.

Throughout the eighteenth century, New Orleans had its own strong musical heritage, in which military-style bands played a prominent role. Black musicians, both slave and free, provided music for balls and parades in that colorful city and eventually dominated the transition of the traditional military funeral

FIGURE 4.4
A band of drummers.

parade to a civic custom. The band attached to the First Battalion of Free Men of Color, which had an active role in defeating the British at the Siege of New Orleans (1815), included people identified as Creole-of-color, meaning that they were partly European and active in the French-dominated culture of the city.

Besides their military functions, early military bands also played to entertain the public at parades and informal concerts. Among the popular tunes included in such programs, a favorite would have been "Yankee Doodle" (Listening Example 16), which has pleased American ears from the time of its origin to the present day. Though perhaps written by an Englishman for the purpose of ridiculing the appearance of New England troops compared with the spit and polish of the British army, it delighted Americans, who added countless verses of text (some say about 190) over the years.

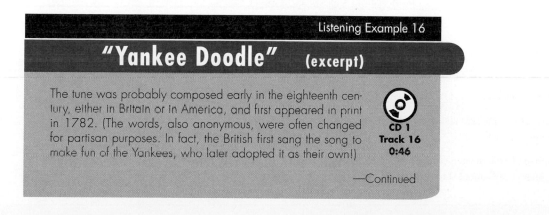

Listening Example 16

"Yankee Doodle" (excerpt)

The tune was probably composed early in the eighteenth century, either in Britain or in America, and first appeared in print in 1782. (The words, also anonymous, were often changed for partisan purposes. In fact, the British first sang the song to make fun of the Yankees, who later adopted it as their own!)

CD 1
Track 16
0:46

—Continued

"Yankee Doodle" (excerpt)

Composer The origin of the tune and the meaning of the title are unknown.

Genre Here, fife and drum music.

Timbre The high-pitched fifes carry the stirring tune, while the drums mark the rhythm with distinctive beats and rolls.

Melody The happy tune, in a major key, moves in a stepwise manner, with few leaps.

Texture Monophonic. The fifes play the tune in unison.

Form Strophic. Each verse has two parts (**a** and **b**). The first section of the tune is played and repeated; then the second section, in a version popular during the Revolutionary War, is played.

Meter Duple.

0:00		The drums play an introduction.
0:05	**a**	First section.
0:15	**a**	Repeat.
0:25	**b**	Second section.
0:35	**a**	The corps begins to sound a second verse as the example tapers off.

Terms to Review

armonica or glass harmonica   fife and drum corps

Key Figures

Thomas Jefferson   Benjamin Franklin   Francis Hopkinson

Critical Thinking

Do you know of any modern statesmen who have been enthusiastic music amateurs?

If you have been to the theater, compare your experience with what the text says about stage entertainment and audience behavior at a typical eighteenth-century American theatrical performance.

PART 1
Summary

The earliest North American music experience was that of American Indians, whose many musics are associated with ritual, dance, ceremony, or work. Most Native American music was and is song, sometimes supported by sound instruments—primarily percussion instruments, such as drums, rattles, and rasps, or their most common melodic instrument, a flute. Contemporary Native American music reflects not only the ancient, traditional songs and dances, but also various new styles, some of which are traditional and some borrowed from North American neighbors. Even the new songs remain a potent source of power in American Indian culture, confirming Indianness, validating ceremonies, and helping keep people "right" and in balance with nature and with the deity who controls all.

Beginning in the sixteenth century, as Europeans came to settle in the New World, Native Americans in Florida and in the missions of the Southwest learned to perform Roman Catholic music and some European secular music as well. Soon German- and English-speaking Protestants established permanent settlements in America, bringing with them their hymns and psalm tunes as well as folk and other secular music. The first book printed in the New World was a psalter, the Bay Psalm Book. Both African and European Americans enjoyed secular as well as religious music, the settlers singing ballads and playing fiddle tunes, the slaves singing work songs and other songs according to African custom.

Early efforts to improve the quality of singing in New England's churches led to the forming of singing schools, some of whose singing masters wrote their own original tunes, thereby becoming known as members of the First New England School of composers. Their music differed in style and purpose from that of their European contemporaries. William Billings, Daniel Read, and their many Yankee pioneer colleagues produced quantities of psalm tunes, hymns, fuging tunes, and patriotic songs for use at singing school, at church, and in the home.

Americans' musical tastes became more secular and more varied throughout the eighteenth century, as music supplied entertainment in the home, at concerts, and in the theater. Many people learned to play instruments and sing simple songs, and musical societies were formed for the purpose of performing instrumental and choral music. Talented amateurs participated in informal recitals and composed songs and keyboard pieces. Moravians produced music of a complexity and quality unprecedented among other early American compositions.

Public concerts and musical theater had also become popular forms of entertainment by the middle of the century. The important professional musicians associated with the early American theater were Europeans who adapted popular European shows to suit the less sophisticated American taste. Band music became increasingly popular as fife and drum corps and military bands played public concerts in addition to performing their military functions.

PART 2

The Tumultuous Nineteenth Century

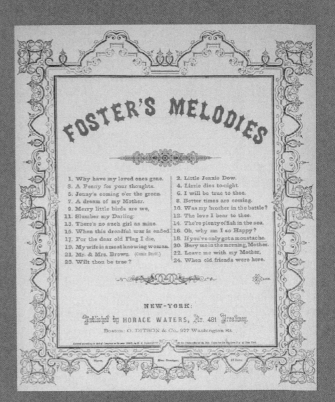

Romanticism in America: Historical and Cultural Perspective

During the nineteenth century, most European writers, painters, and musicians abandoned the coolly reasoned Classical style to reveal in their new art a fierce independence, a fascination with the unknown, and a worshipful love of nature—all characteristics associated with *romanticism* in the arts. From about 1825 to 1900, the emotional, intuitive style called Romanticism (the capital letter distinguishing the nineteenth-century style from romanticism in general) dominated the arts in Europe, and German musicians dominated music in the Western world.

Americans revealed strong romantic tendencies long before the nineteenth century and continue to do so today. Thus the artistic style newly dominant in Europe came quite naturally to this young country, where its spirit seemed always to have been at home. Perhaps the pioneers bred their sense of adventure into later generations of Americans, or perhaps the vast, wild land encouraged the demand for freedom and independence. For whatever reasons, romanticism seemed then, as now, congenial to the American personality.

The Emergence of Characteristically American Art

Although from about the 1830s one could travel from America to Europe by steamship, such travel was neither safe nor reliable, and most Americans remained effectively isolated from European culture. Little diplomatic exchange took place, and few foreigners immigrated to America during the midcentury period. Although many nineteenth-century American musicians shied away from the fresh, original sounds of the Yankee tunesmiths and attempted to emulate European—specifically German—traditions, the young country's literary and visual artists often expressed their romantic ideals in characteristically American ways.

Independence
In the early 1800s, Americans defended their new and hard-earned political and military independence by resisting the French and British in assorted skirmishes and vigorously fighting the notorious Barbary pirates. American patriots further manifested their fierce independence by vowing, in the Monroe Doctrine of 1823, to resist foreign interference anywhere in the Western hemisphere. In 1828, city and frontier folk alike rejected aristocratic leadership by electing a populist hero president of the United States, and under President Andrew Jackson a new American nationalism evolved as artists and writers, encouraged by their patrons' new interest in American art for art's sake, shed their dependence on Europeans and began to produce works on a wide variety of American subjects.

Claiming a refreshing freedom from European dominance, American literary figures developed their own distinctive ways to express the American experience, and a genuinely American literature evolved. The prolific literary activity of this period reflected a new American nationalism, as poets and novelists wrote on American subjects placed in American settings. James Fenimore Cooper's *The Last of the Mohicans,* for example, was one of many Romantic works featuring the American Indian.

In the mid-nineteenth century, Boston housed an important group of writers and philosophers known as transcendentalists, who in the romantic way trusted intuition, rather than reason, as the guide to truth. Sharing the Protestants' and the frontier people's belief in the integrity and ability of the individual, the transcendentalists also fervently expressed in their literary and philosophical works their love of nature and pride in America's natural beauty.

From the time Abraham Lincoln was elected president in 1860 until he was assassinated in 1865, sermons, speeches, poems, articles, and proclamations addressed all sides of the slavery issue. The famous humorist and author Mark Twain (real name Samuel Clemens, 1835–1910) depicted scenes and described relations between blacks and whites as he remembered them from his boyhood along the Mississippi River. An amateur musician who sang and played the piano, Twain frequently referred in his stories to the singing of simple songs and the playing of keyboard instruments. Twain claimed to particularly dislike the piano, an instrument he may have associated with the upper classes, with whom he did not identify. It is also possible that his sensitive ear was offended by the sound of poorly tuned pianos, since few instruments in his day were afforded the regular attention of a professional tuner. In any case, he often wrote approvingly of a simple and increasingly popular keyboard instrument variously called a *reed organ, parlor organ, cabinet organ, cottage organ,* or *melodeon* (Listening Example 36, "St. Louis Blues"). The reed organ, cheaper and requiring less maintenance than a piano, was very popular in Twain's day.

The Unknown
Romantic curiosity and intrigue with the unknown led pioneer men and women to

push America's frontier ever farther west, defying great perils in the high spirit of optimism also characteristic of the romantic personality. During the early years of the nineteenth century, surveyors and engineers explored and carefully mapped the wilderness areas of upstate New York, New England, and the West. The Erie Canal was opened in 1825, and steam railroads soon afforded Americans yet further opportunity to become acquainted with their magnificent land, of which they were justly proud.

Stories and poems concerning abnormal psychology by such writers as Edgar Allan Poe (1809–1849) and Nathaniel Hawthorne (1804–1864) revealed their fascination with the unknown, whereas some Romantic painters, sharing the interest in science and art expressed during the last century by Charles Willson Peale, explored new fields of study and made discoveries of significant scientific and practical worth. James Audubon (1785–1851) gave unprecedented attention to the study of birds, producing an astonishing number of realistic watercolors of American birds in their natural poses and settings.

The Erie Canal.

A melodeon. The player of this instrument, the timbre of which could be varied through the use of levers or buttons called *stops*, pumped one or two treadles to produce the wind that made the sound possible.

Samuel Morse (1791–1872), who like Audubon and C. W. Peale had an interest in and a talent for both science and art, helped make the pre-photographic process known as *daguerreotype* popular with Americans, who often had more interest in something new and mechanical than in objects of purely artistic value. Having studied painting in Europe, Morse produced several fine canvases upon his return to America. Ultimately, however, he became discouraged at Americans' preference for landscapes of local scenery over the large European-style "history paintings" he favored, whereupon he turned his attention to another form of communication and invented the telegraph.

Love of Nature
Nature, formerly viewed as a menacing force to be conquered and tamed, now received reverent admiration in American literature, painting, and music idealizing the natural beauty of the American continent. Writers portraying nature as good and beautiful included the poets William Cullen Bryant and Henry Wadsworth Longfellow and the essayists Ralph Waldo Emerson and Henry David Thoreau, each of whom expressed in American ways ideals similar to those of the British Romantic poets.

American painting in the post-Revolutionary, or federal, period also reflected the new American nationalism and the romantic love of nature, as artists captured the clear light, blazing sky, and vast open spaces of the American landscape. Although American viewers lagged behind Europeans in

Margaretta Angelica Peale, *Still Life with Watermelon and Peaches,* 1828. Oil on canvas, 13 in. × 19⅛ in. (33 cm × 48.5 cm). (Smith College Museum of Art, Northampton, MA. Purchased with funds given anonymously by a member of the class of 1952.)

Angelica Peale (1795–1882), one of very few professional women artists, was widely admired as a painter of still lifes, perhaps considered a more seemly subject than landscape for a woman to interpret. The same democratic spirit that elected Andrew Jackson president stimulated appreciation for scenes in art of everyday life, especially, as experienced in the idealized countryside: corn husking, dancing, and all manner of work and play were charmingly depicted by folk and formal artists.

Painters accompanying explorers and adventurers across the American wilderness depicted the wild beauty of untamed areas, stirring the romantic imagination of city-bound folk. George Catlin (1796–1872), a dedicated artist-explorer, vividly portrayed the vast American wilderness, complete with Indians and wild animals.

appreciating art for its own, not necessarily functional, sake, American artists produced paintings and sculptural works of unprecedented numbers and variety. In painting, landscapes predominated, but Charles Willson Peale's cousin Margaretta

George Catlin, *White Cloud, Head Chief of the Iowas.* Canvas, 58 cm × 71 cm (22⅞ in. × 28 in.)

Fusion of the Arts

Although comparisons are readily drawn among the various arts of any stylistic period, the relationships between literature, painting, and music of the Romantic period are particularly striking in their strength and significance. Nineteenth-century artists in Europe and America drew inspiration from close association with one another and showed unprecedented interest in others' work.

In truth, however, in America as well as in Europe, artists were newly dependent on the approval of a public audience, which lacked both the training and the experience of the earlier limited, even private, audiences of church, court, or salon. Thus during the Romantic period, in this country and abroad, artists relied on each other for moral support, and sometimes for more practical support as well.

The first important group of American painters, known as the Hudson River School, was led for a time by Thomas Cole (1801–1848), whose large landscape paintings capture the spaciousness and grandeur of the Catskill and Adirondack Mountains of New York State. Reflecting the close association between artists so dear to the great Romantics, Cole based his painting *Scenes from The Last of the Mohicans* on the novel by his friend James Fenimore

Thomas Cole, *Scenes from The Last of the Mohicans*.

Asher B. Durand, *Kindred Spirits*. In a scene exemplifying the Romantic image, this beautiful painting expresses love of nature, nationalism, and the close mating of the arts.

Cooper, who is sometimes referred to as a Hudson River painter using prose rather than pigment to depict panoramic American landscapes.

The intertwined relationships among writers and artists is also revealed in *Kindred Spirits* by Asher B. Durand (1796–1886), who succeeded Cole as leader of the Hudson River School. Durand's painting portrays the artist Cole, for whom the painting was a memorial, and the poet William Cullen Bryant sharing admiration for the natural beauty of the Catskill Mountains. Durand intended the painting to depict the rugged moral innocence of the new continent contrasted with what Bryant called the "tamings and softenings of cultivation" that afflicted European culture. Cole, Durand, and Bryant, who knew and admired one another, differed widely in their political views, yet shared a patriotic urge to eradicate American feelings of inferiority toward the Old World. *Kindred Spirits* embodies the feeling of Romantic artists of various media that reverence for the natural beauty of their homeland transcended the feelings of more mundane souls.

Music proved a particularly congenial medium for the romantic blending of the arts: An art song, for example, was the setting of a poem to music, and program music often depicted scenes from literature in musical terms. Certain kinds of musical theater, especially operas and operettas, constituted even more complex combinations of visual, literary, and musical arts. While there was no Hudson River School of musicians, leading composers and music performers of the day traveled to the Hudson River Valley, derived inspiration from its physical beauty, and evoked its spirit, if not its name, in their music.

The Civil War Era

The reform movements begun in the early part of the nineteenth century gathered strength in the 1860s, as tension heightened between blacks and whites and between supporters of slavery and of abolition. Workers, increasingly well organized, forced enactment of tough new labor laws; feminists marched and demonstrated, demanding improved educational opportunities for women, liberalized property rights, equitable divorce laws, and the right of women to vote. Whereas urban Northerners found themselves

Wooden bucket (c. 1825), whose charming painted designs must have seemed to lighten its load.

Edmonia Lewis, *Bust of Abraham Lincoln*.

increasingly repelled by slavery, Southerners considered the system essential to the plantation economy upon which they depended, and there seemed no grounds for compromise on this volatile subject.

Finally forced to confront the problems leading inexorably to the Civil War, Americans reflected in their literary, visual, and musical arts every facet of these and other social issues.

From about 1850 to 1875, American painters shared their European colleagues' fascination with the myriad effects of light, which they learned to use as a means of expression in its own right, their best work capturing the clear atmosphere and wide spaciousness characteristic of the American scene. American artists of the period idealized nature in the romantic way, viewing it as morally uplifting and taking pride in the grandeur of their nation's landscape. Andrew Jackson's optimism and the idealism of the American pioneer were reflected in many moving scenes of mountain splendor and rural calm.

But few American patrons shared the artists' appreciation for American art. The best-known American artist of his day, James McNeill Whistler (1834–1903), spent most of his life in Europe, having become discouraged by the lack of a market for serious art in his own country. Highly eccentric in dress and manner but widely admired for his great talent, Whistler became a leading figure in both European and American art.

American still-life painting matured and flourished, largely independent of European influence, and folk art became more individual and expressive than ever. American practicality and craftsmanship produced fine weather vanes, shop signs, furniture, and other wares every bit as beautiful as they were indeed useful.

Americans during this time also produced distinctive sculpture, sometimes laden with messages of social significance. *The Greek Slave* by Hiram Powers (1805–1873) was seen as an American expression of sympathy for the Greek War of Independence as well as for slaves in the American South. Another work revealing its creator's social consciousness was *The Indian (The Chief Contemplating the Progress of Civilization)* by Thomas Crawford (1813–1857). Among the few professional women artists of the time,

Edmonia Lewis (1845–1909), whose mother was Native American and whose father was black, produced sculpture with social and political relevance, including a stunning bust of Abraham Lincoln in 1867.

Music

Newly liberated from its former semifunctional position in worship or daily life, and newly available to an ever wider public audience, music became an increasingly significant facet of nineteenth-century American life. Religious and secular music, for voices and for instruments, reflected every feature of American experience in that turbulent century. ♪

Religious Music in the Early Nineteenth Century

Consistent with the Romantic emphasis upon individual rights and preferences, the brave men and women of the American frontier developed a fierce (if inconsistent) respect for the integrity of the humblest individual. Puritans, Quakers, and members of other Protestant sects living in the cities of the Northeast, who shared the frontier people's work ethic and concern for the common folk, initiated strong reform movements addressing issues of human and civil rights. Women particularly became active in a number of social causes, including the abolition of slavery, the founding of the American Temperance Society (1826), improvements in the conditions of prisons and asylums, and increased aid to the disabled.

The Great Revival

This zeal for reform spawned the strong religious revival movement known as the Great Revival, or the Second Awakening (see the Great Awakening, p. 50), which rapidly attracted rural Presbyterians, Baptists, Methodists, and others by the thousands to huge, emotional camp meetings, each lasting for several days. Itinerant preachers called circuit riders led the praying, shouting, singing, and often a kind of frenzied dancing at these social, recreational, and religious events—refreshingly democratic affairs in which men and women, blacks and whites, adults and children participated with equal enthusiasm (Figure 5.1).

Shape-Note Notation

Music, too, reflected the concern for reform. For example, around the turn of the nineteenth century, singing school teachers eager to improve the quality of their students' singing devised and promoted a new method of reading music called **shape-note notation.** While the traditional system of music notation is quite easy to learn (see Prelude, pp. 7–8), shape-note notation proved popular and long-lived.

Shape notes evolved from the system of placing the first letters of the four syllables *fa, sol, la,* and *mi* on the staff instead of traditional note heads.

FIGURE 5.1

George Bellows, *Billy Sunday*. This lithograph depicts the famous revivalist preaching to a fervent camp meeting crowd.

FIGURE 5.2

An arrangement of "Old Hundred" in shape-note notation. The words are placed under the melody line.

O come loud anthems let us sing,

◁ = fa (used for the 1st and 4th degree of scale)
○ = sol (used for the 2nd and 5th degree of scale)
□ = la (used for the 3rd and 6th degree of scale)
◇ = mi (used for the 7th degree of scale)

In shape-note notation, each syllable was assigned a different shape (square, circle, diamond, or triangle) and placed in appropriate positions on the staff (Figure 5.2). Although never adopted as the usual way of notating music, the shape-note method proved an effective teaching tool and a comfortable means of reading folk hymns and camp-meeting songs.

Vocal quartets hired by shape-note music publishers to popularize their music collections created strong interest in and a demand for shape-note songbooks, in which songs were printed in three-part harmony with the melody in the middle voice, according to an old-fashioned custom. (Today we usually place a hymn melody in the top voice, with three lower voices providing harmony.) One of the most popular such songbooks, ***The Sacred Harp,*** first published in 1844, is still in use today in many areas. Its first edition included the tunes of popular British ballads, to which Americans had set their favorite religious verses, as well as new American hymns, fuging tunes, and anthems. Southern song compilers printed and circulated the familiar shape-note repertoire after it lost favor in New England, and new shape-note music appeared well into the twentieth century.

Spiritual Songs

Camp meetings occurred not on the strictly regulated and segregated Southern plantations, but in rural and frontier regions, where blacks and whites alike worshiped and socialized freely, sometimes with each other. Virtually isolated from European experience throughout the post-Revolutionary periods, frontier Americans evolved a distinctive music suiting the purposes and pleasing the ears of hardy pioneers. Besides the tuneful ballads with their new religious texts mentioned above, camp-meeting songs included hymns with texts by famous English clergymen, and popular American folk hymns and spiritual songs, or **spirituals.** These strophic settings of simple religious texts to folk or popular tunes, available for those who could read music in the popular shape-note notation, became a treasured source of comfort and inspiration for people living a difficult life in the South, in the country, and on the frontier.

Because folk hymns or spiritual songs (sometimes called gospel hymns) involved a great deal of repetition, even people who could read neither words nor music learned them quickly and easily. Some songs had many verses, in which only one or a few words changed—"father" becoming "mother," "sisters," "brothers," or "friends" in succeeding stanzas, for example. "There'll Be Joy, Joy, Joy" (Listening Example 17) is typical of the simple but rousing white spirituals sung lustily at nineteenth-century revival camp meetings. (We will discuss the performers, the Carter Family, in Chapter 11, Country Music.)

"Amazing Grace"
We do not know who composed "Amazing Grace" (Listening Example 18), surely the favorite of all white spirituals, or folk hymns. The words, written in the 1770s by an English abolitionist preacher and former captain of a slave ship, John Newton, were sung to many different melodies before becoming associated with the lovely American melody called "New Britain." This tune, which appeared in print (in shape-note notation) at least as early as 1831, remains widely known today: It can be found, in fact, on more than 1,100 albums in nearly 1,000 different arrangements. As likely to be performed at times of joy (weddings) as of grief (funerals), the haunting spiritual beautifully expresses our deepest feelings.

The melody of "Amazing Grace" is based on a pentatonic scale, which, as discussed earlier, corresponds to the five black notes within an octave on a keyboard (see p. 32).

Black Spirituals
Especially after the Civil War, many blacks (free or slave) who had been converted to Christianity participated enthusiastically in rousing camp meetings, singing psalm tunes and folk hymns with sincerity and fervor. In songs such as "No More Auction Block for Me" (Listening Example 10), they expressed their fervor for freedom. They also developed distinctive spirituals as simple and folklike as white folk hymns but more rhythmically vibrant. African

"There'll Be Joy, Joy, Joy" (excerpt)

CD 1
Track 17
1:37

Members of the Carter Family perform this well-known gospel hymn, probably from the 1920s. Sara, with her rich, expressive alto voice, sings the melody, while A. P. and Maybelle add the light harmony characteristic of mountain music. "Mother" Maybelle, as she was called, on guitar and Sara with her autoharp introduce the song, add simple accompaniment to the sung verses, and play one verse alone.

Composer   Possibly James Macdermid (dates unknown).

Genre   Gospel hymn.

Timbre   Three solo voices (two female, one male), guitar, and autoharp.

Melody   The key is major, the tune simple, repetitive, and easily memorized.

Texture   Homophonic.

Form   Strophic. Only the first phrase of each verse has new text, introduced here by Sara's deep voice. A. P. and Maybelle join her, in call-and-response fashion, for the rest of each verse, which remains the same. Notice how the frequent repetition of words and phrases makes the song seem familiar almost immediately.

Meter   Quadruple. The occasional rhythmic irregularities (and the raw southern twang) accentuate the physical and emotional power of stirring camp-meeting spirituals such as this.

Tempo   Relaxed.

0:00   Guitar and autoharp introduction
0:04   Verse 1   *There'll be joy, joy, joy up in my Father's house . . .*
0:24   Verse 2   *We'll all be happy there, up in my Father's house . . .*
0:45   Verse 3   Instrumental.
1:05   Verse 4   *Don't you want to go up there, to my Father's house? . . .*
1:24   Verse 5   *There'll be no drunkards there, up in my Father's house . . .*

"Amazing Grace"

This lovely melody from about 1830 is perfection itself; yet it seems endlessly adaptable and easily absorbs various interpreters' slides, scoops, and other effects similar to, and sometimes borrowed from, African music.

CD 1
Track 18
4:19

Composer Anonymous.

Genre Spiritual song.

Timbre Soprano solo (Judy Collins), accompanied by a harp.

Melody Pentatonic. The melody itself is known as "New Britain."

Texture Monophonic/homophonic/polyphonic. The performance begins a cappella. The harp enters rather tentatively when the first verse (treated here as a refrain) first recurs, and gradually assumes a more pertinent role as the song continues. Notice how the harp slightly varies the accompanying harmonies and finally complements the voice with melodic interest of its own.

Form Strophic.

Meter Triple.

Tempo Slow.

0:00   Verse 1:   a cappella *Amazing grace, how sweet the sound . . .*

0:45   Verse 2:   a cappella *Through many dangers, toils, and snares . . .*

1:28   Refrain (text same as the first verse): The harp enters quietly here.

2:12   Verse 3   *'Twas grace that taught my heart to fear . . .*
       The harp strums chords, varying the harmony.

2:51   Refrain   The harp becomes more active, playing more notes but still primarily providing harmony.

3:28   Refrain   The harp assumes melodic interest instead of simply strumming chords. Harp and voice bring the lovely hymn to a quiet, yet dramatic close.

"Nobody Knows the Trouble I've Seen" (excerpt)

The text of this famous spiritual remains subject to variation by different soloists, who differ not only the degree of dialect they choose to use, but the words themselves. (The second line of the chorus, for example, is traditionally sung "Nobody knows but Jesus.") The repetition of a chorus, or refrain, after each verse, as well as the recurring phrase "Oh, yes, Lord," allows a group to comfortably participate in a performance, no matter the words sung to each verse by the soloist.

CD 1
Track 19
1:58

Composer Anonymous.

Arranger Henry Thacker Burleigh (1866–1949).

Genre Spiritual.

Timbre Bass voice (Paul Robeson (1898–1976), with piano accompaniment.

Melody The simple tune, based on the pentatonic (five-note) scale, retains its improvisatory flavor in Robeson's polished performance.

Texture Homophonic.

Form Strophic.

0:00   Chorus   *Nobody knows the trouble I've seen, . . .*
0:37   Verse 1   *Sometimes I'm up, sometimes I'm down, . . .*
1:04   Chorus
1:34   Verse 2   *Although you see me goin' along so, . . .*

American spirituals included joyful praise songs accompanied by hand clapping and other African effects, such as call-and-response, melodic improvisation, and exciting rhythmic complexities. On the other hand, many black spirituals, such as "Nobody Knows the Trouble I've Seen" (Listening Example 19), expressed the deep sorrow black people experienced in their everyday lives. Referred to by blacks as slave hymns or sorrow songs, black spirituals often contained hidden references to hopes for release or escape—from slavery, from oppression, from the harsh realities of the black experience in America, even from life itself. Borrowing familiar imagery from the Old Testament of the Bible, they described their anguish in terms of another oppressed people, the Jews. References to "the promised land" somewhere "over Jordan" could be heard as veiled references to reaching safety in the North, readily understood by fellow slaves but safely obscure to their white owners.

Spirituals as Concert Music During the Reconstruction era (the period following the Civil War), black spirituals acquired a new dimension in the form of hymnlike choral harmonies. Beginning in 1871, spirituals were introduced to the world in this form by the Jubilee Singers, a small choral group touring to raise funds for their impoverished school, Fisk University in Nashville, Tennessee, one of several schools founded for the education of former slaves.

Soon the black spiritual entered the solo singer's repertoire as a kind of black art song, often performed in moving arrangements such as we hear in Listening Example 19, written for voice and piano by **Henry (Harry) Thacker Burleigh** (1866–1949). Thus African American spirituals, many originally improvised and performed in the African style of call-and-response, became and remain familiar to and well loved by black people and white people alike.

Singing Conventions

The Great Revival (Second Awakening) and other strong revival movements gave further impetus to the popularity of the music of the First New England School, which continued to be enjoyed by plain and simple folk in New England, New York, New Jersey, Pennsylvania, Maryland, and the Carolinas—wherever the singing school masters roamed and set up their short-term but highly effective schools. Every summer throughout the nineteenth century, singing conventions attracted shape-note singers in large numbers to come together in churches or campgrounds, where they spent several days singing together, picnicking, and socializing much as in the early days of the singing schools.

But as public schools standardized music instruction, and as improved roads and the automobile brought new travel and entertainment opportunities to young people, musical tastes changed. The eventual purchase of small publishing houses by commercial gospel music companies, more interested in making money than encouraging public singing, contributed to a decline in the number of singing conventions and amateur shape-note singers. Yet singing conventions exist today in rural, urban, and suburban areas across the country, attended in declining numbers but with strong enthusiasm by those who still know and love the traditional songs and the shape-note method of reading them.

Further Movements to Reform Music

Despite the popularity of singing school music and shape-note notation, many educated Americans considered this music inferior to the music of their European contemporaries. Especially, they disparaged the unorthodox music of the First New England School—fuging tunes in particular. The same fervor for reform that gave rise to labor movements and the Temperance Society led many American musicians to scrupulously avoid the irregularities characteristic of the music of the self-taught singing school masters (the very characteristics that render it interesting and attractive to modern ears).

Thus while America's literary figures and visual artists developed indigenous styles of expression, professional American composers turned to Europe for inspiration and instruction, choosing to imitate the German masters who dominated European music at that time. In music collections published in America during the first half of the nineteenth century, European pieces and their American imitations largely replaced indigenous American music; and although faithfully retained by steadfast adherents of the singing school (especially in the South, as noted above), shape notes and other simplified notation systems generally succumbed to the traditional European system of writing music.

Lowell Mason (1792–1872)

A strong proponent of traditional music notation and of music that at least sounded "European," the hymn writer and educator **Lowell Mason** led the movement to reform music in America. The son of a singing school master and schoolteacher, Mason inherited talent both for music and for teaching. Having attended singing school as a child, he continued the study of music as a young man by taking private lessons with a German musician. While making his living by working at a bank, he learned to play several instruments, became a church organist and choirmaster, and began to compose rather conventional but very attractive anthems and hymns.

Believing that children should not have to depend, as he had depended, on the singing school system for their music education, Mason declared that public schools should provide all American children instruction in reading music and singing. It was, in fact, largely owing to his efforts that the Boston public school curriculum first included music, in 1838, and that other school districts soon followed Boston's example. Mason also pioneered in training for music teachers, made voice lessons readily available to adults and children in the Boston area, conducted performances of choral music, published collections of choral music and hymns, composed religious vocal music, and generally promoted the improvement of musical taste and performance in America.

Toward this worthy end, Mason wrote hymns and other religious music he considered of a better (that is, more European) quality than the works of the Yankee pioneers. However, sensitive to the needs of the relatively unsophisticated public, he revealed a keen business sense, sometimes using (or allowing his publisher to use) shape-note notation, although he clearly preferred that people learn the traditional European system of writing music. Also recognizing the public's fondness for fuging tunes and other early American songs of which he disapproved, Mason wisely included some of them in all the volumes he published, ensuring their commercial success and making himself a wealthy man.

Less daring and less original than the efforts of the Yankee pioneers, Mason's attractive hymns appealed to the sentimental taste of his day, and a number of them remain among the most familiar hymns today. "Nearer, My God, to Thee" (Listening Example 20), "My Faith Looks Up to Thee,"

Listening Example 20

"Nearer, My God, to Thee"

Although it makes no reference to Christ, this 1856 hymn continues to be found in nearly every published Christian hymnal and is named by many people as their favorite. Set to Mason's tune, it is said to have brought comfort to people aboard the ill-fated *Titanic* as the ship plunged to its icy grave.

CD 1
Track 20
4:21

Composer   Lowell Mason.

Genre   Hymn.

Timbre   The Mormon Tabernacle Choir, with organ accompaniment.

Melody   Mason's pentatonic melody, which is called "Bethany," lies comfortably within the range of just over an octave. Notice that in contrast to Billings's "Chester" and "When Jesus Wept," in which one syllable of text may run through several notes, Mason's melody almost consistently gives each syllable just one tone.

Texture   Homophonic. Whereas Mason accompanied his melody with simple, academically correct tonal harmonies, based almost entirely on the I, IV, and V chords, this arrangement adds changing harmonies in the choral voices and in the organ accompaniment. Notice, too, the arrangement's varied combinations of voices and alternation between accompanied and a cappella performance.

Form   Strophic. Each verse follows the form **aa' ba':** that is, the second and fourth lines are similar to the first, while the third line is different from them.

Meter   Quadruple.

Text   The words, written by a young American woman, Sarah F. Adams (1805–1848), are based on the Bible story of Jacob, who, while fleeing from his home and his brother Esau, dreamed of seeing angels ascending and descending "steps unto heaven," or to Bethel, "the house of God" (Genesis 28:10–22).

0:00   Verse 1   *Nearer, my God, to Thee, nearer to Thee!* . . .
        The verse begins quietly, the melody in the soprano voices while the others provide harmony, with minimal organ accompaniment.
1:22   Verse 2   *Tho' like the wanderer, the sun gone down,* . . .

—Continued

"Nearer, My God, to Thee"

After a brief organ transition to another key, the second verse is
sung a cappella, the tenors carrying the melody. Notice the
interesting changes in harmony.

2:30   Organ transition.

2:42   Verse 3   There let *the way appear, steps unto heaven* . . .

Men sing the first line, women and then the full choir the second.
Notice the expressive changes in dynamic levels.

3:58   *My God, to Thee!*

The arranger of this version of the hymn added the closing phrase.

"Work, for the Night Is Coming," and "When I Survey the Wondrous Cross"
are still widely known and are included in the current hymnals of many
denominations.

Terms to Review

shape-note notation   *The Sacred Harp*   spiritual

Key Figures

Henry Thacker Burleigh   Lowell Mason

Critical Thinking

If you read music notation, why do you suppose that
many people found shape-note music easier to read than
the traditional method of notating music?

Why do you think the pentatonic pattern playable on the
five black notes of a keyboard has inspired so many
popular melodies, including "Amazing Grace," "Nobody
Knows the Trouble I've Seen," and countless others?

Why might American composers have turned to Europe
for inspiration and instruction at the same time that
American artists, painters, and literary figures were
developing a characteristically American style of
expression?

Popular Music of the Civil War Era

T hroughout the nineteenth century, great waves of immigration from various European countries enriched America's popular culture, as Germans, Italians, French, Swedish, and other newcomers poured their secular as well as their religious songs into the American stream. Instrumental music, too, found popularity as dance tunes of various ethnic heritages entertained informal gatherings in every settled region of the country, and concert bands delighted audiences with amusing novelty pieces. However, then as now, songs dominated music in the vernacular.

Each geographic area of America produced and enjoyed new songs and instrumental pieces expressing the typical local experience. On the frontier, for example, people sang songs about freedom, equality, danger, and the beauty of nature in the wild. Songs commemorated the opening of the Erie Canal, the California gold rush, and other events of intense local and national concern. Slaves in the South produced their own characteristic music, expressive of their particular loneliness and suffering. Seamen sang chanteys; and songs of miners, farmers, railroad workers, and even outlaws joined the American repertoire as well. Lullabies served every segment of the population, and play and party songs entertained rural adults as well as children. More and more, music became a part of the day-to-day American experience (Figure 6.1).

Minstrelsy

Most popular of all the songs representative of this fertile period were those sung in **minstrel shows,** a form of entertainment popular in England in the late eighteenth century in which white men, their skin darkened by burnt cork or coal, caricatured African American figures. Minstrel performances soon became a part of American circus and showboat performances and even appeared between the acts of serious plays. Two basic characters emerged: one representing the plantation slave, with ragged clothes, uncouth manner, and thick dialect, named Jim Crow; the other, a fashionable dandy of elegant dress and manners caricaturing a citified Northern black, named Zip Coon. Jim Crow and Zip Coon, ridiculous and grotesque, became stock characters in

FIGURE 6.1

Henry Ossawa Tanner,
Banjo Lesson.

the countless minstrel shows that defied conscience and good taste to remain popular for decades.

A minstrel show began with a rousing grand march, during which the players entered the stage and formed a semicircle, exchanging comic comments (Figure 6.2). The fiddle and the banjo made vital contributions to the entertainment, minstrels radically transforming the four-string plantation banjo to "invent" the five-string banjo that is often called America's only truly indigenous musical instrument (though Native American instruments, including the tom-tom, bone flute, and medicine rattle, among others, are also indigenous). A retired blackface performer (Joel Walker Sweeney, 1810–1860) helped develop the drumlike hoop body and adjustable tensioning brackets familiar today; and about 1880 the placement of strips of material, called **frets,** on the fingerboard allowed players to stop the strings at a specific, rather than an estimated, pitch, making it easier to perform complex and sophisticated music.

Minstrel shows also invariably included a **tambourine** (derived from an African percussion instrument) and a pair of **bones** (commonly replaced in more recent times by a pair of linked castanets). Often there was also a small accordion-like instrument called a **concertina,** with a number of buttons on each side that control the pitch. The concertina is played by alternately pushing the sides inward and pulling them out, producing the wind that makes the sound.

Often credited as the first popular hit in America, the minstrel song "Jim Crow" was written by a white man known as the father of American minstrelsy,

FIGURE 6.2

Scene from a minstrel show, with "Mr. Bones" on the left and "Mr. Tambo" on the right.

Thomas Dartmouth "Daddy" Rice. ("Jim Crow" later became a hostile term synonymous with discrimination against African Americans.) In 1843, another white man, **Daniel Decatur Emmett** (1815–1904), who had served in the Union army as a fifer at the age of seventeen and later performed in circus minstrel acts, formed the **Virginia Minstrels,** the first completely independent minstrel show. At their debut the Virginia Minstrels, wearing white trousers, striped calico shirts, and blue calico coats with tails, appeared before a wildly enthusiastic audience in New York City. They sang, danced, joked, and told stories in a manner imitative of plantation and Northern blacks as they understood, or misunderstood, them. The **Christy Minstrels,** a four-man troupe formed by E. P. Christy, a famous white minstrel composer and skit writer, toured the American South and West bringing theater (of a sort) to people who had never experienced it in any form before.

Daniel Decatur Emmett wrote one of America's favorite songs, "I Wish I Was in Dixie's Land" (Listening Example 21), conceiving it as a lively plantation song-and-dance routine called a **walkaround,** performed as the finale of a minstrel show. The troupe stood in a semicircle in front of a plantation background, and when the music started, two or more of the members strutted out and alternately sang a stanza while another "walked around" in the inside of the semicircle. Reaching the center, the singers began to dance, accompanied by a musical interlude, after which the entire troupe joined in the frolic.

"I Wish I Was in Dixie's Land"

About 1860, Emmett wrote "Dixie" as a lively plantation song-and-dance routine called a walkaround, performed as the finale of a minstrel show with the concluding instrumental music accompanying the spritely dance steps. The origin of the word *Dixie* is obscure—it probably does not refer to the Mason-Dixon line. Some associate it with a French money note called the *dix* (for "ten").

CD 1
Track 21
3:31

Composer Daniel Decatur Emmett (1815–1904).

Genre Minstrel song.

Timbre Bass voice, joined in the chorus by an alto, with mandolin and folk percussion instruments.

Melody The lively melody, in a major key, begins with a broken major triad (5-3-1).

Texture Verse, monophonic; chorus, homophonic. The mandolin plays a verse, accompanied only by percussion. When the bass enters, the mandolin doubles the melody. For the chorus, an alto voice joins the bass, adding simple harmony. The mandolin and percussion accompany throughout.

Form Strophic. Each verse has two identical phrases (**a**), each sung by the bass, ending "Look away! Look away! Look away! Dixie Land." The chorus (**b,** "I wish I was in Dixie . . . ") succeeds each verse.

Meter Duple.

Tempo Brisk.

0:00		The mandolin strums four chords, then plays a verse of the song, accompanied by the percussion instruments.
0:36	Verse 1 (bass)	*I wish I was in de land ob cotton, . . .*
0:53	Chorus (bass and alto)	*Den I wish I was in Dixie, Hooray! Hooray!*
1:10	Verse 2 (bass)	*Old Missus marry "Will-de-weaber, . . .*
1:44	Verse 3 (bass)	*His face was sharp as a butcher's cleaver, . . .*
2:18	Verse 4 (bass)	*Now here's a health to the next old Missus, . . .*
2:51	Verse 5 (bass)	*There's buckwheat cakes and Injun batter, . . .*

Ironically, the song's catchy tune, simple lyrics, and inspiring patriotic chorus ("In Dixie's Land, I'll take my stand, To live and die in Dixie") made it a virtual anthem of the South, though it had been written by a Northerner, was originally sung in "black" dialect by whites, and first became popular in New York City. "Dixie," in fact, was fervently received wherever it was performed in the country, cheered as enthusiastically by Abraham Lincoln in Chicago as by the most zealous Southern patriot. The performance on our CD is more polished than a minstrel audience would have heard, but we can sense the rousing spirit of the stirring song.

After emancipation, blacks themselves participated in minstrel shows, forming their own companies and writing songs that remain favorites today. The best-known minstrel songs include "Carry Me Back to Ole Virginny," "In the Evening by the Moonlight," "De Golden Wedding," and "Oh, Dem Golden Slippers," all composed by the first well-known black songwriter, **James A. Bland** (1854–1911).

James A. Bland (1854–1911)

The son of a remarkable father, one of the first black men to receive a college education, James Bland attended public school in Washington, D.C. As a teenager, he became a page in the U.S. House of Representatives and enjoyed entertaining himself and Washington notables by singing his own songs to a banjo accompaniment.

After Bland graduated from Howard University with a degree in liberal arts at the age of nineteen, his main ambition was to become a stage performer. Having repeatedly been turned down by minstrel groups that preferred white men playing in blackface, he finally secured a job and for several years toured the country with various minstrel companies. In England with one troupe, he became very popular and even performed for Queen Victoria and the Prince of Wales. Unfortunately, his talent for music was unmatched by good business sense, and though he made a lot of money he died penniless, from tuberculosis, in Philadelphia. His grave in a nearby city's cemetery for blacks remained unmarked until 1939, when the American Society of Composers, Authors, and Publishers (ASCAP) found the site, landscaped it, and erected a monument.

In 1940, the Virginia state legislature made "Carry Me Back to Ole Virginny" the official state song. (The song can be heard on YouTube.)

The Heritage of Minstrelsy Although offensive by today's standards, minstrelsy constituted a highly popular form of entertainment in the pre- and even post–Civil War periods, offering a refreshing contrast to the sentimental songs of the age; and much of the music produced by this unlikely medium retains its appeal. Although derived from African and European customs, minstrel songs and dances were as indigenous to the American experience as were the folk hymns of New England and the South. The best of the minstrel music, often referred to as America's first popular music, had an un-self-conscious and highly infectious charm, exemplified by the minstrel fiddle tune "Turkey in the Straw"—possibly derived from an old Irish ballad but known in 1834 as "Old Zip Coon." (Vintage recordings of both tunes can be heard on YouTube.)

Stephen Foster (1826–1864)

By far the outstanding American composer of popular songs of the pre–Civil War period was the gifted, self-taught musician **Stephen Foster.** Born into the genteel society of Pittsburgh, Pennsylvania, the young Foster heard his sisters sing and play the piano and other instruments and soon was picking out tunes himself. (The philosopher George Santayana (1863–1952) coined the term "genteel tradition" to describe that pretentiously noble, decidedly prudish segment of polite society determined to ignore the unattractive aspects of life— such as the flophouse and the slum—and preserve "culture" as they understood it.) Because music was not considered a respectable profession for a man in his social position, Foster dutifully went to work as a bookkeeper while still in his teens; but he could not resist jotting down some of the tuneful melodies that filled his mind and—to his own amazement—had his first song ("Open Thy Lattice, Love") published when he was just eighteen. Soon he was writing and publishing professionally.

Foster's early sentimental love songs suited the self-conscious gentility of his family and their friends, reflecting and reinforcing the mid-nineteenth-century concept of the female identity: domestic, refined, and well-cared-for by father or spouse. The women in Foster's songs, normally described from a male point of view, are passive creatures, entirely idealized, and often asleep ("Beautiful Dreamer"), or perhaps dead, as suggested in "I Dream of Jeanie with the Light Brown Hair" (Listening Example 22).

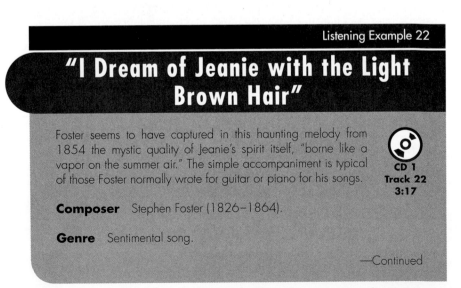

Listening Example 22

"I Dream of Jeanie with the Light Brown Hair"

Foster seems to have captured in this haunting melody from 1854 the mystic quality of Jeanie's spirit itself, "borne like a vapor on the summer air." The simple accompaniment is typical of those Foster normally wrote for guitar or piano for his songs.

CD 1
Track 22
3:17

Composer   Stephen Foster (1826–1864).

Genre   Sentimental song.

—Continued

"I Dream of Jeanie with the Light Brown Hair"

Timbre Tenor voice, accompanied by simple guitar chords, mostly I, IV, and V. The guitar also plays a brief introduction, interlude between verses, and conclusion, never competing, however, with the voice for primary attention.

Melody The mostly pentatonic melody indicates the internal repetition typical of Foster's songs, lending them immediate accessibility and familiarity. Each verse has four melodic phrases, three of which are nearly the same: the first (**a**), second (**a'**), and fourth (**a"**).

Texture Homophonic.

Form Strophic.

Meter Quadruple.

Tempo Slow. The extreme relaxation of the tempo (called *rubato*, for "robbing") occurring at the end of significant phrases enhances the romantic character of the piece, which expresses—in the romantic way—a longing destined never to be fulfilled.

Text (by Stephen Foster)

0:00　**a**　*I dream of Jeanie with the light brown hair . . . .*

　　　a'　*I see her tripping where the bright streams play . . . .*

　　　b　*Many were the wild notes her merry voice would pour, . . .*

　　　a"　*I dream of Jeanie with the light brown hair . . .*

1:37　**a**　*I long for Jeanie with the daydawn smile, . . .*

　　　a'　*I hear her melodies, like joys gone by, . . .*

　　　b　*Sighing like the night wind and sobbing like the rain, . . .*

　　　a"　*Oh! I long for Jeanie, and my heart bows low, . . .*

Foster's own personal favorite songs were of two types: the lovely "plantation melodies," reminiscent of the songs he heard African Americans singing as they worked on the Pittsburgh riverfronts, and—especially—the rollicking, comic songs he wrote for minstrel shows. Foster, in fact, experienced a devastating conflict between the music he felt he *ought* to write and the music he wrote and loved best. His sentimental songs about home ("Old Folks at Home," for example, and "My Old Kentucky Home"—a nostalgic "remembrance" of the plantation life he never lived inspired by Harriet Beecher Stowe's novel *Uncle Tom's Cabin*)—his songs about unfulfilled romantic love (such as "Beautiful Dreamer," "Come Where My Love Lies Dreaming," and "Jeanie"), and his settings of poems about the Civil War were well-enough received. His minstrel songs, however, reflect the ambivalence he experienced as a member of a family with strong personal and professional ties to the political party in favor of states' rights and (at least tacit) support of slavery, and a man whose friends and in-laws supported abolition. Desiring acceptance by polite society, and unwilling to offend his family, to whom he was devoted, Foster resisted his apparent inclination to express his own abolitionist sympathies. (Foster's Civil War songs, in support of Lincoln and restoration of the Union, were published only after his parents' death.)

Yet even his early minstrel songs, while undeniably demeaning to African Americans, avoided the outrageous caricatures commonly presented onstage. One of his songs, "Uncle Ned," dealt sympathetically with the tragic figure of an elderly and terribly abused slave; another, "Nelly Was a Lady," is told in the words of a grieving slave who has been sold away from his wife, has learned that she has died, and is about to die himself from overwork and grief. The very term "lady" applied to a slave was revolutionary for the minstrel stage.

The exuberant "Oh! Susanna" (Listening Example 23) became a national hit following its performance by the Christy Minstrels in 1848, but Foster lost money on the song. Hardly the witless businessman as he is often portrayed (he kept his own account books, calculated anticipated earnings from songs, and wrote out contracts with his publishers—the earliest contracts we know of between American music publishers and an individual songwriter), Foster nevertheless made little money from his music. But this is not surprising, since he was apparently the first American to attempt to earn his living solely from the sale of his songs, and there was no organization at the time to support his efforts to collect fees owed him. If not money, his songs brought Foster lasting fame and adulation. "Oh! Susanna" soon traveled across the country, carried to the Western frontier by thousands of adventurers and homesteaders who loved her as their own.

Listening Example 23

"Oh! Susanna"

This catchy, irresistible tune from 1848, with the internal repetition characteristic of Foster's songs, satisfies rather than tires the listener and has pleased many ears in many times and cultures. The nonsensical verse, too, defies logic and simply entertains, which is all it sets out to do.

CD 1
Track 23
1:15

—Continued

Listening Example 23—concluded

"Oh! Susanna"

Composer   Stephen Foster (1826–1864).

Genre   Minstrel song.

Timbre   Tenor, with banjo accompaniment.

Melody   Pentatonic. (The only two notes not in the pentatonic scale occur in the first line of the chorus on the syllables "Oh! Su . . .".)

Texture   Homophonic.

Form   Strophic.

Meter   Duple. The rhythm is steady, the only variety occurring with the syncopated accent (occurring on an unexpected beat), again in the first phrase of the chorus ("Oh! Su-san-**na!**"). Yet the song has the snap and dash of many a banjo or fiddle tune, compelling us to nod or rap along with its beat.

0:00	Banjo introduction.	
0:15	Verse 1	*I come from Alabama with my banjo on my knee.* . . .
0:30	Chorus.	*Oh, Susanna, don't you cry for me.* . . .
0:38	Banjo interlude.	
0:46	Verse 2	*I had a dream the other night when everything was still.* . . .
1:00	Chorus.	

Foster indeed was a man of paradox: His irresistible minstrel and plantation melodies set America and soon much of the world humming his tunes and singing his words about a life he never experienced, for Foster was neither black nor from the South. Analysis of his best songs reveals little that is innovative or even particularly interesting in their form, rhythm, or harmony. The songs are in simple strophic form, with much repetition of the melodic phrases within each verse; there is little rhythmic variety, except for occasional syncopation, as in the phrase "Oh! Susanna!"; and most of the songs were written with simple guitar or piano accompaniments based on the three primary chords of the tonal system.

Foster wrote his songs when the sentimental parlor ballad was in vogue, and some of them may be described as such. But it is difficult to place many of Foster's songs within a particular category or genre. They are hardly art songs, because the texts are not of the quality associated with that form, but they *are* art in the sense that they are long lived and representative of their composer's distinctive style. Foster's melodies, although folklike, are clearly composed. The songs are popular in the sense that they are enjoyed all over the world, but except for the rollicking minstrel songs, they have not been part of our usual concept of popular music.

It seems a bitter irony that a man so gifted should have been destroyed by his own inability to distinguish between genius and gentility. Unwilling even to acknowledge some of his best songs, he gave them away or allowed them to be pirated. Fearful that even the sentimental "Old Folks at Home" might offend the public sensibilities, for example, Foster asked E. P. Christy to claim its authorship, though he accepted the small royalty for each song sold. Later, as the song and indeed many minstrel songs as well gained in popularity, Foster wished to be recognized as the composer of "Old Folks at Home" and was most disappointed when Christy refused to alter their previous arrangement. It was not until the song's copyright expired in 1879 that Foster's name finally appeared as its author and composer.

Foster married in 1850, but his increasing emotional instability and heavy drinking caused his wife to leave him three years later. Stephen Foster died a pauper, alone and unrecognized, at the age of thirty-eight.

Patriotic Songs

Some of America's most enduring patriotic songs appeared between the Revolution and the Civil War and were associated with events occurring during that tumultuous time. Frequently included in theatrical entertainments then, they became and in some cases have remained widely popular.

The words to "Hail, Columbia," by Francis Hopkinson's son Joseph, were sung to the tune known as "President's March," composed by Philip Phile for the inauguration of George Washington in 1789 and commonly played when that president appeared in public. This stirring patriotic song, like many others, sometimes served political aims. For example, the 1798 war between France and England divided American allegiance, some people rallying to the side of the newly democratic French republic, whereas others felt tied to England by affection and tradition. However, the rousing words to the brand-new "Hail, Columbia," frequently performed at theatrical entertainments in that year, united emotional audiences by exalting the wonders and accomplishments of America and arousing national pride.

"Hail to the Chief," traditionally played by the United States Marine Band to announce the ceremonial entrance of the president of the United States, is generally attributed to an Englishman, James Sanderson, who possibly based his tune on an old Scottish melody. Many sets of words were added over the years, but the tune soon evolved from a popular song of the day to the march with official status that we recognize today. First performed in this country in 1812, it was sung (with a different title and text) in 1815 in honor of George Washington's birthday; in 1828 the U.S. Marine Band played it to honor

President John Quincy Adams when he attended the opening of the Chesapeake and Ohio Canal.

A young lawyer, **Francis Scott Key** (1780–1843), wrote the words to "The Star Spangled Banner" under most dramatic circumstances. During the War of 1812, Key boarded a British vessel moored in Chesapeake Bay in order to plead for the release of an important American prisoner. The British agreed to release the prisoner before sailing for England, but they held both him and Key on board through the night while they attacked the city of Baltimore. In four stirring verses, the emotional young lawyer described the agony of suspense he experienced while witnessing the attack and his overwhelming pride and relief at the sight of the American flag waving high the next morning. Key set his romantic text, which he titled "The Defense of Fort McHenry," to the melody of "The Anacreontic Song" (pronounced uh-nak-ree-**on**-tik) (Listening Example 24), which was the theme song of an English gentlemen's club. Obviously fond of the catchy melody, Key had already used it as the setting for other poems he had written and found it suitable to express his pride, relief, and enthusiasm after the harrowing night of the attack on Baltimore. In 1813, Thomas Carr musically arranged the tune and rechristened it "The Star Spangled Banner."

Listening Example 24

"The Anacreontic Song" ("Anacreon in Heaven")

The composer and the lyricist of this song, written about 1778, were members of the Anacreontic Club—a group of wealthy Englishmen dedicated to the celebration of music with wine and song. The club took its name from an ancient Greek poet who wrote idyllically of Venus, the goddess of love, and Bacchus, the god of wine.

CD 1
Track 24
4:29

Composer   (Probably) British composer John Stafford Smith (1750–1836).

Lyricist   (Probably) Ralph Tomlinson, 1744–1778)

Genre   Drinking song.

Timbre   Male chorus, a cappella.

Melody   Beginning with a broken major chord (the notes sounded one at a time), the melody is extremely angular in contour, covering a wide range with large leaps.

—Continued

Listening Example 24—concluded

"The Anacreontic Song" ("Anacreon in Heaven")

Texture   Homophonic. This performance alternates passages for solo voice, duets of various combination, and full chorus.

Form   Strophic, six verses, of which we include only the first.

Meter   Triple.

Text	Bass	To Anacreon in heaven,
	Chorus	Where he sat in full glee,
	Tenor, then duets	A few sons of harmony sent a petition,
	Bass	That he their inspirer
	Chorus	And patron would be,
	Tenor, then duets	When this answer arrived
	Chorus	From the jolly old Grecian:
	Duets and solo ensembles	Voice, fiddle and flute, no longer be mute,
		I'll lend you my name and inspire you to boot!
	Tenor, bass	And besides I'll instruct you like me to entwine
		The myrtle of Venus with Bacchus's vine.

Little did either Key or Carr suppose that many years later, during the Spanish-American War (1898), the stirring song would be designated the official anthem of the American armed forces. Still less could they imagine that, in 1931, President Herbert Hoover would sign a bill making Key's song the American national anthem. Some have suggested that the melody's wide range and large intervals ("Oh say, can you sing it?") render it more difficult to sing than is appropriate for a national anthem; but defenders stoutly respond that the dramatic nature of the melody and the effort required to sing it properly make it all the more distinctive and ideally suited for this exalted position.

"America the Beautiful"—less bellicose than "The Star Spangled Banner"; unassociated with a particular, long-ago battle; and more appreciative of the land's natural beauty—is sometimes recommended as an alternative American national anthem. A young English literature professor named Katherine Lee Bates wrote the words to "America the Beautiful ("O beautiful for spacious skies") in 1893, after climbing to the summit of Colorado's 14,000-foot-high Pikes Peak and being awed by the view. She later revised the words, responding to suggestions from readers of her poem, which became ever more popular with the advent of radio and the patriotic fervor raised by World War I. When, in 1926, the National Federation of Music Clubs held a contest to select a musical setting for the poem, more than 900 people submitted compositions. Bates never selected a winner, but today we sing her words to "Materna," written in 1888 by a church organist and music store owner, Samuel A. Ward. (The famous song can be heard on YouTube.) Neither Bates nor Ward ever claimed or received any royalties for this magnificent song.

Civil War Songs

In 1860, several southern states seceded from the Union, plunging the country into the Civil War. At such times of grief and turmoil, people turn to art and to music—at popular or at more serious levels—to express their anguish and ease their sorrow. Thus it is not surprising that many memorable songs concerned these particularly tragic years.

Indeed, Civil War songs appeared in a rich variety of folklike, religious, comic, and serious styles. "Dixie," as we have seen, began as a minstrel show walkaround. Some songs, lyrical and dramatic in style, suggested their composers' fondness for Italian opera. Regional favorites, such as "Maryland, My Maryland" (which vied with "Dixie" and "The Bonnie Blue Flag" to become a Confederate national anthem), "Marching Through Georgia" (a celebration of General William Tecumseh Sherman's march to the sea), and "The Yellow Rose of Texas" (originally a minstrel tune praising an African American girl as "the yellow rose of Texas" who "beats the belles of Tennessee"), stimulated patriotic fervor and became popular during the troubled period. (The Bonnie Blue Flag, the unofficial first flag of the South, flew from 1860 to 1861.)

What is surprising is how much music inspired by the Civil War has survived more than a century to please, entertain, and move listeners of other eras who are used to other styles. Some tunes acquired new texts in the twentieth century: Thus Elvis Presley sang "Love Me Tender" to the tune of the love song "Aura Lee," and Bob Dylan set "Blowin' in the Wind" to the tune of the slave song "No More Auction Block for Me" (see Listening Example 10). Other songs survive much as they were introduced at the time of America's greatest national trauma. The familiar bugle call "Taps" is generally said to have been adapted by a Union general (Daniel Butterfield) from an earlier signal for Extinguish Lights (Lights Out) borrowed from the French. The new bugle call spread quickly through Union and also Confederate camps, and after the Civil War became an official bugle call. Today the haunting melody is sounded at funerals, memorial services, and wreath-laying ceremonies, evoking the same emotions it stirred on the campgrounds of the Civil War.

The stirring "Battle Hymn of the Republic" with its rousing chorus beginning "Glory, glory, hallelujah!" is set to a tune once sung as a tribute to the militant abolitionist John Brown ("John Brown's body lies a-mouldering in his grave"). Dozens of irreverent verses had been set to this simple Methodist camp meeting tune that, according to one writer, "stuck to the ears like burrs to the skirt of a blackberry girl." But upon viewing firsthand the desperate plight of blue-clad Union soldiers, many wounded or ill and all of them lonely and

FIGURE 6.3
Julia Ward Howe
(1819–1910).

heartsick, the published poet and author Julia Ward Howe (Figure 6.3) composed her poignant poem "Battle Hymn of the Republic" to be set to the old tune; and her fervent words sung to the strong melody lifted the morale and stirred the spirits of Union troops and prisoners.

After the Civil War, the "Battle Hymn" became one of several patriotic songs (including "The Star Spangled Banner") to serve as an anthem of the reunited nation, its fervent refrain seeming to embody the very soul of American patriotism. Many people experienced profound disappointment when it, together with "America the Beautiful," lost the position of national anthem to Francis Scott Key's patriotic creation. ("Battle Hymn of the Republic" can be heard on YouTube.)

In 1887, Julia Ward Howe wrote, "The wild echoes of the fearful struggle have long since died away, and with them all memories of unkindness between ourselves and our southern brethren. But those who once loved my hymn still sing it." And we still do.

Singing Families

Before and after the Civil War, several singing families toured the United States performing songs of many kinds. Like the twentieth-century European Trapp Family portrayed in the Broadway musical and movie *The Sound of Music,* these traveling groups performed in churches, meetinghouses, and concert halls.

The most popular American singing family, the **Hutchinsons,** first came to public attention when the thirteen Hutchinson children presented a highly successful performance of religious and secular music at a New England meetinghouse in the early 1840s. Later, three Hutchinson sons formed a trio; and when, still later, their sister Abby joined them, the popular quartet toured through New England for several years. When Abby married and retired from the group, other members of the family formed various ensembles, and the Singing Hutchinsons remained famous in America and Europe for decades.

The Hutchinsons' performances included secular, humorous songs in strophic form called **glees,** with the melody in the top voice and the other two or three voices providing chordal harmony. Glees, introduced in Europe during the eighteenth century, were originally sung by men only, but by the mid-nineteenth century many glee clubs formed in American cities included women as well as men. These popular ensembles sometimes sang more serious choral literature as well as glees and other lighthearted fare. Today's high school and college glee clubs generally are small mixed choral groups.

Although their music was refined, genteel, and sentimental, the texts of the Hutchinsons' songs, some of which they wrote or adapted themselves, addressed some of the most radical social causes of their day, such as temperance, women's suffrage, and the abolition of slavery. Consider, for example, the strong message of Jesse Hutchinson, Jr.'s text to the stirring emancipation song, "Get Off the Track" (Listening Example 25).

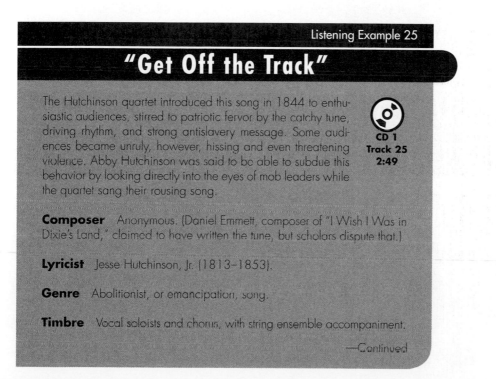

Listening Example 25

"Get Off the Track"

The Hutchinson quartet introduced this song in 1844 to enthusiastic audiences, stirred to patriotic fervor by the catchy tune, driving rhythm, and strong antislavery message. Some audiences became unruly, however, hissing and even threatening violence. Abby Hutchinson was said to be able to subdue this behavior by looking directly into the eyes of mob leaders while the quartet sang their rousing song.

CD 1
Track 25
2:49

Composer   Anonymous. (Daniel Emmett, composer of "I Wish I Was in Dixie's Land," claimed to have written the tune, but scholars dispute that.)

Lyricist   Jesse Hutchinson, Jr. (1813–1853).

Genre   Abolitionist, or emancipation, song.

Timbre   Vocal soloists and chorus, with string ensemble accompaniment.

—Continued

"Get Off the Track"

Melody Major. The tune is that of a popular minstrel song, "Old Dan Tucker."

Texture Homophonic (soloist accompanied by piano; choral harmony).

Form Strophic.

Meter Duple.

0:00		Instrumental introduction. The ensemble lightly accompanies each verse and plays interludes between them. (The full text can be found on the Internet.)
0:09	Bass solo	*Ho! the car Emancipation . . .*
	Chorus	*Roll it along, thro' the nation, . . .*
0:39	Soprano	*Men of various predilections, . . .*
	Chorus	*Get out of the way! Every station! . . .*
1:12	Tenor	*All true friends of Emancipation . . .*
	Chorus	*"Put on the steam!" all are crying . . .*
1:42	Soprano	*Hear the mighty car-wheels humming! . . .*
	Chorus	*"Get off the track!" all are singing, . . .*
2:15	Soprano	*See the people run to meet us;*
	Tenor	*At the depots thousands greet us;*
	Soprano	*All take seats with exultation,*
	Bass	*In the car Emancipation*
	Chorus	*Huzza! Huzza! Emancipation*
		Soon will bless our happy nation.
		(Repeat)
2:41		The instruments play a brief closing section, followed by a choral "Huzza!"

Concert Bands

During the Civil War, **concert bands** (Figure 6.4) played a variety of entertaining novelty pieces. The early-nineteenth-century addition of valves having facilitated the playing of intricate melodies on trumpets, horns, and cornets (all previously relegated largely to adding color and harmony to band music), these instruments now assumed a prominent melodic role in marching and concert

FIGURE 6.4
A concert band, c. 1875.

bands. During the 1850s, in fact, many bands consisted of brass instruments only, leading to criticism by some that military and concert bands of the time offered nothing but "sounding brass and tinkling cymbals," and to an expressed preference for the return of reed instruments to the band ensemble.

Bands provided an important stimulus for music publishing in America, although much of the music printed for American bands throughout the nineteenth century was written by European composers. Besides marches and dance tunes, **programmatic** pieces, describing in musical terms a sequence of scenes or events, were particularly popular at band concerts. "Battle" pieces featuring the sounds of gunshots, cries of the wounded, trumpet calls, and other instrumental warlike effects were especially well received.

After the Civil War, the concert band evolved into a balanced ensemble of woodwind, brass, and percussion instruments. Bands brought famous orchestral and opera music, as well as popular songs and dances, to audiences unable to attend the orchestral halls, opera houses, and popular venues of big cities, and band music became so popular that Americans gradually came to prefer its instrumental timbres to the vocal renditions they had previously favored. This change in musical taste provided a firm foundation on which jazz and the swing age could build.

Patrick Sarsfield Gilmore (1829–1892)

Patrick S. Gilmore, one of thousands who fled Ireland's potato blights and famine to make a new life in America, considered himself American by choice. (When asked if he had been born in Ireland, he joked, "No, I was born in Boston at the age of eighteen.") He began his career as a member of a popular Boston minstrel group, in which he played the tambourine, sang in a quartet, and played cornet solos, while also acting as the group's agent. His business sense served him well as his musical career began to rise: He originated a successful series of summer concerts at the Boston Music Hall, and soon established his own professional ensemble—a new and daring business venture—known as Gilmore's Band. A virtuoso cornet player, he was appointed bandmaster of the Union army and became the most famous bandmaster of the 1860s.

When military bands broke up after the war, Gilmore formed America's first band conceived entirely as a concert ensemble. A master entertainer who organized mammoth concerts in which thousands of performers participated, he also brought outstanding European bands to perform in America. (One concert he sponsored, in New Orleans in 1864, included a band of 500 members; a chorus of over 6,000; a battery of 50 canons; 40 soldiers striking anvils; and the simultaneous ringing of all the church bells in the city.) Finally, Gilmore achieved in his Grand Boston Band the effective balance between brass and woodwind instruments we expect to hear today.

A music publisher and instrument manufacturer, the bandleader Gilmore also composed several topical songs and marches. He usually is credited with having written the popular Civil War song "When Johnny Comes Marching Home Again" (which can be heard on YouTube), though he claimed only to have set timely lyrics to an Irish folk tune that he "happened to hear someone humming" and "taking a fancy to it, wrote it down, dressed it up, gave it a name, and rhymed it into usefulness for a special purpose suited to the times."

Terms to Review

minstrel show	concertina	program, programmatic music
fret	walkaround	
tambourine	glee	
bones	concert band	

Key Figures

Thomas Dartmouth "Daddy" Rice	Christy Minstrels	The Hutchinson Family
Daniel Decatur Emmett	James A. Bland	Patrick S. Gilmore
Virginia Minstrels	Stephen Foster	
	Francis Scott Key	

Critical Thinking

Discuss some of the reasons minstrelsy became so popular just at the time of rising tensions between North and South and between whites and blacks. Which does it reflect more: white people's contempt for, or their fascination with, black culture?

What might be some of the reasons that blacks performed—in blackface—on the minstrel stage after the Civil War?

Do you recognize any echoes of the minstrel tradition in contemporary American culture? In his book *Raising Cain: Blackface Performance from Jim Crow to Hip Hop,* W. T. Lhamon, Jr., suggests (in a picture on the book jacket) a relationship between a minstrel performer dancing in the 1840s and M. C. Hammer performing in the 1990 hip-hop video "Hammer Time." Can you support or refute Lhamon's suggestion?

Would you choose "The Star Spangled Banner" or another patriotic song as America's national anthem? If another, which one, and why?

A young divinity student named Samuel Francis Smith set the words to one candidate for the American national anthem, "America," to a German tune, "Heil Dir im Siegerkranz," also used as the Prussian national song and the British royal anthem as well. (There had been Dutch, Danish, French, Swiss, and Austrian versions, too.) Oliver Wendell Holmes (a close friend of the poet) suggested that had the poet written "Our country" instead of "My country, 'tis of thee" the hymn would not have been "immortal." Do you agree or disagree that the choice of "My" instead of "Our" was a "master stroke"?

Concert Music

Although still less distinct than the highly subjective lines drawn today between *vernacular music* ("for the people") and *art* or *concert music* (for an audience viewed as somewhat select), differences between the popular and the classical worlds of music assumed more significance in the American experience as the nineteenth century progressed. While household music and religious songs retained their vital position in American life, the decades before and after the Civil War witnessed growing interest among composers, performers, and listeners in music for the concert hall.

Musical activity increased significantly across America in the late nineteenth century. This period witnessed the establishment of some of our finest professional music schools, or **conservatories,** and several concert halls and opera houses were built. The Metropolitan Opera House (built in 1882) and Carnegie Hall (built in 1891) attracted enthusiastic audiences to New York City; and Americans across the country enjoyed access to more concert music of a greater variety and finer quality than ever before. Choral and chamber societies presented programs not only on the East Coast but also in cities farther west such as Cincinnati and Chicago. Both serious and light opera became more popular, while the great vocal and instrumental virtuosos continued to attract an ever wider and more appreciative public audience.

Orchestral Music

Although most French and Italian composers had partisans in the New World, nineteenth-century Americans who enjoyed hearing orchestral music preferred the German Romantic style to any other. Romantics (Germans and others) approached the elements of music differently from their classical forebears. Their melodies were long and lyrical rather than short and motivic, their phrases asymmetrical rather than balanced in the classical way. Also, Romantic composers were more likely to repeat their long, songlike melodies with variation or embellishment than to develop brief intellectual melodic ideas. Chordal harmony became fuller and steadily more **dissonant**—that is, the harmonic combinations sounded less stable, more tense—as ears adapted to richer and ever-more-pungent combinations of sound. (Harmonies are said to be *disso-nant* or **consonant,** according to their degree of stability.) Adding new tones to familiar chords, Romantic composers expanded the concept of tonal harmony and achieved newly varied and colorful effects. They also treated rhythm more freely than the Classicists had, sometimes avoiding regularly recurring patterns of a certain number of beats per measure and writing phrases of irregular length—five or seven measures, for example, instead of four or eight.

About the same time that painters began to use color for expressive rather than realistic purposes, composers began to explore the timbres, sometimes called the *colors,* of sounds. Thus nineteenth-century music includes increasingly rich and imaginative instrumental effects. Technological changes increasing the capabilities of woodwind and brass instruments encouraged their wider use in the symphony orchestra, and the percussion section of the orchestra also was greatly expanded, making it necessary to add more strings in order to balance the sound. Accordingly, the Romantic orchestra was not only larger than that of the Baroque or Classical period but also included a richer variety of timbres. When you attend orchestral performances today, you will probably notice that pieces written in the eighteenth century are played by a small or **chamber orchestra,** whereas Romantic pieces require a much larger ensemble.

European orchestras playing in nineteenth-century America generally performed European works, though the celebrated French conductor Louis-Antoine Jullien (1812–1860) gave serious attention to orchestral music by American composers in his concerts performed here. A showman in the tradition of P. T. Barnum (founder of the Ringling Brothers and Barnum and Bailey Circus), Jullien wore white gloves when he conducted, from a gilt music stand, and used a jeweled baton. But however flashy he might have appeared, he led his ensemble in fine performances of great orchestral music. Jullien added American musicians to his orchestra during the year he spent in New York (1853) and, strongly prompted by the local press, included some American works in his programs. For many years, however, no one followed Jullien's brave lead.

The large orchestral ensemble, in fact, held little interest for the young republic. Few American orchestras existed throughout the nineteenth century, although dedicated professional and amateur musicians endeavored to make the orchestral sound appealing to an American audience. The New York Philharmonic Society, the nation's oldest orchestra still in existence today, was founded in 1842 but remained a loosely organized and rather haphazard association for many years.

Finally, a great musician of German background raised the level of orchestral performance and of audience appreciation in America.

Theodore Thomas (1835–1905)

Soon after the ten-year-old **Theodore Thomas** (Figure 7.1) arrived in America from Germany, already an accomplished violinist, he became a member of the New York Philharmonic Society. He played, as well, for various theater and opera orchestras. But he always intended to become an orchestral conductor and in that capacity to raise the level of Americans' appreciation for orchestral music. And so he did.

FIGURE 7.1

Cartoon depicting Theodore Thomas (1835–1905) conducting in Central Park.

Scornful of the casual rehearsal and concert procedures of the New York Philharmonic Society, Thomas formed his own ensemble, hiring only the best musicians, rehearsing them rigorously, and, beginning in 1864, presenting public programs guaranteed to please an audience. His method was to subtly but systematically alter the balance in his concerts between light, familiar pieces and more serious, challenging works as his listeners became more experienced with orchestral fare.

Recognizing Americans' familiarity with varied and entertaining programs, Thomas invited solo **virtuosos**—performers exhibiting technical brilliance—to dazzle the listeners, who then dutifully received perhaps one movement, or section, of a more serious piece. Thomas also was careful not to plan programs that were too long. He traveled widely with his orchestra, bringing symphonic music to people who had never heard it before and extending the season's employment for his musicians; in the summer he offered outdoor "garden concerts," where refreshments were served. The quality of his performances was always superb, and America gradually developed an enthusiastic appreciation for the thrilling orchestral sound. Inevitably, German composers formed the core of Thomas's programs, although he also gave generous attention to outstanding American composers of the day.

With the support of some Chicago businessmen, in 1891 Thomas established the Theodore Thomas Orchestra, later known as the Chicago Symphony Orchestra, which he conducted until his death in 1905. By that time several other American cities had formed their own orchestras, and smaller towns had short orchestral seasons as well. During the next several decades, Americans continued to form numerous school, civic, and professional orchestras and to absorb the great symphonic literature of the world. By the mid-twentieth century, public school, civic, and professional symphonies across the country rendered America a veritable nation of symphony orchestras.

Romantic Virtuosos

Nineteenth-century Americans attended concerts in much the same frame of mind with which they viewed a circus or minstrel show, and they particularly enjoyed dazzling displays of technique by solo virtuosos. Certainly virtuosity is among the qualities of *musicianship*—the broad combination of talents possessed by the consummate performer—including sensitivity to the *style* of the music, differing from one period and one culture to another; *originality* of interpretation; and of course *accuracy*. But the spectacular performance of difficult passages of music, thrilling to see and hear, held sway in the minds and hearts of the mid-nineteenth-century American audience, where Romantic glorification of the individual made virtuoso performers objects of intense hero worship.

The great nineteenth-century virtuosos benefited from the American passion for brilliant performances at the very time Europeans had begun to tire of them. European performers flocked gratefully to America, where an adoring public eagerly applauded their showy performance techniques. Among the best-known and best-remembered of the concert artists who toured America, however, was one of her own: an exotic composer and pianist from Louisiana, Louis Moreau Gottschalk.

Louis Moreau Gottschalk (1829–1869) Among the outstanding pianists of the period, the young American pianist **Louis Moreau Gottschalk** (Loo′-ee Mo-roh′ Got′-shok; Figure 7.2) amazed and entertained audiences on both sides of the Atlantic with virtuosic performances of his own entertaining compositions. Gottschalk, whose English Jewish father had been educated in Germany and whose mother was descended from an aristocratic French family that had emigrated from the West Indies a generation before, was born into the brilliant cultural milieu of New Orleans. (Gottschalk's mother was called a Creole, meaning someone born in this country of a foreign family. Later the word *Creole* referred to people of mixed racial heritage, causing some to believe erroneously that Gottschalk had African American ancestors.) Gottschalk's first and strongest language was French, although he also spoke Spanish and English fluently.

Nineteenth-century New Orleans teemed with a rich variety of cultural experiences, as French, Spanish, Creoles, and African Americans mixed freely in a sophisticated atmosphere unlike that of any other city in Europe or America.

FIGURE 7.2

Louis Moreau Gottschalk
(1829–1869) at the piano.

From this fertile environment, Gottschalk absorbed the musical sounds of each culture, frequently finding inspiration for his compositions in exotic Creole tunes based on French folk and popular melodies.

Unlike Stephen Foster's Victorian family, Gottschalk's sophisticated parents had no genteel compunctions regarding professional musicians. Recognizing their son's precocious talent and the lack of educational opportunities at home, they sent him to France at the age of thirteen to study music. He stayed abroad for eleven years, becoming a great favorite of aristocratic Europeans, who admired his youthful compositions for piano and his astonishing virtuosity. Frédéric Chopin (1810–1849), the famous Polish "poet of the piano," famously predicted that Gottschalk would one day be the "king of pianists." Having amazed and delighted concert audiences in Spain, France, and England, Gottschalk returned in 1853 to America, where music lovers, perceiving his long stay abroad to have made him respectably foreign, responded with unbridled enthusiasm to his performances of his own melodically simple but technically demanding piano pieces.

Next Gottschalk spent several years in the West Indies, whose tropical sounds and flavors he captured in some of his later compositions, returning to America in 1862 to find the country desperately at war. Although a southerner by birth,

Gottschalk sided firmly with the North and began an exhausting concert tour across America, reaching people who had never heard concert music before and contributing most of what he earned to the Union cause. Criticized by an elite few for playing his own tuneful pieces instead of the great classical music of Beethoven, Chopin, and others, Gottschalk replied that he simply played what the audience wanted to hear; but he also commented late in his short life on the marked improvement he perceived in the level of American taste.

Gottschalk never married but was adored by women, who screamed and swooned and fought to grab pieces of his clothing whenever he appeared. Finally forced in 1865 to leave the country (by a scandal in which he probably was quite—or mostly—innocent), he traveled to South America, where he organized huge concerts, much like Patrick S. Gilmore's mammoth band extravaganzas. (During one of his tours of Cuba, he produced a gigantic festival, writing three new pieces requiring a total of 650 performers, including a military band, a Caribbean drumming group, 198 choristers, 68 clarinetists, 33 tuba players, and assorted other musicians. A newspaper warned that "young ladies who are easily frightened or nervous should bring smelling salts, as we predict faintings.") Gottschalk died in South America at the age of forty. His death is usually attributed to yellow fever but actually remains a mystery—as is fitting, perhaps, for this quintessentially Romantic man.

Piano Music

Although Gottschalk composed songs, orchestral works, and even operas, he is particularly remembered for his delightful piano music. By 1800 the piano had almost displaced the harpsichord as the keyboard instrument likely to be found in homes or heard in concert. The piano constituted, in fact, the ideal Romantic instrument, providing access to every facet of emotional expression. The *damper* or "loud" pedal (to the player's right) held the tones, connecting one to another for a **legato** or smooth and lyrical melody line, or allowing the sounds to accumulate to thunderous effect. The *una corda* (one string) or "soft" pedal (on the left), by shifting the keyboard, considerably dampened the volume and altered the color of the sound. And on some large pianos, a center pedal, called the *sostenuto,* allowed the player to sustain some tones while others sounded cleanly above them.

Piano music enjoyed immense popularity in the United States, where the varied concert programs of the day often included a virtuosic piano performance by a resident or visiting concert artist. Lowell Mason's son Henry cofounded the famous Mason and Hamlin piano company in 1854; and Jonas Chickering, William Knabe, and Henry Steinway all lived in America, producing pianos unsurpassed anywhere in the world. By midcentury, the piano was widely available to middle-class homes, and much "household" piano music was available in arrangements simple enough for the average young lady to master.

Best-known among Gottschalk's piano compositions are his pieces based on popular dances and his moving **character pieces,** such as "Berceuse" ("Lullaby") and "The Banjo," which capture the mood or character of their subject in musical terms. ("The Banjo" may be heard performed on YouTube.)

The rhythms and forms of popular dances had long invigorated many kinds of concert music, and Gottschalk continued this tradition by writing several waltzes and mazurkas for the piano. Concert pieces based on these and other traditional dances are intended not to be danced but rather to capture the mood, style, tempo, form, and meter of a popular step.

Gottschalk based his stirring "Bamboula" (an Online Listening Example) on a dance popular with whites and blacks alike in the vibrant city of his birth. He organized "Le bananier" (Listening Example 26) according to a formal design called **theme and variations,** in which a melody or theme recurs throughout the piece varied, perhaps in tempo, timbre, rhythm, meter, accompaniment, ornamentation, and so on, thus providing both unity and contrast. (An apt comparison may be made with the musical theme of a movie, recurring in various ways throughout the film to arouse any number of conflicting emotions.) Notice the "obstinately" repeated pattern, called an **ostinato,** in the left hand. An ostinato may be rhythmic only (hand claps or a drum pattern, for example) or melodic as well.

www.mhhe.com/ferrisaml6e

Listening Example 26

"Le bananier"

The *theme* is a Creole melody from about 1850, in a minor key. The *variations* include changes from major to minor mode, changes in range of pitch, different accompaniment patterns, and various virtuosic embellishments.

CD 1
Track 26
2:48

Composer   Louis Moreau Gottschalk (1829–1869).

Genre   Character piece.

Timbre   Piano.

Mode (scale or key)   Minor. During the piece, the mode changes from minor to major and back again.

Theme   The Creole melody has two parts: the first phrase, **a,** begins with an ascending broken minor triad (1-3-5). The second half of the theme (**b**), higher than **a** in range, begins with three repeated and accented notes.

Texture   Homophonic. The left hand primarily adds harmonic interest to the right.

Form   Theme and variations.

—Continued

"Le bananier"

Meter   Duple. Strong accents and irregular phrase lengths enhance the exotic effect of the tuneful melody.

Tempo   Moderate.

0:00		The left hand introduces an ostinato—here an octave played one note at a time.
0:04	**a**	The minor theme begins in the right hand, accompanied by the ostinato in the left.
0:19	**a**	Repeat.
0:30	**b**	The second half of the theme, higher in range, begins with three repeated, accented notes.
0:40	**b**	Repeat.
0:50	**a**	The theme is heard in a higher range, accompanied by a new ostinato.
1:00	**a**	Repeat, softer.
1:10	**b**	The second half of the theme is delicately embellished by the right hand, accompanied by chords in the left.
1:23	**a'**	A variation of **a** is played, in a major key, accompanied by yet another ostinato.
1:34	**a'**	The variation is repeated an octave higher.
1:44		A section of new material sounds improvisatory.
2:01	**a'**	The major version of the theme is in the left hand, while the right hand performs dazzling runs.
2:19	**b**	The second half of the theme recurs briefly.
2:34	**a**	Fragments of **a** in the left hand and rapid, virtuosic figures in the right conclude the attractive piece.

Rise of Nationalism in Music

The second half of the nineteenth century witnessed strong European nationalistic efforts, as certain nations not bordering directly on Germany began to assert their artistic independence and establish characteristic styles of their own. Artists in Russia, Bohemia, Norway, and Finland soon established strong national styles, as writers, painters, and musicians drew inspiration from and based their works on the colorful folk tales, legends, and religious music of their own local experience. Suddenly the peasant became more interesting than the noble. By the later part of the century, after the ruling aristocracies of several nations had been overthrown and popular states established, **nationalism** became a significant political and cultural movement throughout western Europe.

At about the same time that American paintings began to reflect America's own natural splendors, a few intrepid composers also set out to capture the American spirit in music and to promote performances of American music. These early seeds of nationalism fell on dry ground, however, largely ignored by audiences on both sides of the Atlantic. Europeans admired Americans' mechanical and industrial capabilities but considered them novices in matters of art; and most Americans remained hesitant to defy the established wisdom that Germans knew best how to write music.

Yet a strong nationalistic urge developed among a few dedicated American musicians and listeners as the nineteenth century drew toward its close. In 1892, Jeanette M. Thurber, one of the few Americans genuinely interested in establishing a nationalistic style of composition, invited an outstanding Czech nationalist composer to direct the National Conservatory of Music in New York City. While in America, the prestigious Antonín Dvořák (1841–1904) listened to the music of African Americans and Native Americans with the same fascination with which he absorbed the folk music of his own beloved homeland, expressing amazed regret that Americans seemed relatively uninterested in their "native" sounds. Dvořák did not always distinguish between genuine spirituals developed by African Americans and the derivative minstrel songs; nor did he specifically recommend that American composers quote or imitate black or Indian effects. He strongly suggested, however, that these particular musics offered unique and important sources of inspiration.

To illustrate his ideas of how American music should sound, and to express appreciation for the scenic beauty of the land he was visiting, Dvořák wrote his Symphony no. 9 (*From the New World*) and two chamber pieces. Each of these works includes melodies that seem to be based on the scales of black or Indian music as Dvořák understood them—although he harmonized the melodies and orchestrated the music according to Western custom.

When homesickness compelled Dvořák to return home after less than three years, he had raised very little interest in American-sounding music. This country's multiethnic population and lack of a common heritage made the concept of a nationalistic American music difficult to grasp. At least a few Americans reflected his influence, however, by using black or Indian references in their music. They included the distinguished African American composer Henry Thacker Burleigh (see p. 81), who inspired Dvořák's interest in spirituals.

The market for American music remained minimal, and few composers or listeners of the late nineteenth century showed much interest in music that sounded American. Although by the latter part of the nineteenth century American composers were producing impressive works in all the large instrumental and vocal forms—symphonies, concertos, sonatas, operas, and choral works—and finally were being afforded a respectful, if limited, hearing, most of them not only studied in Germany but also wrote most of their music in the firmly established German Romantic style.

Second New England School

Although New York City remained the center of music performance, the intellectual atmosphere of the Boston area nurtured significant developments in music as well as in philosophy and literature, and New England produced most of the important American composers of the late nineteenth century. The Boston Symphony Orchestra, founded in 1881, loyally supported the efforts of local composers by bringing their music to public attention, often with repeated performances of a well-received work.

Members of the **Second New England School** of composers, much of whose music was comparable in quality as well as in style to that of many of their European contemporaries, shared a dedication to the principles of German music theory and a concern for careful craftsmanship leading some to dub them the "Boston classicists." They contributed to every genre of concert music. Many were church musicians and organists who included organ **transcriptions** of opera arias and symphonic music in their recitals, bringing this literature to Americans who had little access to opera or orchestral concerts. These intrepid pioneer composers also contributed strong compositions for organ and a significant body of choral music to the American music repertoire.

John Knowles Paine (1839–1906) As a young man, **John Knowles Paine,** the oldest member and the leader of the Second New England School, made the decision—unusual for an American of his day—to become a professional musician. Having progressed in his music studies as far as possible with a German teacher in America, he traveled to Germany to polish his skills, giving organ concerts while he not only studied music theory and composition but also composed.

While in Europe, Paine wrote his Mass in D for chorus, soloists, and orchestra, reminiscent in style of a well-known Mass by Beethoven. (A Mass is a setting to music of the most important Roman Catholic worship service.) Although he was a Protestant, Paine took his text from the Roman Catholic liturgy, according to choral music custom. In this first large composition by an American to be performed in Europe (where it was better received than at a later American performance), Paine neither intended nor achieved a distinctively American sound.

Returning to America in 1861 to find the country at war, Paine became the organist at Harvard University, where, eager to share his newly acquired expertise, he offered free noncredit lectures in music (not considered a proper course of study at American universities) to the students. To the surprise of the university administration, Paine's lectures were very well received. Thanks to his efforts, in 1875 America's oldest college became the first to include music in its formal curriculum, and Paine became the first American professor of music.

Paine's much-admired Symphony no. 1, first performed by Theodore Thomas's orchestra in 1876, was the first American symphony to be published—but in Germany rather than America, and only after Paine's death. He wrote many other kinds of music as well, including songs, hymns, an opera, and several fine keyboard compositions for organ or piano, including his cheerful *Fuga giocosa* (Humorous Fugue) (Listening Example 27).

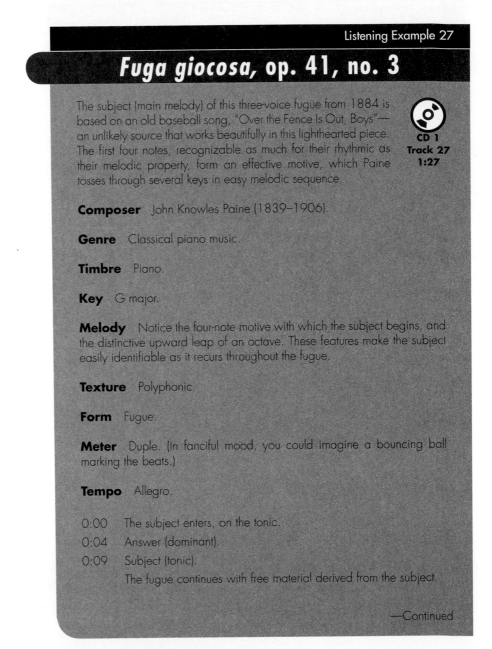

Listening Example 27

Fuga giocosa, op. 41, no. 3

The subject (main melody) of this three-voice fugue from 1884 is based on an old baseball song, "Over the Fence Is Out, Boys"— an unlikely source that works beautifully in this lighthearted piece. The first four notes, recognizable as much for their rhythmic as their melodic property, form an effective motive, which Paine tosses through several keys in easy melodic sequence.

CD 1
Track 27
1:27

Composer   John Knowles Paine (1839–1906).

Genre   Classical piano music.

Timbre   Piano.

Key   G major.

Melody   Notice the four-note motive with which the subject begins, and the distinctive upward leap of an octave. These features make the subject easily identifiable as it recurs throughout the fugue.

Texture   Polyphonic.

Form   Fugue.

Meter   Duple. (In fanciful mood, you could imagine a bouncing ball marking the beats.)

Tempo   Allegro.

0:00   The subject enters, on the tonic.
0:04   Answer (dominant).
0:09   Subject (tonic).
       The fugue continues with free material derived from the subject.

—Continued

Listening Example 27—concluded

Fuga giocosa, op. 41, no. 3

0:18   Notice that the motive descends in melodic sequence.
        You will hear frequent reference to the motive as the piece
        continues.

0:37   The subject returns.

0:47   Sudden chords momentarily alter the texture from polyphonic to
        chordal.

0:49   Sequence.

0:53   Sequence.

1:00   Sequence.

1:10   Rapid runs and chords render the light piece suddenly virtuosic
        and the texture increasingly dense.

1:18   The motive returns and leads briskly to the dramatic end.

Fugue Although originally conceived as a form of European keyboard music, the highly structured **fugue** serves American composers as well. It is suited for music not only for a keyboard instrument, but for every performing medium, including the voice. A fugue is a polyphonic composition with three to five melodic lines or "voices" entering one at a time in imitation of one another, according to specific rules. (In Latin, *fuga* means flight, suggested by the effect of the voices of a fugue "chasing" each other. Think of "fugitive.")

The principal theme or *subject* of a fugue enters alone. After it has been heard all the way through, it is imitated by each of the other voices in turn until each has made its entrance. The first entrance—the subject—is on the tonic; and the second voice, or *answer,* begins on the fifth tone of the scale, called the **dominant.** The remaining voices (usually there are a total of three or four) alternate entrances between tonic and dominant until each voice has been introduced (Figure 7.3). Whereas the voice proceeds with independent material, referring to the subject and answer more or less frequently throughout the piece. There may be a second theme, or *countersubject,* introduced in the same manner as the subject and also recurring throughout the fugue. Thus, although intellectually conceived and tightly structured, the form is quite flexible after the **exposition** is completed.

In the *Fuga giocosa,* notice the manner in which Paine takes a fragment of the theme (the first four notes) and uses it as a **motive**—a short melodic phrase lending itself readily to development. Paine repeats the motive at several different levels of pitch, a technique called melodic **sequence.** (The first phrase of "Three blind mice," for example, is answered by "See how they run," the same melodic figure, but at a higher pitch level—another example of sequence.)

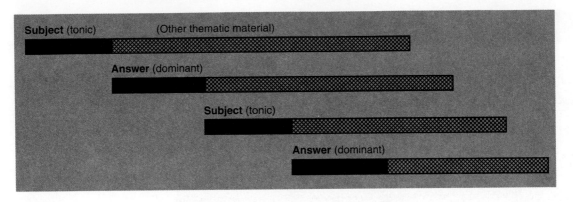

FIGURE 7.3

Exposition of a four-voice
fugue.

Amy Marcy Cheney Beach (1867–1944) A large number
of capable and prolific composers, many trained in Europe, were soon active
in the New England area. A prominent member of the Second New England
School whose music is becoming increasingly well known was a woman,
Amy Marcy Cheney Beach (Figure 7.4). Already recognized as an outstanding pianist before her marriage at the age of eighteen to Dr. H. H. A.
Beach, Amy Marcy Cheney thereafter used her married name professionally.
While not the first American woman to write music, she was the first to rank
with highly educated and sophisticated musicians; and she was, in fact, the

FIGURE 7.4

Amy Marcy Cheney Beach
(1867–1944).

first American woman to write a successful Mass and a symphony. Women of her day and before simply were not afforded the education, the financial or social support, or the patronage required to succeed as professional composers.

Beach's parents and her husband recognized and encouraged her talent, although to a limited extent. She studied piano from a young age but had minimal training as a composer. She rigorously trained herself, however, translating into English important foreign treatises on instrumentation and orchestration. Before her marriage, she performed as a pianist with the Boston Symphony Orchestra and with the Theodore Thomas Orchestra; but her husband preferred that she concentrate on her compositions, a married woman's professional appearance onstage not being well accepted in her day. After her husband's death, Beach resumed her concert career, performing to great acclaim both here and in Europe.

Although her compositions were widely performed and well received on both continents, Beach could not escape references to her sex in reviews of her work, reviewers sometimes criticizing her for trying to sound masculine, or praising her graceful melodies and more gentle symphonic passages as properly feminine in style. Thus, although she handled the symphonic medium very capably, it is little wonder that Amy Marcy Cheney Beach composed more songs, including her charming "The Year's at the Spring" (an Online Listening Example), than any other form, because her contemporaries readily accepted songs as fitting examples of feminine creativity.

www.mhhe.com/ferrisaml6e

In her Symphony in E minor ("Gaelic," Listening Example 28), Beach responded to Dvořák's recommendation to produce American music based on ethnic and traditional idioms. She disagreed, however, that African American or Native American music represented the influences prevalent in her society. In a letter to the Boston *Herald,* Beach wrote, "We of the North should be far more likely to be influenced by old English, Scotch or Irish songs, inherited with our literature from our ancestors." A large portion of Boston's population was Irish American, and Irish tunes had become familiar in middle-class parlors and on theater and concert stages across the country. Beach therefore chose to base her symphony on themes taken from or based on Irish tunes and to imbue the work with a Gaelic flavor. She also wrote that the symphony had a program, depicting the struggles, laments, romance, and dreams of the Irish people.

Listening Example 28 is one section, or **movement,** of the symphony, which has four movements in all. As each act, chapter, or stanza of a literary work is logically organized within itself, so each movement of a symphony or other multimovement work has a particular design, or form. This movement has a three-part (ternary) design, illustrated by the letters **A B A**: A theme is introduced (**A**); the theme is transformed (**B**); the theme returns in its original form (**A**). The movement ends with a **coda,** a closing section sometimes added at the end of a piece or a movement. (In Italian, *coda* means "tail.")

Symphony in E minor ("Gaelic"), second movement

Composed in 1896 and the first known symphony to have been composed by an American woman, the "Gaelic" symphony is said to have inspired one of the other Second New England School composers to state that the work was fine enough to make Beach "one of the boys." The Boston Symphony Orchestra premiered the work, which soon had other performances in cities in the state of New York and in Chicago under the baton of Theodore Thomas.

CD 1
Track 28
8:25

Composer   Amy Marcy Cheney Beach (1867–1944).

Genre   Symphony movement.

Timbre   Symphony orchestra.

Key   E minor.

Form   **A B A** (ternary, or three-part, form) with a coda.

Meter   The **A** sections are in quadruple meter. The middle section (**B**) is in duple meter.

Tempo   **A** is slow, relaxed. **B** is fast (*allegro vivace*).

0:00   Orchestral introduction.

0:26   The oboe, accompanied by other woodwinds, introduces the lovely theme (an Irish tune titled "The Little Field of Barley"). The tune has four phrases.

1:15   The third and fourth of the tune are repeated. Notice the use of rubato (relaxed tempo).

2:02   **B**. Excited string figures begin the middle section. Beach transforms the theme, which dances through the strings lightly accompanied by the full orchestra.

2:20   The theme in its new guise is sounded, and then the instruments toss the melody lightly back and forth. Beach finds the simple tune a source of great variety, as she takes it through several keys.

2:40   **B** returns.

—Continued

Listening Example 28—concluded

Symphony in E minor ("Gaelic"), second movement

3:00 Intimations of **A** occur, but in the mood of **B**.

3:19 **B** returns. (Notice the tinkling sound of the triangle, which joins the fun.)

3:42 **A** contemplates a return.

4:00 The orchestra sweeps dramatically up, and higher still, to end the section abruptly and change the mood in preparation for the return of **A**, of which we hear tantalizing snatches.

5:00 The return of **A** is implied.

5:29 **A**. Woodwinds subtly return the theme to its original form. The plaintive English horn plays the melody.

6:04 The oboe takes it over, as the orchestra gently joins in and slowly swells to a romantic climax, the strings giving their full, lush attention to the theme.

7:11 Two clarinets play a rather tentative descending phrase; the oboe and English horn respond; the orchestra tapers off.

8:01 Coda. The agitated **B** material returns briefly, to bring the movement to a succinct close.

Edward MacDowell (1860–1908)

The composers of the Second New England School wrote effectively in all the symphonic, choral, and solo genres; but, as we have seen, their music predominantly conformed to the sounds of their European contemporaries. **Edward MacDowell** (Figure 7.5), who was too romantic to be called a classicist of any sort, and too individual to be included in a school of composers, became the first American to write concert music in a style distinctively his own.

In his teens appearing equally talented in music and art, MacDowell was sent to Paris to study in both fields. Finally deciding to become a professional musician, however, he traveled to Germany, where he followed the prevailing custom of studying theory and composition. An accomplished pianist, he concertized widely during his long stay abroad, and some of his songs and piano pieces, written in the accepted German style, were published in Germany before he returned to America in 1888.

In 1896, after several years of performing, composing, and teaching in the Boston area, MacDowell accepted the position as head of the newly established music department at Columbia University in New York City, which afforded him the opportunity to implement his ideal of teaching music as related to the

FIGURE 7.5

Edward MacDowell
(1860–1908)—composer,
painter, poet, and lover of
nature.

other arts. We have already noted that Romantics often were talented in more than one of the arts and found particular significance in relationships between music and literature. Thus MacDowell, who not only composed music and painted but also wrote poetry, believed that the arts could not be understood in isolation from one another and established at Columbia a curriculum similar to a modern humanities program.

MacDowell professed not to espouse the nationalists' claim that quoting African American or Indian themes would establish a characteristically American music, suggesting instead that American music should seek to capture the youthful, optimistic spirit of the country. Nevertheless, he was unable to resist references to American Indian music in several of his compositions. For example, each section of his orchestral *Indian Suite* is based on Native American lore or experience, and each uses American Indian or Indian-like melodies, though the harmonies and orchestral effects are entirely European. (A **suite** is an instrumental work consisting of several sections or semi-independent pieces.) Similarly, his famous set of character pieces titled *Woodland Sketches* includes one called "From an Indian Lodge," which imitates American Indian sounds within a Western framework. (The exquisite "To a Wild Rose," from *Woodland Sketches*, is an Online Listening Example.)

MacDowell's piano pieces, including *Woodland Sketches,* reflect his romantic love of nature, painting in musical terms idyllic scenes of woodland lakes and hills. These delicate, intimate, and modest piano miniatures capture the very essence of the sounds and moods of nature as MacDowell loved it.

His vision of music as one of the integrated arts has profoundly benefited American arts to this day, for after his death, MacDowell's widow established a summer colony on their estate at Peterborough, New Hampshire, where artists, musicians, and literary figures are invited to spend uninterrupted summers working within their chosen fields at the **MacDowell Colony.**

Terms to Review

conservatory	theme and variations	exposition
dissonance	ostinato	motive
consonance	nationalism	sequence
chamber orchestra	Second New England School	movement
virtuoso	transcription	coda
legato	fugue	suite
character piece	dominant	MacDowell Colony

Key Figures

Theodore Thomas	John Knowles Paine	Edward MacDowell
Louis Moreau Gottschalk	Amy Marcy Cheney Beach	

Critical Thinking

Compare the effect their families and upbringing must have had on the careers of Stephen Foster and Louis Moreau Gottschalk.

Can you envision a nationalistic American music? If so, what characteristics would you expect it to include?

Why do you suppose nineteenth-century Americans showed so little interest in concert music by American composers?

How might Amy Cheney Beach's professional experience have differed had she lived half a century later?

Does Paine's *Fuga giocosa* sound humorous, as its title suggests? If so, what lends it that flavor?

What do you think of the efforts by several American composers to capture an American sound by adapting American Indian sounds in their vocal, choral, piano, and orchestral compositions? Defend your position by referring to the elements of music. Have you heard similar adaptations in scores for films about Native Americans, and if so, were they effective?

PART 2
Summary

By the turn of the nineteenth century, Americans had become more romantic than classical in their style of expression. The romantic zeal to improve the conditions of life initiated religious and social reform movements as well as efforts to reform American music by making it sound more European. Lowell Mason, who led the movement to reform musical taste in America, wrote attractive—although quite conventional—hymns, brought music education into the public school system, and systematically attempted to raise the level of musical awareness and appreciation.

Lowell Mason's efforts notwithstanding, country folk continued to practice and enjoy their accustomed ways of reading and singing music, and singing schools remained popular in rural areas, using shape-note songbooks such as *The Sacred Harp* as teaching materials. During the Great Revival, people of all ages, both black and white, attended religious camp meetings, where they enjoyed singing rousing hymns and spirituals. Secular songs became popular, too, often reflecting the experience of everyday life. In the cities, theaters offered popular entertainment that was primarily musical. Religious songs, sentimental ballads, songs of social protest, and glees were sung in parlors and concert halls and included in the performances of well-known singing families such as the Hutchinsons.

In minstrel shows, the most popular entertainment of the period leading to the Civil War, white men blackened their skin and imitated the songs, dances, and dialect of stereotypical African Americans. Stephen Foster wrote outstanding minstrel songs of a more sensitive, less demeaning, nature than most; yet genteel society preferred his love songs, Civil War songs, and sentimental ballads about home. Concert bands became balanced ensembles capable of performing transcriptions of orchestral and operatic literature as well as more popular pieces.

Mid-nineteenth-century Americans particularly enjoyed concert music performed by virtuoso soloists. America's own piano virtuoso, Louis Moreau Gottschalk, gained popularity on both sides of the Atlantic. Gottschalk introduced American audiences of the Civil War period to piano music, generally performing his own light but stirring compositions. After the Civil War, conservatories, concert halls, and opera houses were built in several American cities, as concert music grew in significance. Theodore Thomas presented orchestral programs that pleased audiences and gradually raised their level of appreciation, but primarily for European orchestral music.

The seeds of American nationalism, sown during the nineteenth century, bore fruit slowly. Dvořák encouraged Americans to develop a characteristic sound of their own; but the Second New England School produced the first significant American concert music, primarily in the German Romantic style.

Edward MacDowell developed a characteristic, although not distinctively American, idiom of his own. The MacDowell Colony in Peterborough, New Hampshire, continues to invite artists in every discipline to spend summers working there.

PART 3

The Growth of Vernacular Traditions

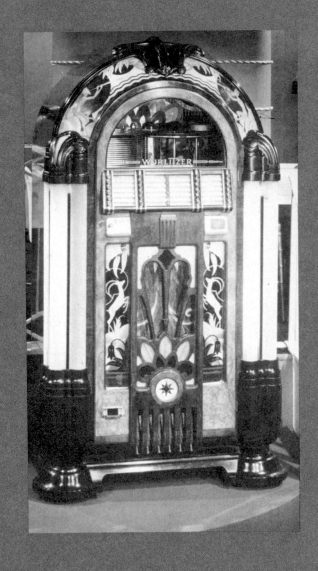

124

Music in the Vernacular: Historical and Cultural Perspective

The common, or vernacular, language of a country is the language spoken by most of its people—the language they hear and use throughout their lives. A culture's vernacular music also is commonly heard and understood, without conscious effort on the part of listeners, and with less training and experience required for its performance than for the performance of so-called classical, concert, or art music. Often the term *popular* is applied to much of the music we shall cover in this section of the text, but that term does not adequately embrace such disparate fields as jazz, folk, rap, country-western, and rock. In fact, *pop* has become a genre in its own right, distinguished from other vernacular sounds.

Walt Whitman (1819–1892)
"I hear America singing, the varied carols I hear."

Vernacular Art and Literature

Besides music, the other arts of the post–Civil War period also captured new American flavors. The picturesque stories of Bret Harte (1836–1902), for example, brought Western local color to appreciative readers in the great cities of the East, while Mark Twain (1835–1910) made everyday scenes of his youth in the Mississippi River region internationally, and hilariously, famous. The poet Walt Whitman (1819–1892) frequently used colloquial language to express the American experience of his day in an eloquent, distinctively American, idiom. Whitman's simple, anguished words in his famous poem "O Captain! My Captain!" reached the hearts of a nation mourning the death of Abraham Lincoln.

After the turn of the twentieth century, other poets variously expressed themselves in colloquial terms. Popular culture thrived from the late 1930s through the early 1950s, when pulp novels, adventure comic books, swing music, and B movies enlivened the humdrum lives of working Americans. Some of the work of the mid-century "beat" poets, who borrowed vocabulary from jazz musicians and sprinkled their verse with obscenities in an effort to bring poetry "back to the streets," was undeniably powerful and moving.

The visual arts, too, showed a new interest in the mundane facts of everyday American life and, by the turn of the twentieth century, the robust vigor of city life replaced the idyllic rural American landscape as the subject of choice for many American artists. Ben Shahn (1898–1969), among many socially conscious painters of the period, imitated newspaper cartoons in the effort to attract large numbers of people to his paintings. By the 1950s, Jasper Johns (b. 1930) and Robert Rauschenberg (1925–2008) were introducing everyday objects (flags, numbers, street signs) into their paintings, and in the 1960s a new art, known as "pop," presented soup cans, Coke bottles, lightbulbs, comic strip characters, and movie stars in hugely glorified detail. George Segal (1924–2000) cast life size plaster figures from live models, outfitted them in familiar commercial products, and placed them in lifelike settings, to amuse and sometimes fool the viewer's eye.

One of America's most distinguished black artists, Romare Bearden (1912–1988), worked in *collage,* a cut-and-paste technique combining objects of varying content and material to form a work of art. A member of the movement known as the Harlem Renaissance, Bearden attempted, as he said, to "establish a world through art in which the validity of my Negro experience could live and make its own logic." Bearden

125

Empress of the Blues by Romare Bearden.

defied conventional rules of art, sharply cutting the human features in his stunning collages with sudden breaks and surprising repetitions that functioned for him, it has been suggested, as a visual equivalent to the jazz he loved. *Empress of the Blues* is one of his most famous works.

Vernacular Music

As we have seen, art or classical music gained favor in the New World only very slowly, over a long period of time, and much of the music already considered in this text belongs in the realm of the vernacular. Native American music never was conceived as an elite form of art; nor were Anglo-American or African American dances or songs. The hymns and psalm tunes written by self-taught amateurs formed a part of their education and recreation as well as their worship. The composer Stephen Foster had no formal music training and did not intend his music for concert performance. Spirituals and alabados were really religious folk songs.

However, although vernacular music has always been a significant facet of American culture, it was during the period between the Jacksonian era and the Civil War (1829–1861) that what we now call popular music emerged. Americans wrestling with rapid industrialization, economic uncertainty, slavery, westward expansion, and other overwhelming issues of social, religious, political, and economical import

found popular songs a helpful means through which they could cope with reality: sentimental songs on such sensitive topics as slavery, women's suffrage, or alcoholism, for example, allowed emotional release without requiring direct confrontation of the issues on a personal level.

At least until recently, vernacular music—like popular art—has evolved in an unself-conscious manner, spontaneously reflecting cultural characteristics indigenous to the region where it occurs. Thus long before art music achieved anything recognizable, however controversially, as an American sound, the young nation's vernacular music revealed strongly characteristic American traits. About the time of the Civil War, when popular culture included minstrel shows, band and circus music, the songs of Stephen Foster, and stirring performances by popular singing families, many songs, dances, and instrumental pieces acquired a new, distinctively American flavor. The rhythms, timbres, melodies, and harmonies of many songs, dances, and instrumental pieces, unfettered by conventional (European) rules, introduced new sounds suited to the pace and moods of American life and articulated in regional American accents. Some music, written down or passed along by oral tradition, was conceived to provide popular entertainment at home, in the theater, or in some other structured setting. Some tunes evolved on an open range, in a cotton field, on a chain gang, or on the field of battle, where they offered self-expression and relief to the lonely and oppressed.

Again until recently, there has been little studied attempt to preserve vernacular traditions. Favorite pieces survived from one generation to the next simply through unchanging, or slowly changing, performance practice, as we observed with the early ballad "Barbara Allen" (Listening Example 5). New sounds also gain recognition as styles, genres, or kinds of vernacular music in their own right, to be short-lived or long-lived according to the vagaries of popular acceptance and of the music business. Some very old tunes remain familiar today, whereas some highly popular songs have been largely forgotten by the fickle public who loved them a few months ago. ♪

The Rise of Popular Culture

The gap between classical and popular music widened during the last half of the nineteenth century. Though differences had been recognized between music for everyday experience and music intended for concert performance, and also between religious and secular music, such distinctions were not necessarily clear: a spiritual sung at a religious service on Sunday might provide personal pleasure on Monday, or be part of a recital on Saturday night. Classical music of the eighteenth and early nineteenth centuries offered tuneful melodies commonly hummed by Americans who perhaps never attended a classical concert or an opera, but who heard the tunes on someone's parlor piano or in a theater or band performance. Songwriters, in fact, often modeled their popular songs on the melodies of Austrian, German, and Italian classical music.

But as time progressed, many European composers steadily increased the complexity and dissonance of their music. Meanwhile, writers of popular songs simplified their melodies and harmonies, making them more accessible, and more acceptable, to a wide audience. And so the two kinds of music grew farther apart.

Concert bands straddled the two music worlds, sprinkling transcriptions of classical and operatic music among stirring marches and folk, popular, and novelty tunes. The year Patrick Gilmore (see Chapter 6) died, a young American violinist named **John Philip Sousa** (Figure 8.1) formed a band destined to surpass in size of ensemble, variety of repertoire, and quality of performance any previous concert band, including Gilmore's.

John Philip Sousa (1854–1932)

When John Philip Sousa's father learned that his thirteen-year-old son was planning to run away from home and join a circus band, the elder Sousa promptly enlisted John Philip in the Marine Corps, where, as an apprentice in the United States Marine Band, he soon learned to play all the band instruments. From the time the Marine Band was founded through an act of Congress signed by President John Adams in 1798, its primary mission has been to provide music for the president of the United States and the commandant of the Marine Corps. In 1801, the prestigious ensemble played for the inauguration

127

FIGURE 8.1

John Philip Sousa on a sheet
music cover.

of President Thomas Jefferson, and it has performed for every presidential inauguration since that time.

Sousa left the band at age twenty to pursue a career as violinist and conductor of theater orchestras; but five years later he became the director of the
Marine Band, and in that capacity he faithfully served five presidents (Hayes,
Garfield, Arthur, Cleveland, and Harrison). He brought the band to a peak of
perfection, regularly astonishing audiences with incredibly soft dynamic levels
and other expressive effects previously thought possible only for the symphony
orchestra. Later, Sousa formed his own Sousa Band, which traveled widely and
earned a worldwide reputation.

Although Sousa wrote songs, programmatic orchestral music, and especially comic operas and operettas that were widely known and popular in his
time, he is best remembered today as the "march king." His marches conform
in most respects to many marches by European composers, but their wealth of
melodic invention and their stirring spirit render them distinctively American
and irresistibly attractive. Sousa is honored not only as a great musician

and composer but also as a fervent patriot. Further, as an early member and supporter of the American Society of Composers, Authors, and Publishers (ASCAP; see p. 89), Sousa made important contributions to the growth of the music business in America. He was enshrined in the Hall of Fame for Great Americans in the John F. Kennedy Center for the Performing Arts in 1976 and inducted into the Washington, DC, area Music Hall of Fame in 2002.

Marches

Although differing widely in mood and tempo, marches—be they military, funeral, patriotic, or concert pieces—normally share duple meter, with a strongly marked beat to correspond with the marching pattern LEFT-right-LEFT right. Meter, which refers to the number of beats in a measure, may be *simple* or *compound* according to the manner in which each beat is divided.

Simple meter means that each of the beats in a measure is divided by *two*. For pieces in *simple duple meter* (for example, "Yankee Doodle" or Sousa's "The Stars and Stripes Forever"), we count the two beats in each measure as *ONE*-and-*two*-and, and so forth.

In *compound meter,* each beat is divided by *three*. For pieces in *compound duple meter* (such as "My Bonnie Lies Over the Ocean," "When Johnny Comes Marching Home," or Sousa's "Washington Post March"), we also count two beats per measure but divide them as *ONE*-and-a-*two*-and-a, or *ONE*-two-three-*four*-five-six.

A march, which may begin with a short (four- or eight-measure) introduction, consists of a series of melodic sections called **strains,** each usually sixteen or thirty-two measures long, and each repeated at least once. One of the strains, scored for fewer instruments and therefore softer in dynamic level, and also typically sweeter or more lyrical than the others, is called the **trio.** Some marches include a section called the **break**—dramatic, highly rhythmic, and often percussive in style and timbre, thus providing effective contrast to the melodic strains.

"The Stars and Stripes Forever" (Listening Example 29), designated in 1987 as the national march of the United States, conforms to this general description of a march. Sousa also wrote a text, seldom heard today, for this famous piece:

> *Hurrah for the flag of the free!*
> *May it wave as our standard forever,*
> *The gem of the land and the sea,*
> *The banner of the right.*
> *Let despots remember the day*
> *When our fathers with mighty endeavor*
> *Proclaimed as they marched to the fray*
> *That by their might and by their right it waves forever.*

The last decade of the nineteenth century witnessed two phenomenal movements in popular American music, each of which proved long-lived and influential far beyond initial intentions or expectations. These two American musics—one (ragtime) primarily instrumental and led by black musicians, the other (the songs of Tin Pan Alley) vocal and led by American Jews—aroused the immediate enthusiasm and the lasting admiration of listeners here and abroad.

"The Stars and Stripes Forever"

**CD 1
Track 29
3:11**

This 1896 march, Sousa's most famous, is unusual in that its trio has the songlike, memorable melody we mostly associate with the piece. The stirring march is recognized around the world and is considered an American classic.

Composer   John Philip Sousa (1854–1932).

Genre   March.

Timbre   Concert band.

Key   E-flat major.

Texture   The first and second strains are homophonic in texture. Simultaneous, independent melodies (*countermelodies*) played during the returns of the trio make the texture there polyphonic.

Form   A A B B C D C D C
 A = first strain
 B = second strain
 C = trio (third strain)
 D = break

Meter   Duple.

Tempo   Moderate.

0:00		Introduction.
0:03	**A**	First strain, beginning with several repeated notes.
0:17	**A**	Repeat.
0:30	**B**	Second strain. Notice the wide range of pitches and several large leaps between tones.
0:44	**B**	Repeat.
0:58	**C**	Trio, softer and more melodic than the other strains, and twice as long. The four phrases occur in the order **a b a c.** You may sense that the trio is in a different key (the subdominant, A-flat major), or perhaps you will simply be aware that its lyrical character is distinct from the martial mood of the first two strains.

—Continued

Listening Example 29—concluded

"The Stars and Stripes Forever"

1:25	**D**	Break, bold and dramatic, with virtually no melodic interest. The lower brass play particularly virtuosic passages. This percussive break provides extreme contrast with the lyrical trio, which therefore sounds fresh on its return.
1:47	**C**	Trio, performed this time with a perky countermelody in the piccolo, providing intense polyphonic, or *contrapuntal*, interest. (The high-pitched piccolo suggests the sound of a fife.)
2:15	**D**	Break.
2:36	**C**	Trio, still in the subdominant key, accompanied by a new countermelody, played this time by the low register trombones. The loud dynamic level, and the military clamor of brass and percussion, lend new character to the lyrical trio melody.

Although Sousa's band played transcriptions of many of the same pieces that Theodore Thomas's orchestra (see Chapter 7) performed, the two directors differed in their goals, Thomas intending to educate his listeners while Sousa wished simply to entertain his. To this end, Sousa often included in his concerts transcriptions of a popular new piano music called *ragtime*.

Ragtime

During the rather hectic last decade of the nineteenth century, talented African American pianists began to play a new, highly syncopated and very danceable music in more or (especially) less reputable places of entertainment. Small bands, too, "ragged" their arrangements, adding spicy syncopations over a steady beat. By 1897, the hot new music was being called **ragtime.**

Early ragtime pianists improvised their music, captivating audiences in nightclubs and bawdy houses with a jaunty, toe-tapping style. In the last years of the nineteenth century, however, as publishers began to show interest in the catchy new music, some ragtime players composed highly structured pieces that we now consider "classic" ragtime. This development remains controversial, some ragtime lovers insisting that writing down and publishing rags debased their essential quality as jubilant, spontaneous creations. But while the term originally had a more general meaning, normally we consider ragtime specifically a written piano music, composed for publication rather than improvised. Uprooted from their homeland and transplanted in a harsh new world, black musicians were restructuring their familiar modes of musical expression to fit their new cultural experiences. Thus in effect, ragtime was a new and essentially American music created by black musicians, based on both white European and black African traditions.

From the marches of European-influenced composers, such as Patrick S. Gilmore and John Philip Sousa, ragtime derived its march form and tonal harmony. Like a march, a rag generally begins with a brief introduction. Next we hear several strains in the order **A A B B C C D D,** each different letter representing a new strain. Usually one of the strains is a trio, often in the subdominant; and many rags, like many marches, end in this key. The pattern is not rigid, however, and certainly does not dictate the content; the first strain may return later in the piece, and many other variants of this basic march form also are possible.

Although some of the early ragtime players were self-taught, others with music training brought their knowledge of European harmony to the popular piano style. Thus, even though early rags were clearly tonal, some of them included rather complex melodies and harmonies using numerous **chromatic** tones—tones other than those of the major or minor scale on which the piece was based.

The rhythms and the flavor of ragtime, however—the characteristics that made it wildly popular in Europe as well as in America—derived from Africa and were practiced by singers, brass bands, and other instrumental ensembles long before ragtime was established as a piano form. Although syncopation had enlivened Western music from its beginning, the spicy nature and consistent application of syncopated rhythms were distinctive characteristics of the vigorous new vernacular music, ragtime.

Late minstrel shows constituted a strong source of inspiration for the hot new piano style: After the Civil War, as noted in Chapter 6, minstrelsy provided a lucrative source of income for black as well as white performers, and blacks formed their own lively shows in which they syncopated, or ragged, banjo tunes. The high-stepping plantation dance called a **cakewalk,** based on the syncopated figure *short-LONG-short,* became a regular feature of the **finale,** or last scene, of a minstrel show. This distinctive cakewalk rhythm also appears occasionally in the music of many composers—Gottschalk's "Bamboula" and "The Banjo," Stephen Foster's "Oh! Susanna," and Daniel Emmett's "Dixie" to name a few. (Because *duration* implies *accent,* we hear the long note of the cakewalk rhythmic pattern as stronger than the short notes that surround it.) This pattern consistently served the ragtime pianist, whose left hand marked the regular duple meter while the right hand played a highly syncopated melody.

Outstanding ragtime pianists included **Eubie Blake,** who died at the age of one hundred in 1983; **James Scott** (1886–1938); and Ferdinand DeMenthe, known as **Jelly Roll Morton** (1890–1941)—among many others, each with his own style of writing and playing rags. Ragtime pianists recorded their performances on **piano rolls** by playing on a special piano that marked dots on a paper, which then could be punched and duplicated, making it possible for eager listeners throughout America and abroad to hear the music "live" on the new **player pianos.** A "pianist" played this novel instrument by pumping two pedals controlling a set of vacuum bellows that forced air through the holes in the paper as it wound over a tracker bar, causing the piano hammers to strike the appropriate piano strings. Player pianos brought recorded performances of the great ragtime players into people's homes before phonographs—and long before radios—became widely available. They also preserved improvised performances by many ragtime players who resisted—more, resented—the move toward "respectability" by those who published their compositions.

Scott Joplin (1868–1917)

The childhood experience of **Scott Joplin** (Figure 8.2), the acknowledged king of ragtime, was rich with music, for his father, a former slave, played the violin, and there were other instruments in the Joplin home as well. The young Joplin studied piano with a German immigrant musician, who also provided him with basic studies in music theory.

While still a teenager, Joplin left his home in Texarkana, Texas, and traveled east to Missouri, earning some money along the way by playing ragtime piano. In Sedalia and later in St. Louis—the early center of ragtime creativity—Joplin addressed both white and black music markets, playing in black bars and saloons while writing sentimental songs and arrangements in the white popular style. A shy and gentle man, he liked composing and teaching far better than playing in the rough environments where ragtime was first popular; and finally, the huge commercial success of his "Maple Leaf Rag" (Listening Example 30), published in 1899, allowed him to concentrate on the activities he preferred. This rag, previously rejected by one publisher, in 1899 finally attracted the attention of another, John Stark, who heard Joplin play it at the Maple Leaf Club. "Maple Leaf Rag" achieved enormous popularity, and Stark became Joplin's most frequent publisher for the next ten years.

FIGURE 8.2

Scott Joplin (1868–1917) was honored with a commemorative stamp by the U.S. Postal Service in 1983 as part of its Black Heritage series.

Listening Example 30

"Maple Leaf Rag"

Composed in 1899, this landmark in American music history earned quick commercial success—unprecedented for a black composer—and became a standard in the repertoire of many famous pianists. Notice the constant beat, maintained in the left hand, and the sparkling right hand's creative play against the beat.

CD 1
Track 30
3:04

Composer Scott Joplin (1868–1917).

Genre Ragtime.

Timbre Piano.

Key A-flat major.

Melody Each strain has its own distinctive, syncopated melody, played by the right hand and accompanied by the left in various fashion.

—Continued

"Maple Leaf Rag"

Texture   Homophonic.

Form   March form, the strains occurring in the order **A A B B A C C D D.**

Meter   Duple.

Tempo   The score indicates *tempo di marcia* (march tempo), but Joplin was adamant that rags must be played at a moderate tempo.

0:00	**A**	The first strain, which begins without introduction, features the short-*LONG*-short cakewalk figure, which first occurs in the second half of the first measure and recurs frequently throughout the piece. The first two measures are repeated. Notice the accented chromatic notes in the next two measures (0:06 and 0:07) and the dramatic ascending figure that follows. (The ornamental flourishes in the left hand are added—improvised—by the pianist.)
0:20	**A**	Repeat.
0:41	**B**	The second strain (**B**), rhythmically similar to the first, is higher in pitch. It begins with a chromatically descending melodic line and is marked *staccato*, meaning that it should be played in a crisp, detached manner.
1:01	**B**	Repeat.
1:21	**A**	The first strain returns.
1:40	**C**	Trio. Notice the rich chordal texture of this strain, as the left hand alternates octaves and chords in a pattern later characteristic of stride piano (see pp. 161–162). The key is the subdominant, D-flat major.
2:00	**C**	Repeat.
2:20	**D**	The fourth strain returns to the tonic and is more similar in texture to strains 1 and 2.
2:40	**D**	Repeat. The lively piece ends with two emphatic chords.

Although very easy to enjoy, good rags may be quite difficult to play. Joplin's own rags reveal a change from the (relative) simplicity of such early rags as "Maple Leaf Rag" and "The Entertainer"—both irresistibly tuneful and entirely unpretentious—to some of his later rags such as "Euphonic Sounds," which sound like music more for the concert than for the dance hall. Although he insisted that rags should be played as written, Joplin regularly improvised complex embellishments in his own playing—which, however, was never very fast, for Joplin knew that a dashing tempo trivialized the strength and dignity of a great rag.

Influence of Ragtime

Ragtime had a striking effect on many kinds of music in both the popular and classical realms. Social dancing was strongly affected as Americans, who even before the Civil War had largely abandoned popular eighteenth-century country dances for couple dances such as the waltz and the energetic polka, after the rise of ragtime avidly adopted the **two-step, or fox-trot.** The frequent syncopations of the popular new dance delighted young people and the fox-trot soon replaced all other dances in popularity.

James Reese Europe (1881–1919), at the time of his death America's best-known African American composer and bandleader, composed some of the most popular fox-trots of his day. Flavoring his dance band music with ragtime, Reese became wildly popular in New York City. During World War I, he led an army band in Europe. The band members not only entertained troops to great acclaim but also served heroically under fire, becoming the most decorated unit in the American Army during that war.

By the early twentieth century, many forms of American popular music reflected a strong black influence, although most of the rags, blues, and jazz recordings were made by white performers. African American vocalists especially were excluded from recording, though instrumental groups, such as those led by Europe and by W. C. Handy (see pp. 155–157), were allowed to record because listeners were less likely than in vocal performances to discern the performers' race.

Soon white composers also were writing songs using ragtime rhythms, such as "Hello, My Baby!" by Joseph E. Howard, "Waiting for the Robert E. Lee" by Lewis F. Muir, and "Yes, Sir, That's My Baby" by Gus Kahn and Walter Donaldson. In the second decade of the twentieth century, many songs with little or no syncopated rhythm and no reference to ragtime in their titles were perceived as ragtime songs, because of the style—brash, breezy, humorous—in which they were sung and played onstage and in recordings. Their lyrics were more colloquial, closer to everyday speech, than the rather formal expressions found in other sentimental love songs of the time. In fact, though, performers capitalized on the popularity of ragtime by "ragging" (syncopating) almost any popular song of the day. Nearly all ragtime songs were written and performed by whites, who thus established a pattern to be repeated through the twentieth century, as white musicians reaped benefits from watered-down interpretations of music originating with blacks. Several European composers also reflected the influence of ragtime by writing syncopated concert pieces with "rag" or "ragtime" in their titles.

At the end of World War I, ragtime had declined in popularity. Some composers were producing rags too complex for popular appeal, and the commercial effort to reach a broad audience often diluted the very characteristics that had made early rags exciting. By then, however, jazz musicians were reflecting the strong influence of ragtime, which—while important entirely in its own right—must also be considered a precursor of that hot new American music.

Meanwhile, popular songs replaced piano music in the affections of the public, which turned from this primarily instrumental music, led by black Americans, to a new brand of vocal music, led by American Jews—the songs of Tin Pan Alley.

Tin Pan Alley

The popular music publishing business expanded rapidly after the Civil War, with publishing houses active in many cities, including Boston, Chicago, Philadelphia, Baltimore, and Cincinnati. Well before the turn of the twentieth century, popular music had become an important business, and songs were being written for the purpose of making money. Songs with piano accompaniment printed as sheet music sold in amazing quantities, made popular by variety shows, music theater performances, and piano rolls (Figure 8.3).

In 1881, the brothers Alex and Tom Harms established a publishing firm in New York City, achieving such commercial success that many other song-publishing companies also based their firms in New York. This music publishing activity first centered on East 14th Street, in what was then the heart of New York's theater district; but by the 1890s, nearly every major music publishing house was situated on or near 28th Street, soon dubbed **Tin Pan Alley,** in reference to the sounds of many pianos playing at once, as house composers worked out new compositions and **song pluggers** demonstrated the music by playing and perhaps singing it for customers. Theater performers also stopped

FIGURE 8.3

Couple enjoying Tin Pan Alley songs on piano rolls.

by when in town to try out and select new songs for their shows, the primary means by which most listeners became familiar with popular music. (In the 1920s, the new recording industry began to assume some of the responsibility for popularizing songs; but although radio stations were playing popular recordings in the 1930s, it was another decade before radios became widely enough available to influence the popularity of a song.)

The Songs Tin Pan Alley publishers produced only popular songs, and these were nearly uniform in style, beginning with a brief piano introduction, which might include references to the melody of the song or might simply set the key and the tempo, and proceeding with the **verse-chorus form** that had become standard well before the time of Tin Pan Alley. Nevertheless, the dozen or so superb songwriters of the period developed their own styles and sounds to produce hundreds of great songs that continue to please listeners today.

The verses of a Tin Pan Alley song narrated a story or described a situation or a portrait, whereas the chorus, which was repeated after each verse, echoed or commented on the story. The songs of the 1890s often told tales of tragedy and loss, although their chorus might not reveal the sad nature of the song text: only those who sang or heard the last verse of a song, for example, might be aware that the loved one extolled in the chorus has died.

Most songs had at least two, and often several, verses, but in time the verses became less and less important, listeners clearly preferring the memorable chorus melodies and often scarcely realizing that a song also had a verse or verses. For this reason, by the 1920s Tin Pan Alley composers were writing shorter verses and fewer of them. Further, since early recordings could contain only three or four minutes of music on a record side, the verses of a song might well be omitted in recorded performances—another reason for composers not to spend precious time and effort writing them. Even when time allowed for a verse, performers often chose to repeat the familiar chorus instead, inviting an audience, if present, to sing along; and finally many Tin Pan Alley composers simply wrote songs without any verses at all.

Although largely writing songs to order, early Tin Pan Alley composers nevertheless produced many wonderful tunes still well remembered today. A large number, including "After the Ball" (1892), "The Sidewalks of New York" (1894), "Casey Would Waltz with the Strawberry Blonde" (1895), "Meet Me in St. Louis, Louis" (1904), and "Take Me Out to the Ball Game" (1908), were waltzes, reflecting the popularity of European operettas and other European music.

The lyrics of many songs from this period reveal social conflicts rising from women's new position in society, as the move from agriculture to industry, from a rural to an urban setting, altered female roles in family and social life. No longer confined to the farm or to country life, better educated and more widely experienced than women of an earlier generation, the "new woman" of the period from 1890 to 1910 assumed an active, independent role, even in courtship and romance. This excerpt from "Ta-ra-ra-boom-dee-ay" (1891,

Sammy Cahn (1913–1993), lyricist
"The popular song is America's greatest ambassador." (1969)

attributed to Henry Sayers) suggests the flirtatious lyrics—descriptive of lightly duplicitous behavior—typical of many songs of that time:

> *I'm not extravagantly shy,*
> *And when a nice young man is nigh,*
> *For his heart I have a try,*
> *And faint away with tearful cry!*
>
> *When the good young man in haste,*
> *Will support me 'round the waist,*
> *I don't come to while thus embraced,*
> *Till of my lips he steals a taste!*

Barbershop Singing Tin Pan Alley songs were often performed by quartets in **barbershop style,** a popular form of musical entertainment of that period. Four unaccompanied male voices, ranging from high to low (tenor, lead, baritone, and bass) sang popular songs in close harmony; quartets competed, in fact, to see which could make the most surprising harmonic changes in a given song "work." The lead voice nearly always sang the melody, the other voices providing harmony above and below. Barbershop singing retains an audience today, and the Society for the Preservation and Encouragement of Barbershop Quartet Singing in America has about 34,000 members in 800 chapters around the country. Women, too, usually called "Sweet Adelines" after the title of a popular song, enjoy singing in barbershop style and have their own very active organizations.

Tin Pan Alley songs lend themselves particularly well to barbershop singing: written within a modest vocal range and with simple (often clever) lyrics, they can be sung comfortably by average voices, and their simple melodies accommodate the creative harmonic changes characteristic of barbershop style, as heard in "Rose" ("A Ring to the Name of Rose") by George M. Cohan, Listening Example 31.

Listening Example 31

"Rose" ("A Ring to the Name of Rose")

CD 1
Track 31
2:29

This arrangement slightly changes Cohan's melody and rhythm, and especially the harmony, using the tight, complex harmonic combinations characteristic of barbershop singing. To the original 1923 text, the arranger has added phrases from a children's song, "Ring around the rosy, a pocket full of posy"—an innocent-sounding nonsense verse that has a sinister connection: Many people believe that "rosy" refers to the telltale mark on the skin of

—Continued

"Rose" ("A Ring to the Name of Rose")

a plague victim, and "posies" to bouquets of flowers held to disguise the smell of mass death. (The next, unsung, line of the verse—ending "All fall down"—may refer to those who have succumbed to the terrible illness.)

Composer   George M. Cohan (1878–1942).

Genre   Barbershop music.

Timbre   A cappella male chorus (The Phoenicians), singing in barbershop style.

Texture   Homophonic.

Form   Verse-chorus.

Meter   Duple. The rhythm of the verse is so relaxed, with use of so much rubato, that it is difficult to define the meter before hearing the swinging chorus.

Tempo   Flexible in the verse, moderate in the chorus.

Text   By George M. Cohan.

0:00   Verse: Note the dramatic changes in dynamic level, the emphasis on harmonies rather than the melody, and the extremely flexible rhythm throughout the verse. All are characteristic of barbershop style.
"What's in a name?" said Shakespeare.

0:54   Chorus: Here the rhythm settles down to a regular metrical pattern, enlivened with frequent syncopation. Cohan lends gentle emphasis to the name "Rosie," for example, by delaying—syncopating—the first syllable.
There's a ring to the name of Rosie, ...

1:47   The second half of chorus is repeated, starting very softly, with light hand claps adding a new touch. There is a long crescendo.

2:09   A surprising reference to a traditional children's play song interrupts Cohan's text. The performance ends on a rousing major chord.

FIGURE 8.4
Irving Berlin (1888–1989).

Jewish American songwriters dominated Tin Pan Alley's years—the period between the two world wars, or from about 1920 to about 1945. Although forming a small percentage of the population in the early years of the United States, Jews had been actively involved as performing musicians and music teachers in urban areas, and had contributed significantly to the popular song industry from its beginning. As their population in this country increased dramatically, Jewish Americans made phenomenally successful careers in various areas of show business, including popular song.

Irving Berlin (1888–1989)

The long-lived **Irving Berlin** (Figure 8.4) was born Israel Baline in western Siberia, but his only memory of his native country was of himself lying huddled in a blanket, watching from the outskirts of town as Cossacks set fire to his Jewish neighborhood. His family fled Russia and settled in 1893 in a poor tenement in New York City. There the small boy began selling newspapers on the streets and soon became fascinated with the popular songs he heard pouring through the doors of busy taverns and cafés. Singing for pennies on street corners and in saloons, and as soon as he was old enough (eighteen) becoming a singing waiter, he soaked up the sounds that later emerged in his own hugely varied body of work: barroom ballads, ethnic songs, folk songs, novelty songs, ragtime, blues, and jazz.

While working on Tin Pan Alley as a song plugger, Berlin began to write songs for vaudeville and other forms of musical entertainment. Like most Tin Pan Alley composers, Berlin felt inspired by ragtime, though, as already noted, most "ragtime songs" only approximated the mood and style of ragtime without following ragtime's systematic opposition of a syncopated melody and an unsyncopated bass.

"Alexander's Ragtime Band" (Listening Example 32), written for a vaudeville show in 1911, became Berlin's first hit song. (Alexander was the name commonly applied to the leader of a black jazz band.)

Listening Example 32

"Alexander's Ragtime Band"

Recorded in 1911, Bessie Smith ("empress of the blues") and Her Band improvise freely on Berlin's happy tune, like the irrepressible jazz musicians they are (see Chapter 9). Although not a ragtime piece, it is ragtime-flavored: the mood is that of ragtime, and the rhythm is syncopated, though not in the systematic ragtime manner.

CD 1
Track 32
2:59

Composer   Irving Berlin (1888–1989).

Genre   Tin Pan Alley song.

—Continued

"Alexander's Ragtime Band"

Timbre   Blues singer Bessie Smith (1894–1937), accompanied by Her Band: cornet, trombone, clarinet, piano, banjo. The band plays a four-measure introduction, accompanies (and competes with) Bessie Smith as she sings, and plays a full chorus alone. All the instrumentalists were outstanding players, but Coleman Hawkins (clarinet) and Fletcher Henderson (piano) became particularly well-known and influential jazz musicians.

Texture   Homophonic. The band interjects occasional melodic comments but basically adds harmonic support to Smith's ringing voice.

Form   Verse-chorus.

Meter   Duple.

0:00   The band plays a four-measure introduction.

0:06   Verse: Bessie Smith begins the verse, accompanied by Her Band.
Oh my honey, oh, my honey,
You better hurry and let's go down there. . . . .

0:30   Chorus: When Smith sings, "Come on and hear," we indeed *hear* the band.
Come on and hear, Come on and hear,
Alexander's Ragtime Band. . . .

1:20   The band plays a full chorus.

2:08   Smith sings the chorus once more.

Totally immersed in American popular music and music theater, Berlin went on to become one of the best-known, most popular, and most enduring of all American songwriters. A self-taught musician, he was only comfortable playing on the black keys of the piano, so that he was limited to playing in one key—strangely, a key (G-flat or F-sharp) many pianists consider particularly difficult. This posed a problem, since a composer must be able to write in different tonalities to match the range of a singer's voice, or to add variety to a piece of some length by **modulating** (changing systematically) from one key to another. Different keys also seem to have varied effects, some sounding warm and rich, for example, and others cool and light, making one key more suitable than another for a particular song. So Berlin had a trick piano built on which he could slide a board to change mechanically the key in which he was playing while still using primarily the black keys on the keyboard.

Besides his prodigious music talent, Berlin also had a strong business mind. In 1914, he was one of a group of prominent music creators who founded the **American Society of Composers, Authors, and Publishers (ASCAP)** to ensure that music creators would be fairly compensated for the public performance of their works. Other early members included John Philip Sousa and Jerome Kern. Today ASCAP, with over 175,000 member-owners, protects the rights of music creators, distributing billions of dollars in royalties and licensing performances of hundreds of thousands of international creators under reciprocal agreements all over the world. Musicians in every field—hip-hop, jazz, country, Latin, symphonic music, musical theater, gospel, rock, electronic—all benefit immensely from the services of ASCAP.

In 1919, Irving Berlin formed his own publishing company, while continuing to write numerous songs, many of them for the Broadway stage. In the 1930s, he moved to Hollywood to write for movie musicals. During his long career, he wrote about 1,500 songs, nearly 1,000 of which remain in print.

There seemed no limit to the range of Berlin's talent or his musical imagination. While the rollicking tunes and jolly rhythms of many Berlin songs reveal his attraction to syncopated popular dance music, others, such as "Always," "How Deep Is the Ocean?" and "The Girl That I Marry," have a warm, romantic character. "White Christmas" is the most frequently recorded song of all time. His songs have become classics of American music, as much a part of American culture as any folk song. "A good song embodies the feelings of the mob," he once said. "And a songwriter is not much more than a mirror which reflects those feelings."

Berlin's patriotic song "God Bless America" has a curious history, having sparked controversy from the time singer Kate Smith introduced it in 1938. The public received the song with wild enthusiasm, and Berlin, thrilled, donated all royalties from it in perpetuity to the Boy Scouts and Girl Scouts of America; but liberal commentators attacked it as jingoistic, flag-waving, and sentimental, whereas on the right, according to a story in *Time* magazine in 1940, the song "brought on a wave of snide anti-Semitism directed at composer Berlin"—the composer, however, of America's most popular Christmas and Easter songs, "White Christmas" and "Easter Parade." Leftists attacked the song's lack of respect for separation of church and state, and right-wingers resented a non-Christian born in another country telling God to bless America. Yet not a few Americans enthusiastically proposed replacing "The Star Spangled Banner" with "God Bless America" as the national anthem.

A painter as well as a musician, Berlin passed his last years in quiet retirement, universally acknowledged—long before the world celebrated his hundredth birthday in 1988—as the elder statesman of American popular song.

Jerome Kern (1885–1945)

Born to a prosperous New York family, **Jerome Kern,** unlike his near contemporary Irving Berlin, had a sound music education. He studied in London for a time, composing songs for the British musical stage, and absorbing something of a European sound that would affect his music always. He intended, in fact, to become a composer of classical music but found himself irresistibly drawn to the popular musical theater and began writing songs for Broadway.

Kern's first songs were simply interpolated into British shows imported to Broadway, according to the custom of that day, when songs usually were unrelated to the plot of a show and therefore could be added or substituted at will. Many composers took advantage of the opportunity to write one or more songs for a show without having to be responsible for the entire score.

Like Berlin, Kern worked as a Tin Pan Alley song plugger and a rehearsal pianist for Broadway theaters before he began writing for his own shows (see Chapter 17, p. 302). His songs often resemble those of Irving Berlin, although many include more complex harmonies and sophisticated chord changes than had been used by Berlin and other early Tin Pan Alley songwriters. Also like Berlin, Kern wrote for Hollywood sound movies, finding them a congenial medium to introduce many of his finest late songs, including "The Last Time I Saw Paris" (from *Lady Be Good,* 1941) and "Long Ago and Far Away" (from *Cover Girl,* 1944). We shall consider music for theater and films in Chapters 17 and 18, but many of Tin Pan Alley's greatest hits, written for plays or movies that have been largely forgotten, still live prominent lives quite independent of the theatrical vehicles that launched them long ago.

Cole Porter (1892–1964)

The early life of **Cole Porter** (Figure 8.5), another major contributor to the golden age of American popular song (1920s–1950s), could hardly have differed more from Irving Berlin's. Wealthy, privileged, and very highly trained (in Paris under classical musicians), Porter took his career as a composer-lyricist seriously, working every bit as hard as anyone dependent upon his job for a living. His witty, sexy, sophisticated lyrics expressed basic human emotions in clever, fresh, and subtle ways—often so risqué as to earn him the nickname "the genteel pornographer."

FIGURE 8.5
Cole Porter (1892–1964).

The film *De-Lovely* (2004), a musical biography of Cole Porter's life, movingly portrayed this gifted, privileged, yet tortured man, who suffered physical pain after his legs were crushed in a horseback-riding accident in 1937, and emotional pain as a homosexual man living a double life. He indulged in numerous affairs with men and seems to have expressed some of his conflicting feelings in tantalizingly ambiguous song lyrics—for example: "It's the wrong game, with the wrong chips; Though your lips are tempting, they're the wrong lips. They're not her lips, but they're such tempting lips, That if some night you are free, Then it's all right, yes, it's all right with me," from "It's All Right with Me" (1952). Yet Porter remained deeply devoted to his wife, who basically accepted him as he was. One of Porter's best-known songs, "Always True to You in My Fashion," may have been addressed to her: "But I'm always true to you, darlin', in my fashion; yes, I'm always true to you, darlin', in my way."

Unlike Berlin's tuneful melodies, many of Porter's sophisticated tunes are quite difficult to sing. Often extremely chromatic, they wind their stepwise way up and down the scale, arriving just where and when they should but posing hazards to the vocalist along the way. "I've Got You Under My Skin," "In the Still of the Night," "You Do Something to Me, "All of You," "Begin the Beguine," and "Just One of Those Things" all illustrate the narrow steps and chromatic intervals typical of a Porter melody; and "Night and Day" (Listening Example 33) makes clear why many musicians prefer to listen to Cole Porter than to perform his music. (Porter is said to have referred to creating a new melody as "delicious torture," a sentiment hardly likely to have been expressed by the practical, down-to-earth Irving Berlin.)

"Night and Day"

Best-known for his spectacular dancing on stage and screen, **Fred Astaire** (1899–1987) also had a gift for beautifully presenting the lyrics and mood of a song. He introduced "Night and Day" in Cole Porter's 1932 musical *Gay Divorce*, which was made into a movie, renamed *The Gay Divorcee*, in 1934. Despite its very narrow vocal range and difficult-to-sing melody, the song was a sensation from the start.

CD 2
Track 1
3:12

Composer   Cole Porter (1892–1964).

Genre   Tin Pan Alley song.

Timbre   Astaire's light, rather thin but attractive tenor voice accompanied by a dance band.

Texture   Homophonic.

—Continued

"Night and Day"

Melody The melody, designed by Porter to fit the narrow range of Fred Astaire's singing voice, seems uniquely suited to the text of both verse and chorus. The verse uses very few notes, and the chorus phrases generally descend by steps or small skips, then rebound to their beginning tones.

Form Verse-chorus.

Meter Duple.

Harmony The harmonies, considered very sophisticated for show music at the time, have become standard fare for jazz musicians to build improvisations upon.

0:00 A brief band introduction sets the mood.

0:07 Verse, "Like the beat, beat, beat of the tom-tom when the jungle shadows fall . . ." As the singer's inner voice, like the beat of the tom-tom, keeps repeating, "you, you, you," the melody repeats one note thirty-three consecutive times. Notice the woodblock accompanying the "tick-tick-tock of the stately clock."

0:33 Chorus. The form is **a a b.**

    a *Night and day, you are the one . . .*

    a *Day and night, why is it so . . .*

    b *Night and day, under the hide of me . . .*

1:50 The band, using muted instruments accompanied by relentlessly throbbing percussion, plays the first two phrases (**a a**) of the verse.

2:42 Astaire returns with **b.**

George Gershwin (1898–1937) Born and bred in Brooklyn, New York, **George Gershwin** (Figure 8.6) worked as a song plugger on Tin Pan Alley while still a teenager, banging out tunes for singers and dancers. Soon his own tunes began attracting the attention of Broadway publishers, and before he was twenty he became a house songwriter for the T. B. Harms publishing firm, one of the most important on the street. An excellent pianist, Gershwin was also in demand as an accompanist for professional singers.

An early Gershwin song, "Swanee," written for a Broadway *revue* (a variety show—see pp. 295–296) when he was twenty-one, received little attention until the popular singer Al Jolson (1888–1950) adopted it as a regular part of his

FIGURE 8.6

George Gershwin
(1898–1937). "True music
must repeat the thought and
inspirations of the people
and the time. My people are
Americans and my time is
today." (1925)

performances. Jolson's dramatic, full-voiced singing style and impassioned delivery made the song an instant hit—the biggest hit song of his career—and brought Gershwin into great demand to write songs for the musical theater. During his short lifetime he wrote the scores for some 30 musicals and composed over 600 songs, many of which, including "Someone to Watch Over Me," "'S Wonderful," and "I Got Rhythm," were defined not only by Gershwin's beautiful melodies and complex harmonies, but also by clever lyrics written by George's brother Ira. Ira Gershwin (1896–1983) wrote the words to one of George Gershwin's most beautiful melodies after his brother's death from a brain tumor at age thirty-nine. He titled this moving tribute to a beloved brother, which has become one of the Gershwins' best-known songs, "Our Love Is Here to Stay." The youngest Gershwin brother, Arthur, was also a songwriter, although he never became very well known.

Gershwin, like Berlin, Kern, and Porter, also wrote for Hollywood movies, bringing to them the same sophisticated skills he had honed on Broadway. But unlike the other great Tin Pan Alley songwriters, Gershwin had strong, even compelling interest in classical music and jazz. Although he was not a jazz musician himself, his musical language has the sounds and the flavor of jazz, and his songs lend themselves particularly well to jazz interpretations. (We will study jazz in Chapters 9, 10, and 15.) Gershwin's richly dissonant harmonies include sometimes humorous, sometimes plaintive turns and embellishments, making his music absolutely recognizable as his own; and his hauntingly beautiful melodies render his songs as meaningful and as well loved today as ever.

Decline of Tin Pan Alley Several factors contributed to the gradual lessening of the influence of Tin Pan Alley on American popular music.

Inevitably, popular taste began to change after half a century of domination by one powerful system. Sentimental songs that retained significance through the years of World War II became less relevant after the war was won, the troops were home, the economy boomed, and youthful tastes came to the fore. Humorous, nonsensical "novelty" songs accommodated the lightened mood; Latin rhythms attracted wide audiences; songs from the country and from the West joined and in some cases replaced the urban song style that had dominated American popular music for so long.

Coincidentally, in 1940 ASCAP enforced a strike against the major radio networks, which would not meet ASCAP's demands for fees significantly higher than those currently paid. For over a year, pending settlement of the strike, radio stations could play no new recordings of Tin Pan Alley music. Desperate for new music to program, the stations readily accepted music offered by a newly formed organization, **Broadcast Music Incorporated (BMI),** whose members were generally younger than and largely unaffected by the professionals of Tin Pan Alley, and whose music reflected varied regional tastes.

The tide was about to turn, bringing a wave—many waves—of new sounds in popular music.

Terms to Review

strain	**piano roll**	**modulate**
trio	**player piano**	**American Society of**
break	**two-step** or **fox-trot**	**Composers, Authors, and**
ragtime	**Tin Pan Alley**	**Publishers (ASCAP)**
chromaticism	**song plugger**	**Broadcast Music Incorporated**
cakewalk	**verse-chorus form**	**(BMI)**
finale	**barbershop style**	

Key Figures

John Philip Sousa	Scott Joplin	Cole Porter
Eubie Blake	James Reese Europe	Fred Astaire
James Scott	Irving Berlin	George Gershwin
Jelly Roll Morton	Jerome Kern	

Critical Thinking

Do you think that Scott Joplin improved or damaged ragtime by turning it from an improvised style to a written piano music?

Discuss the reasons for the rise, and then the decline, of Tin Pan Alley.

How do ASCAP and BMI affect the popular music consumer today?

The Jazz Age

As Americans danced into the beginning of the twentieth century, saloons and dance halls rang with the sounds of ragtime, the two-step, and various Latin dances (see p. 209) soon to become even more popular. Fast tempos, syncopated rhythms, and dance band timbres—beautifully captured by the African American artist Archibald Motley in his painting *Blues* (Figure 9.1)—replaced the sedate ballroom dances played by the string orchestras of an earlier time. As dance rhythms became more complex, solo instrumental lines more independent, and instrumental timbres more varied, Americans discovered that listening to the new music was just as exciting as dancing to it. By 1917, they were calling it **jazz.** (The origin of the word *jazz* is obscure, but in African American slang it had a sexual connotation; its secondary sense was of excitement, energy, and invigoration.)

The popular writer F. Scott Fitzgerald dubbed the 1920s—the decade of dance marathons, speakeasies, a stock market boom, Babe Ruth, Greta Garbo, and Rudolph Valentino—the "jazz age," and so that period is often called today. Of course the roots of jazz lie far earlier, and jazz was not the only music popular in the roaring twenties, but that was when the new music came to wide public attention through the performances and recordings of a large number of tremendously talented musicians who would dominate the field for decades.

The roots of jazz, rich and varied, include white European marches, hymns, and various popular dances; Creole and Caribbean influences; and of course and most significantly, the stirring hot rhythms, dramatic percussive effects, and distinctive vocal and instrumental performance techniques derived from black Africa. Ragtime, which already embodied characteristics derived from white and black music, profoundly influenced the evolving style. It is not surprising, then, that jazz styles vary widely—in mood, instrumentation, tempo, and even artistic intent, although generally jazz is regular in meter, involves **blue notes** ("bent" or slurred melodically ambiguous notes), and is improvised to a greater or lesser extent, depending on the performers' inclinations and abilities. Although rooted in folk and popular styles, jazz rarely entered the popular music mainstream. It reached an enthusiastic segment of the popular music audience, of course, but it belongs to America's art music tradition as well.

FIGURE 9.1

Blues, Archibald Motley. The syncopated rhythms of Motley's swaying musicians and dancing couples superbly evoke and reflect the influence of the music of the jazz age.

Blues

The foundations of jazz, primarily an instrumental music, lie in the **blues,** a vocal form whose origins, although stubbornly obscure, derive from African American traditions and date from sometime in the nineteenth century (Figure 9.2). Just when the blues emerged is the subject of dispute, but certainly after the Civil War intimations of what we call the blues were heard from slaves and from newly emancipated blacks, who often found their lives more rather than less difficult after they received their freedom. Away from their familiar plantation environment, lonely and in desperate need of money, some became migrants, some went to prison, and others held backbreaking, unrewarding jobs such as digging ditches or laying railroad lines. In their new distress, they sometimes expanded field hollers into simple solo songs, laden with emotional content and highly expressive of their loneliness and pain. In effect, they were singing the blues.

Rural or Country Blues
This new kind of solo song, introduced by blacks, was folklike in sound but highly distinctive in character and form. The texts of the early **rural** or **country blues** addressed every aspect of life, but most concerned work or, sometimes, love—unrequited, betrayed, or gone wrong. Blues singers expressed their troubles and told unflinching stories in an unaffected, straightforward

FIGURE 9.2

The origin of the blues.

manner, without sentimentality and often with a wry or whimsical humor that lessened the sadness while increasing the poignancy of their tale of woe.

They could hardly have guessed the inestimable influence their simple music would have upon the development of every genre of American music.

Form. The earliest blues stanzas probably consisted of one line of text sung three times to a familiar or improvised melody. But in time it became customary to sing the first line twice and add a conclusion or response, in the form **AAB** (statement, repeat, response). Because each stanza had three lines, and each line had four measures or bars, the form is called the **twelve-bar blues.** It is the only purely American contribution to musical form.

> *Hard times here, worse times down the road.*
> *Hard times here, worse times down the road.*
> *Wish my man was here to share the load.*

Melodic Characteristics. Blues singers and later instrumentalists adopted the African custom of treating the third, seventh, sometimes fifth, and less often sixth degrees of the scale as neutral or ambiguous tones, the wonderfully flexible blue notes the jazz musician "bends" (lowers or slightly raises) to produce gracefully fluid, emotionally expressive melodic lines. Besides these "bent," "tired," or "worried" notes, vocal and instrumental scoops and slides or glissandos, also derived from black African singing, further colored the performance of early blues melodies.

Blues Harmony. In time, a simple harmonic pattern emerged in which the tonic, subdominant, and dominant chords occurred in unorthodox order, providing a strong, simple, and distinctive harmonic framework for blues musicians to improvise around.

> *Line 1: stays tonic*
> *Line 2: IV goes to I*
> *Line 3: V goes to IV goes to I*

It is in the third line that the distinctive harmonic irregularity occurs, as V—which implies a movement toward tonic—surprisingly "regresses" to IV. The verbal explanation sounds technical—all the more interesting, when one considers that the distinctive chord pattern evolved from simple custom.

Improvisation. This asymmetrical, strictly tonal, textually simple form beautifully served the improvising musician in several ways. Vocal and instrumental timbres were limited only by a performer's imagination and the availability of musical instruments, and possibilities abounded for subtle rhythmic adjustments over the solidly steady beat. Each of the characteristics of text, form, melody, and harmony described previously further supported the musician's improvisational efforts:

1. Each line of text took about 2½ bars to complete, leaving 1½ measures of thinking time to be filled with half-spoken, half-sung nonsense syllables, later called **scatting** or **scat singing,** or by improvisation on accompanying instruments.
2. Repetition of the first line of text gave the singer additional thinking time to plan the response.
3. Melodies could be embellished and colored by scoops, slides, blue notes, and other creative and expressive effects.
4. The basic harmonic pattern allowed ample harmonic variety, the simple chords supporting without getting in the way of creative ideas.

Soon the rural blues evolved from intensely personal introspection to a form of shared entertainment, sung around campfires or in the poorest living quarters to ease spirits when the labor of the day was done. Any available instrument might accompany the voice, perhaps answering the singer and filling out a line with its own melodic interest. This call-and-response effect is among the African traditions essential to the blues; others include the deeply personal expression and various expressive manners of vocal embellishment. While the chords and structured regularity of the blues reflect white customs, these always remain subject to a performer's individual interpretation and never govern or limit a musician's creativity.

The great country blues singer and guitar legend **Robert Johnson** (1911–1938) recorded only twenty-nine songs, but his influence has been long-lasting and far-flung. His guitar playing, mediocre in his early years, became so virtuosic he was rumored to have sold his soul to the devil; today signs all across the Mississippi Delta claim to mark "the spot" where Johnson struck the deal! Johnson was only twenty-seven when he died, poisoned by a jealous husband (or perhaps girlfriend) while performing his compelling music at a juke joint.

Performing his blues piece "Hellhound on My Trail" (Listening Example 34), Johnson handles the form casually, adding a measure here or there as it suits him.

"Hellhound on My Trail"

CD 2
Track 2
2:34

The bluesy mood of this 1937 piece fits the impassioned nature of the text, voiced by a lonely traveler far from home and missing his "little sweet woman." The varying length of the lines indicates the informality and improvisatory nature of country blues, and the frequent blue notes and intricate melodic embellishments add to the individuality and the passion of Johnson's performance.

Composer and Performer   Robert Johnson (1911–1938).

Genre   Country blues.

Timbre   High, rather pinched, nasal, male voice, accompanied by guitar.

Melody   The descending melodic line suggests a sigh, depression, a low, lonely mood.

Texture   Homophonic. The strummed guitar chords add harmony—which sometimes sounds strange to modern, or city, ears.

Form   Twelve-bar blues. Each verse follows the form **a a b.**

Meter   Quadruple.

Tempo   Slow, "loping" in the manner of a tired horse.

Text   Notice the manner in which Johnson fills out each line with repetitions of fragments of the text and with eloquent commentary on his guitar, which also sets the mood with its introduction.

0:09	**a**	*I got to keep movin'. Blues fallin' down like hail.*
0:24	**a**	*Blues fallin' down like hail. (incomplete)*
0:36	**b**	*And I can't keep no money with a hellhound on my trail.*
0:50	**a**	*If today was Christmas Eve, and tomorrow Christmas Day,*
1:03	**a**	*If today was Christmas Eve, and tomorrow Christmas Day,*
1:13	**b**	*I would need my little sweet rider [lover] just to pass the time away.*
1:25	**a**	*You sprinkled hot-foot powder [a voodoo spell?] all around my door.*
1:35	**a**	*You sprinkled hot-foot powder all around your daddy's door.*

—Continued

Listening Example 34—concluded

"Hellhound on My Trail"

1:46	**b**	*It keeps me with a ramblin' mind, Rider, every old place I go.*
1:58	**a**	*I can tell the wind is risin', the leaves tremblin' on the tree.*
2:11	**a**	*I can tell the wind is risin', the leaves tremblin' on the tree.*
2:21	**b**	*All I need is my little sweet woman to keep my company.*

Classic Blues Blues conceived primarily as entertainment, performed in theaters and clubs and on commercially distributed recordings, is called **classic blues.** Whereas country singers accompanied themselves, usually on guitar or banjo, classic blues performers often had a band backing them up, and the piano assumed increasing importance. More professional, more stylized, more universal than the earlier primitive or rural blues, classic blues found a wide audience among white as well as black Americans.

The outstanding singers of rural blues were men, famously including Huddie Ledbetter (see p. 249) and Blind Lemon Jefferson among many others; but the early classic blues singers were mostly women, and nearly all of the great blues lyrics are written from a woman's point of view. Again in contrast to folk or country blues, which embraced a wide range of topics, most classic blues lyrics concern love—especially love "gone wrong." By the 1920s, theatrical performance was becoming recognized as an acceptable profession for women (white or black), and the field offered many unprecedented social and economic opportunities.

Gertrude "Ma" Rainey (born Gertrude Pridgett, 1886–1939), one of the most imitated and influential classic blues singers and composers, established something of a link between early rural blues and sophisticated blues performances recorded for commercial distribution. Having performed in both styles, Ma Rainey, sometimes called Madame Rainey and the mother or the queen of the blues, taught **Bessie Smith** (1894–1937), who became perhaps the most famous of all classic blues singers (Figure 9.3). Bessie Smith is remembered today for the intense personal feeling with which she imbued her performances, embellishing melodies and bending tones—as in Listening Example 35, "Lost Your Head Blues"—to communicate the deepest emotions to her rapt and sympathetic audiences.

Ma Rainey, Bessie Smith ("Empress of the Blues"), and a number of other great classic blues singers brought a new professionalism and theatrical polish to blues, which soon became a highly profitable medium of entertainment. Of the great classic blues recordings, Bessie Smith's earned the most money for her recording company, but although Columbia Records paid her well, she never received any royalties for her efforts, and she died, after an automobile accident, nearly penniless.

FIGURE 9.3

The American blues singer and songwriter Bessie Smith (1894–1937).

"Lost Your Head Blues"

This 1926 straightforward delivery of complaint, unburdened by sentimentality and relieved by slight, wry humor, is characteristic of the blues. Also listen for expressive slides and blue notes throughout the piece in both trumpet and voice. The performance seems tightly organized and professionally delivered, yet both voice and trumpet suggest literally endless possibilities for interpretation of this famous blues piece.

CD 2
Track 3
2:54

Composer Probably Bessie Smith (1886–1939).

Genre Classic twelve-bar blues.

Timbre Blues vocalist Bessie Smith, with trumpet and piano accompaniment. Lightly dissonant piano chords lope along throughout the performance, supporting both voice and trumpet while remaining uninvolved in the dialogue between them.

Melody Bessie Smith weaves her flexible vocal line over and around the solid support of the accompanying harmonies. The melody remains fairly constant for each verse, although always subject to Smith's supple vocal manipulations. Especially in verses 3 and 5, Smith ranges slightly afield, but never far from the original melodic line.

Harmony I, IV, and V chords.

Texture Homophonic.

Form Twelve-bar blues. There are five three-line verses. To each line of each verse sung by Bessie Smith, the trumpet responds, in turn answering, mocking, and encouraging the singer.

Meter Quadruple.

Tempo Moderately slow.

0:00   The trumpet and piano play a four-bar introduction.
0:11   *I was with you, baby, when you didn't have a dime. . . .*
0:44   *Once ain't for always, two ain't for twice. . . .*
1:16   *When you were lonesome, I tried to treat you kind. . . .*
1:49   *I'm goin' to leave, baby, ain't gonna say goodbye. . . .*
2:21   *Days are lonesome, nights are long. . . .*
Notice the slight slowing in tempo at the end of the last line, signaling the conclusion of the song.

Urban Blues

It was only a matter of time before the professional publishing and recording industries recognized the commercial potential of the blues, and blues pieces began to be published as sheet music. White composers started to write blues, and the word *blues* appeared in the titles of many pieces, including some that were not blues at all. Published blues first appeared about 1912, and by the 1920s so-called blues **race records** (the unfortunate industry term for recordings intended for an African American audience) were being mass-produced.

As the blues entered the popular music stream, blues composers adapted the twelve-bar form in a manner they supposed would better appeal to a mainstream (white) audience. Intended for performance by professional musicians, the so-called **urban blues** could be more complex in form and more sophisticated in harmony than the earlier rural blues; and although some or even most of the stanzas of urban blues retained the three-line form, one or more verses had the conventional four- or eight-line (sixteen- or thirty-two-bar) form. Soon urban blues, recorded by professional blues singers, were being disseminated to a wide and increasingly appreciative public. As the great blues singers made some of their finest recordings with the outstanding jazz musicians of their day, close connections were established between instrumental jazz and urban blues, which shared a folk or popular heritage, a regular beat, subtle rhythmic variations, versatile blue notes, and fluent improvisation.

Although **William Christopher (W. C.) Handy** (1873–1958), the African American bandleader and composer who called himself "father of the blues," hardly invented the form, he certainly led it into the world of commercial popular music. As a young man, Handy (Figure 9.4) learned to play a cornet and

FIGURE 9.4

W. C. Handy (1873–1958) (at left) with Duke Ellington (1899–1974).

(to his Methodist father's dismay) joined a minstrel troupe. He then formed his own dance band, which played in Memphis for a while before moving to Chicago and finally to New York. There Handy began writing and publishing urban blues, including the best-known example, the beautiful "St. Louis Blues" (Listening Example 36).

Listening Example 36

"St. Louis Blues"

Notice how complex the formal arrangement of this blues piece from 1914 has become in contrast to the improvised twelve-bar country blues. Here we have a sophisticated vocal and instrumental performance of a published composition, in which the verses vary in melodic content and even in the number of lines per verse. Bessie Smith delivers the words in her big, robust voice with great rhythmic freedom, bending pitches (as on "sun" in the first phrase of the song), with Armstrong echoing her effects on his trumpet.

CD 2
Track 4
3:09

Composer W. C. Handy (1873–1958).

Genre Urban blues.

Timbre Blues vocalist (Bessie Smith), accompanied by Fred Longshaw on reed organ (see picture on p. 70) and by Louis Armstrong (see pp. 158–160) on trumpet. Although the reed pump organ suggests the rustic flavor of country blues, the young Louis Armstrong already reveals his mastery as a jazz musician, competing on his trumpet with Bessie Smith for virtuosity and emotional expression.

Melody The song has considerable melodic variety, the first two verses having the same melody but the third and fourth each offering new melodic material.

Texture Homophonic. The competing melodies occur consecutively, not simultaneously.

Form Modified twelve-bar blues:

Verses 1 and 2 follow the twelve-bar form.
Verse 3 has four lines; the first two rhyme, as do the last two.
The song ends with a fourth stanza, in twelve-bar form.

Meter Quadruple.

—Continued

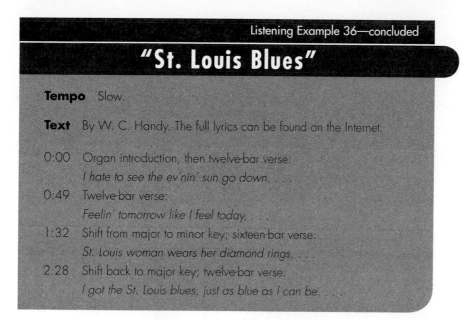

Listening Example 36—concluded

"St. Louis Blues"

Tempo Slow.

Text By W. C. Handy. The full lyrics can be found on the Internet.

0:00 Organ introduction, then twelve-bar verse:
I hate to see the ev'nin' sun go down. . . .

0:49 Twelve-bar verse:
Feelin' tomorrow like I feel today, . . .

1:32 Shift from major to minor key; sixteen-bar verse:
St. Louis woman wears her diamond rings, . . .

2:28 Shift back to major key; twelve-bar verse:
I got the St. Louis blues, just as blue as I can be. . . .

New Orleans Jazz

As musical instruments left over from Civil War military bands became readily and cheaply available, black musicians began playing them in their own manner, improvising freely on favorite familiar tunes. In New Orleans, small brass bands played for parades, concerts, and even funerals, developing a famous tradition that survives today. Having performed solemn music to accompany the funeral party both to the cemetery and—for a dignified interval—on the way back to town, the band breaks into joyous music whose familiar tunes and hot rhythms virtually compel the mourners' healthy return to everyday life.

In time, the bands' instrumental techniques became more individual, the tempos faster, and the mood more high-powered and intense. Although some musicians read music, most did not and simply improvised freely on familiar tunes. In a word, they were playing jazz. Soon small bands or **combos** (Figure 9.5) of black musicians were providing indoor entertainment, their hot new dance music combining the steady beat and stirring tempo of European march and dance tunes with the subtle and complex syncopations of black African and Caribbean effects.

As already noted (see p. 107), New Orleans, which had alternately been under French and Spanish rule and to which many Afro-Latin people had fled from Caribbean settlements such as Haiti and Cuba, offered a rich cultural climate. Its music included popular French, Spanish, Creole, and black tunes; serious and comic opera; and airs from marching, dance, and concert bands. The city generously nourished the exciting new vernacular sound, with the notorious Storyville red-light district of gambling saloons, bordellos, and dance halls offering ample job opportunities for jazz musicians. Thus it is not

FIGURE 9.5

Members of a jazz combo.

surprising that New Orleans produced a large number of astonishingly talented jazz musicians who soon attracted others to their city, making it the first important center of jazz.

Most **New Orleans jazz** combos consisted of three to eight people playing clarinet, cornet or trumpet, and trombone, with a rhythm section including banjo, tuba, and drums. Later, combos playing indoors rather than on the streets added a piano and sometimes replaced the tuba with a string bass. Having selected a hymn, rag, march, popular song, or blues and agreed upon the harmonic patterns to be repeated throughout, the musicians began improvising around the tune: The cornet handled the melody; the clarinet wove countermelodies around it; the trombone provided supporting harmonies; and the rhythm section marked the beat, a straight four-to-the-bar, with an accent on *ONE* and a secondary accent on *three*. Early New Orleans performances were basically collective improvisations played in this manner, the soloists taking turns improvising complex variations on given (known) melodies while the other musicians provided rhythmic and harmonic support.

Louis Armstrong (1901–1971)

Louis Armstrong (Figure 9.6) survived a violent childhood in New Orleans to become a gentle, kindly, good-natured man and an incredibly talented musician. He played the cornet in King Oliver's band as a boy, and in the early 1920s followed Oliver to Chicago, where Armstrong formed his own band (the Hot Five, later the Hot Seven) and began making important jazz recordings, including the performance of his wife's composition "Hotter Than That" heard in Listening Example 37.

FIGURE 9.6

Louis Armstrong (1901–1971).

"Hotter Than That" (excerpt)

Lil Hardin, an outstanding jazz pianist who became Louis Armstrong's second wife, performed regularly with the Hot Five, the group that recorded this piece in 1928 and many other early Armstrong hits. The other instrumentalists include Lonnie Johnson, whose blues-based guitar improvisations are somewhat unusual, because previously electric amplification guitars had played a limited role in jazz. Here, however, the guitar provides exciting moments.

CD 2
Track 5
1:31

Composer Lillian Hardin Armstrong (1898–1971). Louis Armstrong and the Hot Five instrumentalists improvise imaginatively, with great virtuosity, on the composer's tune and its harmonic structure.

Genre New Orleans jazz.

Timbre Louis Armstrong's voice, plus cornet, trombone, clarinet, piano, guitar. The cornet, trombone, and clarinet take turns improvising while the other instruments provide a rhythmic accompaniment. Armstrong's cornet solos dominate, of course. And in his scat singing he "plays" his voice like another instrument, revealing a seemingly limitless range of creative and expressive techniques.

Texture Homophonic.

Form A series of improvised solos on the thirty-two-bar tune.

Meter Quadruple.

Tempo Fast.

0.00 Introduction: Armstrong's cornet dominates the eight-bar introduction, accompanied by all the other instruments, collectively improvising.

0:09 Chorus 1: Cornet solo, accompanied by piano and guitar.

0:27 Chorus 2: The cornet solo continues.

0:46 Chorus 3: Clarinet solo accompanied by piano and guitar.

1:03 Chorus 4: Another clarinet solo.

1:20 Chorus 5: Armstrong's scat singing, accompanied by guitar, as the excerpt tapers off.

Switching to the trumpet, Armstrong developed previously inconceivable virtuosic techniques for that instrument, producing pure, clarion tones that had never been heard before.

Even more significant than his virtuosity, however, were Armstrong's original and highly creative solo improvisations, as beautifully expressive as they were technically brilliant. The extraordinarily wide emotional range of his playing greatly expanded musicians' and listeners' concept of what jazz was all about, leading the great bebop trumpet player Dizzy Gillespie (see pp. 175–177) to express the feeling of many musicians when he said of Armstrong, "No him, no me."

Armstrong also sang (in a manner of speaking), scatting in an amazingly creative, often humorous, always expressive way. Finding sadness or humor or elation in a song, he let it issue forth as a purely natural, purely human statement. In this and in every way, he personalized his performances as no one had before, taking the music and making it his own.

Chicago Jazz

During the 1920s, after the authorities shut down New Orleans's lucrative Storyville district, many outstanding jazz artists moved to Chicago, which then became the new performing and recording center for jazz. Chicago's large population, thriving speakeasies, and fledgling recording opportunities—as well as a plentiful supply of jobs in the railroads, stockyards, and mills—soon attracted jazz musicians from all over the country.

In Chicago, many young white musicians became enamored of the sounds of the New Orleans combos and, in the sincerest form of flattery, set out to imitate them. **Dixieland,** the term for this white imitation of New Orleans jazz, in time came to be applied to all early jazz, although musicians distinguished between New Orleans Dixieland and Chicago Dixieland. The Chicago combos usually added a saxophone to the New Orleans instrumentation and replaced the banjo with a guitar; further, big-city tension and drive characterized Chicago jazz, which often began and ended with more complex improvisations than New Orleans musicians used and which emphasized the role of soloists to a greater degree. A marked backbeat often enhanced the excitement of the newer style. It has been suggested—but one can never know—that the white musicians actually strove to outdo their models (Figure 9.7).

Before the end of the roaring twenties, the heart of jazz shifted again, this time to New York City, where numerous combos and many jazz pianists continued to evolve distinctive sounds. Another important regional style—Kansas City jazz—was already evolving but reached its peak in the next decade, the 1930s, which we will cover in Chapter 10.

Jazz Piano

Jazz pianists, whose instrument sounded its own harmonies and who could practice independently of other musicians, enjoyed greater opportunity than other jazz instrumentalists to maximize their individuality; and indeed a

FIGURE 9.7
The Original Dixieland Jazz
Band.

number of jazz pianists developed distinctive styles extremely influential in
the transition from ragtime to jazz. **Jelly Roll Morton**, mentioned in Chapter 8
as an outstanding ragtime player, combined ragtime and *boogie-woogie* techniques to produce his own inimitable jazz piano style, with rhythms looser and
melodies less embellished than those of ragtime. (Morton is often also spoken
of as the first jazz composer. Certainly he was the most innovative "hot tune
writer," to use his expression, until Duke Ellington began composing in the
1930s.) Earl Hines (1903–1983) played with a swinging, flexible style usually
associated with band instruments rather than with the piano. And Art Tatum
(1910–1956), one of the most admired pianists in jazz history, combined his
gifts for complex and ingenious harmonic changes and incredibly powerful
technique with elements of the piano style called *stride*.

Boogie-Woogie

As accompanying instruments assumed ever more sig-
nificant roles in performing the blues, the next logical step was adapting blues
to instrumental forms. Thus before 1920, certain ragtime pianists carried the
twelve-bar structure, and often the characteristic harmonic progressions of the
blues as well, to the piano.

Unlike the written ragtime pieces, **boogie-woogie** or **piano blues** was freely
improvised, the new jazz pianists accompanying a syncopated melody in the
right hand with a characteristic highly rhythmic left-hand ostinato. This **eight-
to-the-bar** accompanying pattern (subdividing the four beats of a measure into
eight pulses, usually in the pattern LONG-*short*-LONG-*short*-LONG-*short*-
LONG-*short*) resulted in complex cross rhythms, which—combined with a
brisk tempo and a new driving intensity—quickly made boogie a music popular to dance and listen to. (Many fine boogie-woogie performances can be
heard on YouTube.)

Stride Piano

Stride piano retained the regular left-hand metrical pattern of ragtime, alternating low bass notes on one and three with midrange

chords on two and four under an improvised melody in the right hand. **James P. Johnson** (1894–1955), the "father of stride piano," certainly furthered the transition from ragtime to jazz, with playing that was more dissonant, more loosely structured, more strictly improvisational, and more highly syncopated than other jazz piano music of the 1920s. Although Johnson composed other kinds of music as well, including "The Charleston," which flappers joyously danced through the roaring twenties, he is best remembered for his great stride compositions such as "Carolina Shout" (Listening Example 38).

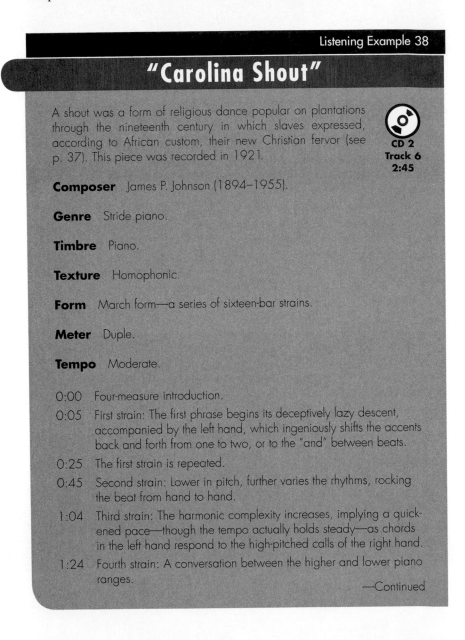

Listening Example 38

"Carolina Shout"

A shout was a form of religious dance popular on plantations through the nineteenth century in which slaves expressed, according to African custom, their new Christian fervor (see p. 37). This piece was recorded in 1921.

CD 2
Track 6
2:45

Composer James P. Johnson (1894–1955).

Genre Stride piano.

Timbre Piano.

Texture Homophonic.

Form March form—a series of sixteen-bar strains.

Meter Duple.

Tempo Moderate.

0:00 Four-measure introduction.

0:05 First strain: The first phrase begins its deceptively lazy descent, accompanied by the left hand, which ingeniously shifts the accents back and forth from one to two, or to the "and" between beats.

0:25 The first strain is repeated.

0:45 Second strain: Lower in pitch, further varies the rhythms, rocking the beat from hand to hand.

1:04 Third strain: The harmonic complexity increases, implying a quickened pace—though the tempo actually holds steady—as chords in the left hand respond to the high-pitched calls of the right hand.

1:24 Fourth strain: A conversation between the higher and lower piano ranges.

—Continued

"Carolina Shout"

1:42 Fifth strain: Shorter, more fragmented phrases further intensify the last three strains, as the vigorously striding left hand offers ever-new variations on the beat.

2:01 Sixth strain.

2:20 Seventh strain.

2:38 A cascading four-bar coda brings the stunning piece to a satisfying close.

Fats Waller (1904–1943), who studied with James P. Johnson, developed his own legendary jazz piano style, more driving, intense, and virtuosic than his mentor's. Although Waller went on to become one of the great jazz entertainers and a composer of hundreds of tunes, he never surpassed the beauty of Johnson's technically demanding stride pieces. And although Waller's stride piano playing was a direct descendant of ragtime, Waller rarely wrote out his pieces in full, generally writing only a simple melody line and the most fragmentary additional notations. (All that was required to copyright an original tune was a melody and a title.) Some of his compositions were published as sheet music during his lifetime, and he did record some piano rolls, but neither form is considered representative of the performances Waller would have realized from the same pieces.

Sweet Jazz

Throughout the 1920s, as the center of jazz innovation and performance shifted from New Orleans to other cities, especially Chicago and New York, a tame but attractive music that came to be known as **sweet jazz** reached a wide audience through the sophisticated, classically tinged performances of the Paul Whiteman Orchestra, the most popular dance band of its day. **Paul Whiteman** (1890–1967), a white classically trained violinist who adored jazz but lacked the gift to create the uninhibited improvisations of the jazz musicians he admired, formed his band in the early 1920s to play jazzy arrangements of popular and even classical melodies.

Although Whiteman was known for a time as the "king of jazz," his music bore only a marginal relationship to real jazz. Most of the notes were written out for his musicians, who did not indulge in creative flights of improvisational fancy; but their jazzy timbres and syncopated rhythms suggested to listeners the flavor of jazz. Most significantly, sweet jazz introduced the art of the arranger, which was to become even more important in the era of the big bands.

As sweet jazz soothed troubled audiences during the Great Depression, real jazz—hot, and mostly black—went underground. But during the 1930s jazz finally found a popular audience, as big band music came into its own. Now Americans were ready to swing!

Paul Whiteman (1890–1967) "Jazz came to America three hundred years ago in chains."

Terms to Review

jazz

blue notes

blues

rural or country blues

twelve-bar blues

scatting, scat singing

classic blues

race records

urban blues

combo

New Orleans jazz

Dixieland

boogie-woogie or piano blues

eight-to-the-bar

stride piano

sweet jazz

Key Figures

Robert Johnson

Gertrude "Ma" Rainey

Bessie Smith

W. C. Handy

Louis Armstrong

Jelly Roll Morton

James P. Johnson

Fats Waller

Paul Whiteman

Critical Thinking

What characteristics do country blues, classic blues, and urban blues share? In what ways do they differ?

What characteristics do vocal blues and piano blues (boogie-woogie) share? How do they differ?

Why do you think the outstanding rural blues singers were men and the great classic blues singers women?

How would you compare sweet jazz with real jazz? Why do you suppose Paul Whiteman was called the "king of jazz"? What audience would his music have most appealed to?

Jazz 1930–1960

J azz reached a peak of popularity in the mid-1930s, a relatively optimistic period when the Great Depression gradually receded and America's involvement in World War II lay ahead. Recordings and radio programs having made the sounds of sweet jazz widely familiar by then, multitudes of people—both white and black—craved more adventurous listening, and with Prohibition ended, real jazz came to be performed in an atmosphere more congenial to the general public than the small, illegal speakeasies of the 1920s. Crowds flocked to hear the big bands play, and by 1935 *big band* music resounded from radios, recordings, juke boxes, and dance halls all over the country.

Big Band Swing

While sweet jazz soothed more timid listeners, black jazz musicians added instruments to their small combos and developed the vibrant sound that came to be known as **big band** jazz, or **swing.** The new sound was of such huge appeal to whites and blacks of virtually every stratum in society that jazz and popular music came together for a time, and swing constituted *the* popular music of the 1930s.

Both "big band" and "swing" need clarification. The earliest big bands actually had only five or six members, but the standard soon became twelve to eighteen players, in three sections of instruments:

1. Brass (trumpets, trombones).
2. Woodwinds, called **reeds,** in which the player causes small flexible pieces of cane to vibrate (saxophones, sometimes also a clarinet).
3. Rhythm (a guitar and/or double bass, piano, drums).

Swing, like many terms in art, has several meanings, some rather technical. For example, *swing eighths* are strings of eighth notes performed in uneven rhythm, alternating long and short notes of subjective rather than measured length. This contributes to the flexible give-and-take, or expressive *rubato,* within the steady jazz beat. But *swing* also refers to a mood, a lilt, a magical effect that great jazz achieves and that sympathetic listeners recognize and respond to. When all elements of a jazz performance come together and work, the music swings.

Eventually the big, or swing, bands experienced the stimulating interaction between black and white musicians characteristic of many developments of jazz, for although the makers of recordings and the managers of commercial radio stations still severely segregated popular music intended for blacks or whites, African American music inevitably became more familiar to and popular with a greatly widening audience. White people often traveled to Harlem, a black neighborhood in uptown New York City, where they could hear the finest jazz musicians in the world collectively improvise, or **jam.** And even people who hardly understood the complex new music found themselves intoxicated with its nearly indefinable trait called swing.

Art of Arranging Whereas early jazz combos functioned well with free improvisation, the larger groups of players needed to follow some kind of structured plan, relying upon arrangements that were either written down or thoroughly worked out in rehearsals. Musicians who did not read music could follow the *chart,* a "map" of the arrangement indicating the structure of the piece, the chord progressions, and the time for soloists to stand (unless they were the pianist or drummer) and freely improvise.

Because many such arrangements were based on New Orleans originals, listeners perceived much the same music as New Orleans and Dixieland jazz; but the larger combos, more sensuous orchestration, and more structured atmosphere made the new sound more intelligible to a wide audience. Because most of the big band musicians had more formal music training than most of the jazz pioneers, big band harmonies were more adventurous and their pieces more highly structured than those of early jazz. Solo improvisations, still hot, were brief, the band playing together much of the time.

The great ragtime and jazz pianist Jelly Roll Morton was one of the first bandleaders to provide arrangements for his band, beginning in the mid-1920s. Even more influential for later jazz bands, however, were the arrangements of **Fletcher Henderson** (1897–1952), who made large groups *sound* as if they were improvising and in fact left room for improvisation, within limits. A fine pianist with a degree in chemistry, Henderson in effect transformed the large "sweet" dance band into a jazz band, skillfully alternating the independent use of each section (trumpets, trombones, saxophones, rhythm) with outstanding solos. So successful were his innovations that they were copied by nearly every dance band of the big band era and in fact remain standard for many high school and college jazz bands today.

Count (Bill) Basie (1904–1984), who defined jazz as "music you can pat your foot to," became one of the most popular of all big band arrangers and leaders. The music of this quiet, unobtrusive pianist and leader dominated the **Kansas City jazz** scene. Musicians coming from Chicago, New York, New Orleans, and elsewhere found Kansas City a hospitable environment for gradually developing a distinct style of jazz, a pared-down, lighter, more relaxed music than jazz created in either New Orleans or Chicago. Instead of interweaving musical lines in the complex web of sound characteristic of New Orleans combos, Kansas City arrangements were based on simple musical phrases, called **riffs,** which were repeated over and over again. The music had a light, airy feel—less dense and more spacious than other styles.

With his refined "less is more" style of piano playing, Basie proved that *space*, or *silence*, is as important to music as *sound*. He chose his notes—whether as pianist or arranger—meticulously, giving each utmost significance. Basie's band was particularly admired for its rhythm section, in which guitar, bass, and drums were so closely integrated as to produce a perfectly balanced sound. And Basie's unique style of piano playing gave further reason for some to consider his ensemble the best swing band of all.

The brilliant tenor saxophonist **Lester Young** (1909–1959) seemed uniquely comfortable with Basie's style. In "Taxi War Dance" (Listening Example 39),

---

Listening Example 39

"Taxi War Dance" (excerpt)

Many outstanding jazz soloists played with Count Basie, but Lester Young acquired the nickname "Pres" or "Prez"—for president of tenor saxophone players—in appreciation for his superlative talents. Here the two virtuosos demonstrate their remarkable musicianship, in this piece from 1939.

CD 2
Track 7
2:50

Composer and Arranger Count Basie (1904–1984) and Lester Young (1909–1959).

Genre Kansas City jazz.

Timbre Four trumpets, three trombones, three saxophones, piano (Basie), guitar, double bass, drums.

Texture Homophonic.

Form A series of thirty-two-bar choruses, each featuring particular soloists.

Meter Quadruple.

Tempo Moderate, relaxed.

0:00   Introduction: Basie introduces a rolling figure in the lower piano range, which continues.

0:05   The trumpets make brief emphatic comments, accompanied by trombones and drums, over Basie's rolling accompaniment.

0:09   Chorus 1: Lester Young begins his relaxed, swinging saxophone improvisation by quoting the beginning of Jerome Kern's "Ol' Man River."

0:44   Chorus 2: The trumpet figure and rolling piano riff return, and we hear a melodic trombone solo accompanied by the rhythm section.

1:24   Chorus 3: The trombones play a four-note motive (a distinctive rise, then a fall, in pitch), answered by the trumpets. This figure recurs several times, interspersed between solo passages for tenor sax and other instruments, as the piece continues.

we hear Young answering Basie's spare, rolling piano figures with his own light, elegant melodic saxophone phrases.

The white clarinetist and bandleader **Benny Goodman** (1909–1986; Figure 10.1) brought big band music to national attention through his many recordings and radio programs. Although Goodman's unprecedented inclusion of outstanding African American soloists in his band was warmly appreciated, his exploitation of the contributions of black musicians sometimes caused resentment. Many of the Goodman band's best arrangements, for example, were by Fletcher Henderson, but although the band made Henderson's arrangements extremely popular, Henderson never earned the money that Benny Goodman and his band accrued. Both Goodman and Henderson had received classical music training; both insisted on disciplined musicianship from their band members; and the fact that Goodman's band became more popular than Henderson's was a source of some bitterness by the end of the decade.

Goodman later divided his playing and recording between big bands and various smaller ensembles, for while big bands remained highly popular well into the 1940s, the range of jazz styles expanded greatly during that decade, offering musicians and listeners alike a wealth of exciting new musics.

Most popular of all the big bands, and probably the easiest to recognize, was the **Glenn Miller** band. Alton Glenn Miller (1904–1944; he detested and dropped his first name) knew he had limited talent as a trombone player and devoted his attention to arranging, at which he clearly excelled. In 1940, for example, he recorded forty-five songs that made it onto the top-seller

FIGURE 10.2
Duke Ellington (1899–1974).

charts—a figure neither Elvis Presley nor the Beatles ever matched. He developed a distinctive sound—a clarinet lead supported by four saxophones—rich, sensuous, and nearly irresistible.

At the height of his popularity, Miller, age thirty-eight, enlisted in the Army Air Corps and, as leader of the Army Air Forces Band, made it his mission to update military music to a style that the World War II troops would enjoy. Miller disappeared in a small military plane flying from England to recently liberated France, possibly the victim of friendly fire. Yet his music, including the classics "Moonlight Serenade," "String of Pearls," and "In the Mood" among too many others to mention, endures as the musical symbol of an entire generation, and today—nearly seventy years after his death—there are "Glenn Miller bands" and Glenn Miller fans all over the world.

Edward Kennedy "Duke" Ellington (1899–1974)

In 1922, **Duke Ellington** (Figure 10.2) moved from his hometown, Washington, D.C., to New York City, where he formed his own small dance band. By 1927 he had transformed the ensemble into the ten-member Duke Ellington Orchestra, playing hot New Orleans jazz at the popular Cotton Club in Harlem. The talking brass instruments, wailing clarinets, ritualistic drumbeats, beautiful melodies, and precise orchestration of the Ellington sound astonished black and white listeners alike. Ellington hired the best musicians available and deftly exploited the unique sounds of each in his gifted orchestrations, writing for specific musicians to capitalize on special talents they sometimes did not know they had. Although he was already famous as a great jazz pianist, Ellington is said to have used the jazz band as his real "instrument," exploring its entire range of sounds with unprecedented imagination and creativity. By juxtaposing instruments in nontraditional combinations and using them in the extreme limits of their range, he transformed their sound, sometimes effectively obscuring their identification.

Far more than an arranger, Ellington is recognized as a serious composer, producing symphonic works such as "Black, Brown, and Beige" (1943), international pieces such as "Latin American Suite" (1968), and large-scale sacred works incorporating dancers, choruses, and gospel singers together with his own band, as well as the lovely songs to which generations have danced and romanced. Drawing from many seemingly irreconcilable American musics, including field hollers, Shaker hymns, fiddlers' dance tunes, minstrel songs, ragtime, Tin Pan Alley, New Orleans jazz, and—especially—the blues, Ellington created a particular American tapestry of mood and style.

Listening Example 40 presents "Mood Indigo," a haunting tune Ellington composed in 1930 and arranged innumerable times for many combinations of instruments.

Listening Example 40

"Mood Indigo"

CD 2
Track 8
3:03

Most striking about "Mood Indigo," aside from its dreamy melody written in 1930, is the seemingly endless creativity with which Ellington arranged parts for his instruments. Played with mutes, or in the extremes of their ranges of pitch, the instruments become difficult to identify, achieving sounds previously not associated with them or thought possible for them to achieve.

Composer   Duke Ellington (1899–1974).

Genre   Big band arrangement.

Timbre   Big band—five trumpets, three trombones, five saxophones (two tenor, two alto, one baritone), two clarinets, bass, drums, and Duke Ellington at the piano. Even in this brief rendition, the colors of the sounds change continuously, rendering the timbres endlessly interesting in their own right. Listening to Ellington perform other versions of "Mood Indigo" (available on YouTube) provides further insight into his incredibly versatile and imaginative approach to orchestration.

Melody   Ellington's lovely chromatic melody adapted readily to music for dancing or for listening to. Lyrics added later made the piece also a popular song of lasting appeal.

Harmony   The harmonies at times result from juxtaposing one key over another (called *bitonal* harmonies), a highly sophisticated and unexpected technique in this early jazz piece.

—Continued

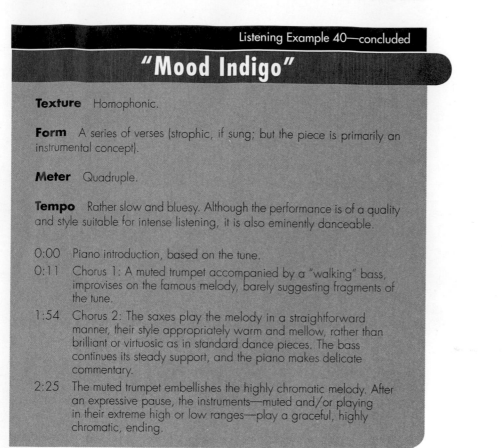

Listening Example 40—concluded

"Mood Indigo"

Texture Homophonic.

Form A series of verses (strophic, if sung; but the piece is primarily an instrumental concept).

Meter Quadruple.

Tempo Rather slow and bluesy. Although the performance is of a quality and style suitable for intense listening, it is also eminently danceable.

0:00 Piano introduction, based on the tune.

0:11 Chorus 1: A muted trumpet accompanied by a "walking" bass, improvises on the famous melody, barely suggesting fragments of the tune.

1:54 Chorus 2: The saxes play the melody in a straightforward manner, their style appropriately warm and mellow, rather than brilliant or virtuosic as in standard dance pieces. The bass continues its steady support, and the piano makes delicate commentary.

2:25 The muted trumpet embellishes the highly chromatic melody. After an expressive pause, the instruments—muted and/or playing in their extreme high or low ranges—play a graceful, highly chromatic, ending.

During the early days of rock and roll, Ellington's jazz was heard less often, but at the 1956 Newport Jazz Festival his orchestra made a tremendous hit, leading to a best-selling album, *Ellington at Newport,* and to prestigious new concert dates. From then Duke Ellington's fame soared to unprecedented heights. We will meet him again in the discussion of concert jazz.

Women in Jazz

We have discussed some of the great women blues singers, and other outstanding female soloists were soon to be featured singers with famous big bands. But few women had successful careers as jazz instrumentalists. Women wishing to play jazz in those days faced formidable odds: it was widely assumed that they did not have the strength, temperament, or talent to measure up to the men. Nevertheless, one gifted pianist, and a blazingly hot all-female band, disproved these assumptions.

Mary Lou Williams (Mary Elfrieda Scruggs, 1910–1981), another noted arranger for big bands, was a rare exception in the developing world of

FIGURE 10.3

The jazz musician and composer Mary Lou Williams (1910–1981).

jazz—a highly successful woman instrumental soloist (Figure 10.3). Having played the piano in public since the age of six, she married a carnival band member, and when her husband left the band to join another she hired a replacement for him and ran the group herself. Later she worked as a freelance arranger for several bands, including Benny Goodman's, and became a staff arranger for Duke Ellington, producing highly original and distinctive arrangements while also performing as a pianist both here and in Europe.

Having contributed to all the evolving styles of popular piano music, from ragtime to bebop and beyond, Williams performed fluently in all of them. After arranging and composing for Duke Ellington for many years, she became his close friend in later life and played at his funeral; and in 1996, she was honored with the first of an annual series of Mary Lou Williams Women in Jazz festivals at the Kennedy Center in Washington. A street in Kansas City is named after her.

The outstanding female band resulted from the situation during World War II, when all-woman bands (all-girl bands, as they were called then) flourished as men went off to war, and people grew accustomed to seeing women in various nontraditional roles. Well-known all-white female bands included one led by Phil Spitalny (note the male leader) and another led by Ina Ray Hutton. Most impressive of all, however, were the **International Sweethearts of Rhythm.** Predominantly black, with Chinese, Indian, Hawaiian, and white representation as well, they were also all-female and thus were largely ignored by white audiences, films, and print media, who would not take a bunch of women seriously as jazz musicians. Yet at Harlem's Apollo Theater and Savoy Ballroom—drawing probably the most demanding jazz audiences in the land—they made a tremendous, and a lasting, hit.

Rise of Big Band Vocalists

A new generation of young Americans unfamiliar with early jazz danced to the happy sounds of big band music through the 1940s. Many older people enjoyed the music as well, finding the repertoire familiar because the big bands, like the earlier combos, based their music upon marches, hymns, and the made-to-order songs of Tin Pan Alley, whose formula had altered only slightly since the 1890s.

Reactions against big band music began to set in, however, even while crowds continued dancing to its swinging beat, as increasingly complex band arrangements, emphasizing rhythm and swing rather than melody, sometimes rendered the source tune unidentifiable. Though the repetition of riffs held arrangements together while effectively heightening the intensity of the mood, the swing crowd began to resist challenging instrumental arrangements in favor of simple songs.

Although primarily an instrumental concept, early jazz had important reciprocal relationships with popular song: Early combos improvised on the melodies or harmonies of popular songs, and many songs of the 1920s and 1930s were jazz-flavored. The big bands played arrangements of old and new songs from Tin Pan Alley. Thus it is not surprising that at some point in the 1930s, big bands began to work closely with vocalists. Slowly the style of big band music changed as bands assumed the role of accompaniment and as great instrumental soloists vied for popularity with outstanding vocalists, regularly alternating instrumental and vocal choruses. Ella Fitzgerald (1918–1996) became famous for her scat singing, and crooners such as Rudy Vallee and Bing Crosby became increasingly popular as the technology of microphones and recording engineers allowed their more intimate personal styles to be projected to an audience. In time, crowds came not so much to dance as to hear Crosby, Frank Sinatra, and other popular singers, for whom the bands provided support. A lush string sound returned to favor, replacing the brassier sound of big band jazz; and by the mid-1940s singers accompanied by orchestral ensembles supplanted the big swing bands in the affections of the white public.

Billie Holiday (1915–1959)

Billie Holiday (born Eleanora Fagan) trod softly between the worlds of jazz and pop, although her interpretations of many great blues songs were undeniably those of a great jazz singer. Jazz scholar Nat Hentoff said that Lady Day, as she was respectfully known, could simply say hello, and the sound and rhythm of that one word became the very definition of jazz. Among her most striking innovations was her way of "microphonizing" her voice—using the microphone, at that time a new enhancement, not only to amplify but to alter her voice and add expressive effects.

A tragic figure who died possessed of just seventy cents despite having earned a lot of money during her career as singing and recording artist, she once recorded an unforgettable ballad, "Strange Fruit," concerning lynching. The words of the ballad—devastating to hear or read—have a strange history of their own. They were written not by a black but by a first-generation

Jewish American whose parents had come to the United States from Russia. Abel Meeropol (1903–1987), whose pen name was Lewis Allen (and who later adopted the two children of Ethel and Julius Rosenberg, whom he had never met, after their parents' execution in 1953), was inspired by a picture of a lynching to write the poem and to set it to music. (The words to "Strange Fruit" can be found at several websites.)

Bebop

In the early 1940s an angry new style emerged, largely unnoticed at first but destined to exert great influence on the future of jazz. The new music, called **bebop** or **bop,** began as a revolt by a few virtuosic black musicians against the domestication of jazz by the swing bands of the 1930s. Bebop musicians reacted against the polished performances of written, rehearsed "jazz"; they resented limitation to the short stylized solos of big band music, the dependence on written arrangements, and the lack of freedom to improvise. They further resented the disproportionate financial rewards granted to white musicians less creative and less innovative than many underrecognized blacks. The tight, difficult, virtuosic music they conceived as a return to the ideals of early jazz (improvisation, virtuosity, and close interaction between soloist and combo) is generally considered the first truly modern jazz.

Like much of the concert music of the 1940s and later, bebop was performed by a small ensemble of virtuoso musicians. The music consisted of stark, clear, technically demanding instrumental lines. The angular melodies moved by large unpredictable leaps instead of narrow steps, and the solos were so rapid-fire that they were too fast to dance to—and almost too fast to listen to. Rather than following prearranged or familiar harmonic progressions, bop musicians challenged one another to chart new harmonic paths and make them work. Their chords, large and richly dissonant, startled ears accustomed to tame, consistently pleasant sounds. Further, they sometimes improvised on the *harmony* of a famous tune rather than on the *melody,* which remained obscure to puzzled listeners. The best bebop musicians in fact achieved a revolutionary sound that effectively changed the course of jazz.

The typical bebop combo consisted of trumpet and saxophone, double bass, piano, and percussion. The melody instruments (trumpet and sax) sometimes began a composition by playing a pop, blues, or original melody in unison, then alternating with increasingly complex improvisations while supported by the other players. The double bass, which marked the beat, sometimes took melodic responsibility as well in the walking bass pattern inherited from the swing era, while the piano and percussion supplied unexpected, irregular accents.

A saxophonist who died young and a trumpet player who remained active until shortly before his death at seventy-six were among the innovators and outstanding exponents of bebop.

Charlie "Bird" Parker (1920–1955)   As a youngster in Kansas City, Missouri, **Charlie Parker** (Figure 10.4) absorbed the sounds of Lester Young, Count Basie, and other outstanding jazz musicians active there. Later

FIGURE 10.4
Charlie Parker (1920–1955).

Parker moved to New York City, where he jammed in Harlem's clubs with pianist **Thelonious Monk** (1920–1982) and trumpeter Dizzy Gillespie (see below), inspiring and inspired by them to develop the complex new music.

Not only was Charlie "Bird" Parker an amazing saxophone virtuoso, his sax tone dry and biting and his melodies highly jagged in contour, but he also introduced new rhythmic, melodic, and improvisational techniques that lifted jazz to a different plane. A knowledgeable musician, he sometimes quoted fragments of popular and classical compositions, moving rapidly from such familiar phrases to soaring flights of melodic virtuosity. Parker often performed with a fiercely rapid tempo and an unrelenting emotional intensity that left the weak behind but offered adventurous listeners glorious new insights to jazz.

Addicted to drugs and alcohol and ill for much of his short life, Parker—whom some consider the most influential of all jazz musicians—died when he was only thirty-four. In 1988, the movie *Bird* brought the story of Charlie Parker to popular attention; but among serious jazz afficionados, his memory and influence have never faded.

John Birks "Dizzy" Gillespie (1917–1993)

Dizzy Gillespie (Figure 10.5) improvised rhythms of a complexity unprecedented in Western culture, reached notes no one knew the trumpet could play, and devised harmonic changes defying the accepted rules of harmony. But even more important, his music touched the human spirit with passion and beauty.

Gillespie enjoyed African Cuban rhythms and sounds, which he included in such pieces as his big band number "Manteca," among the earliest pieces

FIGURE 10.5

Dizzy Gillespie
(1917–1993).

www.mhhe.com/ferrisaml6e

to bring Latin American sounds to modern jazz. Less zealous than Parker and apparently comfortable with a variety of jazz styles and techniques, Gillespie remained an active performer until shortly before his death, his famous balloon cheeks highly visible on television programs and in concerts around the world. (Performances by both Parker and Gillespie can be viewed on YouTube, and Gillespie's "Shaw 'Nuff" is an Online Listening Example.)

Parker and Gillespie's performance of "KoKo" (Listening Example 41) demonstrates the incredible virtuosity, musicianship, and compatibility of these outstanding musicians.

Listening Example 41

"KoKo"

CD 2
Track 9
2:53

At a session in 1945 intended to record a swing standard titled "Cherokee," by Ray Noble, Parker and Gillespie improvised halfheartedly on the tune until Parker, tired of the familiar melody, decided to improvise instead on the *chords*. Therefore, instead of beginning as usual with the "head," or reference to the standard tune, Parker used bits of his own melodic material, skillfully weaving them over and through the rather unusual chord changes of "Cherokee." The resulting historic recording—one of Parker's greatest solos—is based on no prewritten melody at all (incidentally requiring Parker's recording company to make no royalty payment for "Cherokee," because chords, unlike melodies, did not bear a copyright). Neither is Parker's "KoKo" related to Duke Ellington's earlier composition of the same name.

—Continued

"KoKo"

Composers-Improvisers   Charlie Parker (1920–1955) and Dizzy Gillespie (1917–1993).

Genre   Bebop

Timbre   Alto saxophone (Charlie Parker), trumpet and piano Dizzy Gillespie, drums (Max Roach), bass (Curley Russell).

Melody   There is no prewritten melody. Rather, the musicians improvise over the (unusual, therefore interesting) harmonies, rather than the melody, of "Cherokee."

Texture   Homophonic.

Form   A series of choruses, each featuring one or more solo instruments.

Tempo   Extremely rapid.

0:00   Introduction: The alto sax and muted trumpet begin the elaborate, rather eerie, introduction, playing in unison, accompanied by lightly brushed drums.

0:06   A brief muted trumpet solo, accompanied by complex accents on the drums.

0:12   Alto sax solo.

0:19   The sax and muted trumpet play in parallel harmony. The drums continue to comment.

0:25   Chorus 1: Parker soloes, accompanied by drums, a fast walking bass, and (soon) sparse piano chords, played by Gillespie, who has put down his trumpet and moved to the keyboard.

1:15   Chorus 2: Parker maintains his extremely brisk tempo and astonishing virtuosity.

2:08   Chorus 3: An intricate, virtuosic drum solo varies the texture and sonority—and gives Gillespie time to return to his trumpet.

2:30   The alto sax and muted trumpet play in unison, accompanied by brushes on the cymbals. We hear a muted trumpet solo, then an alto sax solo, both backed up by cymbals.

2:49   The parallel harmony of alto sax and muted trumpet heard in the introduction return to round out and conclude this remarkable piece.

Although popularity was never a primary goal of the bebop musicians, their style might have attracted a wider audience had the public been able to experience its evolution. At the very time Parker and Gillespie were leading the bebop revolution, however, a recording artists' strike caused a ban on commercial recordings of popular music that lasted for about two years (see p. 147). Thus even the devoted jazz audience was largely nonplussed by the sophistication and complexity of the first bebop recordings produced when the strike finally ended. One tends not to like what one does not understand, and there were many who did not understand bebop.

But bebop is an important music, which not only challenged and stimulated talented musicians and conscientious listeners but also ushered in the age of modern jazz. Meant for listening more than dancing, bebop had significant implications for musicians interested in establishing relationships between concert music and jazz.

Jazz as Concert Music

A number of Americans writing music in the vernacular tradition have applied their knowledge of classical techniques to popular pieces; and many composers have simply refused to distinguish between classical and popular musics in terms of either quality or preference. Among those we have studied, John Philip Sousa, the march king, also composed operettas and symphonic works; Scott Joplin, the king of ragtime, wrote operas; and George Gershwin wrote one opera and several symphonic pieces (including *Rhapsody in Blue* and Concerto in F, both Online Listening Examples), as well as the many Broadway show tunes we still hear and romance to today.

www.mhhe.com/ferrisaml6e

Thus during the 1940s, as jazz steadily grew more serious, dissonant, intellectual, and complex, some jazz musicians absorbed influences from contemporary classical music, reversing the process by which classical musicians had borrowed jazz techniques for their own purposes. No longer music for dancing and entertainment alone but for serious listening as well, jazz had become, in fact, a kind of classical or concert music in its own right. By the early 1950s, jazz was performed frequently in concert, especially on college campuses and at huge jazz festivals. Both black and white jazz musicians, and their listeners as well, took a more intellectual approach to jazz than had earlier been customary, and jazz criticism became a recognized field. Today, as we shall see in Chapter 15, certain jazz composers collaborate with poets, choreographers, and classical musicians to produce serious concert works.

Jazz Composition
Because the essence of jazz is improvisation, musicians wishing to combine classical and jazz techniques faced a new challenge: They had to create a balance between what was written, what was improvised by the soloists, and what an ensemble achieved collectively. Certainly

there were precedents for requiring performers in the classical tradition to improvise:

1. During the Baroque period (1600–1750), composers wrote the melody and bass lines of a composition, leaving the harmonies to be filled in by a lute or keyboard player.
2. In the early Classical period (1750–1825), soloists improvised one or more cadenzas in performing a solo concerto.
3. Church organists often are expected to improvise music that connects one part of a service, or one verse of a hymn, to another.

In all these cases, however, musicians improvised within established guidelines appropriate for a given style of music. Jazz as classical music was a *new* concept, and musicians involved in its evolution faced new situations. The symphonic jazz of the 1920s, such as George Gershwin's *Rhapsody in Blue* (an Online Listening Example), was simply concert music with some of the flavors of jazz; and the big band arrangements approached the concept of composed music but were hardly original compositions. By the 1940s, however, jazz composers were doing more than arranging familiar tunes—they were writing original jazz compositions, and at that point jazz entered the world of art music. Some will question whether concert jazz is jazz at all; but the question remains unimportant if we value each style and each piece of music according to its merits, no matter what label it carries.

Duke Ellington, whom we have already met as an outstanding big band leader and as the composer of "Mood Indigo," also wrote serious concert, or classical, music. His scope, in fact, was enormous: In addition to his beautiful ballads and inspired band arrangements, he composed tone poems, ballet suites, concerto-like miniatures for star sidemen, sacred music, topical revues, film scores, and extended jazz works; and at the time of his death he was writing a comic opera, *Queenie Pie,* intended for public television. Finally staged in Philadelphia and Boston in 1986, *Queenie Pie* has received occasional performances in other cities since.

Ellington has, in fact, been referred to as America's most prolific composer of the twentieth century, in both number of pieces (almost 2,000) and variety of forms. In title and content, his serious compositions often reflected the black experience in America with extraordinary depth, wit, tenderness, and strength. Among his best-known symphonic works, for example, *Black, Brown, and Beige,* subtitled "A Tone Parallel to the History of the Negro in America," premiered by Duke Ellington and his orchestra at Carnegie Hall in 1943, has been played by many other major orchestras since. Ellington returned to Carnegie Hall on a near-annual basis until 1948; and when the nation mourned the death of President Franklin D. Roosevelt in 1945, Ellington's orchestra was the only dance band selected to pay tribute in a memorial radio broadcast.

Ellington wrote "Concerto for Cootie" (Listening Example 42), one of his most beautiful compositions, to feature the trumpeter Charles "Cootie" Williams. A **concerto** is defined as a multimovement composition for orchestra and one or more soloists—that is, a piece consisting of several semi-independent sections, or movements. Ellington chose, however, to write a one-movement piece.

www.mhhe.com/ferrisaml6e

"Concerto for Cootie"

Pleasure in altering sounds—with mutes, buzzes or ringings, playing in extremely high or low ranges, and by any number of creative ways—is thought to derive from African traditions. Certainly Ellington was a master of this particular art or technique, as we hear in "KoKo" (Listening Example 41) and also here, in this 1940 piece.

CD 2
Track 10
3:19

Composer   Duke Ellington (1899–1974).

Genre   Concert jazz.

Timbre   Saxophones, clarinet, trumpets, trombones, bass, drum.

Texture   Homophonic.

Form   A B A.   The **A** section has four phrases (**a a b a**). Although not written in the Classical concerto form, which has three movements, this one-movement piece retains the masterful interplay between soloist and orchestra characteristic of the Classical form.

Meter   Four beats to the bar.

Tempo   Relaxed.

0:00   Introduction: The trumpet (Cootie Williams) begins the piece on the downbeat with a phrase later adapted to begin Ellington's popular standard "Do Nothin' Till You Hear from Me."

0:18   **A:** (**a**) Williams presents the beautiful **A** theme in several ways, skillfully altering the timbre of his instrument by using various mutes and playing techniques.

0:42   (**a**) The accompaniment as well as the trumpet's timbre changes each time the theme recurs, producing rich and varied sonorities.

1:08   (**b**) Williams achieves a raucous, taunting, *funny* sound with his horn.

1:26   (**a**) The theme returns with a particularly rich and mellow band accompaniment.

1:56   **B:** The dramatic **B** theme differs from **A** in key and timbre. Williams plays it with the open horn, creatively extending and elaborating upon the melody.

2:37   **A** returns, and the piece ends with a brief coda.

Progressive Jazz

In 1949, pianist-arranger **Stan Kenton** (1912–1979) led a twenty-piece orchestra in a jazz concert at Carnegie Hall, where his tightly organized and beautifully balanced ensemble played with elegance and precision. Kenton's name for this music, **progressive jazz,** became the name of a new jazz movement. Kenton also made other important contributions to modern jazz, including serious exploration of Latin American drums and rhythms in his big band jazz. (See p. 213.)

While Kenton and Woody Herman promoted progressive jazz in the East, **Dave Brubeck** (b. 1920) was in the forefront of progressive jazz on the West Coast, where performances such as that in "Take Five" (Listening Example 43)

Listening Example 43

"Take Five"

Besides atonality and polytonality, Dave Brubeck also frequently uses irregular meters—five or seven beats per measure, instead of the usual two, three, or four. His jazz quartet achieved unprecedented popularity and sales for a jazz recording with this engaging 1959 piece, in which "five to the bar" sounds exactly "right."

CD 2
Track 11
5:23

Composer   Paul Desmond (1924–1977), saxophonist with the Dave Brubeck Quartet.

Genre   Progressive jazz.

Timbre   Dave Brubeck Quartet (piano, sax, bass, drums).

Texture   Homophonic.

Form   A B A

0:00   **A:** Drums play a four-bar introduction, followed by a piano pattern, or "vamp," for a tantalizing eight bars.

0:21   The piano marks the beginning of each measure with a low, accented pitch, as the sax plays the famous sixteen bar theme, accompanied by the rhythm section.

0:50   The theme returns.

1:06   Improvisatory-sounding section, in which Desmond's sax explores ranges and rhythms in a manner constantly surprising, all the while backed by the steady rhythm section relentlessly repeating the five-beat accompanying figure.

1:50   **B:** An intricate drum solo.

4:21   **A** returns.

brought his quartet increasing fame and prestige. Brubeck, a pianist and composer who played with Dixieland and swing bands as a youngster, majored in music in college and then studied composition with the French composer Darius Milhaud (1892–1974; this name is pronounced mee-OH), one of several important European composers who sought to escape the horrors of World War II by living and teaching in America, profoundly affecting the course of our music history. Milhaud, who was particularly interested in jazz and had written several symphonic pieces with jazzy rhythms and timbres, encouraged Brubeck to apply jazz techniques to his concert compositions.

But Brubeck also absorbed ideas from European art music. For example, intrigued by the manner in which Baroque keyboard players improvised chords over a given bass line, he produced polyphony reminiscent of the Baroque style. Brubeck's harmonies, however, are those of his own century, including effects that are **atonal** (without a tonic) and **polytonal** (with two or more tonics); and his rhythms are the complex rhythms and sometimes polyrhythms of modern jazz. He frequently uses **irregular meters**—five or seven beats per measure instead of the usual two, three, or four.

Cool Jazz

At the same time that Desmond and Brubeck were evolving their "progressive" ideas, other jazz musicians were developing a style they called **cool,** closely related to and sometimes indistinguishable from progressive jazz. In reaction to the complexity and exclusive nature of bebop, they organized larger bands that included the sensuous sounds of symphonic instruments such as the French horn and oboe. More elegant and less hot than bebop, cool jazz clearly reflected the influence of European concert music—especially the Impressionistic harmonies of Claude Debussy and the sharp dissonances of Russian composer Igor Stravinsky.

The important musicians involved in cool jazz included **Miles Davis** (1926–1991, Figure 10.6), who in 1949–1950 led the nine-piece orchestra

FIGURE 10.6

Miles Davis (1926–1991).

(nonet) that recorded the album later titled *Birth of the Cool*. Not much noticed at the time, the album later made a major impact on jazz musicians and fans. The project was Davis's; he organized the recording sessions, directed, called rehearsals, hired the halls, and wrote or cowrote some of the music. "Boplicity" (Listening Example 44) demonstrates this more cerebral, less impassioned way of playing jazz.

"Boplicity"

CD 2
Track 12
3:00

"Boplicity," a 1945 example of cool jazz, retains or adapts some characteristics of bop. The music is restrained, understated, in a new way; yet it remains relentlessly objective. Miles Davis clearly appreciates the importance of silence as well as tones, and he plays with great restraint. The instruments sound drier, less intense, producing a "cool" sound compared with the hot effects of bebop. A piece of smooth, easy listening, "Boplicity" projects more simplicity than bop, while yet respecting the basic premises of the music it purports to challenge. Slower-paced, less emotional, more cerebral, and quieter than the impassioned sounds of bebop, "Boplicity" integrates many characteristics of bebop with the taming effects of arrangement, combining orchestral colors with the independence of a small band.

Composer　Miles Davis (1926–1991) and Gil Evans (1912–1988).

Arranger　Gil Evans (1912–1988).　Davis wrote the melody, and Evans scored the written ensembles, adding horns and tuba to provide rich new timbres to the jazz ensemble.

Genre　Cool jazz.

Timbre　The Miles Davis Nonet (nine-member ensemble) included trumpet, trombone, alto and baritone saxes, French horn, and tuba, bass, drums, and piano. The members of the nonet varied, but the musicians involved in this recording included Gerry Mulligan on baritone saxophone and John Lewis on piano. In this arrangement, the rhythm instruments basically accompany the others.

Form　Three **aaba** choruses.

Meter　Quadruple.

Tempo　Moderate (slower than bop), very steady.

—Continued

"Boplicity"

0:00	**a**	The trumpet introduces the theme, accompanied by the nonet.
0:14	**a**	The theme is repeated.
0:28	**b**	We hear a new phrase—one bar in the alto sax, one in the baritone sax, then the trumpet resumes playing melody, accompanied by the ensemble.
0:43	**a**	The theme returns and concludes with an extra flourish—a one-bar "tag."
0:59	**a**	The baritone sax improvises a new melody over the same chord changes as in the first section. (At 1:08, the steadily walking bass is easily heard.)
1:12	**a**	The baritone continues.
1:26	**b**	Alto sax, then tenor sax, trombone, and baritone improvise over the chord changes.
1:36	**a**	The trumpet takes the melody.
1:58	**a**	The trumpet leads the last phrase of the section.
2:12	**a**	Piano and bass draw attention, then the trumpet continues.
2:27	**b**	The piano leads this phrase.
2:40	**a**	The original melody returns for eight bars, before the nonet plays a gently dissonant close.

But cool jazz was only one of the many styles Miles Davis explored, as he continued to make important contributions to jazz over the years. He became particularly interested in expanding the melodic possibilities of jazz by basing melodies on scales other than the major, minor, or blues scales. Each seven-note pattern within the range of an octave, depending on which note we begin on, produces a different pattern of half and whole steps. Each of these scales, or **modes**—of course including the major and minor—gives a particular character to the music based upon it. We have already noticed differences between the major and minor scales; but Davis chose to explore *other* modes, and the *modal* music on Davis's album *Kind of Blue* had a strong influence on many jazz musicians of varied tastes. A virtuoso trumpet player, Davis was also an outstanding bandleader, composer, and innovator who continued throughout his life to experiment with creative ideas in jazz.

Hard Bop

In the late 1950s, certain black musicians reacting against the detached, intellectual, "white" sounds of West Coast cool jazz combined driving rock-related rhythms with the "amen chords" of gospel to produce **hard bop.** Earthy, emotionally exuberant, intensely physical in concept, hard bop derives from the blues and embodies strong rhythms and bluesy phrasing. Melodies are straightforward, harmonies are simplified, and the rigid beat is punctuated with strong backbeats. Whereas bebop musicians generally improvised around the structure—although not the melody—of a popular or familiar tune, the less cerebral, aggressive hard bop often worked around new, unknown melodies.

The drummer **Art Blakey** (1919–1990), who worked with many of the biggest names in jazz, formed his own hard bop group, the Jazz Messengers, in the late 1940s and retained the name for other groups active in 1950s-style music. His 1955 recording of Horace Silver's "The Preacher," a funky blues piece with elements of gospel, clearly reflected the increasing influence of rhythm and blues (see pp. 227–228) and gospel on jazz.

Ever more varied, increasingly sophisticated, jazz acknowledged at the end of the 1950s—as it does today—continuing awareness and appreciation of its roots. YouTube affords us the remarkable and priceless opportunity to view today performances by the jazz masters of yesterday, as impressive and as beautiful now as when they were new.

Terms to Review

big bands	riff	polytonality
swing	bebop	irregular meters
reeds	concerto	cool jazz
jam	progressive jazz	modes
Kansas City jazz	atonality	hard bop

Key Figures

Fletcher Henderson	Mary Lou Williams	Jelly Roll Morton
Count Basie	International Sweethearts	Dizzy Gillespie
Lester Young	of Rhythm	Stan Kenton
Benny Goodman	Billie Holiday	Dave Brubeck
Glenn Miller	Charlie Parker	Miles Davis
Duke Ellington	Thelonious Monk	Art Blakey

Critical Thinking

Discuss the relationship between Fletcher Henderson and Benny Goodman. Is Goodman to be praised for having hired Henderson as an arranger, or criticized for having exploited the black musician's talents?

Have opportunities improved significantly in recent years for women in jazz? If so, how?

Of the styles studied in this chapter, which do you prefer and why? Which are likely to have the most influence on future musicians?

Country Music

s various vernacular musics evolved in America's urban and rural environments throughout the nineteenth century, people living in certain remote areas of the eastern hills continued to sing and play their traditional music much as it had been performed in the countries and in the times of their ancestors. Relatively isolated from mainstream popular music and largely unaffected by modern trends, they passed the old tunes and performing customs from one generation to the next by oral tradition, thus faithfully preserving many early folk ballads—especially those, like "Barbara Allen" (Listening Example 5), brought to America from the British Isles.

After the Civil War, however, new influences invaded even isolated mountain areas, inevitably affecting the music as well as every other aspect of life. Migrant workers seeking jobs laying railroad lines, mining coal, or working for the textile mills being established in remote hill areas, where tough union rules could safely be ignored, brought new kinds of music and new musical instruments with them into the hills. Of particular significance was the five-string banjo, on which one string played a constant or repeated pitch, or **drone,** ideal for accompanying hill or country music (Figure 11.1).

Conversely, mountain people began to take temporary jobs in the cities, from which they brought home new subjects for songs and new musical sounds. Soon new "folk" songs evolved, similar to the traditional ballads but characteristically American in subject and style. Sometimes people lost track of the origin of a song, so that one included in the folk repertoire might actually have been composed rather than improvised, memorized, and passed down in the traditional way.

From Country to City

In the early 1920s, commercial recording companies began to send talent scouts into the hill country both to search for folk singers and instrumentalists with a distinctive sound and to entice country musicians to come to the cities, where the market for recordings of "old time" music was increasing. In 1925, four musicians from Virginia recording under the name Hill Billies gave rise to

FIGURE 11.1

A musician playing a five-string banjo.

186

the term **hillbilly music,** somewhat scornfully applied to the music of country fiddlers, harmonica players, and singers of traditional country ballads. For a time, "old-time," "hillbilly," and "country" all referred to the rich store of traditional music coming down from the hills.

Hill musicians traveled with tent shows, medicine shows, and vaudeville shows (see pp. 293–295). They amazed audiences with their virtuosic performances at fiddlers' contests; and at country fairs they sang songs concerning the elemental subjects of human experiences—love, work, family life, death—in a semidetached, impersonal manner that made their music all the more moving. City listeners soon perceived the wealth of beauty and entertainment this unfamiliar style offered, and the audience for country music continued to expand.

As commercial radio evolved, hillbilly music proved widely popular, and "barn dance" radio shows sprang up not only in the South, but through the Midwest as well. The most famous of these shows, the **Grand Ole Opry,** which debuted on a station in Nashville, Tennessee, in 1924 and had much to do with the establishment of Nashville as a base for the country music industry, remains a vital country music institution today.

The trend toward popularity and commercialization, however, inevitably signaled the end of the old way—the oral tradition—of preserving original folk songs and performance practices. The commercial market required a constant supply of new pieces, and professional country musicians adapted to this demand by writing new songs and learning to perform them in a manner acceptable to a city audience. Story songs, or ballads, were particularly well received, and many were about dramatic topics of the day: a coal mine disaster, a murder, a hanging, the sinking of a famous ship. By the mid-1920s, as recordings of country music became widely available and brought the country sound to an ever wider audience, even hill people themselves began to lose track of which folk songs were traditional and which were created by modern professionals.

In 1927, two different strains of hillbilly music reached the public: one introduced by a soloist from the Deep South, and the other made popular by a singing family from the mountains of Virginia.

Jimmie Rodgers (1897–1933) **Jimmie Rodgers** (Figure 11.2)

came from Mississippi but wandered through several states in the course of his brief career. He had little formal training but many creative ideas, and he was willing to try anything suggested by the record producers who promoted him. Although accompanied on his recordings by various and unusual combinations of instruments, Rodgers probably was most effective when he accompanied himself on the guitar, providing appropriately simple support for his clear, pleasant tenor voice, which he sometimes used in the falsetto range. He also had a natural **yodel**—a rapid alternation between full voice and falsetto—later imitated by many country singers. The thirteen songs called "blue yodels" for which Rodgers was particularly famous had the form and harmonies of the twelve-bar blues, with his distinctive yodel added at the end of each verse, as in "Blue Yodel no. 9," Listening Example 45.

FIGURE 11.2

Jimmie Rodgers (1897–1933) and the Carter Family, pictured during a recording trip to Victor Studios in New Jersey.

Listening Example 45

"Blue Yodel no. 9"

This unlikely collaboration from about 1930 between Jimmie Rodgers and Louis Armstrong—two legendary and highly distinctive figures in American music—suggests their mutual admiration and respect. Louis Armstrong's wife at the time, Lillian Armstrong (see "Hotter Than That," Listening Example 37), accompanies them on the piano.

CD 2
Track 13
2:37

Composer   Jimmie Rodgers (1897–1933).

Genre   Country.

Timbre   Vocal soloist (Jimmie Rodgers), accompanied by trumpet (Louis Armstrong) and piano (Lil Hardin). The piano provides steady accompaniment for Rodgers, while the trumpet responds to and interacts with the voice.

Texture   Homophonic.

Form   Strophic, with a comfortably irregular number of bars per line and lines per stanza.

Meter   Quadruple.

—Continued

Listening Example 45—concluded
"Blue Yodel no. 9"

Tempo   Moderately slow, "bluesy," relaxed.

0:00   Six-measure trumpet and piano introduction.

0:14   Jimmie Rodgers sings the first stanza, accompanied by the piano. Notice that the trumpet enters, usually just past the halfway point of a line, to offer instrumental response and commentary. The trumpet also answers Rodgers's yodel, interspersed between stanzas.

Standin' on the corner, I didn't mean no harm. . . .

0:47   (Yodel)

0:53   The second stanza has three lines, unusual in verses other than for twelve-bar blues. Again, the trumpet intersperses comments and completes the lines.

I said, "You'll find my name on the tail of my shirt; . . .

1:23   (Yodel)

1:27   The trumpet takes a three-line twelve-bar verse, accompanied by the piano.

1:53   The last stanza has four lines, beginning with:

My good gal loves me, everybody knows. . . .

2:26   Rodgers's yodel, then the expressive horn and steady piano, conclude the song.

Known as the "singing brakeman," Rodgers drew on his experiences as a former railroad man for some of his songs. Others concerned love gone wrong, cowboys, the Southern home he missed, and country folk whom his listeners either recognized or idealized. While country songs more commonly paid homage to mother than to dad, Rodgers, whose mother died when he was only six, paid sentimental tribute to the father who raised him in "Daddy and Home" (an Online Listening Example).

Although Rodgers performed professionally only for about six years, dying of tuberculosis at the age of thirty-six, he became extremely popular during his short career, during which he established the solo song as an important part of hillbilly music. He had the honor of becoming the first person elected to the Country Music Hall of Fame, established in Nashville, Tennessee, in 1961.

www.mhhe.com/ferrisaml6e

The Carter Family   The **Carter Family** (see Figure 11.2) represented
a different tradition from that of Jimmie Rodgers: Whereas he typified the

hard-living solo wanderer, they symbolized the close, conservative family. Rodgers's relaxed, bluesy voice made the solo country song popular, while the Carters performed as a group, their harmony close and their voices tense.

Alvin Pleasant Delaney (A. P.) Carter (1891–1960), his wife Sara, and his sister-in-law (Sara's cousin) Maybelle, who came from the mountains of Virginia, sang traditional songs, ballads, and hymns in the rather pinched, nasal voices and the close, tight harmony characteristic of mountain people. They accompanied themselves with guitar, on which Maybelle Carter developed considerable virtuosity; and with autoharp, a simple folk instrument whose strings are strummed or plucked with one hand while the other hand depresses buttons to form chords.

The Carters often favored the rhythms of ragtime and early jazz and even spiked their songs and their instrumental music with a zesty **backbeat** (accents on beats *two* and *four* instead of the usual *one* and *three*). Their varied song repertoire included topical ballads describing train wrecks and other notable disasters, and sentimental songs praising mountain flowers, simple country churches, and lovely pale maidens, as well as hymns and joyful camp meeting spirituals, such as "There'll Be Joy, Joy, Joy" (Listening Example 17).

During the 1920s and 1930s, members of the Carter family collected, arranged, and recorded hundreds of American traditional songs, spirituals, and folk songs, thereby laying the foundation for modern country music. Bluegrass, honky-tonk, Western swing, and rockabilly—discussed in this text—are among the Carter Family's direct heirs. Further, several generations of Carters have continued to perform country music professionally. June Carter (1929–2003) became widely known in her own right as a singer who delivered great country songs, earthy or spiritual, with the plaintive wail of a mountain girl. Appearing regularly on Nashville's Grand Ole Opry in 1950, she befriended Elvis Presley and Hank Williams (she was godmother to Hank Williams, Jr., as well as to Roy Orbison's sons) and met Johnny Cash, who would become, in 1968, her third husband.

Johnny Cash's daughter Roseanne Cash has been a major country music performer since the 1980s. She is a master at mixing country, folk, pop, and rock influences in her Grammy-winning music. Roseanne's stepsister Carlene, who kept the Carter name, carried her country music to England, where she recorded with assorted rockers. Today she continues to combine the sounds of rock and country in her own distinctive way.

Styles of Country Music

By the late 1920s, most Americans had radios, which brought hillbilly or old-time music and (white) religious country music, called **gospel** into homes across the country. (Black gospel music is discussed in Chapter 13.) Spiritual songs, well-loved from camp meeting days, found a new identity as part of the country music family. Thus the typical radio program of the 1920s included sentimental parlor songs (such as "I Dream of Jeanie with the Light Brown Hair," Listening Example 22), old English and American ballads (such as "Barbara Allen," Listening Example 5), work songs, and gospel hymns, performed by country singers, usually accompanied by a fiddle or banjo and sometimes by a guitar. String bands, consisting of several fiddles, one or more banjos and guitars, and sometimes a string bass, played rollicking dance tunes. Popular radio shows also included "dance songs," in which string bands alternated verses with a solo voice.

Country music readily absorbs ethnic and regional styles, adapting them to become a part of the country sound. As rural music evolved across America, reflecting local experience and preference, a great body of modern country and folk musics appeared, of seemingly endless variety and charm. Some of this music reflects people's perception of and reaction to the urban developments that change the country way of life: the opening of mines in the hill country, the building of highways through country fields, economic depressions, and the commercialization and urbanization of modern life, all spurred folk expression. Texans' country music reflected sounds from their neighbors to the south and east—the mariachis of Mexico and Louisiana's Cajun music and zydeco. Hawaiian music, too, reached the western states and eventually moved east across the mainland, becoming an important component of country-western music.

American Folk Ballads

Topical songs—personal stories relating current political or social events—have always had a place in American folk music, but their topical nature discouraged their survival beyond memories of the events they described, and few of those we remember today are much more than a hundred years old. About the turn of the twentieth century, however, the growth in the trade union movement and passionate interest in numerous social causes produced a large number of topical songs, most of them aimed at city audiences rather than rural audiences, and most with a decidedly leftist bent. Throughout the early years of that century, railroads, representing progress and the future, acquired a sheen of glamour and proved a popular subject for ballads, including the very familiar "Wabash Cannon Ball," written and recorded by Roy Acuff in 1936. Although composed, written down, and commercially disseminated, such ballads had much of the flavor and appeal of the traditional folk ballads discussed in Chapter 2 and are reminiscent of the broadside ballads on topics relevant to an earlier age.

One of the most popular and enduring American ballads, "The Ballad of Casey Jones" (Listening Example 46), describes a train wreck that actually occurred in 1900—although not exactly as the song relates the tale. The famous ballad has an uncertain history: A laborer named Wallace Saunders (or Wallis Sanders), who had known and liked the engineer Casey Jones, seems to have set the story of the wreck to an old railroad song called "Jimmie Jones,"

"The Ballad of Casey Jones"

CD 2
Track 14
3:02

This song, published in 1902, tells the story of an engineer, John Luther Jones, nicknamed Casey for his hometown—Cayce, Kentucky—who had safely delivered the fast passenger express known as the Cannonball to Memphis, Tennessee. Tired from his long run from Canton, Mississippi, Jones intended to rest for the night; but learning that the engineer scheduled to run the Cannonball south was ill, Jones agreed to take over the run, which finally began an hour and a half late. Proud of his record for meeting schedules, Jones determined to make up the lost time and nearly succeeded in doing so by running his train at more than 100 miles an hour at a time when speeds of 70 or 80 miles an hour were considered highly daring for passenger trains. But his reckless speed caused him to miss signals warning that several cars of a derailed freight train lay sprawled across the tracks straight ahead of him. Had he slowed as he properly should have, approaching the end of his run, a collision could have been averted; but Jones saw the danger too late, commanded his fireman to save himself by jumping off the train, and stayed in the cab himself to meet certain death. Desperately squeezing the throttle and brakes to slow the train to less than 50 miles an hour before it finally slammed into the train ahead, he spared his passengers injury, and all escaped unharmed. Jones alone died.

Composer Wallace Saunders wrote the words and set them to an anonymous tune. Saunders's words, however, have been re-interpreted by many singers and would not have been exactly those of Johnny Cash's version.

Genre Ballad.

Timbre Male vocal solo (Johnny Cash), accompanied by banjo and background choral harmonies. The banjo plays brief interludes between each chorus and the next verse, emphasizing the stirring backbeat.

Texture Homophonic.

Form Verse-chorus.

Meter Quadruple.

Tempo Fast.

0:00   A mournful train whistle, followed by a percussion instrument's rhythmic "chugging," introduces the ballad. The banjo sets the beat, and Johnny Cash begins the song.

—Continued

Listening Example 46—concluded
"The Ballad of Casey Jones"

0:24   Verse 1.   *Come all you rounders if you want to hear*
               The story 'bout a brave engineer, . . .

0:46   Chorus: A small group of singers provide background harmonies and sing the first words of each phrase of the chorus.   *Casey Jones climbed in the cabin . . .*

0:58   Banjo interlude, emphasizing the stirring backbeat.

1:03   Verse 2: Notice the rise in key level for the second half of the second verse, with a corresponding rise in emotional tension.
               Through South Memphis Yards on a fly . . .

1:29   Chorus.

1:46   Verse 3: Here, Cash momentarily abandons the melody to dramatize his tale with a kind of dramatic declamation.
               Dead on the rail was a passenger train. . . .

2:11   Chorus.

2:28   Verse 4 (four lines only): The last verse features another rise in key.
               Headaches and heartaches and all kinds of pain . . .

2:39   Chorus: After the chorus, the train whistle returns to end the ballad as it began.

altering the events, however, to advance the drama, thereby making Casey Jones a folk hero.

Saunders, who was black, never received a penny for the song, which white entertainers made into a grassroots hit and which in time acquired a catchy chorus, repeated after each verse. Today, a century after the famous crash occurred, this early American song lets us relive the heroic last moments of a flawed but courageous man, whose legend survives today.

Bluegrass
In the 1930s and 1940s, **Bill Monroe** (William Smith Monroe, 1911–1996) blended old-time string band music with the holler of the blues and the improvisation of jazz to create a music called (since the 1950s) **bluegrass,** a virtuosic instrumental style rooted in mountain music such as the Carter Family performed. This revival of a traditional music took its name from Monroe's string band, called the Blue Grass Boys (Figure 11.3), named for his home state of Kentucky, whose music on the radio and in recordings soon became widely popular and commercially important.

Bluegrass is unique among country musics, which consist mostly of song, in being primarily an instrumental concept. The bluegrass ensemble includes a fiddle, a guitar, a string bass, a five-string banjo, and often a mandolin—a

FIGURE 11.3

Bill Monroe (1911–1996) playing the mandolin with his Blue Grass Boys at the Nightstage in Boston, MA.

www.mhhe.com/ferrisaml6e

popular Italian instrument that produces a delicate yet vibrant sound when its strings are plucked. The **acoustic,** or natural, instruments of a bluegrass band make the characteristic timbres light, but the fast tempos and virtuosic playing provide plenty of excitement.

Besides being a virtuoso performer on the mandolin, Monroe also set a new vocal standard with his haunting calls and high-pitched harmonies (the high lonesome sound) based on hymn-singing techniques learned in his youth, as heard in "It's Mighty Dark to Travel" (an Online Listening Example). However, even with bluegrass ballads, sung in the high tones and with the close mountain harmony introduced to urban music by the Carters, the emphasis is on important instrumental interludes or breaks. No less than other country musics, bluegrass has absorbed varied influences and adapted its sound to suit evolving tastes. The verse-chorus form of bluegrass ballads reflects the style of Tin Pan Alley; the virtuosic instrumental playing owes homage to jazz; the manner in which Monroe and his musicians sometimes took turns playing lead and making virtuoso displays suggests the inspiration of western swing (see pp. 197–198).

The virtuosic performances in Listening Example 47 ("Earl's Breakdown") reveal the reasons bluegrass remains among the most appreciated styles of country music today. The musicians **Lester Flatt** (guitar) and **Earl Scruggs** (banjo), who left Bill Monroe's Blue Grass Boys in 1948 to form their own group (the Foggy Mountain Boys), developed a distinctive style of bluegrass, and greatly popularized this stimulating country music: The smooth vocal harmony of Flatt and Scruggs's band, as well as Scruggs's dazzling banjo technique and Flatt's guitar trick called the Lester Flatt G-run, in which the guitar concludes another instrument's solo break with a strong bass figure, all attracted a wider audience to classic bluegrass. Monroe strongly resented the success of Flatt and Scruggs, but during the folk revival of the early 1960s (see pp. 248–251), he accepted the title they and other young musicians bestowed on him: "father of bluegrass." Monroe continued to perform at the Grand Ole Opry until shortly before he died.

"Earl's Breakdown"

In jazz, the term *breakdown* means an instrumental interlude, and especially in bluegrass it indicates a chance for the soloists to show off their spectacular technique. In this 1963 piece, it is Scruggs's three-finger picking style of banjo playing that riveted the attention of fans. However, a good bluegrass musician knows when to shine as the performing star and when to enhance a colleague's playing by providing creative and appropriate backup; and a good bluegrass listener appreciates every line of music.

CD 2
Track 15
3:00

Composer Earl Scruggs (b. 1924).

Genre Bluegrass.

Timbre Guitar (Lester Flatt), banjo (Earl Scruggs), mandolin, fiddle, bass.

Texture Homophonic.

Form Verse-chorus.

Meter Duple.

0:00   Verse 1: The banjo presents the tune, which has two parts, accompanied by the other instruments.

0:15   Chorus 1: Scruggs uses a tuner to bend the pitches expressively.

0:30   Verse 2: The fiddle offers virtuosic variations on both parts of the tune.

0:44   Verse 3: Another fiddle solo.

0:58   Verse 4: Scruggs takes the tune back, with chromatic variations, again bending the strings in his distinctive style.

1:13   Chorus 2: Banjo solo.

1:26   Verse 5: The fiddle ranges ever more widely in pitch, treating only the first half of the tune.

1:41   Verse 6: The mandolin takes a turn, introducing a new picking style.

1:56   Verse 7: Banjo solo.

2:09   Chorus.

2:24   Verse 8: Fiddle solo.

2:39   Verse 9: Banjo solo.

2:53   Banjo solo, leading to end.

During the 1960s, the vibrant sound of the acoustic string instruments and the brilliant playing of the instrumentalists made bluegrass particularly popular on college campuses, in coffeehouses, and at folk festivals around the country. Bluegrass has flavored television shows—*Beverly Hillbillies* (theme song by Flatt and Scruggs), *Petticoat Junction, Green Acres*—and films: *Bonnie and Clyde,* and the famous "Dueling Banjos" of *Deliverance,* for example. In 1954, Elvis Presley recorded a revved-up rockabilly version of Monroe's song "Blue Moon of Kentucky." More recent references to bluegrass include Steve Wariner's "Domino Theory" (1990), sung in the high-pitched tones of mountain music and accompanied by mandolin, steel guitar, and fiddles. The title cut of Vince Gill's album *High Lonesome Sound* (1996) beautifully updated the traditional bluegrass sound. In 1995, the songwriter-singer-instrumentalist Steve Earle accompanied "Train a-Comin'" with unamplified instruments only, and his CD *The Mountain* (1999), on which he played his songs accompanied by the Del McCoury Band (mandolins, banjos, guitars, fiddles, and upright basses) became a standard-bearer of contemporary bluegrass.

The film *O Brother, Where Art Thou?* (2000) and its soundtrack brought bluegrass, gospel, and other "old-time" music to large numbers of new enthusiasts, providing a market for the music of young and middle-age musicians who like to perform traditional music. Prominent among today's performers in bluegrass style, **Alison Krauss,** a fiddle virtuoso from Illinois, sings with a silvery voice that lacks the regional accent and twang distasteful to many younger listeners. She and her band Union Station have won many awards and maintain a seemingly nonstop schedule of performances. (The outstanding solo musicians in this band include Jerry Douglas, a virtuoso performer on the **Dobro**—a wood-body resonator guitar with a metal cover plate over the sound hole and an aluminum cone for amplification. An accomplished composer as well as a gifted performer, Douglas has become known all over the world, and the Gibson guitar company has named a Dobro model after him.)

And so the old style, rooted in rural traditions and continually adapted to contemporary tastes, enjoys new life in various versions today. The passionate fans who gather each summer at bluegrass festivals around the country burn with a zeal approaching that of the faithful attending old-fashioned religious camp meetings.

Country Pop and the Nashville Sound

When rock and roll exploded on the popular music scene in the early 1950s (Chapter 13), the country music industry faced imminent disaster. Country singers did not immediately abandon traditional styles, of course, but recording executives and performers soon realized that two new audiences needed to be addressed: youngsters excited by the new sounds of rock and roll, and urban adults uncomfortable with the raw sounds of traditional country music. Both audiences resisted country music instrumentation—the hillbilly fiddle and the wailing steel guitar—but accepted country songs if accompanied by an electric guitar and drums (for young people) or piano and strings (for adults). The latter group responded to *country pop,* or the *Nashville sound.*

When RCA records opened independent studios in Nashville in the late 1950s, **Chet (Chester Burton) Atkins** (1924–2001), one of the most admired and influential guitarists in the world, was appointed head of the Nashville division and set out to change the sound of country music. The unexpected but undeniable commercial success of Patti Page's recording of "Tennessee Waltz" (1950; a song inspired by the popularity of Bill Monroe's recording of "Kentucky Waltz" in 1948) moved Atkins to acknowledge the advisability of obscuring the boundaries between country and pop and producing songs that would score on both the popular and the country music charts. Intending to establish an "easy listening" country sound, Atkins toned down rhythm sections and added background voices to soften the harsh effect of traditional country music. The sophisticated, polished sound he achieved became known as the **Nashville sound.**

Nashville had been the preeminent center of the country music business since 1942, when Roy Acuff (1903–1992)—a mountain boy from east Tennessee who symbolized the link between old-time early-morning radio, medicine shows, and hotel-room recording sessions on the one hand and modern commercial country music on the other—founded the first modern music publishing company there. Now Nashville met the threat of rock and roll by combining country themes with pop instrumentation. Nashville soloists singing of traditional country topics jived up their rhythms and often added a background chorus of voices singing not in the close mountain harmony of the Carters but in a trained professional style, much like the doo-wop singers of Motown rock and roll (pp. 233–235). Chet Atkins sang country songs and played his guitar in a style close to that of Tin Pan Alley.

Even as some country musicians modified their twang and polished their performances, presenting country-style songs in a pop format in order to survive as commercial entertainers, **cover recordings** of country hits made by Tony Bennett, Frankie Laine, and other popular singers appeared on the popular music charts. The smooth voices and polished styles of Eddy Arnold and Jim Reeves, often accompanied by a string orchestra, also represented country pop.

By the early 1960s, the success of Chet Atkins's Nashville sound and of country pop in general caused Nashville to become, with New York City and Hollywood, a recording capital of popular music. Criticized as superficial by some, country pop has nevertheless flourished in the early years of the twenty-first century, as Faith Hill, Shania Twain, LeAnn Rimes, Tim McGraw, Randy Travis, Kenny Rogers, and Garth Brooks, among others, enjoy huge popular and financial success in the field.

Western Swing

Even before bluegrass and the Nashville sound established their popularity in the Eastern United States, country music moved west, where it developed further distinctive styles. In the 1930s, people displaced from their jobs by the economic turmoil of the Great Depression, or forced to abandon farms located in the drought-stricken Dust Bowl, left their accustomed environments and roamed west, carrying with them their traditional music customs, if little else. This kind of forced migration continued in the 1940s, during World War II, as people leaving familiar rural areas to find jobs

FIGURE 11.4
Bob Wills (1905–1975).

www.mhhe.com/ferrisaml6e

in the cities brought along their taste for country music. In the West, Mexican, Cajun, Hawaiian, and cowboy music flavored a new brand of country music, called **country-western.**

Whereas country music in the Eastern United States generally reflected the conservative mood and morality of the Christian home, the western country flavor was closer to that of the dance hall. Texans responded to the big band craze of the 1930s and 1940s with a dance band style of their own, called **western swing:** To the piano, sax, brasses, and jazz rhythm section of the Eastern big band, Texans added fiddles and the steel guitar, while their singers added yodeling in the style of Jimmie Rodgers. Fast tempos, hot rhythms, and wonderfully virtuosic instrumental solos also indicated a strong jazz influence on western swing.

Bob Wills (1905–1975; Figure 11.4), the major figure in the development of western swing, performed country fiddle tunes, Hispanic folk music, African American folk blues, jazz—and more. His band, the Texas Playboys, fluctuated in membership and in numbers over the years but always featured musicians of talent and accomplishment. Wills, who played fiddle and mandolin, punctuated the band's performances with jive talking, falsetto asides, and cries of "ah-ha!" as heard in his signature tune "New San Antonio Rose" (an Online Listening Example). Wills's innovative combination of horns, fiddles, and steel guitar grabbed the public's ear, and "New San Antonio Rose" became a huge national success in the 1940s.

Bob Wills and the Texas Playboys played straight fiddle tunes, cowboy numbers, hit parade songs, jazz instrumentals, blues numbers, Mexican music, and more. Mixing all these styles together presaged the tendency of today's popular musicians to achieve an eclectic mix of various musics—including western swing. Today the wildly exciting Hot Club of Cowtown, for example, combines Bob Wills's western swing with the hot stylings of a French jazz violinist (Stephane Grappelli) to produce a swinging music suited for dance and fun. (Hot Club of Cowtown can be heard on YouTube.)

Honky-Tonk

While Texas dance halls rang with the sounds of western swing bands, another country-western style developed in the intimate Texas bars and clubs called honky-tonks. The patrons in these small crowded rooms were more interested in listening than dancing to the **honky-tonk** songs, which addressed in the frankest terms harsh subjects relevant to the experience of returning servicemen and uprooted or separated families: infidelity, divorce, alcohol, home sickness, separation, loneliness, prison. Singers delivered the rough, realistic lyrics in an earthy, matter-of-fact manner typical of the country style.

Accompanying bands, if any, had a distinctive instrumentation borrowed from the blues, jazz, or Hawaiian ensembles, but electrified in order to be heard in the noisy honky-tonks. An amplified piano, loud enough to carry above the noise of rough drinking crowds, often provided the sole accompaniment. Electrification, in fact, proved essential to honky-tonk music, and nearly all the instruments— even the fiddle—were likely to be electrified in the honky-tonk band.

Historically, the stars of honky-tonk were white men from the Southwest, including Ernest Tubb, Lefty Frizzell, Buck Owens, Merle Haggard, George Jones, and George Strait. However, Charley Pride, the only black country music performer to have a long and distinguished career, has found honky-tonk a congenial medium, as have the Hispanic singers Freddie Fender and Johnny Rodriguez.

Greatest of all honky-tonk stars was **Hank Williams, Sr.** (1923–1953; Figure 11.5), though Williams cannot be confined to one style. As influential as Jimmie Rodgers and as passionately admired, Williams became a legendary figure in country music. Williams's songs and his performances blended blues, gospel, and mountain music to produce his own brand of honky-tonk. His voice—thin, nasal, and flat in a characteristic country way—yet had intense emotional appeal, enhanced by a modified yodel and an occasional "tearful" break. He sang his own songs, rooted in emotional and physical pain (he suffered from spina bifida). Written in plain language, his songs appealed directly to the hearts and souls of his radio and concert listeners, who made him during his short life the best-known and most financially successful country singer. (Hank Williams can be heard performing some of his songs on YouTube. One of the most famous, "Your Cheatin' Heart," is an Online Listening Example.)

A sentimental man with deep religious faith and a silly sense of humor, Williams is best regarded as a tragic genius. The Grand Ole Opry, which brought him to fame, finally dismissed him for drunkenness and erratic behavior, and he died alone in the back of his chauffered car on the way to do a show in 1953. His heart failure may have been caused by an overdose of morphine, or perhaps his body simply wore out from pain and a troubled life.

In 1961, Hank Williams joined Jimmie Rodgers as one of the first three inductees into the Country Music Hall of Fame.

For a time, honky-tonk shied away from the wrenching honesty that, like the blues, helped its listeners confront hard times and even death. But recent

www.mhhe.com/ferrisaml6e

FIGURE 11.5

Hank Williams, Sr.
(1923–1953).

honky-tonk responds to the new public frankness on subjects such as sex, drugs, and violence with strong new lyrics, often delivered by female singers.

Cowboy Songs
From the time of the earliest talking pictures, Americans flocked to western films, and by the mid-1930s the craze for westerns was full-blown. Films portrayed the West as Hollywood envisioned it: full of wide-open spaces, dramatic scenery, beautiful and virtuous women, and despicable villains, invariably vanquished by brave and handsome cowboys—many of whom sang romantic cowboy songs.

Some of the Hollywood singing cowboys actually were from the West. **Gene Autry**, born near Tioga, Texas, in 1907, was working as a telegraph operator when, one night in 1927, the great humorist Will Rogers overheard him singing and strumming his guitar and encouraged him to try his luck in New York. Unsuccessful in New York, Autry got a job with a radio station in Tulsa, where he was known as "Oklahoma's yodelin' cowboy," a tribute to the "singing (and yodeling) brakeman" Jimmie Rodgers. A good businessman as well as a highly talented musician, Autry started his own publishing company and film production company and became the first movie star to get into television. Today the Autry Western Heritage Museum in Los Angeles, California, presents a multiethnic history of the American West and its impact on pop culture.

Tex Ritter, another famous singing cowboy, also came from Texas; but many of the songs he, Autry, and other "cowboys" sang were written by Tin Pan Alley professionals. Among the most famous of these were "Tumbling Tumbleweeds" (featured as a tremulous harmonica solo in the film *City Slickers* in 1991) and "Cool Water," both written by Bob Nolan, a founding member of a famous singing trio called the Sons of the Pioneers. Most of the songs sung by Roy Rogers, who, like Autry, starred in about a hundred western films, were also written by Nolan. Of course there were real cowboy songs as well, many of them with lilting Irish tunes to which nineteenth-century immigrant Irish cowboys set new words describing life on the American range. These, together with the songs composed for western films, became part of the country-western repertoire.

By the late 1940s, cowboy songs had largely faded in popularity. Gene Autry, who earlier had recorded songs from the African American blues tradition ("Black Bottom Blues," "Wild Cat Mama," and "Traveling Blues," for example), went on to sing songs in the popular rather than the western vein. (He is best known today for "Here Comes Santa Claus," which he cowrote with Oakley Haldeman; and "Rudolph, the Red-Nosed Reindeer," written by Johnny Marks.) Tex Ritter's biggest hit, "High Noon" (written by Dimitri Tiomkin), was high on the pop charts rather than the roll of country-western hits.

The western sound that Autry helped popularize has experienced something of a revival, however, partly spurred by movies such as *Sleepless in Seattle* (1993), which included "Back in the Saddle" (cowritten by Ray Whitley and Gene Autry) on its multiplatinum soundtrack, and *The Horse Whisperer* (1998). (Contemporary cowboy balladeer Don Edwards can be seen and heard on YouTube.)

Hawaiian Music

Hawaiian music, rooted in old religious chants and hymns, absorbed rhythms, sounds, and instruments brought to Hawaii by missionaries, tourists, and settlers from many other lands. Particularly, Hawaiians enjoyed the guitar, brought by Mexican cowboys in the mid-1800s, adapting the instrument, however, to accompany hula and Hawaiian songs and hymns. By loosening (slackening) the strings, Hawaiians invented the **slack key guitar,** giving the instrument a characteristic resonance and allowing new styles of fingering and picking. Charles Philip "Gabby" Pahinui (1921–1980), the acknowledged master of the slack key guitar, acquired fans around the world for his virtuosic style of Hawaiian music, heard in "Mele of My Tutu E," Listening Example 48.

Listening Example 48

"Mele of My Tutu E"

Hapa haole songs—mostly in English with Hawaiian terms sprinkled in—first appeared in the early 1900s, when there was much confusion as to how Hawaiians could communicate their culture to others. Native Hawaiians were being discouraged by mainland authorities from speaking their native language. (It was actually illegal to school your children at home in Hawaiian.)

CD 2
Track 16
2:57

—Continued

"Mele of My Tutu E"

And composers not proficient with the Hawaiian language wrote about the beautiful islands in English. It is easy to understand why hapa haole songs, such as this one from about 1945—easy to listen to, fun to dance to, and relatively easy to understand—became very popular with tourists to the tropical paradise. (The complete lyrics to this song can be found on the Internet.)

Composer and Lyricist   Danny Ku.

Genre   Hapa haole song.

Timbre   Three male vocalists, steel guitar, slack key guitar, percussion. The instruments play an introduction, a closing section, and four verses of their own, as well as accompanying the vocalists and playing a small "tag" at the end of each verse.

Texture   Homophonic.

Form   Strophic.

Meter   Quadruple.

0:00   Instrumental introduction.
0:08   *Ho'okahi* (alone) *Sunday afternoon . . .*
0:39   *She was singing an old melody . . .*
0:57   Two instrumental verses.
1:29   *Tutu e ina ka'awa e . . .*
1:47   Two instrumental verses.
2:18   *Tutu is going home now . . .*
2:47   Instrumental conclusion.

The Hawaiian **steel guitar** is even better known and has had more influence on various country musics. This instrument, with metal strings raised above the fret board, is held horizontally in the lap. The player presses a steel bar against the strings, rather than pressing them to the fret board with the fingers as on a traditional guitar; and by sliding the metal bar along the strings with the left hand, the player achieves a gentle slide, suggestive of and congenial to a country twang. Invented and popularized in Hawaii around the turn of the twentieth century, the steel guitar caused a sensation at the Panama-Pacific International Exposition of 1915 in San Francisco, and from there it spread throughout the United States, exerting a profound and lingering influence on country music. By the end of the 1930s, the Hawaiian steel guitar—electrified

FIGURE 11.6
A ukulele.

or acoustic—was well established in southwestern country bands and was becoming a part of Southeastern country music as well.

The **ukulele,** a small guitar with four strings (Figure 11.6), also attracted much enthusiasm at the Panama-Pacific Exposition, where the Hawaiian Pavilion featured Hawaiian songs, hula, and instrumental music. Portuguese immigrants brought the ukulele to Hawaii in 1879, and according to one legend, Hawaiians, enchanted at the way fingers flew over the strange new instrument, called it "ukulele," meaning "jumping fleas." By the 1920s, as Hawaiian music became hugely popular on the mainland, Tin Pan Alley performers accompanied many of their songs with a ukulele. Interest waned for a time, but recent years have seen ukulele festivals sprout up not only in Hawaii, but on the mainland as well: The Northern California Ukulele Festival and the Uke Festival in Massachusetts draw large crowds every year.

Hawaiian music, popular in its own right, also has profoundly affected mainland country music (and pop). Songs such as "Sweet Leilani," "Hawaiian Wedding Song," and "Blue Hawaii" (all available on YouTube) wooed a receptive audience, and the steel guitar, slack key guitar, and ukulele have played a more subtle but vital role in promoting country music. "Hapa haole" songs, such as "Mele of My Tutu E" (Listening Example 48), won easy popularity with their combination of Hawaiian flavor and English lyrics.

Cajun Music   Evicted by the British from their homeland in Acadia (Nova Scotia) in the mid-eighteenth century, the French Acadians (later called Cajuns) sought asylum in the bayous of Southwest Louisiana, finally settling in a remote area south of New Orleans. There, relatively isolated from most of

American society, they continued to speak French, slowly evolving a *patois,* or mixed language, of their own.

The success of hillbilly recordings in the 1920s sent record companies' talent scouts to Louisiana searching for additional regional styles to record, and soon outstanding Cajun musicians were attracting an enthusiastic listening public. In 1932, as national record companies actively promoted commercial recordings of regional music, a folklorist named **John Lomax** (1867–1948) also traveled to Louisiana, where he recorded genuine traditional Cajun music for the Library of Congress. Meanwhile, however, radio brought new musical influences, such as blues and hillbilly, to Cajun regions, and Cajun musicians began to follow the example of Jimmie Rodgers, the Carter Family, and later Bob Wills, often translating popular country and country-western songs into French. Thus the Texas-Cajun influence was in fact a two-way affair.

Although the sensitive listener may detect a hint of tragedy in **Cajun music,** the sound is prevailingly lighthearted, with dance rhythms and catchy melodies dominated by the wonderfully raucous sound of the accordion. The Cajun accordion, with ten melody buttons (instead of piano keys) on one side and two bass accompaniment buttons on the other, produces a loud, vibrant sound requiring singers to produce a high, strained tenor voice that will carry over the roaring accordion and droning fiddles. Often one hears shouts ("Oh, ya, yaie!") reminiscent of bluegrass sounds.

After years of recycled arrangements performed by aging musicians, Cajun music is enjoying a vibrant renaissance; today's Louisiana dance halls are filled with young dancers and young musicians bringing a hard-rocking approach to the traditional acoustic instruments. Traditional waltzes and other dances, such as the two-step in Listening Example 49, also resound from the dance halls with rhythms and timbres as spicy as highly seasoned Cajun food.

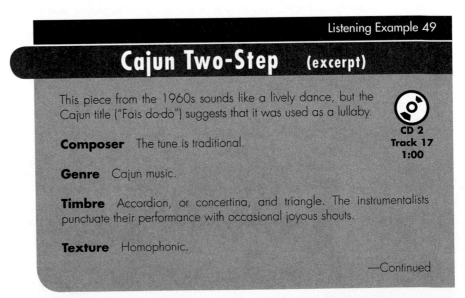

Listening Example 49

Cajun Two-Step   (excerpt)

This piece from the 1960s sounds like a lively dance, but the Cajun title ("Fais do-do") suggests that it was used as a lullaby.

CD 2
Track 17
1:00

Composer   The tune is traditional.

Genre   Cajun music.

Timbre   Accordion, or concertina, and triangle. The instrumentalists punctuate their performance with occasional joyous shouts.

Texture   Homophonic.

—Continued

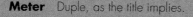

Listening Example 49—concluded

Cajun Two-Step (excerpt)

Form The two-step is a dance organized much like a rag or march in a series of four-measure strains. The taped excerpt includes **AABBAAB,** and we sense, probably accurately, that the dance could continue almost indefinitely were it not for constraints of concert or recording time.

Meter Duple, as the title implies.

Tempo Fast. The insistently rapid tempo contributes to the exuberant nature of the piece.

0:00	**A**	The accordion, accompanied by triangle, introduces the melody.
0:09	**A**	Repeat.
0:18	**B**	A new phrase.
0:27	**B**	Repeat.
0:35	**A**	The original tune returns.
0:44	**A**	Repeat.
0:53	**B**	The second phrase returns, as the excerpt tapers off.

Zydeco A more recent accordion-based music, **zydeco** (zy-deh-COH), distinguished by spicy-hot Caribbean and Latin rhythms, is the music of southern Louisiana's Creoles—a term of various meaning but here applying to *gens de couleur libre* ("free persons of color"). The term *zydeco* is a corruption of the first two words of the French phrase *les haricots sont pas salés,* meaning "the snap beans aren't salted," a traditional indicator of hard times. But there is no misery to the rich zydeco sounds of accordion and harmonica, accompanied by a tambourine and sometimes by a *frottoir,* or a rub board (a washboard-like instrument that the musicians may strap to their chests for ready access) marking the hotly syncopated rhythms. An electric guitar and bass, drums, and sometimes even a saxophone enliven the sound. Heard mainly along the Gulf Coast, where a blend of African American French Creole traditions has created a rich gumbo of musical flavors, contemporary zydeco bands combine the energy and amplification of the hottest rock groups with the exotic melodies and dialect of the Cajuns to produce their own intoxicating music.

Mainstream artists, too, show the influence of the compelling Cajun and zydeco musics. Paul Simon's tribute to zydeco and its late "king," Clifton Chenier—"That Was Your Mother"—was one of the highlights of Simon's multimillion-selling album *Graceland,* for example. When asked what drew her to Cajun, country singer Mary Chapin Carpenter (who won a Grammy in 1992 for her Cajun-flavored "Down at the Twist and Shout") replied, "In no particular order: percussion, fiddle, spices, waltzes, Acadian accordion, the tempo, lyrics of love and spirit, gumbo, wails, Highway 10, darkness, dance halls."

Women in Country

The road life, honky-tonk settings, and all-male bands typical of country music did not encourage participation by women, at least during the first half of the twentieth century, when women's seemly, or proper, place in American society was rigidly defined. Most of the women who made early successful careers in country music were heavily influenced by pop stars and may be seen as cross-over artists bridging country and pop: Thus **Patsy Cline** (1932–1963), who came from a country background and had a strident, powerful country sound, gained high positions on both pop and country charts. **Kitty Wells** (b. 1919), known as the "queen of country music" through the 1950s, faced strong competition from a number of great female singers in the succeeding decade. **Loretta Lynn** (b. 1935), who also favored honky-tonk instrumentation, and who appealed to beleaguered housewives with such songs as "The Pill," perhaps had the strongest claim to inherit Wells's title.

In the 1990s, women established a commanding, even dominant, presence in country music, both as writers and as singers of "new country." Mixing old-fashioned values and country instrumentation with frank sexuality and samplings of other vernacular sounds, women have reigned securely at the top of the country charts ever since.

Growing up, **Dolly Parton** (b. 1946) sang traditional ballads and gospel songs with her eleven brothers and sisters. Besides her pure, clean soprano voice, she also has a genuine talent for songwriting and remains a dominating (and stunning) presence on the country music scene. **Reba McIntyre** (b. 1955), who broke new ground by singing country-style songs about contemporary city people, established celebrity status through television and movies even before starring on Broadway in 2001 in a revival of *Annie Get Your Gun* (music by Irving Berlin). In 2007, *Billboard* magazine named McIntyre their first Woman of the Year.

Harmony singing, too, has shown a new strong female influence. Close, tight country music harmonies between a man and a woman, as in the duets of George Jones and the late Tammy Wynette, or Porter Wagoner and Dolly Parton, constituted a kind of musical dialogue, the combination of enormously different but compatible voices implying sexual tension, resolved or not. But even more characteristic of country harmonizing are same-sex combinations, in which the blending of voices is tantalizingly close. The collaboration of Dolly Parton, Emmylou Harris, and Linda Ronstadt put three enormously talented but strikingly different country singers together in an amazingly successful sound. **Emmylou Harris** has avoided the Nashville marketing machine and performs a distinctive mix of folk, bluegrass, country, and rock with artists of varying styles. **Linda Ronstadt** has a background in Mexican and Spanish music and began her career singing rock and roll. A true crossover artist, she has sung operetta and classical songs as well as several styles of country. All three women have a wide range of emotional expression, and their combined vocal talents are impressive indeed. Their first album, *Trio,* released in 1987, is an outstanding example of traditional harmony singing. (The album includes the lovely song "To Know Him Is to Love Him," by Phil Spector, available on YouTube.) As a point of interest, their performance of "After the Gold Rush," on another album, is accompanied by the unlikely combination of synthesizer, strings, and Ben Franklin's instrument, a glass harmonica (see p. 62). (Another point of irrelevant but intriguing interest: Spector was convicted of second-degree murder in 2009 for a crime he committed nearly six years earlier.)

Recent Country

More sophisticated in performance and broader in scope than ever, country music continues to hold a wide audience as, "new country" vies with "traditional country" on radio stations and in the hearts of country music lovers. A new traditionalism leads some country stars to replace synthesizers, string sections, and pop drumbeats with acoustic guitars and fiddles, and some seek to recapture the friction and grit of original honky-tonk. Fiddling and banjo contests regularly draw huge crowds to folk festivals and state fairs. The catch in the throat, the plink of a mandolin, the woozy swoop of a steel guitar, even a modest mountain twang have returned to current country; and western swing, and—especially—bluegrass have a strong presence in country music today. The bluegrass influence is apparent in the music of many outstanding country musicians who combine various styles of their choice to create music of their own. We have already mentioned Alison Krauss, who blends bluegrass, jazz, rock, and folk; and Jerry Douglas, who performs bluegrass, rock and roll, jazz, blues, and classical music on his Dobro. Béla Fleck does amazing things with bluegrass, jazz, classical, and rock on his five-string banjo. The virtuoso fiddler Mark O'Connor blends bluegrass with funk and jazz. All these current musicians and more can be found on the Internet, often with clips of their music available at the click of a mouse.

Here, it is time for you to leave the textbook and, using the names offered above as starting points, explore country music in your world today.

Terms to Review

drone	acoustic	slack key guitar
hillbilly music	Dobro	steel guitar
Grand Ole Opry	Nashville sound	ukulele
yodel	cover, cover recording	Cajun music
backbeat	country-western	zydeco
gospel	western swing	
bluegrass	honky-tonk	

Key Figures

Jimmie Rodgers
the Carter Family
Bill Monroe
Lester Flatt
Earl Scruggs
Alison Krauss

Chet Atkins
Bob Wills
Hank Williams
Gene Autry
John Lomax
Patsy Cline

Kitty Wells
Loretta Lynn
Dolly Parton
Reba McIntyre
Emmylou Harris
Linda Ronstadt

Critical Thinking

What do you think has caused many country musicians to seek to "return to the roots" of country music?

Do you prefer traditional country or modern interpretations? Why?

Do you prefer acoustic (bluegrass) music or electrified (honky-tonk) style? Why?

Why does country seem to lend itself to describing life's most elemental feelings and experiences? Is it the instrumentation? Regional accent? Rhythm? Delivery style? Something else?

Latin Popular Musics

Music from Latin America, having enriched the popular and concert music of the United States for at least a century and a half, is of more significance to North American popular music today than ever before. In the Southwest, where venerable Spanish traditions remain strong, traditional dance music is played much as it has been for many generations. In other parts of the country, Latin American dance music has strongly affected North American pop and jazz. And today "Latin pop" is a category in its own right—a strong one—on the *Billboard* trade magazine popular music charts.

Early in the twentieth century, Latin popular dances took the United States by storm, first as exotic curiosities, next as fads, and finally entering the mainstream of American popular music. The first of the Latin rhythms to affect American pop was the Argentinean **tango** (Figure 12.1), a graceful yet torrid dance aptly described as "a vertical expression of a horizontal desire." Sedate in tempo but highly sensuous in performance, the tango was introduced to Broadway audiences in 1911 and was made widely popular as danced by Irene and Vernon Castle in a 1913 musical (see p. 304). The tango (which may be viewed on YouTube) represents a sophisticated fusion of European and African ingredients.

Lyrical tango *melodies* often suggest the influence of Argentina's large Italian population. The basic tango *rhythm* is that of an older Cuban dance, the **habanera** (named for Havana, Cuba), which subdivides eight eighth notes (four beats) into 3 + 3 + 2. The habanera beat has been of enormous significance to popular music in the United States; for example, in the mid-nineteenth century Louis Moreau Gottschalk used the rhythm in several of his popular piano pieces (see pp. 109–110); Jelly Roll Morton claimed that New Orleans ragtime players often applied the "Spanish tinge," as he called this beat, to their left-hand accompaniments; and in 1914, W. C. Handy used the rhythm in the four-line verse—the "tango section"—interspersed between the blues stanzas of "St. Louis Blues" (Listening Example 36). Since those early days, the habanera beat has been heard as the basic rhythm of numerous pop styles.

In the 1930s several Latin dances entered American pop through big band music, especially that of the popular bandleader **Xavier Cugat** (Figure 12.2),

FIGURE 12.1

The Argentinean tango.

FIGURE 12.2

Xavier Cugat and Carmen Miranda, stars of Latin music in concerts and film musicals of the 1930s and 1940s.

who was born in Spain but raised in Cuba. Several renowned Latin performers, including Desi Arnaz and Carmen Miranda (see Figure 12.2), began their careers at about that time, appearing in popular stage shows in the 1930s and later in film musicals.

Three Latin areas—the Caribbean, Brazil, and Mexico—have particularly influenced the popular, classical, and religious music of North America.

The Caribbean

The slave trade bringing blacks to North America carried many slaves to the Caribbean islands (and even more to Brazil). Slaves in these Latin American areas managed better than their northern counterparts to preserve their cultural traditions, partly because the traditional drumming largely forbidden in the North was tolerated south of the border, and also because the African tribal religions blended far better with the Christian Catholicism prevalent in Latin America than with the Protestantism characteristic of the North.

Since 1898, when Puerto Rico became a protectorate of the United States, a steady influx of Puerto Ricans have arrived to settle primarily in New York City. Cubans, too, have come to New York in some numbers, although far more have settled closer to home and to where they land by boat, in Florida. Chicago and Los Angeles also have sizable populations of Caribbean peoples, including those from Haiti, Trinidad, and other areas of the West Indies. Both Cubans and Puerto Ricans brought numbers of African-derived musical and dance forms to the United States; but because Spanish colonizers transported far more African slaves to Cuba than to Puerto Rico, the black Cuban population is sizable and the African influence on its culture particularly strong.

Santeria: The Way of the Saints
The traditional rhythms of Cuban *batá* drums accompany the most sacred and complex rituals of Santeria, a religion created in the New World by slaves brought from West Africa to work on Caribbean sugar plantations. (Batá are double-headed, hourglass-shaped drums, generally thought to be in the shape of the thunder ax of the god they represent. Both heads of the drums are sounded with the hands.) Nominally converted to Catholicism, slaves often fused their traditional beliefs and rituals—vital connectors to their past—with elements of their new religion. In this way in Cuba, the religious practice called Santeria evolved.

In the United States, Santeria has attracted not only members of the Cuban and Puerto Rican communities but many African Americans and a growing number of Anglo-Americans as well. Santeria songs, each associated with a particular deity, normally are sung without harmony in call-and-response fashion between leader and group, the leader often improvising phrases in an open, relaxed vocal style characteristic of some African practice. The rhythms of the accompanying batá drums also have specific ritual significance, each rhythm constituting a musical prayer that honors and represents a specific god. Because batá drumming is an oral tradition, living in the minds of performers rather than on a printed page, batá ensembles continue to evolve their own individual performance style and technique, always rooted, however, in ancient African tradition.

Bomba
Among the first Latin dances to become popular north of the border was the **bomba,** a distinctive African-derived Puerto Rican couple dance allowing the man great flexibility and freedom to display his dancing skills while his female partner performs relatively fixed steps. They dance to a song

FIGURE 12.3

The subtle, syncopated clave rhythm.

CLAVE RHYTHM

whose text—performed in call-and-response fashion—usually concerns every-day or topical events, accompanied by drums plus optional maracas, *guiro* (a notched gourd, open at one end, scraped with a stick or with metal wires), and cowbell. A pair of sticks strikes a fixed rhythmic pattern on the side of a drum or other hard resonant surface, as the male dancer and lead drummer respond to and compete with each other in rhythms of increasing complexity.

Rumba

Rumba is actually a generic term for a group of Afro-Cuban musical and dance forms. Couples dancing a rumba hold each other slightly apart, shoulders level, while moving their hips provocatively from side to side. The basic rhythm of two or four beats to the measure is divided according to the *clave* rhythm, tapped out by cylindrical sticks called *claves,* which underlies all Cuban dance music: The first of two measures is in habanera rhythm, and the second measure sounds on beats two and three (Figure 12.3). The tempo varies but is never very rapid.

Rumba is the style at the deepest roots of Cuban music, having arrived in Cuba with African slaves. Soon African languages were replaced by Spanish, and the melody lines adapted scales and figures from Spanish songs. This synthesis seeded virtually all the Cuban music that followed, including son, chachacha, conga, mambo, even salsa, as well as cabaret music, pop songs, and Cuban classical compositions. Around the world rumba reached into rhythm and blues, disco, Spanish flamenco-pop, and African guitar-rock. As vital today as at its beginning, rumba continues to evolve: younger musicians with conservatory training emphasize their instrumental technique; jazz flourishes sometimes infiltrate the drumming; elements of rap are moving into the vocals.

Traditional Cuban instruments add to the exotic flavor of the rumba: *Bongos* are pairs of drums of different size, held between the knees and usually played with the fingers and hand, sometimes with a stick. *Conga* drums, largest of the Latin instruments, also often are played in pairs, the sound produced by their muleskin head varying according to whether it is struck by the heel, palm, or fingers of the hand. Pairs of metal drums called *timbales* are mounted on a stand and struck with a stick. *Maracas* are pairs of gourds filled with pebbles or seeds and shaken or rotated by handles attached to one end.

While Cuban and Puerto Rican musicians performed rumbas during the 1930s in New York's uptown Latin district known as El Barrio, Xavier Cugat and other bandleaders entertained downtown ballroom crowds with a rhythmically simplified hybrid Latin and American version of the dance. Soon the rumba's extreme popularity led Tin Pan Alley songwriters to join the Latin bandwagon, producing such wonderful songs as Irving Berlin's "Heat Wave" and Cole Porter's "Begin the Beguine." (The *beguine* is a native dance of the West Indies.)

Cu-Bop

By the 1940s, Cuban instruments and instrumentalists were strongly affecting jazz. Among the most popular influences was that of yet another dance, the **conga,** performed in a line or chain essentially as a march but with a heavy accent every fourth beat emphasized by a side kick by the dancers. Having added a great Cuban conga drummer to his Afro-Cuban jazz orchestra, Dizzy Gillespie, in a bebop concert at Carnegie Hall in 1947, introduced **cu-bop,** merging Latin rhythms with his bebop style.

From then on, Gillespie, Duke Ellington, Stan Kenton, and other U.S. musicians flavored much of their music with Brazilian, Cuban, and other Latin influences. At the heart of Cuban (and African) drumming is the superimposition of rhythmic patterns: Over a constant underlying pulse, other pulses are layered and then varied, creating rhythmic expectation through repetition and then subverting it. This is also a large part of what a jazz soloist does, and jazz musicians readily adapted such techniques to their performances. Stan Kenton's band greatly increased the intensity and excitement of some of their music by employing a typical Latin rhythmic effect called *double-timing,* which subdivides the beat (as into eighths instead of quarters), implying a faster tempo without actually increasing the rate of speed, because the musicians play twice the number of notes per beat.

Mambo

Tito Puente (1923–2000), born in New York City to Puerto Rican parents, became known as the mambo king for his sophisticated "downtown" versions of yet another Latin dance craze, the **mambo.** A bandleader of Afro-Cuban music and a percussionist, Puente had studied at Juilliard and other professional music conservatories and tempered his Latin rhythms with cooler European harmonies, timbres, and tempos. He was influenced by swing and by his religion, Santeria, reflected in his album *Top Percussion* (1957).

Hot or cool, the mambo, developed in this country by Latin and Latin-influenced musicians, merged Afro-Cuban sounds with those of big band jazz. Couples danced the mambo moving forward and back, either holding each other in rumba fashion, touching one hand only, or not touching at all. The slower, simpler **chachacha,** popular in the 1950s, is closely related to or even a form of the mambo, adding a double step between the fourth (last) and first beats. The mambo's influence proved farther-reaching than its originators or even the mambo king might have envisioned. Having merged with big band jazz and having inspired many Tin Pan Alley songs recorded by such popular singers as Perry Como and Nat "King" Cole, the mambo also strongly affected rhythm and blues in the 1950s and introduced Latin rhythms into early rock. Bo Diddley, Ray Charles, and James Brown number among the many musicians who absorbed the Latin percussion sounds and rhythms into their own unique musics.

Salsa

By the late 1970s, a Cuban music that had been considered a sub-style of popular music for decades emerged as a major ingredient in virtually every vernacular field, receiving with its new status a new name as well—**salsa.** The word, meaning "sauce," had long been applied to peppy Cuban sounds, but the young people who coined it as a name seemed to think of the music it defined as something new. In fact, as its popularity spread, salsa drew from a wider range of Latin sounds than before while yet remaining closer to Cuban music than any other Latin style. Today the term *salsa* is sometimes used generically to denote all Afro-Latin popular musics.

Salsa indeed was dance band music, but with instrumentation, rhythms, and a general flavor quite unlike the swing band sound. Its timbres were primarily those of voices and trumpets or, alternatively, flutes and violins; and its complex rhythms continually absorbed varied Puerto Rican and South American elements, which sophisticated jazz musicians enthusiastically incorporated into their highly virtuosic performances (see Listening Example 50).

Listening Example 50

"Ojos" ("Eyes")

CD 2
Track 18
4:50

"Ojos" is a 1978 song about hope, about the poor, about young people who rise above seemingly hopeless social conditions. This performance exemplifies how salsa musicians absorb varied influences (in this case from jazz) and apply them to this basically Cuban style. The trombonist, composer, and bandleader Willie Colón, born in New York City but of Puerto Rican heritage, replaces the traditional trumpets or flutes of salsa with trombone and blends jazz harmonies and jazz-style soloing into his salsa performances. Thus the brass instruments in this performance sound much like those of big band jazz. The Panamanian Rubén Blades (whose mother was Cuban, and who often is referred to as the Latin Bruce Springsteen) adds a showman's flair to his vocals. Blades, a four-time Grammy winner, has recorded in both English and Spanish and has collaborated with Lou Reed, Elvis Costello, and Sting; he has acted in and written songs for a number of movies, and in 1998 performed on Broadway in Paul Simon's musical *The Capeman*.

Composers Rubén Blades (b. 1948) and Willie Colón (b. 1950).

Lyrics Johnny Ortiz.

Genre Salsa.

Timbre Tenor vocal (Blades); brass (with trombone playing the lead lines instead of salsa's traditional trumpets or flutes); percussion, including conga drum, timbales, bongos, maracas, and claves. A piano plays repetitive syncopated patterns.

Texture Polyphonic. Listen for melodic independence between the solo voice and the instruments.

Form Two-part: *canto* (narrative) and *montuno* (rhythmic, more instrumental than vocal in concept).

—Continued

"Ojos" ("Eyes")

Meter Quadruple. Listen for the pervasive clave rhythm—which has, however, been too thoroughly internalized by these sophisticated musicians to be readily identified by the casual listener.

Canto The first section, much like the verse of a Tin Pan Alley song, presents the narrative content of the song, accompanied by the band. There are three eight-bar phrases.

0:00   Brass introduction, eight bars.

0:15   Blades begins his solo: verse 1.

0:34   Verse 2.

0:52   Verse 3.

Montuno The second section alternates instrumental and vocal performances.

1:11   The trombone, accompanied by the other instruments, plays a verse (eight bars).

1:28   During the vocal solo, a chorus of male voices intersperses calls of "Ojos" (eight bars).

1:47   Another vocal verse. Notice that the intensity and rhythmic complexity of the piece increase as the performance proceeds (eight bars).

2:05   Vocal (four bars). Enjoy the intricately woven and highly syncopated rhythmic patterns governed by the clave rhythm.

2:13   Instrumental phrase (four bars). Feel the subtle change in rhythm, still over the clave pattern. Hear the strong ostinatos played by the piano.

2:22   Instrumental verse (eight bars). Try to follow one or more independent instrumental lines at a time, noticing the manner in which their accents fall on, or between, different beats.

2:39   Instruments (eight bars), encouraged by Blades's improvised shouts.

2:55   Instruments play the original melody (eight bars).

3:12   Vocal solo, with choral "Ojos" in the background (eight bars).

3:30   Vocal solo (four bars).

3:38   Instruments, with "Ojos" in background (sixteen bars).

4:10   Vocal solo. Notice how the vocal line becomes rhythmically and melodically freer and more complex toward the end of the piece.

4:35   The instruments neatly close the piece by referring back to the beginning.

By the 1980s and 1990s, as a younger generation of Puerto Ricans born in New York turned away from traditional salsa toward rhythm and blues and hip-hop, the sounds of salsa changed, acquiring a distinct African American inflection. The match of young freestyle singers with classic salsa rhythms has proved powerful indeed, as revealed by the brisk sales of recordings by two popular young salsa artists, Marc Anthony (Marco Antonio Muñiz) and India (Lindabel Caballero).

Brazil

It seems logical to relate the relaxed, easy pace of Brazilian music to the sounds and inflections of the Portuguese language spoken in Brazil. In any case, Brazilian dances—gentler, slower, and less intense than the exciting Cuban and Puerto Rican musics—achieved their own popularity in the United States, though never to the degree of the hot Caribbean sounds.

Samba and Bossa Nova

The Afro-Brazilian **samba,** sometimes called the national dance of Brazil, arrived in New York around 1949 and quickly became popular as sung and danced by the glamorous Carmen Miranda. The word *samba* has various religious connotations, and samba has been the main dance at Rio's Carnival, wildly celebrated before Lent each year.

Bossa nova emerged in the 1960s at least in part as a reaction among the youth of Rio's middle and privileged classes against the perceived commercialism of samba. Derived from, or a variation of, samba, it was sometimes called jazz samba, since it fused elements of cool and progressive jazz with sophisticated Brazilian rhythms.

Less vibrant and more melancholy than Cuban-flavored music, the bossa nova adapted beautifully to the world of jazz, where its flexible rhythms and colorful instrumentation continue to stimulate sophisticated musicians. But much like bebop in the United States, the subtle bossa nova met initial resistance from traditionalists who did not understand its elusive flavors and new sounds. Also like bebop, it is a music primarily for listening. In fact, unlike the rumba, the samba, and other Latin musics popular north of the border, bossa nova is not a dance but a rhythm—rather, a number of subtle, flexible polyrhythms. Whereas samba featured exotic stars singing and dancing in front of a flashy band, bossa nova performers sang softly, accompanied by a single guitar or at most a four-man band. The style was intimate and very sophisticated.

The term *bossa nova* first emerged in the lyrics of a song by **Antônio Carlos Jobim** (1927–1994), a leading figure of the bossa nova movement. *Bossa* was slang for something particularly distinctive; *nova* means "new." The song that introduced the phrase was "Desafinado" (Listening Example 51), meaning "Off Key," and the lyrics say that by singing "off key" the singer was trying to attract the attention of his beloved. (Most familiar of all to a general audience in the United States was another bossa nova by Jobim, the lovely and very popular "Girl from Ipanema" (with vocalist João Gilberto).

In the early 1970s, several important groups and individuals adopted the quietly sensuous rhythms and melodies of bossa nova to flavor their own

"Desafinado" ("Off Key")

Gilberto's calm voice seems uniquely suited to present the long, sinuous, chromatic melodic line, accompanied by subtle but insistent rhythms in the drums, bass, piano, and guitar. Everything about this 1958 performance seems gentle; the softly dissonant harmonies, lightly syncopated rhythms, and even the Portuguese language all fall easily on the ear. However, Jobim deliberately conceived some harmonies to make the singer seem "off key." Thus this song that sounds so easy to sing demands performers with an extremely acute sense of pitch and rhythm.

CD 2
Track 19
4:11

Composer   Antônio Carlos Jobim (1927–1994)

Lyricist   Newton Mendonça (1927–1960).

Genre   Bossa nova.

Timbre   João Gilberto (vocalist, guitarist) and Stan Getz (jazz tenor saxophonist).

Texture   Homophonic.

Form   Strophic.

Meter   Quadruple. The syncopated melody (deemphasized by Gilberto's half-sung, half-spoken delivery) is set against competing guitar rhythms, leaving the listener uncertain where to locate the main beats.

Tempo   Slow, relaxed.

0:00   *Se você disser que eu desafino, amor . . .*
       If you say that I sing out of tune, love, . . .

0:30   *Se você insisted em classificar meu comportamento de antimusical . . .*
       If you insist in classifying my behavior as antimusical

0:56   *O que você não sabe nem sequer pressente . . .*
       What you don't know or even suspect . . .

1:23   *Só não poderá falar assim do meu amor . . .*
       Only you will not be able to speak like this of my love . . .

1:55   Stan Getz gives an instrumental version of the piece, similarly accompanied by drums, bass, piano, guitar. The muted tenor sax, like Gilberto's singing voice, has the warmth and subtlety of a sultry tropical night.

3:47   We barely hear Gilberto's soft syllables in the background, as the piece draws to a mellow close.

FIGURE 12.4
Stan Getz (1927–1991)
playing tenor sax.

distinctive music. Weather Report famously added Brazilian percussionists to the ensemble. Brazilian singer Flora Purim, who appeared equally comfortable performing both jazz and Brazilian music, sang first with Stan Getz (Figure 12.4), next with Gil Evans, and finally with avant-garde pianist Chick Corea and his group Return to Forever. Purim's husband, percussionist Airto Moreira, also joined Corea's group, enhancing their sounds with the Latin bells, rattles, and shakers he had used earlier when performing with Miles Davis. And through the 1980s, the subtlety and flexibility of bossa nova had strong appeal for Pat Metheny's jazz-rock groups, free jazz musicians, and bop.

Mexico

The southwestern states of Texas, New Mexico, Arizona, and California absorbed many sounds from nearby Mexico, where folk music and popular music strongly reflect the songs and dances of African slaves. The country music of the Southwest naturally shows the Mexican influence. Woody Guthrie, who began playing music in Texas in the late 1920s (see pp. 247–248), sometimes adapted Mexican topical ballads, or *corridos,* to his own inimitable style; and the Mexican *ranchera* (ranch song) "El Rancho Grande" became a standard of western swing bands. It has even been suggested that the "blue yodel" of Jimmie Rodgers and others may have been stimulated by Mexican singing styles.

Any number of dances also traveled back and forth between Spain and Mexico, acquiring changes in name, instrumentation, and performance style as they continued to develop. *El cutilio* (an Online Listening Example) is a traditional Spanish social dance, or *baile,* that was popular in the Southwest before and after the Civil War and remains so in that region today. Unlike the religious *alabados,* rarely heard today, *bailes* continue to delight people of every age and social situation. Performed now as then to celebrate engagements, weddings, birthdays, and other joyful events, these rollicking dance tunes lighten the hearts of those who hear them—although few remember how to dance the intricate steps popular more than a hundred years ago.

Tejano and Norteño Music

In the mid-nineteenth century, Europeans from Germany, Poland, and what is now the Czech Republic migrated in large numbers to Texas and northern Mexico, affecting the language, literature, art, and cuisine as well as the music of those regions. Among the effects their strong influence brought about were the addition of the accordion to popular bands and the oom-pah-pah beat of polkas to Spanish songs and dances. The distinctive music tradition that evolved from this blend of styles is known as **norteño** in northern Mexico and **tejano** in south Texas.

By the 1950s, tejanos were singing in Tex-Mex rather than traditional Spanish; during the 1960s and 1970s an orchestral sound infiltrated many tejano bands; and by the 1980s keyboards were included as well. The murder in 1995 of a shining young star, **Selena Quintanilla-Pérez** (1971–1995), brought tejano music to national attention, and the sound has become more familiar and more popular as it continues to evolve. The accordion still dominates some ensembles, but more and more tejano groups are mixing salsa, meringue, techno, and pop in their sound.

Tejanos were closely involved in the development of corridos and another accordion-based music, conjunto.

Conjunto

During the late nineteenth century, as Mexican Americans spread not only throughout the southwestern United States but also well to the north and east, they carried with them their traditional norteño music. Their **conjunto** (con-hoon´-toe) ensembles, usually including besides the accordion a guitar and sometimes a double bass and drums, played polkas, waltzes, and other European dances popular in Mexico and along both sides of the border. By the 1950s they also accompanied the singing of rancheras, corridos, and other traditional Mexican songs. During the mid-twentieth century, conjuntos (Figure 12.5) entertained in cantinas through the Southwest, sometimes adding a saxophone to further color their distinctive sound.

FIGURE 12.5

The 1950s was a peak period for Mexican American music, and among the leading norteño groups was Los Alegres de Teran.

FIGURE 12.6

Strolling mariachis entertain
passersby.

FIGURE 12.6

Strolling mariachis entertain passersby.

In recent years, some conjunto musicians have resisted the traditional polka sounds, blending other musical styles, including jazz, into their performances. Besides saxophones, some have added keyboards and synthesizers to their ensembles, creating *conjuntos orquestales*. Through these and other effective means, such as traveling widely, teaming up with other musicians, and adding conjunto beat to other popular musics, conjunto musicians have attracted enthusiastic new audiences to their *música alegre* ("happy music").

Mariachis
By the late 1970s, folk, country, and rock rhythms and instrumentation increasingly reflected vibrant Mexican traditions, including the sounds of strolling **mariachis** (Figure 12.6). They perform an important Mexican folk music frequently heard in the southwestern United States. Originally a string ensemble, mariachis now add one to three trumpets to the violins, guitar, and perhaps *guitarron* or bass guitar (the instrumentation is quite flexible) making up the traditional ensemble. It is thought that because their joyous music was so often played at weddings, they may have derived their name from a corruption of the French word for marriage, *mariage*.

In the late nineteenth century, mariachis traveled from village to village in northwestern Mexico for saints days and fiestas, their rousing melodies and indigenous rhythms becoming a patriotic symbol of Mexican nationality. Today mariachi musicians dressed in traditional spangled outfits with butterfly-shaped ties and sombreros perform in this country at baptisms, birthday parties, and funerals, as well as the joyous weddings with which their name may be associated. ("Jarabe tapatío," [The Mexican Hat Dance] is an Online Listening Example.)

www.mhhe.com/ferrisaml6e

Latin Music Today

Once an exotic flavoring added to light classical or early popular music, Latin music has become a vital force of great complexity, variety, and significance in the music of the United States, signified by the current popularity of such stars as Gloria Estefan, Ricky Martin, Jennifer Lopez, Christina Aguilera, and Shakira.

Cuban band music, brought to popular attention through the success of the audio CD and film *Buena Vista Social Club,* can be heard performed in an up-to-date style by the big band Cubanismo, which fuses Cuban traditional music with more modern arrangements and suggestions of music from other countries. North of the Mexican border, Latin rock is making an impact reminiscent of the influence of rock and roll south of the border years ago. In fact, *rock en español* embraces everything from Mexican rappers to Argentinean melodic singer-songwriters, all making an imprint on the American market.

The band Santana having ruled the Grammy awards in 2000 (they won eight), the National Academy of Recording Arts and Sciences created a new Latin branch, which presented the first Latin Grammy Awards later that year. By 2009, the Latin Grammy Awards included the categories Best Latin Pop Album, Best Tropical Album, and Best Latin Urban Album. Significantly, the Broadway show *In the Heights,* with music full of salsa, meringue, and hip-hop, won the 2008 Tony Award for Best Musical and captured the 2009 award for Best Musical Show Album, with no qualification as being a vehicle for Latin music.

Terms to Review

tango	cu-bop	bossa nova
habanera	mambo	norteño
bomba	chachacha	tejano
rumba	salsa	conjunto
conga	samba	mariachis

Key Figures

Xavier Cugat	Antônio Carlos Jobim	Selena
Tito Puente		

Critical Thinking

Do you think the radio stations in your area give adequate air time to Latin popular music?

Of the three influential areas covered here—the Caribbean, Brazil, and Mexico—which has most affected the music with which you are most familiar?

Which do you think will be the strongest trend in the future: Latin pop influenced by music from the United States, or "Latin-tinged" U.S. popular music? Why?

PART 3
Summary

The form of John Philip Sousa's marches—a series of melodic strains—was also the form of ragtime, a written piano music combining black rhythmic effects with European harmony and form. Ragtime pianists play syncopated melodies in the right hand accompanied by a simple duple pattern in the left. By the time of World War I, rags were being widely published by Tin Pan Alley, as the popular music industry was known, and many popular Tin Pan Alley songs had the sound and spirit of ragtime. The great popular songwriters included Irving Berlin, Cole Porter, and George Gershwin, each of whom wrote for Broadway musicals as well as for Tin Pan Alley.

When black musicians combined the forms, harmonies, and timbres of white popular musics with Creole, Caribbean, and black African rhythmic and melodic techniques, they produced a hot new music for dancing and later for listening called jazz. The blues, an early manifestation of jazz, began as a black folk song style but evolved to a sophisticated and influential form of popular music. Boogie-woogie transferred the form and harmonic structure of the blues to the piano.

New Orleans nurtured the first important black combos, in which soloists improvised on a given tune while other combo members backed them up. Later, in Chicago, white Dixieland bands imitated the New Orleans sound. White as well as black teenagers and young adults danced to early jazz, but the white middle-age public preferred sweet jazz during the turbulent Depression years. Although not technically jazz at all, these genres introduced the art of the arranger and helped prepare America to swing with the big bands of the 1930s.

In the mid-1930s, jazz reached its peak of popularity, which lasted for about a decade. Big bands played arranged rather than improvised versions of blues and pop tunes, their harmonies more adventurous and their pieces more structured than in earlier jazz styles. Charlie Parker and Dizzy Gillespie led a musicians' rebellion against the commercialism and popularity of big band swing, establishing bebop, a music for listening, not dancing, which ushered in the age of modern jazz. And in the 1940s, the interest of the general audience and many serious jazz musicians turned away from big bands as singers replaced them in popularity.

Since 1950, jazz musicians have formed alliances with the world of concert music, producing symphonic works with jazzy flavors, jazz pieces in classical forms, and third stream pieces in which jazz and classical music meet, yet retain their independent qualities. Among the individuals particularly influential in concert jazz, Duke Ellington, considered one of America's greatest composers, wrote music for both the concert hall and the church; Dave Brubeck extended the rhythmic concepts of jazz pieces by using unusual meters. Progressive jazz introduced a symphonic concept, and cool jazz added a sensuous element to jazz.

Country music, rooted in rural and mountain folk traditions, became commercial when Jimmie Rodgers popularized hillbilly songs and the original Carter Family brought mountain harmony to the city. Recordings, and later radio shows, spread country music to an ever wider audience. Country musicians absorbed many influences as they moved to different states, and soon new styles evolved. Texans danced to western swing and listened to honky tonk, and the cowboy songs of western films joined the hillbilly repertoire to produce a new genre, country-western music. With the exception of bluegrass, an instrumentally dominated revival of mountain folk music, country music consists primarily of song.

Latin dances invigorated the American pop music scene beginning in the 1930s, when big bands popularized several dances from the Caribbean, Brazil, and Mexico. The tango, bomba, rumba, and other Latin dances soon became a seemingly inherent part of the North American popular experience. Brazil's samba and bossa nova offered quietly sensuous rhythms and melodies to North American groups, and Mexican mariachis became an inherent component of southwestern music.

PART 4

Vernacular Musics Since Rock and Roll

Andy Warhol's cover for the album *The Velvet Underground and Nico.*
© 2001 Andy Warhol Foundation for the Visual Arts/Artists Rights Society [ARS], New York.

With the coming of rock and roll, American popular music diversified as never before. Pop and country-western struggled to hold their own against the powerful new music; but in time various styles, including disco, new wave, gospel, rap, jazz, and innumerable regional and ethnic musics, found audiences and vied for popularity with rock and among themselves.

Vernacular Art

The 1950s spawned the *beat generation,* a term invented by Jack Kerouac and originally represented by a small group of excessively talented friends who provided some of the twentieth century's most inspired poetry and prose. Allen Ginsberg, William Burroughs, Jack Kerouac, and their like-minded friends and colleagues stood for nonconformity, a concept in vogue in Europe as well (think of England's angry young men and Jean-Paul Sartre's existentialists). James Dean in the movies and Chuck Berry and Elvis Presley on the radio gave vent to the same spirit motivating the literary beats, who also, however, tempered their expression with an Eastern (specifically Buddhist) philosophy.

The visual arts, too, found new means of expression and established new artistic ideals. The famous Pop artist Andy Warhol (1928–1987) puzzled and intrigued his contemporaries, and he continues to compel our attention today. Working with silk-screen prints made from images taken from newspaper and magazine photos, Warhol ran colors through the screen directly onto his canvas, achieving surprising—some said audacious—new color harmonies. His finest pictures are "serial" paintings, multiple repetitions of the same image on a single canvas. For subjects he chose ubiquitous objects of popular American culture: movie stars, advertising logos, political figures, and popular musicians, many of whom he counted among his personal friends. It has been said that art and music are separate mirrors that reflect some of the same things, and certainly Warhol identified closely with some vernacular musicians of his day. In 1965, the punk rock group Velvet Underground accompanied the showing of one of Warhol's artworks, and the next year he painted a banana for the cover of their first album (*The Velvet Underground and Nico,* released in 1967; see photo on p. 224).

Vernacular Music

During the twentieth century, popular or vernacular music became a significant cultural concept and an important business, as it remains today. Recent decades have produced an unprecedented variety of popular music, including grunge, hip-hop, alternative rock, women in rock, new country, teenybop, Latin pop, and rave, all of which have not replaced but rather joined rhythm and blues, classic rock, light pop, and all the other musics that belong to and express our popular culture.

The 1990s proved to be one of pop's most experimental periods, when experimentation was aided by technological advances that brought down the costs of recording, and by computerized inventories that allowed stores to carry more stock. In the early years of the twenty-first century, the downloading of music has changed the nature of the pop marketplace, challenging major labels to find new ways to make money in what may soon be the post-CD era.

And so we are in the midst of a prodigiously productive period, richer than any earlier time, and richer than any other contemporary culture, in the variety, quantity, and quality of our vernacular music. ♪

Rock and Roll

T he baby boom of World War II produced, in the 1950s, a teen boom of unprecedented numbers, wealth, and influence. Little interested in the sentimental popular music of the Depression and war years, these numerous young people craved excitement and a music expressive of their own frustrations and needs, a music to which they could dance. And for the first time in American history, the teenage population had money enough to command the attention of the popular music industry.

The Generation Gap

Several postwar conditions fostered an unprecedented sense of independence and even rebellion among American youth. Many failed to understand in such prosperous times the frugal ways of their parents, who had survived but not forgotten the Great Depression and years of wartime austerity. Military families experienced frequent relocation, particularly unsettling to children and teens. Young people in more stable conditions often had mothers working outside the home, filling jobs vacated by men still in the military, or continuing jobs to which they had become accustomed during the war or upon whose income they felt dependent. These and numerous other social and economic conditions caused a serious, unprecedented gap in communication and understanding between adolescents and their parents.

The spirit of rebellion also waxed strong among young African Americans returning from war to find the equality they had experienced on the battlefield bluntly denied them in the domestic workforce. Spurred by the injustice of social discrimination, the civil rights movement steadily gained momentum, and black power became a force to be reckoned with.

Meanwhile, popular music after World War II became increasingly diversified, generally moving away from instrumental music back to song. This young generation perceived swing bands as too polished, the performers' dress too formal, and the shows too structured to please them. The sentimental ballads of mainstream pop, suitable for the slow dances popular among young adults, could not satisfy the restless teenage audience, and the complexity of modern jazz—primarily instrumental, often dissonant, intended more for listening than for dancing—simply antagonized them. More and more young white people preferred the vital, stirring sounds of black gospel music and *rhythm and blues* to the music their parents had enjoyed.

Rhythm and Blues

For many years, the popular music recording industry, as mentioned previously, applied the term *race records* to popular musics, ranging from country and urban blues to jazz, white-style ballads, and gospel, performed by and marketed primarily for blacks. Much black popular music was based on the form and harmonic pattern of the blues; most of it was in quadruple meter, with strong backbeats on the normally weak second and fourth beats of the measure; and most of it was danceable. Religious or secular, it generally involved syncopated rhythmic improvisation, call-and-response between a leader and a group or congregation, and vocalizations utilizing African techniques—extremely high and low ranges, falsetto, numerous blue notes, and expressive vocal catches strengthening the emotional character of the music. A recently released album—*Recording Black Culture,* with field recordings of black music made by the eminent African American folklorist John Work III in the late 1930s and early 1940s—reveals that black popular musics of the time—string bands, quartets, blues, and gospel—have the timbres, the rhythms, the very essence of what became rhythm and blues and rock and roll.

Although performed in an idiom deemed unacceptable for mainstream markets, black popular music steadily developed an enthusiastic audience among young white listeners. Finally, in 1949, the industry trade journal *Billboard* abandoned the offensive term *race records,* grouping all the popular music intended for a black audience under the term **rhythm and blues (R&B),** and for several years that was the phrase generally applied to black popular music.

Rhythm and blues ensembles, whether swing-style bands or small combos, were loud, usually featuring an electric guitar and sometimes other electrified instruments as well. The music had a strong vocal orientation, with at least one singer and often an all-male vocal group involved, the need for singers to shout or scream to be heard above the instrumentalists contributing to the emotional intensity of the music. The lyrics of most R&B songs—though frankly, unself-consciously, and even blatantly sexual—remained primarily good-natured. **Joe Turner** ("boss of the blues," 1911–1985) and **Willie Mae "Big Mama" Thornton** (1926–1984) were among the best-known and most admired R&B performers.

Although white listeners readily accepted the soothing music of certain black male ensembles, they did not yet accept black music per se: The performances of such **doo-wop** ensembles as the Mills Brothers and the Ink Spots, featuring high falsetto voices, smooth harmonies, and subtle rhythmic backgrounds sung to nonsense syllables, were relatively white in style. The Platters' doo-wop recordings "Only You" and "My Prayer" are other well-known examples of early doo-wop music. The black soloists Lena Horne, Nat "King" Cole, and Ella Fitzgerald also had hits on the pop charts in the late 1940s and early 1950s, but most of their repertoire was from Tin Pan Alley, and their performances, too, generally conformed to white practice. (All of the groups and individuals mentioned here can—and should—be heard on YouTube.) But black listeners tended to prefer rhythm and blues, and by 1950, increasing numbers of young whites did, too.

Finally, the unexpected but quite congenial blending of rhythm and blues with another non-mainstream music—country-western—invigorated and in fact revolutionized American popular music.

Country Music Meets R&B
Black rhythm and blues and white country-western shared a number of important characteristics. Both lay outside the popular mainstream; both were rooted in the South; both were danceable; both consistently involved the guitar (acoustic, electric, or amplified); both featured frank lyrics and earthy delivery styles; and both were sung in dialects different from that of the standard white urban population.

Thus it is not surprising, given the restless climate of young listeners hungry for something hot and new, that in the early 1950s these two dissident styles met and fused to produce the most widely and most wildly hailed popular music the world had known: rock and roll.

Birth of Rock and Roll

Convinced that white listeners would reject the raucous sound, producers and directors generally refused to program rhythm-and-blues hits on mainstream radio. But a disc jockey in Cleveland, Ohio, named **Alan Freed** soon realized that many white teens preferred R&B hits to mainstream popular music, and beginning in 1951 he played increasing numbers of rhythm-and-blues records on his radio programs, which reached a broad general audience. Freed also promoted live stage performances of music in R&B style, with both blacks and whites present on the stage and in the audience.

Then two young white country singers with black delivery styles entered and forever altered the popular music picture. The terms *rock* and *roll* had long been familiar, and sexually suggestive, in black popular music; but Alan Freed is credited with coining the term **rock and roll** for the new style with which Bill Haley and Elvis Presley revolutionized the popular music world.

Bill Haley (1925–1981)
When **Bill Haley and His Comets,** initially a country-western group, began to combine white western swing with elements of black rhythm and blues, they seemed temporarily displaced musicians—at home in neither popular music camp. They did not know it then, but they were playing a brand-new music—rock and roll, soon to replace all others in popularity. In 1954, their cover recording of Joe Turner's R&B hit "Shake, Rattle, and Roll"—widely played by radio stations that would not have touched the R&B version—quickly soared to the top of the popular music charts. And the next year, the Comets' recording of "Rock Around the Clock," used as the theme for the movie *Blackboard Jungle,* became the first international rock-and-roll hit.

FIGURE 13.1
Elvis Presley (1935–1977).

Elvis Presley (1935–1977)

Elvis Presley (Figure 13.1), another country boy, followed much the same course from country to rock and roll, but the astonishing degree of popularity he achieved was unprecedented then and, for a solo singer, remains unsurpassed. Through a combination of talent, persistence, and luck, Presley achieved a recording contract and soared to the top of his profession with dizzying speed.

Presley's early **rockabilly** or country rock records actually found more favor with blacks than whites, but his appeal soon became interracial and international. The term *rockabilly,* suggesting a hybrid of rock and hillbilly, was first printed in a trade journal in 1956, the year that Presley made a cover recording of "Hound Dog," recorded earlier by Big Mama Thornton. Whereas her record was not played on any but "race" radio stations, Presley's was widely heard and soon reached the top of first the black and then the white pop charts.

Elvis, almost entirely self-taught, played little more than simple chords on his guitar; but he had a beautiful and amazingly versatile voice to which he added warmth and intensity by the use of vibrato. Another early recording, "Heartbreak Hotel" (also 1956), proved the range of his expressive gifts, from wild and raucous to wrenchingly warm and tender.

Early Characteristics

African Americans migrating north to Chicago after World War II found a wealth of music happening there as jazz musicians, country and urban blues musicians, boogie-woogie pianists, and others played for self-entertainment, for commercial clubs, and for the recording studios. Some of the new arrivals began to develop their own distinctive kinds of rock and roll, more closely related to rhythm and blues than was Presley's, which was rooted in country-western music. Their accompanying instruments included one or more amplified guitars, a saxophone, and sometimes a trumpet, over which a singer screamed or shouted. The meter was quadruple, with

FIGURE 13.2

Chuck Berry (b. 1926).

strong backbeats, and the tempo danceable. Bo Diddley (Otha Ellas Bates, later known as Ellas McDaniel, whose nickname is assigned various and conflicting origins though it probably comes from the single-string instrument called a diddley bow) played his electric guitar with terrific rhythmic vitality, achieving an extreme range of sounds in an age before technology made such effects commonplace. Little Richard (Richard Penniman) thumped his piano and screamed his lyrics, sacred or profane, with equal fervor.

Chuck Berry (b. 1926, Figure 13.2), among the most talented early black stars of rock and roll, fused with rhythm and blues more country-western elements than had other outstanding black musicians of the mid-1950s. A great guitarist and a talented songwriter who wrote most of the material he performed, Berry was also an effective singer, shouting protest and rebellion in a high, clear tenor voice over his highly amplified guitar. Berry became as famous for his "duckwalk" across the stage—knees bent, head thrusting forward and back as he played his guitar—as Elvis was for his pelvic gyrations; but more significantly, Berry's music strongly influenced both the Beatles and the Rolling Stones, who later sang his songs and imitated his distinctive style. Berry's many hit recordings included "School Days" (1957, Listening Example 52).

End of the First Era

The end of the 1950s proved a dark time generally for the promising new music, rock and roll: Elvis Presley had been drafted into the army; Little Richard walked away from rock and roll (temporarily, for religious reasons, returning after several years to resume his highly successful career); Buddy Holly died in a plane crash. Scandal plagued several stars, notably Jerry Lee Lewis, who had married his very young third cousin; and Chuck Berry, who had been arrested for taking a minor across state lines.

"School Days"

"School Days" from 1957 offers a slice of American teenage life in the 1950s, depicting the regimented school experience, the grateful escape to the local juke joint, and the joyful release of hearing rock music. It is an infectious homage to rock as a liberating force and a passionate expression of youthful energy and spirit. Throughout the song, the uneven subdivisions of the strongly accented beats, lending the rhythm a "shuffle" effect, nearly compel a physical or, at least, an emotional response from the listener.

CD 2
Track 20
2:34

Composer   Chuck Berry (b. 1926).

Genre   Rock and roll.

Timbre   Male vocal solo (Chuck Berry), accompanying himself on guitar, with piano and drums.

Texture   Homophonic. Listen for call-and-response between Berry and his guitar.

Form   Strophic.

Meter   Quadruple. Throughout the song, the uneven subdivisions of the strongly accented beats that lend the rhythm a "shuffle" effect. There is a gentle backbeat.

Tempo   Brisk, as suits the light mood and the high energy level.

Text   The fast-paced lyrics describe the routine of a 1950s high school student; they describe a student's school day of torments, starting with class and classmates, then little time for lunch, and a mean-looking teacher, with a far more meaningful afternoon—listening with his girlfriend to the latest hits on a jukebox. The lyrics are available on the Internet.

0:00   Verse 1: The first verse rouses the student from bed to face another hectic day at school. Berry's guitar chord jars like an alarm clock, and his first word swoops upward, mimicking the text. The guitar responds to the voice, often imitating the melodic phrase.

0:23   Verse 2: The second verse is rushed, as befits the poor boy's chaotic day.

0:45   Verse 3: Finally—release!

1:06   Verse 4: The joy of listening and dancing to rock and roll!

1:30   Berry's instrumental break dramatizes the scene he's just described, nearly compelling the listener to get up and dance.

2:08   Verse 5: Celebration of the liberating power of rock music.

White performers, seeing their profits slip away to the R&B market, began to make tame, toned-down cover versions of R&B songs, with sexual references less blatant and rhythms less hot; and radio stations that had never programmed "black music" willingly played the "whitened" cover recordings, which they considered more suitable for the general audience. The popular television program *American Bandstand,* hosted by Dick Clark, featured white teen idols such as Paul Anka, Bobby Darin, Fabian, and Frankie Avalon singing respectable, urban versions of rhythm-and-blues hits.

The **payola** investigations of 1959 to 1960, which revealed that disc jockeys were routinely accepting money and gifts for playing (plugging) certain records, tarnished even the popular Dick Clark and virtually destroyed Alan Freed: Convicted of "commercial bribery," Freed received a fine and a suspended sentence; was blackballed by the music industry; and died, penniless, of the effects of alcoholism, at age forty-three.

As rock and roll lost its hard edge and energy, pop became more bland than ever, sending the 1960s off to a slow, unpromising start.

Surfing Music

Social unrest and violence reached unprecedented heights during the early 1960s, as the civil rights movement made dramatic breakthroughs, often at tragic cost, and President Kennedy spoke movingly of a new frontier, challenging young people to make heroic sacrifices in order to realize high ideals. But to warm, relaxed, materialistic youths living in sunny southern California, Kennedy's challenge sounded remote and unreal. Their ideal existence consisted of sun, fun, and—essentially—the beach. And **surfing songs** describing the relaxed California life also provided vicarious pleasure to young whites living in less idyllic parts of the troubled country.

The Beach Boys, formed in the early 1960s by **Brian Wilson** (b. 1942), included two of his brothers, a cousin, and a friend. Wilson, who led the group and wrote some of the songs, had a pleasant falsetto voice, and the Beach Boys sang their simple songs with smooth and soothing harmony.

But soon the Beach Boys evolved into sophisticated concert and studio musicians, effectively articulating such teen concerns as school spirit and fast cars besides the (supposedly) comfortable California surfing life. Temporarily sidelined by a nervous breakdown, Brian Wilson poured his talent into songwriting to produce, in 1966, *Pet Sounds,* which became an influential theme album in a market whose albums primarily had consisted of single, unrelated songs. Later the same year, the Beach Boys released their best-selling single, "Good Vibrations," accompanied by such nontraditional rock music sounds as sleigh bells and the electronic *theremin* (see p. 330).

After 1966, the Beach Boys changed both their leader and their image, growing long hair and beards and adding sophisticated electronic effects to their music, now darkened by protest songs. In the 1980s, the Beach Boys enjoyed something of a comeback, but in 1983 Dennis Wilson drowned, and the later Beach Boys' albums made limited impact on the volatile rock market.

Their lasting fame and influence seemed fated to reside in their songs of sun, sand, and surf. Yet in 2004, the man who on *Pet Sounds* poignantly sang "I just wasn't made for these times" achieved a triumphant return with the release of *Smile,* an album left unfinished in 1967. Long known as "the greatest album that never was," it has brought Brian Wilson acclaim as one of America's finest songwriters.

Motown

Surfing music meant little to young African Americans facing challenges of a more serious kind. Angered to see white performers reaping huge profits from covers of black hits and from bland surfing songs, some black musicians set out to earn a higher share of the wealth. Most notably, in 1959, a young black songwriter named **Berry Gordy, Jr.** (b. 1929), formed a company called **Motown** for the purpose of marketing black rock and roll as aggressively and as lucratively as the products of white musicians.

Motown brought together an amazing group of songwriters, singers, producers, and instrumentalists in the "motor town," Detroit, which became to rock and roll what Nashville was to country. Under Gordy's guidance, the new company turned out hit records as efficiently as assembly lines turned out cars, each one technically perfect, efficiently marketed, and of broad crossover appeal. Gordy custom-designed his singers, carefully supervising their repertoire and requiring them to take classes in diction, grooming, stage presence, and choreography. Thus the Motown sound was lighter, smoother, and less sexy than other, blacker, rock and roll. Motown groups like the Supremes, the Temptations, and the Miracles drew on rhythm and blues and gospel, but they also drew on the pop conventions of Tin Pan Alley, designed to appeal to young whites as well as (or more than) blacks in order to draw a mass audience. There was usually a lead singer and a background vocal doo-wop group, who enriched the sonority by singing nonsense syllables in pleasant harmony. Whereas early Motown records used very simple instrumentation, strings and other orchestral instruments accompanied later performances.

The outstanding Motown group, the female trio the Supremes (Figure 13.3), with their famous lead singer Diana Ross perform "Stop! In the Name of Love" (Listening Example 53). Well-known male vocal groups sponsored by Motown included the Four Tops and the Temptations. Michael Jackson (who died tragically in 2009) was only five years old when Motown discovered him and his brothers, a family group—the Jacksons—perfectly illustrating both the virtues and the liabilities of Motown, for the conformity and uniformity Gordy demanded left his stars little room for individual development. Stevie Wonder, who also recorded for Motown, became the first member of the group to achieve artistic independence and gain control over his own recordings.

An outstanding business man, Gordy intentionally softened gospel shouts and R&B tones, seeking financial success by making Motown recordings appealing to white listeners. In fact, although Motown made a lot of money

FIGURE 13.3
The Supremes. Left to right: Mary Wilson, Diana Ross, Florence Ballard.

Listening Example 53

"Stop! In the Name of Love"

This 1965 song is said to have had its origin in a real-life dispute between Lamont Dozier and his girlfriend, who was about to leave him when he called out to her—the title of the song. (She returned.)

CD 2
Track 21
2:52

Composers Brian Holland, Lamont Dozier, and Eddie Holland (Motown's premier songwriter/production team, known as H-D-H).

Genre Motown recording.

Timbre The Supremes (female vocal trio), accompanied by the Funk Brothers backup band: keyboard, guitar, bass, drums.

Texture Homophonic.

Form Modified verse-chorus. The chorus, or refrain, serves as the "hook," a catchy four-measure phrase that begins the song and recurs after each sixteen-measure (four-line) verse.

Meter Quadruple. Notice the constant steady pulse, with accents applied about equally between downbeat and backbeat throughout the

—Continued

"Stop! In the Name of Love"

song, with no hint of the sophisticated cross-rhythms and polyrhythms of African music.

Tempo Moderate

0:00 Refrain: Sung by the Supremes (four measures). Using a portion of the refrain as introduction was characteristic of the Motown sound.

Stop! in the name of love
Before you break my heart . . .

0:10 Instrumental phrase: Four measures.

0:20 Verse 1: Sung by Diana Ross (sixteen measures). We hear the Supremes in the background, and toward the end of the verse they sing a brief phrase ("Think it o-o-ver") that serves as a further unifying factor—besides the refrain—throughout the song.

Baby, baby,
I'm aware of where you go. . . .

0:52 Refrain: The Supremes sing it twice, adding the motto "Think it o-o-ver," also twice.

1:17 Verse 2: Diana Ross, with the Supremes in the background. As Ross sings the fourth line of the verse, the Supremes join her, repeating "Think it o-o-ver."

I've known of your
Your secluded nights. . . .

1:51 Refrain: As before.

2:16 Verse 3: Diana Ross sings just two lines of the verse, and all bring the song to an end with repetitions of the refrain and the unifying motto.

I've tried so hard, hard to be patient,
Hoping you'd stop this infatuation. . . .

for black singers (despite often taking unfair advantage of them), the music they produced was actually more popular with white than with black listeners, and by the mid-1960s, black musicians were effectively asserting themselves with their own new music, *soul.* (Motown was sold to Boston Ventures in 1988.)

First, however, an invasion from abroad revitalized the fading American rock and roll.

The British Invasion

The remarkable group that came to be known as the **Beatles** (in punning reference to Buddy Holly's Crickets, whom they greatly admired, and "beat" music) began as a Liverpool gang more interested in finding trouble than in changing the course of rock and roll. John Lennon formed the group, which included Paul McCartney and soon George Harrison.

In 1962, having replaced their early drummer Pete Best with the already popular Ringo Starr, the Beatles shared a London performance with Little Richard, recently returned to rock and roll, and became an overnight sensation. They attracted a producer, quickly became famous in England, and very soon were rocking the musical world with their own brand of rock and roll.

Back to Black Rock

The relationship between black and white rock and roll has been and remains curious and complex. With roots in both cultures, rock was primarily a black concept; yet white country singers who sounded black made the style popular, and the Beatles gave it the shot of energy that rescued it from early death. American blacks, however, soon sought to regain the initiative they had temporarily lost to English groups and soloists.

Gospel Gospel music, also called *religious blues,* descends from the religious spirituals developed by the slave culture, celebrated later in camp meetings, and later yet in concert environments. The music evolved in northern urban African American churches, where poor blacks, having migrated from the South after the Civil War, developed a new kind of religious song and a way of singing. *Gospel* actually refers to a family of religious musics, white and black, including the white spirituals discussed in Chapter 5 and the white spiritual songs heard on early country music radio programs; however, only black gospel music has profoundly affected popular music, becoming in effect a branch of rhythm and blues and contributing vitally to both jazz and rock.

The line between sacred and secular is often thin, and gospel generally refuses to draw that line, simply combining religious expression with techniques generally associated with secular music. **Thomas A. Dorsey** (1899–1993), generally considered the father of gospel music, was moved by personal tragedy (the death of his wife and infant son in childbirth) to turn from his career as a blues pianist and composer to writing gospel blues. More personal, sentimental, and emotional than spirituals, gospel songs compel participation. By the mid-twentieth century, performers were punctuating their singing with slides, growls, dips, shouts, blue notes, and falsetto, heightening individual expression and raising the emotional level to extremes. **Sister Rosetta Tharpe** (1915–1973) gives a joyful performance of "Down by the Riverside" (Listening Example 54), exemplifying the infectious appeal of black gospel music.

Whereas Dorsey's music and the performances of numerous early male gospel quartets could be described as *blues-flavored gospel,* in 1955

Listening Example 54

"Down by the Riverside"

"Down by the Riverside" is a traditional spiritual or gospel song (the terms sometimes are interchangeable), but the manner in which Sister Rosetta Tharpe performed it and other well-known gospel songs had more influence on rock and roll and on rhythm and blues than on church music. She was as famous for her feisty R&B guitar playing as for her gospel singing, and her upbeat music and charismatic performance style earned her an important place in rock history.

CD 2
Track 22
2:29

Composer   Anonymous.

Genre   Gospel song, spiritual.

Timbre   Solo voice and guitar (both Tharpe), male chorus, piano, bass.

Texture   Homophonic.

Form   Verse-chorus.

Meter   Quadruple.

0:00   The chorus hums a chord and accompanies and responds to Sister Tharpe as she sings the introduction to the song, as the instrumental ensemble play lightly in the background.
       I feel so bad in the morning. . . .

0:23   Verse 1: Solo, choir.
       I'm going to lay down my heavy load . . .

0:44   As the trio sings the chorus, Sister Tharpe interjects phrases from the text and strums her guitar.
       I ain't gonna study war no more . . .

1:05   Verse 2: Solo accompanied by choir and instruments.

1:26   Chorus: Tharpe, choir, instruments.

1:45   Jazzy, "honky-tonk" instrumental (guitar, piano, bass) verse.

2:05   Chorus: Solo and trio, accompanied by instruments.

Ray Charles (1930–2004) added highly secular lyrics to an old spiritual, producing a *gospel-flavored blues hit,* "I Got a Woman." (The lyrics can be found on the Internet.) Charles's fusion of gospel and blues scored high on the rhythm and blues charts, and soon some gospel male quartets (sometimes quintets or sextets) turned to the denser, more driving hard soul gospel sound.

Shouting with a raucous call-and-response fervor, they became a vital part of the American entertainment business after World War II. While some gospel singers (Mahalia Jackson, for example) continued singing religious gospel songs, others (Sam Cooke, Aretha Franklin) turned from sacred to secular music. All the elements of black gospel music—including a steady beat underlying strong rhythmic complexity, hand clapping, percussive accompaniment, call-and-response, melodic improvisation, and enthusiastic unrestrained body movements and dancing—found their way into rhythm and blues.

Today's black gospel, although derived from early traditions, sounds very little like the spirituals sung, shouted, and danced in camp meetings over a century ago. Electric bass, keyboards, and even a hip-hop flavor bring gospel to rock mainstream airwaves, to the joy of some and the dismay of traditional gospel fans, who see the trend as leaning more toward making money than saving souls. Gospel's virtuoso instrumentalists blend jazz, rock, country, funk, and hip-hop gestures; and gospel choral singing, full-throated and dramatic, is a thrilling sound. Soloists ignite audiences with the power and range of their voices and with their intricate melodic invention rivaling the improvisations of jazz. Of course the recordings have never sounded better, because of higher production standards.

Soul   By the mid-1960s, "Black Power" and "Black Is Beautiful" were potent slogans in the United States, where blacks generally had less interest in integrating with whites than in establishing their own cultural identity. Many, resentful of the basically white flavor of the Motown sound, began to perform a kind of updated rhythm and blues, which they named **soul,** a post-1950s term for black pride and the term with which the music trade magazine *Billboard,* in 1964, replaced rhythm and blues.

At first, soul evolved as a new blues, sung by small vocal groups with harsh voices and a rough delivery style, accompanied by small combos, usually including a saxophone. The added intensity of conviction, passion, and sincerity characteristic of the new black music, blending secular lyrics and gospel energy, remained inherent even in the broader stream of music to which the term *soul* came to be applied.

American blues, gospel, soul, pop, and jazz singer **Aretha Franklin** (b. 1942, Figure 13.4), known as "Lady Soul" and the "Queen of Soul, " began her music experience singing in church and, like many soul singers, transferred the emotional gospel style to popular and rhythm-and-blues songs. Having achieved the status of a living legend, Franklin performed for President Bill Clinton in 1993 and moved the crowd with her inspiring rendition of "America" ("My country, 'tis of thee") at Barack Obama's presidential inauguration in 2009.

The "father of soul," Ray Charles (Ray Charles Robinson, 1930–2004), received excellent music training in his teens, though blind from glaucoma from the age of seven. A fine pianist and singer, who also played the saxophone, Charles was among the first blacks to become technically expert with studio recording technology, thereby enhancing the quality of recordings by himself and other blacks. He also had a great gift for involving an audience in his performances, singing secular songs with the abandon of gospel music and using call-and-response to capture

FIGURE 13.4
American blues, gospel, soul, pop, and jazz singer Aretha Franklin (b. 1942).

listeners' attention and participation. A knowledgeable and complex musician who continued to work year-round until shortly before his death, Charles blended the improvisation of jazz, the beat of rhythm and blues, and the emotional fervor of gospel in his own infectious, inimitable style.

In 1965, **James Brown** (1933–2006), the "godfather of soul," also known as "Mr. Dynamite," recorded "Papa's Got a Brand New Bag" (Listening Example 55), pointing soul in a fiery new direction. Like Ray Charles, James Brown became a good businessman, who financed his own highly successful album *Live at the Apollo* (1963) when his record company failed to back him.

Listening Example 55

"Papa's Got a Brand New Bag"

In this 1965 recording, Brown emphasizes African-influenced polyrhythms more than melody, moving soul in the direction of funk. The song has been interpreted in several ways, aside from an expression of joy in a new girlfriend: as homage to an older man unafraid to try some new steps on the dance floor; as celebration of Brown's recent legal victory releasing him from

CD 2
Track 23
2:06

—Continued

"Papa's Got a Brand New Bag"

a burdensome contract; or perhaps as an announcement that Brown is abandoning R&B and inaugurating the era of funk. Brown was a subtle artist and may have intended all or none of these interpretations.

Composer and Lyricist   James Brown (1933–2006).

Genre   Soul/funk.

Timbre   Vocalist James Brown accompanied by bass, horns, drums, and guitar.

Texture   Homophonic.

Form   Twelve-bar blues, adapted with the independence of funk. After a brief instrumental introduction, Brown sings six verses, praising "Papa's brand new 'bag'" and the way she dances. Brown generally conforms to the form and harmonic changes of twelve-bar blues; however, the second line of text in each verse is original, rather than a repeat of the first line as in classic blues. Notice, too, that the third verse consists of only eight bars instead of twelve. Further, we do not hear the competition or interaction between voice and instruments typical of classic blues performances.

Meter   Quadruple. The accompanying instruments play overlapping, independent rhythmic patterns (*polyrhythms*), punctuating the vocal line and adding rhythmic as well as timbral interest.

0:00	Verse 1 (12 bars):	An instrumental announcement begins each verse.
		Come here, sister. Papa's in the swing. . . .
0:24	Verse 2 (12 bars).	*Come here, mama, and dig this crazy scene. . . .*
0:48	Verse 3 (8 bars).	*He's doin' the Jerk. He's doin' the Fly. . . .*
1:02	Verse 4 (12 bars).	*Come here, sister. Papa's in the swing. . . .*
1:24	Verse 5 (12 bars).	*Oh papa! He's doin' the Jerk. Papa, he's doing the Jerk. . . .*
1:46	Verse 6 (tapers off).	*Hey, come on. Hey! Hey! Come on. . . .*

Brown, however, never enjoyed the commercial success Charles achieved. The African roots of soul are apparent in his harsh, intensely emotional singing, and by the 1970s, he had redefined soul and gospel into a new style, *funk.*

FIGURE 13.5
American rock, soul, and funk group Sly and the Family Stone.

Funk **Funk** began as a new expression of black consciousness, rooted in soul, often with lyrics referring specifically to interracial issues. (The word *funk,* from African American slang, suggests raw, sweaty, earthy, back-to-roots.) When a number of white musicians responded to the lure of funk by copying it, funk formed in a sense a bridge between sympathetic whites and blacks.

Although related to the blues in mood and instrumentation, funk follows no prescribed harmonic pattern as guitars, keyboards, or both fill in simple, repetitive harmonies above a strong bass-guitar line. Rhythms, dense and often highly complex, are punctuated by an intriguing variety of drums. All four beats to a measure may be accented evenly, in striking difference from the strong backbeats characteristic of much rock music.

The recording of "Thank You (Falettinme Be Mice Elf Agin, 1970)" by Sly Stone (Figure 13.5) introduced the bizarre spellings imitated by some later funk musicians. George Clinton, leader of the group called Funkadelic, is considered a rigorously pure funk musician, but many other groups participate in funk with less consistency and dedication. Thus Earth, Wind, and Fire is considered a jazz-funk group, whereas the Commodores are a smooth funk band with crossover appeal to the disco audience (see pp. 273–274). The funk music of Kool and the Gang includes their recording "Funky Stuff" (1970) and, from later in the 1970s, "Celebration."

From Rock and Roll to Rock

Thanks to the wonderful new world of YouTube, nearly every group and individual performer mentioned in this chapter can be not only heard, but *seen* performing today. You can compare R&B recordings by Big Mama Thornton and Joe Turner with the cover recordings by Elvis Presley and Bill Haley and His Comets. You can rock with Chuck Berry, wax nostalgic with the Ink Spots, relax with the Supremes, and experience the emotional intensity aroused by the great soul musicians.

But the heady early days of rock and roll were brought to a close by a series of ominous, often tragic, social events. Riots in the ghettos of Harlem and Watts in 1965, further race riots in 1967, and the murder of Martin Luther King, Jr., in 1968, again changed the mood and the music of youth. As students held sit-ins at colleges across the land protesting against discrimination, authoritarianism, and eventually the war in Vietnam, popular music closely reflected the new mood. The vivid new music replacing the carefree early rock and roll was collectively called **rock,** of which many and diverse branches or brands evolved.

Psychedelic Rock

Psychedelic rock began, in San Francisco, about 1965 as an attempt to reproduce the sensations experienced by someone under the influence of LSD ("acid" in street slang). Because the music was to be felt as well as heard, the sound was amplified to unprecedented levels, the extremely—even excruciatingly—loud volume and heavy distortion of sounds causing emotional, psychological, indeed psychedelic effects in the listener. Improved amplification systems and other technical advances made stadiums and large arenas the ideal venue for huge concerts, perfectly suited to the psychedelic rock experience. During performances, which often were extremely long (time being meaningless to someone in a psychedelic trance), dramatic light shows, emissions from smoke and fog machines, and other special effects produced their own psychedelic aura, rendering such concerts theatrical events in which music constituted only one of the entertainment elements, and in which the audience was expected to be totally involved. References to drugs, sometimes expressed in code to avoid censorship, became more and more overt: "White Rabbit," performed by Jefferson Airplane, never pretended to be about anything else.

Psychedelic Blues

Two blazingly gifted stars—one a singer, one a guitarist—changed the concept of musical sound and experience in their astonishing performances of psychedelic blues. When Janis Joplin passionately sang of her sad and hopeless life, or Jimi Hendrix set fire to his guitars onstage, the audience literally felt the performers' pain.

Janis Joplin (1943–1970, Figure 13.6), a white woman inspired by Bessie Smith and Willie Mae "Big Mama" Thornton, imbued every song she sang with the passion and sincerity of the blues. With a voice sometimes described as coarse sandpaper, Joplin became the most powerful female performer of the rock era, expressing with eloquence, but never overcoming, the agony of her sad and hopeless life.

An impoverished half African American, half Native American left-handed guitarist from Seattle, **Jimi Hendrix** (1942–1970, Figure 13.7) captured the spirit of despair and frustration of American (and British) youth in the late 1960s with his scorching electric guitar. Indulging freely in the drugs he believed enhanced his passion and performance skills, he delivered all the anger and violence of the era in his thunderous electric blues, famously dousing his guitar with lighter fluid and setting it on fire at the Monterey Pop Festival in 1967.

FIGURE 13.6

Janis Joplin (1943–1970).
Psychedelic rock was a
means of expressing frustration
with the values of an older
generation.

FIGURE 13.7

The American musician Jimi
Hendrix (1942–1970).

Gifted beyond verbal description, Hendrix used his enormous talent to
develop guitar techniques beyond the imagination, and the ability, of fellow
guitarists. Although solidly rooted in the blues, which Hendrix played to
masterful effect, his music forged a new world of previously unheard sounds.
To the extreme electronic feedback and distortion being used by other

like-minded guitarists, Hendrix added his own distinctive vocabulary of riffs, bent notes, scales, and electronic effects, making his music truly personal and in fact inimitable.

Heavy Metal The late 1960s produced several American groups inspired by the wild, frenzied performances and distorted guitar sounds of the British Led Zeppelin (which developed a huge and nearly fanatical following in the United States) and by the explosive innovations of Jimi Hendrix, whose style became identified as **heavy metal.** The new sound, extremely loud and often electronically distorted, achieved American identity through Blue Cheer, formed in 1966, and Iron Butterfly, whose recording of "In-A-Gadda-Da-Vida" ("In a Garden of Eden"?) added distorted guitar to the sound of an electric organ. Early metal, with ensembles consisting of drums, bass, and one or two guitars, catered to young, white, working-class, often alienated males seeking realization of their fantasies of power and aggression. Economic crises, political corruption, the scaling back of social services, and perceptions of changing gender roles and family structure all fed the aggressive new music. In time the style matured and to some degree diversified; but the essence of early metal was male and powerful.

Alice Cooper, as both the musician Vincent Furnier (b. 1948) and his band were known, delivered overtly sexual heavy-metal rock theatrics. Their sensational tactics (Furnier often donned a boa snake) won further acclaim in the early 1970s, when theatricality dominated rock performances.

A Future Unassured

Toward the end of its second decade, rock was being celebrated at major rock festivals across the country, the most notable of which, held at Woodstock, New York, in August of 1969, was attended by more than 400,000 people. But some festivals spawned violence and tragedy: Four people died at Altamount Speedway near San Francisco, and three were killed at the "Celebration of Life" on the banks of Louisiana's Atchafalaya River. Rockers hardly seemed to know how to celebrate their hard-won recognition; and although rock music had grown strong and varied, its future seemed insecure as the 1970s began.

Terms to Review

rhythm and blues (R&B)	payola	funk
doo-wop	surfing songs	rock
rock and roll	Motown	psychedelic rock
rockabilly	soul	heavy metal

Key Figures

Joe Turner

Willie Mae "Big Mama"
    Thornton

Alan Freed

Bill Haley and His Comets

Elvis Presley

Chuck Berry

Brian Wilson

Berry Gordy, Jr.

The Beatles

Thomas A. Dorsey

Sister Rosetta Tharpe

Ray Charles

Aretha Franklin

James Brown

Janis Joplin

Jimi Hendrix

Alice Cooper

Critical Thinking

What is your view of cover recordings of rhythm-and-blues hits (such as "Tutti Frutti") by white singers (such as Pat Boone)? Why were the covers successful? How did their success affect black performers? How did the quality, and the style, of the white performances compare with the R&B recordings? Do you see moral implications of this practice? Business implications?

How does the popular music market today compare with the youthful market of the 1950s? Do young people have the same impact—or more, or less? How do those who were teenagers in the 1950s affect the popular music market today?

In what ways do you think Motown served black musicians? In what ways might Motown have damaged them?

Rock Flirts with Country

fter World War II, teenagers, white and black alike, preferred to invest their spending money in the new black-inspired music, rhythm and blues. As rock and roll increasingly dominated the popular music market, the audience for traditional country music fell away: Record sales decreased and radio listeners vanished.

Flirtation between the two genres, however, soon began to attract favorable attention. Rockabilly, the style in which the exciting new singing sensation Elvis Presley performed, responded to the new threat by combining country themes with the rhythms and instrumentation of rock and roll. **Johnny Cash** (1932–2003) was never part of the country music establishment, though his best-known songs, including "I Walk the Line" and "The Green, Green Grass of Home," always sounded like country music. Cash (who sings "The Ballad of Casey Jones," Listening Example 46) jammed with rockers Elvis Presley, Jerry Lee Lewis, and Carl Perkins in the mid-1950s, and the strong rhythm and lively instrumentation of solo recordings by Cash attracted members of the rock and roll audience. With strong ties to rockabilly, he recorded his own versions of songs made famous by rap and heavy metal artists; and in 1992 he was inducted into the Rock and Roll Hall of Fame.

Tennessee Ernie Ford's 1955 recording of "Sixteen Tons," written by the brilliant country guitarist Merle Travis, soared rapidly to the top of the best-selling charts, and a decade later the Beatles recorded country singer Buck Owens's "Act Naturally" as the B side of their single "Yesterday." Soon other country artists felt compelled to modify their styles by adopting techniques of rock and roll. Some Nashville soloists substituted a "hot" guitar for their banjos and mandolins, and their instruments now included electric guitars, drums, and electric bass as well.

Johnny Cash, the "man in black," who said in a song of that name in 1971 that he wore black to remind himself and his audiences of society's injustices, can be seen as country music's first *protest singer*. Devoutly religious and strongly allied with many social movements and causes, Cash related in his deep, virile, bass tones grievous injustices against prisoners, Native Americans, and innocents caught up in war.

Urban Folk Music

At the same time that bluegrass musicians sought to perpetuate traditional country music values, **urban folk** musicians were performing folklike music in a polished, suave manner designed to appeal to fans of popular music. Some set new words to traditional tunes; others composed new songs in the folk or country style. Increasingly, singers used folk music as a forum for social protest and for the expression of their political beliefs.

These urban folk enthusiasts drew inspiration from an earlier generation of radical professional musicians, who viewed the folk song as a valuable means to achieve their social goals. During the early years of the Great Depression, which began in 1929, actors, writers, and musicians sought to create a proletarian society, in which workers would organize—often as members of the Communist Party—to improve their economic and social condition. Three composers mentioned elsewhere in this text—Charles Seeger, Marc Blitzstein, and Henry Cowell—were among those who aimed to create a new music for the masses, generally viewing the folk song as a valuable means to this end.

One of many songwriters provoked by the Great Depression to write movingly of injustice and inequality in American society, the singing hobo **Woody Guthrie** (1912–1967) became a folk hero to his own and later generations.

Woody Guthrie (1912–1967) The singer-songwriter Woodrow Wilson "Woody" Guthrie (Figure 14.1) evolved from a simple hillbilly singer into a sophisticated composer and performer of protest songs while surviving the Great Depression as a hobo riding the rails or thumbing rides on the highways of America. Having seen his own family devastated by forces beyond their control (dust storms, fire, bank failures, illness), Guthrie determined that only by banding together—in trade unions and otherwise—could common people survive. He expressed this belief poignantly in his songs, many set to traditional folk and religious tunes.

In the winter of 1940, while barely recovering from the trauma of the Great Depression and witnessing the suffering of others, Guthrie came to despise Irving Berlin's stirring patriotic ballad "God Bless America" (p. 142). Guthrie protested against what he considered the cloying sentiment and overblown sophistication of Berlin's song by composing the ballad we know as "This Land Is Your Land," which Guthrie originally called "God Blessed America for Me." To Berlin's romantic pastoral imagery ("From the mountains / To the prairies / To the oceans, white with foam"), Guthrie retorted with six verses of his own, beginning, "This land is your land, this land is my land, / From California to the New York island, / From the redwood forest to the Gulf Stream waters; / God blessed America for me." But Guthrie's song continued with a far more complete depiction of America's ills as well as its beauties, as in this verse: "One bright sunny morning in the shadow of the steeple / By the relief office I saw my people— / As they stood hungry, I stood there wondering if / God blessed America for me." Guthrie set his moving verses to a

FIGURE 14.1
Woody Guthrie (1912–1967).

tune perhaps derived from a Baptist hymn, "Oh My Lovin' Brother," though scholars dispute that derivation.

Little realizing the popular potential of his song, Guthrie did not publish it until 1944, during the late period of World War II, by which time he had changed the title to "This Land Is Your Land" and the refrain (the line repeated at the end of each verse) to "This land was made for you and me." He continued to change the song, substituting new verses of pungent social commentary even as he slowly succumbed to Huntington's disease, which eventually killed him. In his last years, Guthrie expressed frustration that his song had become widely known and popular—but without its protest verses.

Protest was not a traditional characteristic of country music, but social commentary was, and Guthrie's stirring poems and songs on a variety of topics inspired the folk revivalists of the late 1950s and the succeeding socially turbulent decade. Many people consider Woody Guthrie America's greatest folk poet.

Urban Folk Revival During the 1950s and early 1960s, the urban folk revival evolved into a very popular movement, attracting huge crowds of mostly young, often socially conscious, and sometimes politically active young people. Among those inspired by Woody Guthrie was **Pete Seeger** (b. 1919), the son of a famous musicologist specializing in American folk music (Charles Seeger). Pete Seeger left college to collect folk songs, learned to play the banjo, and traveled with Guthrie in the years before World War II. (Pete Seeger sings "Barbara Allen" and "Shenandoah," Listening Examples 5 and 6.)

Later the younger Seeger formed the Weavers (so named to reflect "the qualities of rhythm and work"), a folk group dedicated to preserving the tradition of political-activist protest songs. The Weavers' first great hit, "Goodnight Irene," was first popularized by **Huddie Ledbetter (Leadbelly,** 1885–1949), a gifted black blues singer and songwriter. Leadbelly was discovered, while serving a term in jail for assault with intent to murder, by the musicologist John Lomax and his even more influential son **Alan Lomax** (1915–2002). Not a traditional folk song, "Goodnight Irene" was written and published in 1886 by a black railroad porter, Gussie Lord Davis; but Leadbelly had learned it in a much altered version. Impressed with the song (as Leadbelly performed it) and with Leadbelly's talents, the Lomaxes helped to secure the talented blues musician's early release from prison and to launch him on a performing and recording career. Leadbelly's fervor for civil rights led him to join Pete Seeger, Woody Guthrie, and others prominent in the urban folk revival movement.

The Weavers' popularity would seem to have rendered them impervious to attacks from the increasingly suspicious political right; but the cold war and the McCarthy era's Red Scare hysteria forced them, temporarily, to restrict their appearances to union halls, civil rights and peace benefits, and college campuses. Finally, in 1955, Pete Seeger faced censure by Congress. Hauled before a subcommittee investigating supposed subversive influences in entertainment, Seeger refused to cooperate and was blacklisted from television for his leftist leanings. His fortunes soared, however, at the end of the decade, when he left the Weavers and forged a highly successful solo career.

Ironically, perhaps, in the late 1990s Seeger was inducted into the Rock and Roll Hall of Fame. Asked recently about his reaction to this unlikely event, Seeger replied, "Rock is what future centuries will probably say was the twentieth-century folk music."

As popular attention was diverted to the Kingston Trio's recording of "Tom Dooley" (1958)—a murder ballad innocent of political overtones—the urban folk revival came into full bloom, forming an important tie between country music and mainstream pop. The Kingston Trio and other suburban, collegiate, clean-cut groups, including the Limelighters, the New Christy Minstrels, and (especially) Peter, Paul and Mary, joined such city-bred singers of protest songs as Joan Baez, Bob Dylan, and of course Pete Seeger to produce commercial music for a sophisticated urban audience. Performing in coffeehouses, in city nightclubs, and on college campuses, they also effectively revived interest in early folk music—at least among themselves. The Kingston Trio's "Tom Dooley" (a song discovered, like "Goodnight Irene," by Alan Lomax) had first been recorded in the 1920s by a blind fiddler descended from the sheriff who had arrested the murderer Tom Dula; the version by the Kingston Trio (available on YouTube) sold 4 million records. In 1963, the Weavers recorded an

adaptation by Bob Dylan of an old slave song, "No More Auction Block for Me" (Listening Example 10), now titled "Blowin' in the Wind." **Joan Baez** (b. 1941; Figure 14.2) made serious studies of folk and country music, learning traditional songs and performance customs and bringing them to a receptive modern audience. Baez's recordings of the Carter Family's songs, for instance, introduced them to a new audience and also to musicians who composed original "folk" songs modeled on such country classics.

Bob Dylan (b. 1941)

Bob Dylan (Figure 14.3), born Robert Zimmerman in Duluth, Minnesota, followed his idol Woody Guthrie to New York. There Dylan began performing in clubs and recording his original folklike protest songs while learning as much as possible from Guthrie. Dylan's singing voice was harsh and his guitar self-accompaniments were unsophisticated; but the passion in his voice and the stirring messages of his texts—written by himself, some on intensely personal issues—made him the favorite figure of the folk revival. For a time he had a close relationship with the singer Joan Baez, who rose to folk stardom before he became known and who generously supported his early performances. But within a few years, Dylan abandoned Baez and took his own independent path.

Having linked country music with mainstream pop by presenting folklike music in a pop atmosphere, the urban folk revival now initiated another significant change in the popular music industry, inspired by the songs of Bob Dylan. Before Dylan, the folk revivalists, like performers in the Tin Pan Alley tradition, had mostly performed songs composed or handed down by others; but Dylan's original songs inspired others in the folk revival movement to write their own material. Thus, rather than performing new arrangements of traditional tunes, the folk revivalists now produced original "folk" songs.

FIGURE 14.3

Bob Dylan (b.1941) performing at the 2002 Newport Folk Festival.

Dylan was soon to connect with rock as well, not only in the sense that early rock performers wrote most of their own material but—surprisingly—by making a transition from leader of urban folk to electric rock performer.

Folk Rock

The mood of protest having strengthened, rock crowds demanded from performers more than entertainment, and by 1965 urban folk singers who included protest songs in their performances at colleges and in night clubs were addressing rock audiences as well, reflecting the serious new mood by blending light rock effects with tuneful melodies and protest lyrics in what became known as **folk rock.** Mellow groups such as Peter, Paul and Mary, unable or unwilling to update their lyrics and their style, quickly became less relevant and less popular.

Several groups joined the folk rock movement: The Mamas and the Papas added a light rock flavor to their familiar style of folk music; Crosby, Stills, Nash, and Young also updated their sound by adding light rock effects; Simon and Garfunkel and the Fifth Dimension performed in folk rock style as well. But the Byrds, even more strongly affected by Bob Dylan's new approach, became the group most closely allied to the folk rock style, using the amplification and distortion of instrument sounds for expressive effect. Their recorded versions of Dylan's "Mr. Tambourine Man" (Listening Example 56) and

"Mr. Tambourine Man"

The Byrds' 1965 recording of "Mr. Tambourine Man," released *before* Dylan's version of his song, made folk rock widely recognized and popular. The Byrds chose to include only one of the four verses Dylan wrote for the song; perhaps they found the others, expressing loneliness and the desire to find relief in the sound of the tambourine, too personal for group performance. In any case, the Byrds' version is less than half the length of Dylan's recording of this well-known song. (Dylan may be heard performing his own version on YouTube.)

CD 2
Track 24
2:29

Composer and Lyricist   Bob Dylan (b. 1941).

Genre   Folk rock.

Timbre   Four male vocalists, twelve-string electric guitar, drums, tambourine, electric bass (the Byrds).

Texture   Homophonic. The Byrds sing the song's familiar refrain in their close, country-style harmony, the main melody sometimes lying below a higher melodic line, or countermelody, as often occurs in country music. Their simple chords occur in slightly surprising order compared with the harmony of earlier popular music.

Form   Verse-chorus.

Meter   Quadruple.

Tempo   Slow, relaxed.

0:00   During the four-bar instrumental introduction, the drums and tambourine punctuate the sounds of the twelve-string electric guitar and electric bass with a strong backbeat.

0:09   Chorus: The Byrds sing the appealing chorus in their smooth, close-harmony style, accompanied by instruments including the tambourine and the "jingle jangle" electric guitar.
Hey! Mr. Tambourine Man, play a song for me, . . .

0:42   Verse. The soloist (singer-guitarist Roger "Jim" McGuinn) sings the verse, consisting of an unusual ten lines, with an irregular number of beats per line, and with an "unresolved" ending.
Take me for a trip upon your magic swirlin' ship, . . .

1:32   Chorus.

2:02   Close: The guitar and bass gently fade away.

Pete Seeger's "Turn! Turn! Turn!" made a very strong and lasting impact on a wide audience. (Dylan may be heard performing his own song on YouTube.)

Joan Baez (see Figure 14.2) was among those who intensified the emotional content of their songs and addressed topics of current controversy and concern. Drawing upon her examples and those of Woody Guthrie and Pete Seeger, other folk musicians also began adding elements of rock to their performances, thereby reaching a wider audience. And to the confusion of some fans, Bob Dylan switched from urban folk to folk rock in 1965, replacing the acoustic instruments of his early days with an electric guitar and a rock rhythm section.

Newport Folk Festival, 1965

In the early 1960s, the Newport Folk Festival was the central annual event for those who loved folk music. Guitar pickers, blues singers, old-time fiddlers, and banjo players from all over the country joined gospel singers, Cajun bands, bluegrass groups, and folk stars like Joan Baez and Pete Seeger for several days of concerts, workshops, and jam sessions. Most saw folk music as a tool for social change, and by 1963 they revered Bob Dylan, whose songs—including "With God on Our Side" and "Blowin' in the Wind"—movingly addressed social issues of the day.

But Dylan responded to the catastrophic events of 1963 through 1965—the assassinations of President John Kennedy and of Malcolm X, the killing of civil rights workers in the South, the growing involvement of American troops in Vietnam, and the doubling of the draft quota—by starkly altering his message and his style. His subject matter changed from protest to songs about personal relationships, often expressed in complex imagist poetry. His look changed, too, from casually scruffy attire to leather jackets, Cuban-heel boots, and sunglasses. His fans, expecting to hear the old Bob Dylan perform at the Newport Folk Festival in 1965, were outraged when he appeared wearing a black leather jacket and played an electric guitar backed by a rock rhythm band with the sound system cranked up to an ear-splitting level.

Yet by the 1990s, Dylan seemed to have come full circle, recording albums of traditional folk and blues material ("Good as I Been to You," "World Gone Wrong," and "Time Out of Mind"). His album *Love and Theft* (2001) also includes the sounds of blues, jazz, folk, and rockabilly. Today his poetry is attracting acclaim in its own right; some even think that the powerful messages of protest and reform in Dylan's moving poetry are destined to survive his music. A British poet laureate referred to Dylan as one of the greatest artists of the twentieth century; and the American composer John Corigliano (who wrote the music for the film *The Red Violin,* 1999) has set Dylan's words to his own music in a group of songs titled *Mr. Tambourine Man: Seven Poems of Bob Dylan.*

Alternative Country

Country music faces a veritable identity crisis today. The term **alternative country** covers no specific style but refers to the preference of some country musicians to express country concepts in progressive ways, or nontraditional concepts with a country sound. Alternative country's own magazine, *No Depression* (named after the Carter Family's song "No Depression in Heaven"), declares that it covers "alternative country music (whatever that is)."

In the early 1970s, some rock and jazz musicians began to share the instrumental techniques of bluegrass music; and in 1971, four prominent bluegrass musicians led by fiddler/mandolin player **Sam Bush** (b. 1952) formed the New Grass Revival, a band dedicated to fusing elements of jazz, rock, and blues (improvisation, electrified instruments, something Bush described as "the hippie look") with bluegrass style. Their success led to the adoption by other bands of the generic term *newgrass.* (In 2008 the Kentucky legislature passed a resolution honoring Bush as a founder of newgrass music.)

Since the 1990s, alternative country has attracted a small but dedicated group of enthusiasts dedicated to rivaling the polished, professional sounds of mainstream country music coming from Nashville by blending punk (see pp. 274–277) and rock and roll effects with country sounds. Successful releases by Dwight Yoakam, George Strait, and other "modernist" country singers came out of California, which now competes with Nashville for influence in the country market. In 2000, at the Academy of Country Music Awards (based on the West Coast), George Strait and Alan Jackson performed "Murder on Music Row" (Music Row refers to Nashville, where the Country Music Association presents its own annual awards), a stinging indictment of all that West Coast people find wrong with country radio today: "The steel guitars no longer cry and the fiddles barely play, but drums and rock-and-roll guitar are mixed up in your face." Songs such as the Kentucky Headhunters' hit "Rock 'n' Roll Angel" illustrate a new confidence that allowed country musicians in the 1990s to refer good-humoredly to their formerly dreaded competition. Yoakam and others regularly give the hillbilly twang a happy rock-and-roll spin.

A new activism appears in the music of some country stars. In 2002, prompted by the attacks of September 11, 2001, Toby Keith wrote a song, "Courtesy of the Red, White, and Blue"—subtitled "The Angry American"—expressing his father's patriotism and his own faith in the United States. In 2003, the Dixie Chicks (Figure 14.4) expressed another point of view, famously criticizing the president of the United States (and paying for their frankly expressed views with lost performance opportunities).

Today both rock and country audiences seem willing to accept elements of each other's music. In the summer of 2004, the rocker Matt (Uncle Kracker) Shafer toured successfully with the country music star Kenny Chesney and the country trio Rascal Flatts, and since then numerous other rock and country performers have found common ground. Country and rock merge as well on modern country radio and in some of Nashville's

FIGURE 14.4

The Dixie Chicks (left to right: Emily Robison, Natalie Maines, and Martie Maguire) performing at the NOKIA Theatre in Los Angeles on October 18, 2007.

videos, as audiences simply looking for a good time enjoy the two-way love affair.

And so, country music, one of the roots of rock and roll, seems to be forging an ever-more-compatible relationship with the vibrant style it helped to spawn.

Terms to Review

urban folk music	**alternative country**	**newgrass**
folk rock		

Key Figures

Johnny Cash	Huddie Ledbetter (Leadbelly)	Bob Dylan
Woody Guthrie	Alan Lomax	Sam Bush
Pete Seeger	Joan Baez	

Critical Thinking

Do you think Bob Dylan will be best remembered in the future for his music or for his poetry?

Jazz Since 1960

As emerging new styles joined without replacing established trends in jazz, the jazz experience increased in complexity and sophistication, although hardly in popularity. From the time bebop entered the fray—well before rock and roll swept the popular music industry off its feet—jazz has belonged as much to the classical as to the popular music world. Jazz pianist, composer, and scholar Billy Taylor refers to jazz, in fact, as America's classical music.

Throughout the 1960s, jazz musicians explored relationships between classical and popular music, placing less emphasis on outstanding solo performances accompanied by players who obligingly yielded the spotlight until their turn came to take it, and favoring instead collective improvisation by several, or even by all, ensemble members at the same time.

Free Jazz

During the 1960s, a number of jazz musicians sought new approaches to improvisation, which remained at the core of the concept of jazz. Some shared the conviction that jazz was not necessarily—or primarily—about individual solos, but about rhythm and interplay best expressed by the **collective improvisation** of several or all members of the ensemble. In 1960, **Ornette Coleman** (b. 1930) introduced free collective improvisation in an album titled *Free Jazz,* which defied the perception of jazz as generally accessible to the ordinary listener; for **free jazz** was a difficult music, challenging to performers and listeners alike, with no familiar chord changes, no references to popular songs or blues, and no steady beat. In free jazz, each musician improvised independently, aware of and responsive to the other players but bound by no preset obligations. Even the initial phrases of a composition, played by the ensemble's soloists together, were not necessarily in unison.

Free jazz further released musicians from the strictures of tonality, of recurring rhythmic patterns or a fixed pulse, and of predetermined themes. (They did, however, have short melodic motives—riffs—that they could insert in the improvisation and that others could join in on.) It has been suggested that free jazz expressed in musical terms the same sorts of freedom

FIGURE 15.1

The album cover for Ornette Coleman's *Free Jazz,* with art by Jackson Pollock.

African Americans were demanding and finally achieving in many areas of life during that turbulent decade. And the new assertive independence free jazz offered rhythm instruments might be compared to the respected positions African Americans were now assuming in life. The new music also bore a relationship to chance music (discussed in Chapter 23), and Coleman stated that he thought his playing had some rapport with Abstract Expressionist art. The cover of Coleman's recording *Free Jazz* features, in fact, a reproduction of white lights, a 1954 drip painting by the Abstract Expressionist artist Jackson Pollock (Figure 15.1).

Free jazz also reflects an interest in non-Western music, which intrigued many twentieth-century composers of classical music. Having no chord changes to play relieved free jazz ensembles of the need to include a piano, with its restrictive keyboard limited to the tones of the black and white keys. This in turn freed musicians to explore non-Western scales and encouraged them to include instruments from other cultures in their ensembles and to play Western instruments in nontraditional ways. The use of *microtones* (lying between the tones of a piano keyboard) and certain rhythmic techniques derived from the music of India heighten the emotional effect and intellectual challenge of Coleman's performances.

The jazz saxophonist and composer **John Coltrane** (1926–1967, Figure 15.2) became in a sense the spiritual leader of free jazz during the last years of his short life. Coltrane's free spirit, however, caused him to change his stylistic preferences throughout his career. Early known for producing "sheets of sound," because he played so many notes at rapid-fire tempos (as on *Giant Steps,* 1959), he explored other areas of interest in later works. For example, having worked

FIGURE 15.2
John Coltrane (1926–1967).

with Miles Davis on the influential album *Kind of Blue,* Coltrane furthered his interest in modal music, and also reflected the hypnotic pulsating quality of Indian music, in *My Favorite Things* (1960).

Widely known and admired for the beautiful tone and the variety of effects he achieved on his tenor and soprano saxophones, Coltrane countered Ornette Coleman's concept of collective improvisation by playing individual solos of unprecedented length, most famously in "Chasin' the Trane" (1961). Generally dissonant and complex, Coltrane's music features frequent harmonic changes and some polytonal passages.

In 1964 Coltrane produced the very spiritual, emotional album *A Love Supreme.* Here he seemed to identify with rebellious youth of the 1960s seeking new cultural and spiritual identities based on non-Western traditions. Effectively combining religious ecstasy with tranquillity and meditation, this hypnotic mixture of music and chanting became one of the best-selling and best-loved jazz albums of all time. We hear an excerpt from Part I of *A Love Supreme* in Listening Example 57.

Third Stream

Third stream *combines* jazz and classical music in a manner that—unlike the *blending* of classical and jazz effects in symphonic, cool, and progressive jazz—allows each style to retain its characteristic qualities. The composer who first attracted attention to this new idea, which had not yet been named, was **John Lewis** (1920–2001), a classically trained African American pianist interested in the forms of European art music, especially of the Renaissance and Baroque periods. Lewis founded the Modern Jazz Quartet (MJQ) in 1952 (Figure 15.3) and wrote many compositions for that ensemble, often using forms—such as *canon, fugue,* or *variations*—of the earlier periods he admired. Some of Lewis's compositions were to be performed by the MJQ with a symphony orchestra or with another classical music organization, the members of

A Love Supreme—Part I, "Acknowledgement" (excerpt)

Coltrane's 1964 *A Love Supreme*, a four-part devotional *suite* (collection of pieces forming a composition) became one of the best-loved and best-selling jazz albums of all time. Here Coltrane reflects the influence of non-Western traditions as he explores new ways to express spiritual, cultural, and intellectual concepts. YouTube offers Coltrane's complete performance of this lovely piece, including the hypnotic musical and spoken versions of the chant, "a love supreme . . ."

CD 2
Track 25
4:36

Composer John Coltrane (1926–1967). Coltrane conceived the themes and the style, mood, and philosophy of the piece; but his quartet seemingly drew inspiration from Coltrane's mind (heart, soul), for there was no written score.

Genre Spiritual or sacred jazz.

Timbre John Coltrane Quartet; tenor saxophone (Coltrane), piano, bass, drums.

Texture Polyphonic. Each line has its own melodic integrity.

Meter Basically quadruple, but free and flexible, changing as the piece progresses. Listen for complex polyrhythms skillfully performed by each of the instruments throughout the piece.

Form "Acknowledgement" is the first of four sections, which make up a suite. (The other three parts are "Resolution," "Pursuance," and "Psalm.") Part I begins with clearly distinguished eight-bar phrases but continues in a free, rhapsodic fashion suited to the contemplative nature of the piece.

0:00   After a gong begins the rhythmically free introduction, Coltrane's tenor sax explores a figure that serves as a rhapsodic invocation, a call to prayer, quietly accompanied by dissonant piano chords and shimmering metallic sounds. The introduction tapers off with a few breathy sax notes and gentle rolls on the piano. Notice the variety of richly sensuous timbres in this brief opening passage.

0:32   Eight bars: The bass introduces the four-note main theme (filling the range of a fourth), based on the words "a love supreme."

—Continued

Listening Example 57—concluded

A Love Supreme—Part I, "Acknowledgement" (excerpt)

0:48   Eight bars: The piano enters, over the bass and soft percussion.

1:04   The quartet continues the spiritual quest, alternately meditative, contemplative, passionate, ecstatic, and at peace. Concentrate as you listen to each of the instruments in turn. Notice their independence and the melodic and rhythmic intricacy of each line. Hear how Coltrane explores the extreme limits of pitch ranges and how the various ranges affect the timbre of his sax. The very simple bass lines would seem inadequate to support the complexity of all that is built upon them, yet everything holds together beautifully.

Our excerpt tapers off, due to time constraints, but you may find the complete movement at several sites on the Internet. Listening to the remainder of the piece, notice that before abandoning his sax to chant the phrase "a love supreme," Coltrane plays the strangely moving four-note motive in each of the twelve keys—perhaps to suggest the complete availability of the love supreme. His chanting lends a mystic, hypnotic flavor to this emotionally varied piece, which gradually lessens in intensity of emotion and ends quietly.

FIGURE 15.3

The Modern Jazz Quartet (MJQ). Drums, Connie Kay; piano and director, John Lewis; bass, Percy Heath; vibraphone, Milt Jackson.

the jazz quartet improvising some of their music while the classical ensemble played what was written. Thus each group remained true to its traditions, and the collaboration formed a new style of music combining classical forms with jazz improvisation and the feel of swing.

The term for the new style was introduced in 1957 by **Gunther Schuller** (b. 1925), who, for a time at least, believed that jazz and classical music should be treated as separate but congenial entities. In 1957 he referred famously to classical music as the "first stream" of music and jazz as the "second stream," calling their combination in a manner allowing each to retain its characteristic qualities *third stream* music.

Third stream music as Schuller conceived it remained in vogue for only a short time; but the collision—or cooperation—it represents between classically trained musicians, who depend on fixed ideas of standard Western notation, and jazz musicians, who predicate their art on pliability and invention, persists. Ornette Coleman, who remains interested to this day in the concept that used to be called third stream, has been writing classical music since the 1950s, when he produced several string quartets; and in the 1960s he combined jazz and classical concepts much as John Lewis and Gunther Schuller were doing. His piece for symphony orchestra and solo jazz improvisers titled "Skies of America," written in the mid-1960s, gives the conductor something of an improvisatory role as well: choosing between an array of notated inserts to be cued to the orchestra by means of hand signals. Of course the piece poses quandaries for classically trained orchestral musicians accustomed to relying on a straightforward interpretation of the notes printed in a score: Thus when Coleman suggested at a rehearsal of the piece by the New York Philharmonic in 1997 that the musicians might choose to play notes *other* than those he had written, a violinist complained that this concept was very hard to understand, to which Coleman replied, smiling, "Just because it's hard to understand doesn't mean it's not true."

The 1970s

Before 1970, it is possible to define a dominant, though hardly exclusive, style characteristic of each decade: We may see the 1920s as the jazz age, the 1930s as the era of swing, the 1940s reacting to bebop, the 1950s staying cool, and the 1960s exploring relationships between jazz and classical music. Although no one style reigned exclusively at any time, and all existed concurrently with other important kinds of jazz, each of those decades is associated with a particular approach to jazz distinguishing it from other such periods. It is even possible to discern an alternation between *classically* cool and *romantically* emotional music decade by decade: the emotional intensity of the roaring twenties, followed by the soothing sounds of big band music, succeeded by the challenge of bebop, countered by *The Birth of the Cool,* to which the 1960s offered the intellectually rigorous free jazz.

From 1970 to 1980, several important movements not only coexisted but seem to have had relatively comparable influences on the jazz of succeeding periods. The decade experienced a comeback of swing, which remains strong today; European chamber music–style combos appealed to many musicians and listeners; and bebop made a powerful and lasting return. But two other movements vied for attention during the 1970s: *world music* and—especially—*fusion*.

Fusion (Jazz-Rock)

Jazz and rock, which came from the same roots (blues, gospel, work songs), both faced crises as the 1970s began. Jazz seemed to have lost its identity, foundering somewhere between classical and foreign ethnic musics; and rockers, mourning the deaths of some of their greatest stars, struggled to find the means to address the tragic social and political events of the day (see p. 271).

Miles Davis's ensemble incorporated rock rhythms in some of their music beginning in the mid-1960s; and early in the new decade numerous other jazz musicians, who after all had grown up to the sounds of rock and roll, also began to invigorate their music with the rhythms of what had become the most compellingly popular music in history. Introduced in Great Britain in 1963, the movement sprang to life here with Miles Davis's recording of *Bitches Brew* (1969). Davis fanned the flames begun by *Bitches Brew* with *On the Corner* (1972), referred to by some critics as "antijazz." The album features an amazing array of instruments, including an Indian sitar, and a rock (funky) drumbeat shocking to some listeners, thrilling to others. (The dense textures and complex rhythms derived from rhythm and blues gave rise to the term *funk* or *funky* in its 1970s connotation.)

Jazz-rock, or **fusion**, or **jazz-rock-fusion**, as it is variously called, melds rock rhythms and the use of electronic instruments with collective improvisation, extreme ranges of volume (from very loud to whisper-soft), and rapid shifts in meter, tempo, and mood that are uncharacteristic of rock. Further, fusion is an instrumental music, without the vocals generally inherent to rock. But the use of bass guitar or electric bass instead of jazzers' traditional stand-up bass allowed fusion groups to play faster and to alter their sounds with electronic effects; and the manner in which snare drums and bass drums replaced the rhythmic effects previous jazz ensembles had assigned to piano and cymbals raised the rhythmic section to a position of dominance unprecedented in the history of jazz.

By the mid-1970s, some jazz ensembles included electronic organs and other keyboards, on which many jazz pianists enjoyed working, as well as a variety of synthesizers. Electroacoustic instruments—those on which sound is mechanically generated and then electronically amplified and altered—were often included as well. (Electric instruments belonging to the second category include piano, clarinets, guitars, saxophones, trumpets, and drums.) These ideas were not new: Benny Goodman's sextet featured an electric guitar in 1939, the electric organ first gained popularity in black rhythm and blues, and the multitalented singer pianist Ray Charles (see pp. 238–239) played an electric piano for "What'd I Say" in 1959. But electric instruments affected jazz to a new degree in the 1970s. Recording technology also acquired unprecedented importance for jazz musicians, rendering the sound engineer an artist as well as a technician, responsible for manipulating the musicians' sounds to best advantage.

Weather Report, an outstanding fusion band of the 1970s and 1980s, was formed by two musicians (Joe Zawinul and Wayne Shorter) who had worked with Miles Davis on *Bitches Brew*. The band stunningly presents the virtuosity and rhythmic complexity associated with jazz-rock fusion. One of the earliest and most influential jazz-rock groups, Weather Report remained active for over fifteen years. (Song samples from Weather Report's album *Night Passage*, 1980, can be heard at Amazon.com.)

Two influential jazz pianists, each of whom—like so many jazz innovators of the 1970s and later—had also worked with Miles Davis, became particularly prominent in fusion. **Herbie Hancock** (b. 1940) found inspiration from and achieved huge success with electronic instruments. His album *Headhunters* (1973) became the first jazz album to be certified gold and remained for a time the best-selling of all jazz albums. The electric bass and keyboards and synthesizers on this album gave jazz a radical new sound, sometimes called *jazz-funk*. *Headhunters* attracted a sizable international following for its creator, but Hancock has continued to explore acoustic jazz, jazz-rock, funk, "space music" (which sounds like background music for a science fiction film), and other sounds and styles that interest and challenge him.

The influential jazz pianist **Chick Corea** (b. 1941, Figure 15.4) became prominent in fusion, forming, in 1970, a popular and influential fusion group, Return to Forever. A highly accomplished acoustic piano player, Corea turned more and more to a wide variety of electronic keyboard instruments during

FIGURE 15.4

Pianist Chick Corea (b. 1941) onstage at the San Sebastian Jazz Festival, Spain, July 25, 1998.

the 1970s. He also reflected the other major movement of that period, interest in world music, incorporating the influence of Latin American rhythms in his compositions and performances. (See p. 218 for Corea and the bossa nova.)

Integration of Foreign Sounds Fusion, which implies a bringing together, also brought about serious schisms within the world of jazz, as musicians chose between acoustic and electronic instruments, between the flexible rhythms of free jazz and a soul- or gospel-influenced steady beat, and among a huge variety of concepts of music from foreign cultures. In the late 1960s, John Coltrane sparked interest in bringing characteristics of many foreign ethnic musics into jazz, and after his death this became a compelling concept for a number of outstanding jazz musicians, who integrated music from India, Brazil, Arabia, Bali, Japan, China, various African cultures, and many other cultures into their own distinctive performances. European concert music also attracted many jazz musicians, some of whom moved to Europe, where they lived for several years.

One such musician was **Don Cherry** (1936–1995), who worked with Ornette Coleman and John Coltrane, and performed and recorded in Europe and in New York during the 1960s. Having traveled extensively in Asia and Africa, Cherry settled in Sweden in the early 1970s and became active there in music education and performance. Referring to himself as a "world musician," Cherry played many ethnic instruments from Tibet, China, India, Bali, and other countries in addition to the trumpet for which he first became known. In 1978, he and two colleagues—a Brazilian percussionist and an American who played sitar, tabla, and percussion—formed a trio, Codona, that performed a seemingly boundless array of ethnic musics for school children, enthusiastic adult audiences, and recordings.

The 1980s

For jazz musicians, the 1980s proved a fragmented period of enormous diversity, exploration, and discovery. New information about other music traditions, together with sophisticated new technology, greatly extended the range of jazz identity. World music remained important. Electronic techniques expanded their applications. In many cases, a single musician or group participated in a number of kinds of jazz, establishing no definitive identity with any one.

After years of productive acoustic collaborations with outstanding jazz musicians, Chick Corea turned to electronic instruments in the 1980s, appreciating the opportunities they afforded to produce new means of expression and to communicate to a wider audience familiar with electronic sounds. Each member of Corea's Elektric Band (which consisted of a sax, an electric guitar, an electric bass, and drums in addition to Corea's acoustic piano and electronic synthesizer) was a virtuoso with his own distinctive style of playing. Some members of the band tended more toward jazz, some toward rhythm and blues, yet the band always had an integrated sound. One devoted listener described the band as "one part rock, two parts jazz, and one part aerobics class!"

Among the great diversity of jazz styles, however, two fields of interest seem particularly characteristic of the 1980s: crossover jazz, or the blending of jazz and various other musics; and a strong revival of interest in traditional styles.

Crossover Music

The blending of jazz and classical music, defined as third stream by Gunther Schuller, has faded into and out of favor over the years. John Lewis's Modern Jazz Quartet, for example, seen as a black response to the intellectualism of the Dave Brubeck Quartet, and as New York's answer to West Coast cool jazz, gained popularity and stirred up controversy; the group played their "Last Concert," as they titled the performance and its subsequent album, in New York in 1974. Sensing a change of sensibilities in 1981, however, the Modern Jazz Quartet regrouped for a tour of Japan, which was so well received that they resumed touring. In 1984 they returned to the studio to resume their recording career as well.

Fusion, another form of crossover, remained strong in the 1980s, though not as popular as it had been in the 1970s. Herbie Hancock shocked and inspired listeners with his album *Future Shock* (1983), including the astonishing "Rockit," a fusion of jazz, funk, and electronics that became a massive hit and inspired an early MTV video.

A major artist of the period, who remains important today, is the jazz guitarist **Pat Metheny** (b. 1954). He initiated a rock band format that produced album after album of melodious jazz-rock. Metheny, like so many great jazz artists, has a seemingly inexhaustible range of interests and talents. In 1985, he composed the score for the movie *The Falcon and the Snowman,* which led to his recording "This Is Not America"—a Top 40 hit—with David Bowie. Having explored the musical possibilities of the twelve-string guitar and the digital sampling synthesizer called a *synclavier,* Metheny continues to move between pure jazz and pop jazz, to high acclaim.

Traditionalism

Throughout the 1980s, as some jazz musicians blended jazz with rock, folk, pop, and foreign sounds, others resisted such combinations and the white European concert sounds of much crossover music, returning instead to earlier styles, variously updated to modern tastes. In 1982, the jazz trumpet player Wynton Marsalis (see pp. 267–268) founded a quintet that seemed to mark the beginning of this neoconservative trend in jazz. The traditionalists favored a return to pre-fusion acoustic values and to the disciplined, though elastic, harmonies and rhythms of earlier styles.

New Orleans, Chicago, and Dixieland jazz acquired a new generation of fans, while the dancing public enjoyed popular swing hits such as Glenn Miller's "In the Mood" and "String of Pearls." Never widely popular, bop and so-called post-bop offered traditionalists of the 1980s a structured yet progressive sound—daring, but not too new. The return to the steady beat associated with swing and other traditional jazz was likely to be tempered, however, with freely flowing, flexible rhythms and meters. These are indigenous to much music in Africa, but applying them to the music we call jazz was new.

The 1990s and Beyond

The 1990s became the first decade in the history of jazz to have no defining movements. Relationships to rock loomed ever more important as the twentieth century drew to a close, and soul, funk, world music, and crossover remained strong as a new fusion—jazz-rap—evolved. Fusion, in fact, continues to become ever more complex, as musicians explore and expand styles, techniques, and technology. For example, when the British jazz group Us3 released their album *Cantaloop 2004,* updating their sampling of Herbie Hancock's 1994 recording "Cantaloupe Island," a press release described the new recording as "jazz-influenced urban sounds leaning heavily on a Latino R&B vibe" with vocals by a Brooklyn rapper and a singer who had been born in South Africa and was then based in London.

"Stretch It," Part I (an Online Listening Example), from Corea's album *Inside Out* (1990) illustrates the virtuosity and the rhythmic sophistication of fusion, which explains why it remains a vital jazz style today. With its melodic and rhythmic intricacies, its phrases rising and falling in turn, this little piece leaves us with a feeling of grateful uplift. (Amazon.com offers samples of this and more of Corea's music from various periods of his career.)

A new style, called *no wave* or *noise,* evolved alongside all the others. According to the reed player, composer, and jazz scholar **John Zorn** (b. 1953), no wave seeks the emancipation of noise. Pieces in this style are extremely brief, very fast, and loud. Some people have described this music as a collage of very short, isolated sound events.

Zorn is among an impressive number of contemporary jazz musicians who are following Duke Ellington's lead in finding ways to integrate composition and improvisation. Although no one has yet attained the renown or adulation accorded to Ellington during his lifetime, or accomplished Ellington's seemingly effortless negotiation between popular culture and the fine arts, several visionary composers are attracting the attention and admiration of critics and fans of jazz. Many of them are masterful improvisers; several are scholars; all seem interested in putting to their own various uses many or all of the various ethnic, technological, traditional, and experimental resources offered in the early years of the twenty-first century.

Henry Threadgill (b. 1944)

Henry Threadgill, a multi-instrumentalist who principally plays saxophone and flute, has traveled and performed with gospel musicians and blues bands. In the early 1960s, he became associated with a highly influential collective called the Association for the Advancement of Creative Music (AACM), formed to help Chicago musicians present their new, commercially unacceptable, music. In the 1970s, he formed the group Air, a trio that explored African music, ragtime, and assorted other traditional musics. Since 1980, he has formed a number of groups using unusual instrumentation such as the Very Very Circus, which included trombone, two tubas, two guitars, and drums. This unique combination of instruments fuses the music of avant-garde jazz, funk, salsa, and East European marches into a highly original and distinctive sound. Living today in Goa, India, Threadgill maintains a rigorous composing and performing schedule, recording less frequently than before. (YouTube offers early and recent performances by Henry Threadgill with various groups.)

Anthony Braxton (b. 1945)

Anthony Braxton, also a former member of AACM, reached a milestone in jazz history by recording a double album of solo alto saxophone music, *For Alto,* released in 1971. Soon other alto sax players followed his lead by making their own solo recordings. Endlessly exploring and restlessly seeking creative new means of expression, Braxton has also written for huge orchestral ensembles and opera. A highly intellectual composer, he has devised systems for composing music, some based on mathematical relationships, diagrams, or formulas as a means of generating improvisation within the framework of an orchestral composition. He sometimes reflects ideas related to the ideas of John Cage and chance music (see pp. 392–393). In some of his pieces, parts can be played by different instruments depending on what is available or desired for a particular performance, and some of his compositions can be played together. (Anthony Braxton's *92 + (30, 32, 139) + (108c, 108d) for Creative Orchestra* is an Optional Listening Example, and his music is widely available on YouTube.)

www.mhhe.com/ferrisaml6e

Wynton Marsalis (b. 1961)

Wynton Marsalis (Figure 15.5) is a classicist who believes that bebop is the foundation of modern jazz and who continually defends, updates, and modernizes early jazz styles in his own compositions. A Juilliard-trained trumpet virtuoso who achieves an extremely

FIGURE 15.5
Wynton Marsalis (b. 1961), playing in 2004.

beautiful quality of sound, Marsalis is also known as an educator and composer. In 1987, he cofounded a jazz program at Lincoln Center, which he directs today, and which now sponsors hundreds of events in at least fifteen countries. Having toured for a time with Art Blakey's Jazz Messengers, Marsalis took time off to steep himself in the roots of the tradition he so admired, and his deep study of blues, gospel, work songs, and the work of Louis Armstrong and Duke Ellington brought to his playing and to his composing new passion, depth, and technical brilliance.

Concerned with restoring "respect and seriousness" to jazz, Marsalis also believes the future of jazz holds more emphasis on composition than on soloing, and like many other jazz composers today, he writes music intended to last. Indeed, jazz recordings in general are turning toward more closely arranged projects than were undertaken in earlier times, when outstanding soloists reigned supreme.

In 1994, Marsalis's book *Sweet Swing Blues on the Road* received high praise. He has won Grammy Awards for both jazz and classical recordings, and in 1998 he became the first jazz musician to receive the Pulitzer Prize for music, for his extended composition "Blood on the Fields." However, this recipient of numerous national and international awards remains a controversial figure among jazz fans and musicians, some of whom consider him too intellectual and too narrow-minded as to what constitutes "real jazz." Nevertheless, his inspired trumpet playing, gifted teaching, tireless proselytizing for jazz, and impressive compositions suggest that his will continue to be a significant name in jazz.

Jazz Today and Tomorrow

The important American music we call jazz continues to evolve, offering performers and listeners a full range of creative experience. Tradition and innovation variously inspire today's jazz musicians and fans.

The blues, for example, was the subject of a special celebration during 2003, declared, by congressional proclamation, the Year of the Blues. This was a commemoration of W. C. Handy's first hearing, in 1903, a man playing slide guitar with a knife and singing a plaintive blues. As a result of this life-changing experience, Handy later began publishing commercial blues, establishing the relationship between blues and the music business. Today we recognize the blues as a basic structure (which, however, the greatest blues musicians often ignore), a feeling, an attitude, an exacting discipline—a virtually indefinable and seemingly indestructible American music.

Important to the jazz business today are the numerous collectives organized to support jazz musicians. Since the early days of jazz, collective organizations have helped musicians make a living, creating jobs (gigs) and, beginning in the 1960s, new compositions; but now they play a stronger role than ever. Collectives find grant money for commissioning compositions and recordings, sponsor concerts, and build audiences for new jazz music.

Jazz instrumentation continues to evolve, as musicians explore new technology and world sounds. The electric organ, for example, which played a small role in early jazz, has become increasingly relevant in jazz (and in other popular musics as well) today. Thomas (Fats) Waller played jazz on a giant pipe organ in the 1920s, and in the 1940s and 1950s jazz organ trios consisting of electric organ, guitar, and drums (sometimes augmented by a tenor saxophone) imitated an orchestral sound. Now synthesizers and portable digital organs make the instrument's sound readily available, and the commercial success of the recent sampling of organ-heavy soul jazz recordings from the 1960s has created a new audience for the Hammond (electric) organ itself. Particularly influential was the playing of Wild Bill Davis (1918–1995), considered the creator of the modern jazz organ. (He can be heard on YouTube.)

The arranging impulse largely dropped out of jazz performance from the 1960s through the 1980s, but now, stimulated by Wynton Marsalis and other jazz musicians, it is back. As already mentioned, while great jazz soloists still stir up frenzied enthusiasm among their fans, there appears to be a trend to move away from emphasis on virtuosic solos to a collective endeavor, in which the focus within an ensemble is controlled by the bandleader and shifts from one musician to another. Thus performances today often seem to be more about rhythm and interplay than about solos or even melodies.

A prominent chamber ensemble, the Turtle Island String Quartet, adventurously fuses the classical string quartet with popular contemporary American styles, including bluegrass, swing, and bebop, as well as funk, rhythm and blues, hip-hop, salsa, and others. The quartet (which can be heard online) also explores classical Indian music, creating entirely new sounds with a blend of classical, world, folk, jazz, and pop music.

Innumerable jazz festivals around the country and around the world celebrate local and international talent, often presenting several days of concerts, workshops, demonstrations, dance parties, parades, and jazz camaraderie. Students and professionals offer their music and hear the music of others, teaching and learning together in a concentrated and stimulating atmosphere, as musicians and fans steep themselves in the sounds and flavors of today's jazz. Virtually any day of the year will find a jazz festival—or several festivals—joyously under way.

Since John Lewis and Gunther Schuller began integrating jazz and the classics into a third stream; since John Coltrane and others began improvising on scales from India and rhythms from Africa; since Miles Davis sanctioned the use of rock and funk riffs in *Bitches Brew*—it has become increasingly unrealistic to confine jazz to narrow definitions. Composed or improvised, conceived to entertain or to challenge the intellect, jazz in its various, changing guises continues to be a vital feature of the American musical landscape.

Terms to Review

collective improvisation   third stream   jazz-rock, fusion,
free jazz   jazz-rock-fusion

Key Figures

Ornette Coleman   Herbie Hancock   Henry Threadgill
John Coltrane   Chick Corea   Anthony Braxton
John Lewis   Don Cherry   John Zorn
Gunther Schuller   Pat Metheny   Wynton Marsalis

Critical Thinking

Discuss the seeming oxymoron "jazz composition." How do jazz composers meld composition and improvisation? Are you familiar with the music of any other periods where these concepts were joined. Improvised keyboard parts during the Baroque and improvised cadenzas in Classical concertos are examples.

Why do you think jazz musicians today seem more interested in collective performance than in solo virtuosity? Which is more interesting to you?

Why do you think foreign (world) music has affected the music of more jazz musicians than rock, country, or pop musicians?

Does jazz today relate to the nearly hundred-year-old jazz tradition?

Does jazz relate to today's experience?

Popular Music Since 1970

uring 1970, a year of devastating social and political significance in the United States, frustrated protesters against the war in Vietnam, most notably on college campuses around the country, provoked hostility throughout other strata of society. When National Guard troops at Kent State University shot at student protesters, killing four and wounding at least nine, student riots broke out but soon succumbed to a despairing sense of demoralization and helplessness. Meanwhile other groups, including women, Native Americans, Chicanos, and gays, inspired by the civil rights movement of the 1960s against the conservative "silent majority," caused further unrest in American society.

Rockers were deeply affected by the mood of the time, further darkened by the deaths of several prominent rock figures—Jimi Hendrix (1970) from an overdose of sleeping pills, Janis Joplin (1970) from an overdose of heroin, and Jim Morrison of the Doors (1971) from a heart attack. Musical innovation temporarily lessened as rockers absorbed these shocks and looked ahead; and some groups, for whom the sound engineer had become an essential partner in performance, abandoned live performance entirely.

As the British invasion continued, the Rolling Stones became enormously popular in America, covering American blues and soul recordings at first, then diversifying to become a highly eclectic band. The American rock and pop scenes, too, diversified, producing new styles and branches of styles, as musicians struggled to express and affect their troubled times.

Nevertheless, solo singers, many of whom wrote their own songs, acquired significance as the new decade began.

Singer-Songwriters

"The Boss," **Bruce Springsteen** (b. 1949), probably the most successful rock star of the late 1970s, pointed rock in a new direction in 1982, with his album *Born in the U.S.A.* (whose title song was a bitter indictment of the treatment veterans received upon returning home from Vietnam). Springsteen further revitalized music in the mid-1980s with his stirring songs on socially relevant topics, whose messages were further implemented by Springsteen and other

271

like-minded rock stars in the rock-sponsored benefits for starving masses in Ethiopia, "We Are the World" and "Live Aid." In 1995, Springsteen commanded new attention and respect with his profoundly moving songs in the film *Philadelphia*. (Song samples and lyrics from Springsteen's albums are readily available on YouTube.)

Women singer-songwriters often have had to fight the record industry, which has a long tradition of making over its female artists. Much like Diana Ross of the Supremes in the early days of Motown, today's female singers may endure studio scripting, sculpturing, and choreographing to an extreme degree. Yet Carole King, Mary Chapin Carpenter, Sheryl Crow, Lucinda Williams, and Emmylou Harris, among many others, became and have remained successful. (Tracks from some of their recordings can be heard at their websites.)

Among those resisting dominance—by studios, by men, even by customary chord progressions or lyrics—**Joni Mitchell** (b. 1943) has used the conventions of blues, rock, and folk to write unconventional songs about her own most personal experiences. Her style and her voice have changed over the decades, as her interests ranged from nature to narrative to political indignation.

Art Rock

Rockers and jazzers increasingly collaborated among themselves while also incorporating effects of the music of other cultures. **Blood, Sweat, and Tears,** a rock quartet with a brass section and later with a saxophone as well, produced a sound closer to jazz than to rock, and the even more popular group **Chicago** included rock musicians who incorporated in their music some elements of jazz. Although rock and classical music seem a less likely combination than vernacular rock and jazz, the interest in fusion also encouraged collaborative experiments among musicians in those fields, with varying degrees of success. The superficial quoting of themes from familiar classics, as in the Dutch rock group Ekseption's "The Fifth," based on themes of Beethoven, seems musically insignificant, and most arrangements of classical pieces that use rock instrumentation and rhythms have not proved of much or of lasting interest.

Some ensembles, however—several if not most of them British—have achieved an effective blend of serious concert music and rock, called **art rock.** (The term *art rock* does not imply that other rock styles lack artistic qualities: It is simply a convenient way to describe the combination of rock with concepts of "classical," "concert," or "art" music. Each of those terms is flawed as well, and the conscientious musician uses them with qualification.)

Emerson, Lake & Palmer related rock to classical music in several intriguing pieces. The Moody Blues produced an art rock album with the London Festival Orchestra in 1967 and Genesis, King Crimson, Pink Floyd, and Yes are among other English groups who have explored the concept of art rock. A Dutch group, Focus, and a New York ensemble, Ars Nova, also have experimented with this combined style.

Disco

Disco, which began as *discothèque* in France after World War II, may be seen as the result of a romance or a clash between the popular cultures of Europe and America, and between the social elite and the cultural underworld. It is a difficult music to place, having begun in French jazz clubs, turned to rock music in the United States in the 1960s, and topped the pop charts in 1975.

Swing and jazz clubs in France, banned by the Germans in wartime because of their American, black, and Jewish associations, became symbols of dissent in the French underground, enhancing their aura of illicit excitement and thrill. The first American discothèque, which opened on New Year's Eve 1960, catered to a desire among wealthy jet-setters for an entertainment atmosphere less staid than New York's famous Stork Club and El Morocco. Soon more clubs opened, in New York and in other American cities, all however retaining highly exclusive requirements, including expensive membership dues.

By the mid-1960s, the discothèque had spawned a multitude of dance crazes, including the Twist, the Jerk, and the Watusi among many others, and the role of the disc jockey evolved from the anonymous one of simply playing records to sensing and directing the mood of a crowd throughout the evening. Discothèques of the late 1960s offered enormous dance floors, multiple rock bands playing live music (instead of records), huge rotating mirrored light balls, and extreme sonic overload, all inducing virtual hallucinogenic states. But as the role of discothèque attendees altered from frenzied dancer to passive observer, the discothèque phenomenon seemed about to fade away.

In the 1970s, however, it was dramatically reanimated by gay men, blacks, Hispanics, and other urban contingents suppressed during the 1960s and reveling in their newly liberated position. Thus relaunched, and rechristened *disco,* the popular dance phenomenon maintained a highly visible presence throughout the new decade (Figure 16.1). Much of the disco culture concerned drugs and sex, and the hedonistic philosophy that nothing is wrong if it feels right (or as Mae West once said, "Too much of a good thing may be a great thing"), remained at the core of disco culture; but this philosophy also produced the first distinctive disco music. Dissatisfied with short rock singles not primarily intended for dancing, disco DJs and dancers of the 1970s sought extended pieces with continuous danceable rhythms based on the black R&B roots of pop music. The early 1970s produced several hit disco songs, and in 1975 Van McCoy and "The Hustle" went to the top of the pop charts, signifying the mainstreaming of a culture that had prided itself on various kinds of exclusivity, from the wealthy elite to black and gay men.

The new crowds attending Studio 54, which opened in New York in 1977, still had to pass the "entrance requirements" of the club's owners; but at the end of that year, the astounding success of the film *Saturday Night Fever* further buoyed disco's rising fortunes. The movie's double-album soundtrack eventually became the biggest-selling record of all time (later replaced by Michael Jackson's *Thriller*), and by 1978 40 percent of all the music on *Billboard*'s Hot 100 was disco. The songs of the Bee Gees, biggest of all mainstream disco

FIGURE 16.1

Overhead view of the crowd dancing at Studio 54 in New York City, October 31, 1981.

stars, had traditional pop music themes with no relationship to the hedonistic, highly sexualized culture of most early disco.

For a time, rock fans felt threatened by disco, which they viewed as synthetic, aristocratic, and fake; but in the end disco provided the common enemy against which rock fans rallied. The Disco Demolition Rally at Chicago's Comiskey Park stadium in July 1979 blasted out of control, as rock fans broke up mountains of disco records as well as much of the stadium itself, giving Comiskey much the same role in defeating disco that the bloody Altamont concert had played in ending the counterculture of the 1960s. After Comiskey Park, the disco market crashed, doomed as well by a wave of political conservatism and the fear of AIDS.

Punk

In the 1970s **punk** evolved from the raw, raucous garage band music of the 1960s and from the New York City avant-garde scene. While teenagers banged out their emotions and frustrations on whatever instruments—sometimes including garbage can lids—they could get hold of, slightly older and more sophisticated musicians, poets, and artists in New York also were expressing anger and disillusionment with the social and cultural conditions of their day. The imminent threats of war, nuclear disaster, economic turmoil, and out-of-control technology fed their anger and despair; and the hippies' preaching of love to all, the sophisticated arty sounds of art rock, heavy metal's pyrotechnical displays of instrumental virtuosity, and the synthetic sounds of disco fueled their fury. Like the rebellious *beats* of the 1950s (notably including Jack Kerouac, Allen Ginsberg, and William Burroughs) and earlier the Dadaists—a group of European artists protesting against the horrors of World War I—New York's avant-garde musicians of the 1970s turned to irony and anti-art to vent their frustration. Recordings of the simple, repetitive, angry garage band music stimulated their conception of the defiant new music, which contended that nothing sort of overturning society could improve the sorry state of the world.

Punk was born in a small New York bar called CBGB (full name, CBGB & OMFUG, for Country, Blue Grass, Blues, and Other Music for Urban Gourmets), where five men calling themselves the **New York Dolls** (Figure 16.2) began performing in 1971. The musical elements associated with punk include a rigid eighth-note rhythmic throb and a vocal range so narrow as to approach a drone; but ultimately of more interest, perhaps, is punk's association with the art world. A significant number of punk musicians attended art school and brought to their music modern art concepts of shock value, performance as art, and fashion, which profoundly affected the music they performed and how they performed it.

To the alienated attitude, the repetitious unemotional delivery, the pessimistic subject matter (drugs, prostitution, sadomasochism), and the angry new sound of the garage bands, the New York Dolls added glitter (they wore lipstick, heavy eye makeup, and high heels) and a lighter touch. Heavy guitar distortion and a pounding beat contributed to the wild excitement of their audiences. Commercial success largely eluded them, however, as other bands, including Television, the Patti Smith Group, and the Ramones, continued their movement.

FIGURE 16.2

The influential American glam rock band, the New York Dolls.

Avant-garde art particularly influenced **Television,** a punk band strongly attracted to Andy Warhol and the Velvet Underground (see p. 225) and to the free jazz improvisation of John Coltrane. One member of Television, Tom Verlaine (Tom Miller), took his stage name from the French Symbolist poet Paul Verlaine (1844–1896), who represented meanings in his delicate, sensitive verse by the imaginative use of words for their sensuous effects. Although punk was by definition anti-intellectual, Television added to their music a degree of complexity and an aesthetic dimension unique among punk bands.

Patti Smith (b. 1946), a professional writer of poetry, plays, and articles, took her group to CBGB's in 1975, singing angry, gutsy vocals with lyrics and a delivery style calculated to shock her audience. The Patti Smith Group attracted a great deal of attention; but better-known and ultimately more influential were the **Ramones,** who modeled their image on the New York Dolls and took their name from "Paul Ramon," an early stage name of Paul McCartney. (Each member of the band, formed in 1974, assumed the last name Ramone.) Uninterested in art, free jazz, or literature, the Ramones projected raw energy, spirit, emotion, and fun; and their short, simple, fast, hard-driving songs stayed high on the charts into the early 1980s.

In the mid-1970s, Malcolm McLaren, the British owner of an antifashion London clothing store and sometime manager of the New York Dolls, brought the pessimistic, anarchic punk sound to England, where British young people, experiencing far more serious social and economic conditions than their peers in the United States, took the angry new music to their hearts. McLaren's British band, the Sex Pistols, became wildly successful at home and influential in the United States. Soon American society was avidly imitating punk fashion, as models spiked their hair and ostentatiously fastened gaping holes in their trendy clothes with flashy—sometimes gold—safety pins. The striking visual effects of punk dress, hair, and makeup strongly influenced art and fashion around the world.

In the 1990s, several California punk rock bands—including the Offspring, Rancid, and Green Day—made punk no longer the music of a righteous minority. Singing of alienation, resentment, and self-destruction to very short, catchy tunes accompanied by speed-strummed guitars and walloping drums, they brought the humor and tuneful adrenaline of punk to a mass public. The female punk trio Sleater-Kinney, formed in 1994 in Olympia, Washington, vehemently expressed a sense of exclusion and marginalization from a woman's point of view. Meanwhile, the punk look—leather, studded dog collars, and razor-shredded clothing—evolved to include body piercing and punk hairstyles spiked up to seven inches long and vividly colored in unlikely hues such as purple, pink, or green.

In 2004, the Dolls made a strong comeback, despite the deaths of two original members. (A third died soon after the Dolls' historic reunion.) The new Dolls, described by their frontman David Johansen as perhaps more "spiritual," or as he says more "worldcentric" than in their early New York–neighborhood days, continue to perform, tour, and record today. Meanwhile, punk lives on, as it began in the 1970s, through live shows in small places such as bars and pubs, rather than through huge arena concerts or commercial recordings on major labels. In the society of punk, personal interaction between a band and its audience remains essential.

New Wave

The term **new wave** was loosely applied to several sounds of the mid-1980s, some of which reflected certain characteristics of earlier styles. Neither angry nor political, new wave groups defused punk by imitating its manner but not its substance. That is, adopting punk's unconventional dress and bizarre stage movements, new wave musicians criticized society without resorting to shock tactics.

Although it contained some of the elements of punk, new wave was far broader in concept, constituting more a philosophy of life expressed through music than a distinctive musical style. Much of the music of one outstanding American new wave group, **Talking Heads,** is based on the simple harmonies and complex rhythms of some African musics; but the music of other well-known new wave bands, including **B-52s, Cars,** and especially **Police,** responds to different sources of inspiration. The term always referred to new or progressive music, conceived with the aid of modern studio and electronic techniques.

In 2008, the B-52s—all in their fifties—were performing and recording new as well as familiar songs. (In 2007, their first hit, "Rock Lobster," was performed in the film *Knocked Up.*) The band's sound has added a more modern sheen, including a shimmering new electronic feel; but the two women still wear their trademark wigs—lest the audience riot, they say. As one member expresses it, "Our most important legacy is that people had fun."

Grunge

Teenagers of the 1990s, called generation X by the press, continued to find rock a congenial medium in which to release their fears and frustrations brought about by economic uncertainty; family instability; violence on television, on the movie screen, and in the streets; gangs; racial warfare; and social injustice. Some craved an angry, harsh, aggressive sound reflecting their own disturbed feelings, much as baby boomers had turned to early rock and roll.

In the Northwest, **grunge,** sometimes called the Seattle sound, combined the aggression of heavy metal with a melodic element reminiscent of the Beatles. The pacesetter grunge band **Nirvana,** led by **Kurt Cobain** (1967–1994), achieved a hybrid of pop, metal, and punk that became a national phenomenon. Pearl Jam followed Nirvana to the top of the chart in 1991; and in 1993, the early grunge band Soundgarden hit the top with *Superunknown.* The despair of the post–baby boomers was heightened by the deaths, from drug overdoses, of some grunge soloists, and especially by the shotgun suicide of Kurt Cobain, probably the most important figure in the movement.

Electronic Dance Music

During the 1980s, many bands and several individuals with distinctive sounds became rich and famous. Prince (known then as "the artist formerly known as Prince"), Michael Jackson, Lionel Richie, Madonna, Cyndi Lauper, and Sting (formerly of Police), among the best-known names of mainstream rock in the 1980s, maintained various degrees of popularity through the 1990s. Synthesizers and other electronic instruments increasingly varied the sonorities of live and recorded performance, and concerts and recordings achieved new levels of sophistication.

The first years of the new century experienced a return of interest in the popular culture of the 1980s, a source of nostalgia for older rockers and stimulating to youngsters curious about their parents' youthful experience. Thus in 2001, disco and new wave underwent a dance-floor revival, as electronic producers mimicked the pop songs they had grown up loving, to produce a new abstract (without lyrics) dance music as easy to hear as to dance to. Electronic timbres devised by classical composers (to be considered in Chapter 20) once seemed unearthly and unacceptable to pop and classical audiences alike, but now merely reflect the everyday reality of cell phones, cash machines, car alarms, and innumerable electronic and digital tones our ears take for granted.

Rock and electronic music evolved together, both depending on instruments that plugged in, both addressing disembodied audiences through radio and records. As rockers started to hear music as signals and processing, and quickly took to distortion and feedback as desired ends to be attained, the techniques of cutting, mixing, sampling, looping, layering, and sequencing soon became commonplace in rock. Melodically, rhythmically, and harmonically simpler than electronic music devised by the classical electronic avant-garde, dance music produced by synthesizers, samplers, computers, and drum machines has been increasing in popularity year by year. Often surreal and hypnotic, and invariably loud, the music is designed to make people dance, to take them from reality to another place. Variously called *house, techno, electro, nu-wave,* and other names as well, electronic dance music forms an important part of America's landscape in the early twenty-first century.

Pop Music and Politics

Political pop music was at its peak in the early 1960s and 1970s, when controversies over civil rights and the Vietnam War inspired protest songs from artists such as Bob Dylan ("The Times They Are a-Changin'"), the band Buffalo Springfield ("For What It's Worth"), and Marvin Gaye ("What's Goin' On?"), which were widely heard on pop and rock radio stations. Since that time, mainstream music has generally been more concerned with having a good time than engaging in politics, but in 2004, with wars in Iraq and Afghanistan and an upcoming election, pop musicians again were motivated to take political stands. Eminem released a strong political video ("Mosh"), and John Fogerty, Dan Bern, Missy Elliott, and P. Diddy were among many other musicians who urged people to vote.

Politicians in 2008 often used pop music for their own purposes—playing a popular hit at rallies and other campaign events, for example—which sometimes caused controversies between licensing issues and the right of free speech. Many pop, rock, and hip-hop artists publicly endorsed the candidate of their choice, with or without the approval of the candidate. Musicians performed for political events, wrote politically charged lyrics, and even sampled speeches from Barack Obama's campaign. Songs with sensitive political (or other) content, such as will.i.am's song and video based on the Obama campaign's familiar phrase "Yes, we can," are readily available on YouTube as well as other sites.

Looking Forward, Backward, and Abroad

New technology affords an array of sophisticated effects, as synthesizers and other electronic instruments increasingly vary the sonorities of live and recorded performance, and concerts and recordings achieve new levels of sophistication. Previously inconceivable collaborations involving dead artists—Lauryn Hill with Bob Marley, and Celine Dion with Frank Sinatra, for example—sell well.

Acculturation, too, becomes ever more significant, as improved communication and expanded travel bring fascinating new sounds to the Western vernacular music experience. In the 1980s, Paul Simon, Peter Gabriel, the Clash, and Talking Heads were among artists who enriched their sounds by drawing from international sources. Today's advances in technology and communication make it even easier for musicians to hear music from other nations and incorporate it into their own work.

Yet many rock musicians have returned to their roots, producing rhythm and blues, rockabilly, soul, and psychedelic music, even as a new generation, representing many cultures, races, and experiences, carries forward the remarkably varied and durable music we call rock. Nostalgia for earlier, familiar sounds continually vies with the urge to explore new music.

Hip-Hop and Rap

South Bronx, New York, in the 1970s was a neighborhood in ruin. Misguided efforts at urban renewal displaced many residents, took away jobs, and left a wasteland of mostly empty apartments run by slumlords, who often burned the buildings for insurance profit. As African American, Afro-Caribbean, and Latino families moved into the devastated neighborhoods, remaining white youths formed gangs to threaten the newcomers, who soon formed their own gangs, first in self-defense, then for aggression. Much in the way that slavery gave birth to the blues, jobless, poor, and hopeless urban conditions spawned the **hip-hop** culture.

And hip-hop indeed is a culture, usually defined as including B-boying (break dancing), graffiti writing (spray can paintings, often done on moving objects such as subway cars or large vehicles), DJing (disc jockeys playing

FIGURE 16.3
DJ Kool Herc (b. 1955)
performing on June 14, 2008,
outside the Brooklyn Public
Library.

and manipulating records at dance parties), and MCing (a master of ceremonies, or mike controller, *rapping* over the records). **DJ Kool Herc** (b. 1955; Figure 16.3), one of the earliest DJs and a founder of hip-hop, says the culture further includes the way one walks, talks, looks, and communicates. Hip-hop, in fact, is a way of life.

Hip-hop came to the Bronx out of Jamaica, and one of its most characteristic sounds—rapping over spinning records—derived from the harmonically simple, melodically lilting, socially conscious music called *reggae.*

Reggae   During the 1960s, as Jamaicans adjusting to their recent independence from Great Britain wrestled with assorted political and economic crises, Jamaican youths drew from global popular culture to express their national pride with a new, hybrid music. **Reggae,** as they called it, fused characteristics of North American rock and of African music with elements drawn from a black religious movement called Rastafarianism (named for Ethiopia's emperor Ras Tafari—"Ras" means "duke"—later renamed Haile Selassie [1892–1975]) to form a kind of "acculturated rock," which became popular in England in the late 1960s and in the United States a decade later. **Bob Marley** (1945–1981), a leading Jamaican reggae performer, became very well known and highly revered in North America and abroad.

Reggae is roughly related to rhythm and blues, although reggae's African polyrhythms are more complex, the bass lines stronger, and the tempos more relaxed than those of R&B. Reggae combos consist of electric guitars, an electric organ, an electric bass guitar, and drums, with electronic studio techniques sometimes making significant contributions as well. In Kingston, Jamaican DJs (disc jockeys) entertained crowds by maintaining a steady stream of patter—a poetic storytelling—as they changed records, even talking over the records as they spun. This technique, called **toasting,** was destined to have far-reaching effects on the development of rap music in the 1970s and 1980s. The practice was so widespread, records were soon being produced with full songs on one side (A) and the music from the A side *without the vocal* on the other (B), so DJs could toast without competing with lyrics.

Reggae—a Jamaican spin on African American–influenced rock—reveals the possible complexity and enrichment afforded by such wide acculturation. Reggae also exemplifies a popular music with strong religious connotations, for it is closely associated with Rastafarianism. Many reggae songs have urgent political content: Some promoted the "back to Africa" movement that emerged in the 1960s; in the 1970s, Marley sang of equality, unity, and love, all with an underlying threat of revolutionary violence; and today's hard-core reggae fans still favor the searing political indictments that infused much of Marley's music.

The Rise of Hip-Hop
Jamaicans immigrating to the South Bronx in the 1960s brought with them the sophisticated turntable techniques they had developed in Kingston, where mobile sound systems had largely replaced live bands: With only a turntable, powerful amplifiers, and homemade speakers, a DJ could bring dance parties to street crowds unable to afford club entertainment. In the South Bronx, DJs honed their performance techniques to become outstanding showmen by incessantly twisting turntable knobs, *backspinning* (playing one record while turning a second one backward), altering the playing speeds, even scratching the records (moving them in both directions under the needle) to improvise new percussive sounds as they spun. DJs played many kinds of music, from remixed versions of R&B hits through several Jamaican styles, including reggae. They revved dancers to frenzied enthusiasm by playing just the *breaks*—brief instrumental phrases between vocal sections—over and over, switching rapidly back and forth between two copies of a record playing at the same time (Figure 16.4).

Novel in the early days of hip-hop, *scratch DJs,* also known as *turntablists,* have become artists in their own right. The turntable, in fact, may be the most important musical instrument of the current era—several universities offer professional instruction in turntable techniques. The music heard in dance clubs today—called drum-and-bass, house, or trip-hop, among other names—is usually sample-based and electronically composed, and is therefore a DJ's creation. There is even a system now to notate the scratches making up DJs' compositions, allowing top scratch DJs to publish and copyright their compositions and aspiring DJs to see and learn the music. (The exhilarating 2002 documentary film *Scratch* traces the evolution of turntablism.)

FIGURE 16.4

A DJ spins a record at an
outdoor festival in San
Francisco.

FIGURE 16.4

A DJ spins a record at an
outdoor festival in San
Francisco.

Rap In the 1970s South Bronx, people fascinated with the street turntable
show often stopped dancing to watch, whereupon DJs, to stir up the action by
the dancers, hired MCs (for master of ceremonies, or sometimes mike controller)
to fire up the crowd with shouts of "Get up!" "Jam to the beat!" and so on. When
the MCs began speaking to the rhythm of the music and trading increasingly
clever and complex rhymes with one another and with the DJ, **rap** was born.

Rap, which has raised perennial questions about relationships among art,
politics, and public morality, draws from African, Afro-Caribbean, and African
American rhythmic styles; from urban street jive; from black radio DJs from the
1950s through the 1970s; from the heavyweight champion boxer Muhammad Ali;
and from a rich assortment of other historical and cultural influences. In black
music, vocal timbres, rhythms, and vocal inflections all convey meaning, and
MCs (rappers) exploit the entire range of tonal semantics in their delivery styles.

Throughout the 1970s, rappers and DJs preserved their performances
on *mixtapes,* homemade tapes made at street dances and later at dance club
shows. It seemed impossible to capture the hip-hop scene on commercial
recordings—as these were too brief and limiting to encompass the visual
and participatory experiences essential to hip-hop culture. Then in 1979,
the independent label Sugar Hill Records auditioned three unknown rappers
and immediately signed them to improvise the recording "Rapper's Delight"
(Listening Example 58), which featured the three MCs rapping over the
breaks of Chic's song "Good Times."

Social Concerns In the 1980s, rappers began writing socially conscious
lyrics addressing ghetto conditions and economic inequalities in the United
States, which they delivered in their individual "flow" styles—their particular

Listening Example 58

"Rapper's Delight" (excerpt)

"Rapper's Delight" quickly reached American Top 40, introducing America and the world to hip-hop music. To their astonishment, DJs discovered that dancers preferred the record to a live performer. One DJ actually lip-synched to the recording, fooling and then delighting his audience.

CD 3
Track 1
3.22

Improvisers   The Sugarhill Gang: Henry "Big Bank Hank" Jackson, Guy "Master Gee" O'Brien, and Michael "Wonder Mike" Wright.

Genre   Rap.

Timbre   The rappers perform over an excerpt or *sample* (here, the rhythm track) of the 1979 disco hit "Good Times," recorded by the band Chic, performed for "Rapper's Delight" by session musicians in the recording studio (though some suggest the sound is so close to the original recording portions may be tape loops).

Texture   Polyphonic. The instruments add primarily rhythmic interest but those with melodic capability have melodic independence.

Form: Strophic. Each of the three rappers improvises a "verse," performing a clever, amusing, rhythmic recitation over the background music.

Meter   Duple, with a heavy backbeat.

Tempo   Moderate.

Text   The rappers brag about themselves, describe dance moves, tell funny stories, and exhort the listeners to respond.

manner of combining rhythmic play, rhyme scheme, phrasing, accents, timbres, and pitch inflection. Although rap began as a predominantly male activity, Missy Elliott is among several successful female rappers today. While many male rappers extol men's domination over women, Sister Souljah's lyrics have addressed drug abuse, black-on-black violence, and national politics; and Queen Latifah's album *Black Rain* is packed with socially responsible messages about safe sex, relationships, and love. **Salt–N–Pepa** (Figure 16.5) have offered stinging criticism of male promiscuity and spoken of female self-empowerment—though their third album, *Very Necessary* (1993), rhymed the praises of men.

The question whether hip-hop is a culture or a craft arose as immensely successful white rappers—such as Vanilla Ice, the Beastie Boys, and later Eminem, among others—claimed that hip-hop is something one can learn to

FIGURE 16.5
Salt–N–Pepa.

do regardless of one's cultural or ethnic heritage. These rappers emphasize clever, rapid-fire lyrics supported by music strictly designed to show off the complicated rhythms of the words. Certain black hip-hop musicians counter that hip-hop is a culture one is born into, which cannot be limited by the specific sounds produced. Thus Missy Elliott, who sings as much as she raps, and the Roots, an eight-piece hip-hop band using traditional instruments in place of turntables and samples, consider themselves full-fledged hip-hop artists born and bred: They simply prefer a more musical style of hip-hop.

As hip-hop moved downtown from the Bronx to Manhattan dance halls, and then all the way to the West Coast, new styles evolved. The more brutal *gangsta rap* of the late 1980s, often praising misogyny and violence, attracted devoted listeners, both black and white, but drew condemnation from courts and law enforcers. Tupac Shakur, murdered in 1996 at age twenty-four, had rapped about violence, social realism, fate, and pain. Moments of tenderness and compassion in his songs are overwhelmed with fierce black-against-black anger and brutality, and he followed expressions of respectful praise for women with harangues about "bitches" and "hos." The white rapper Eminem (Marshall Mathers, hence "M'n'M"), a master of gallows and gross-out humor, gleefully aims cruel gibes at gays, women (including his mother and his wife), and assorted real people in public life; yet many admire his ingenious wordplay, inventive beats, daring candor, and wicked humor. The language with which Ice-T, Ice Cube, and the Geto Boys rap about gang warfare and driveby shootings is offensive to many, but the situations they so blazingly describe certainly exist.

Back to the Roots Some rappers, of course, produce lighthearted, playful songs, and in the 1990s rap-based cartoons appeared on television.

Rap soon joined mainstream popular culture on television (starting with Will Smith in *The Fresh Prince of Bel-Air*) and in Hollywood films (with Ice-T, Queen Latifah, Mos Def, and Eminem, among others). **Ice Cube** (born O'Shea Jackson in 1969), having become a successful actor, screenwriter, and movie producer, worked simultaneously in the summer of 2003 on the family friendly movie *Barbershop 2: Back in Business* (as actor and executive producer) and on the angry album *Terrorist Threats,* full of socially charged rage. He continues to perform in movies and television and to release new recordings.

Today sophisticated northern urban rappers tap the rich resources of earlier black music: Some, for example, play versions of the music enjoyed by black fieldworkers in the Deep South more than fifty years ago. **Kirk Franklin** (b. 1970) skillfully melds hip-hop and traditional gospel conventions in performances such as his popular hit "Stomp," a collaboration with the group God's Property, featuring the rhythm track to the Funkadelic's funk anthem "One Nation Under a Groove" and a guest rap by Salt (Cheryl James) of Salt–N–Pepa. Franklin's explosive vocal presentation has been compared to that of James Brown or Ray Charles—both of whom were criticized for blending sacred and secular effects.

The song "Shake Ya Tailfeather," performed by Sean Combs (P. Diddy) in the movie *Bad Boys II,* derives its title from "Shake Your Moneymaker," written by slide guitar master Elmore James about 1960. In those days, royalties went to publishers and record companies instead of to blues artists, who often suffered severe economic deprivation. Today's rappers, in contrast, demand professional deals that allow them to own their works and get rich.

And so we turn to the business of music.

Music Business

New technologies continually alter—for better or worse—the business of music, and technological advances, which have occurred more rapidly in recent years than ever before, have affected every phase of this industry. It is possible today for almost anyone, with equipment ranging from moderately priced resources to sophisticated instruments and digital machines, to create, perform, produce, market, and record music from a home studio. It is even possible, with e-jamming software, for independent musicians to play and record together—for fun, or for business—with other musicians in near or distant locations, brought together by Internet connection. Software programs preclude the need to read or notate music, or to perform at a virtuosic level; nor is it necessary for amateur musicians to hire additional performers, sound engineers, or anyone at all: An individual can simulate a combo, band, or singing group at will. Thus music teachers, side musicians, recording engineers, and others find themselves less in demand than before.

On the other hand, new technologies also offer opportunities for those with technical expertise. Some artists, for example, choose to subject their performance to the manipulations of a sound engineer, who with correction software can control many aspects of a recorded sound. Sound engineers practice sonic manipulation not only for correction, but for variety and interest and to make a recording more marketable. While one singer may choose to preserve an original take, flaws and all, for its emotional intensity and integrity, another may wish the sound engineer to correct the pitch if it is slightly out of tune, or to erase—or add—a vocal tremor, at will.

The business of music must continually adjust, as familiar products and processes become outdated, and new creative possibilities for musicians and wider choices for consumers evolve.

Sharing Music
In 1999, the Internet-based software program Napster provided means for fans to share and swap music files via the Internet, and immediately the music industry felt the impact. Legal challenges forced Napster to close down its free service, but the advent of the portable digital audio player called the **iPod** in 2001 quickly revolutionized the music business. Downloading music from computer to portable player was not a new concept, but the efficient interface between the iPod and Apple's online iTunes Store made the process quick, easy, and readily affordable. Compact, elegant, extremely portable, and with a huge storage capacity, the iPod quickly replaced earlier, less efficient digital music players.

Napster, too, eventually established for-pay modes of disseminating digital music files, making them available at very reasonable cost to consumers: Typically, one can purchase single album tracks, from sharing services or from Apple's iTunes Store, for ninety-nine cents each. Many of today's fans willingly suffer the loss of the liner notes and credit information included in an album or CD package for the savings in cost and the convenience of buying only the songs they wish from an album.

Music purchased from the iTunes Store, made available to Apple by the "Big Four" music companies—Sony, Universal, Warner, and EMI—has been subject to a digital rights management (DRM) system, intended to prevent the music from being played on unauthorized devices. But in 2009, the companies were exploring the possibility of removing the DRMs, largely because they have not proved effective. Similarly, efforts are ongoing to remove restrictive U.S. copyright laws, which currently cover original works for ninety-five years. The ease with which digitized music is shared on the Internet has heightened the intensity of argument between those who believe copyright protection properly rewards creative people and the companies that hire and promote them, and those who believe they should be able to legally share, remix, and re-use music of their choice.

As CD sales quickly declined, due to the availability of free and inexpensive downloads, those depending on CD sales for a living faced the need to forge creative new means of earning money.

Marketing Music
Traditionally, artists submitted to sometimes crushing control by their commercial labels, who often exploited their artists' talent and provided them with minimal compensation. The labels did, however,

launch the careers of many legendary performers. We discussed Motown Records in Chapter 13; and the 2008 movie *Cadillac Records,* starring R&B artist Beyoncé Knowles, describes the 1950s role of pioneering blues label Chess Records in establishing the careers of several artists and helping to usher in rock and roll.

In 2008, Atlantic Records passed a dreaded milestone: More than half of its music sales in the United States were from digital products, like downloads on iTunes and ring tones for cell phones. As the music industry faces the fact that digital revenues are unlikely to compensate for declining sales of CDs, some major recording companies and a few independents are exploring a new type of business relationship known as *multiple rights* or *360 deals,* in which artists share with their label their earnings not just from album sales, but from concerts, merchandise, and other sources as well, in exchange for increased investment on the label's part in developing the artist's career. The label might give the artist more money upfront, provide touring subsidies, allow more time to develop a career, and market ring tones and assorted merchandise. In return, the company shares its talent's earnings from lucrative product endorsements, apparel lines, and live concerts.

Today some musicians bypass commercial labels by recording with independent companies instead. Since today's tightly controlled corporate-owned radio stations play the songs record companies pay them to play (a practice known as "pay to play"), music from smaller labels generally does not make it to the airwaves. However, wide access to the Internet has provided unprecedented opportunities to hear music produced by independent labels, here and abroad. Many musicians are successfully marketing their music through Internet blogs, general music websites, and their own websites and MySpace and Facebook pages, avoiding music labels altogether. Some artists are experimenting with different cost models: offering free downloads of their music or allowing consumers to choose their own price for an album. In 2007, the British band Radiohead released their recording *"In Rainbows"* directly to fans via the Internet for whatever their buyers chose to pay. Since their recording company paid them only a very small amount (about a dollar) per album, they believed they would earn more from fans opting to support their music by paying more than that. (This apparently did not happen, however, since Radiohead withdrew their online offer three months later.)

Thus music has become democratized, free from the demands and manipulation of big-name commercial companies and from the need to become commercially successful by satisfying a large mainstream audience. Now it is possible for complex, eclectic, diverse, experimental music—unacceptable to Top 40 venues—to find welcome, and generate income, on the Internet.

The business of music will continue to evolve, as it always has, along with technology. Meanwhile, back-to-roots movements vie with the spirit of futurism to stimulate creativity in the world of pop. Thanks to technology, to multiculturalism, and to the accomplishments of previous generations of pop musicians, the pop scene today is richer and more varied than ever before.

Terms to Review

art rock

disco

punk

new wave

grunge

house, techno, electro, nu-wave

hip-hop

reggae

toasting

rap

iPod

Key Figures

Individuals

Bruce Springsteen

Joni Mitchell

Patti Smith

Kurt Cobain

DJ Kool Herc

Bob Marley

Ice Cube

Kirk Franklin

Groups

Blood, Sweat, and Tears

Chicago

New York Dolls

Television

Ramones

Talking Heads

B-52s

Cars

Police

Nirvana

Salt–N–Pepa

Critical Thinking

Does your personal music collection include albums by any of the performers discussed in this chapter? What does your collection reveal about your preference for one or more particular styles of popular music? Has your preference changed significantly over the last five years? If so, how? Do you find the music being produced today more or less interesting than other popular musics (country, jazz, rock, pop) covered in this chapter and in earlier chapters of this text?

Do you consider hip-hop a craft (that can be learned) or a culture (that must be experienced from birth)?

How do you view duets between live and dead performers? Are these duets still the work of the original artist? Do they confuse or weaken the original artist's intentions? Does it matter? Are the duets comparable to sampling a lick from another artist's recording?

Why would people pay for music when they can get it free? Should musicians own the rights to their work? Should the companies that produce them, or that record them, own the rights? If a singer makes a cover recording of an earlier record, who should own the rights and make the profits from the new product: the first or second singer? The first or second record company? The composer? Other?

Part 4
Summary

In the 1950s, white country-western music combined with elements of black rhythm and blues to produce rock and roll, as the popular music industry responded to the desires and the dollars of American teens. Bill Haley and Elvis Presley, white country singers with a black style of delivery, made the new music widely popular, and soon cover recordings of R&B hits were earning significant money. Rebelling against the whites' windfall from the genius of black music, Motown produced records that pleased whites but earned money for black performers, while soul brought music of a new intensity and sincerity to rock and roll. The British invasion begun by the Beatles continued with the Rolling Stones, who came from comfortable English backgrounds but whose music reflected the experiences of poor black Americans.

The urban folk movement reflected continuing relationships between rock and country. Bob Dylan, Joan Baez, and others composed and performed folk-like songs on topical subjects of the day. Alternative country rivals the polished sounds of commercial country by blending punk and rock-and-roll effects with country sounds.

Jazz in the later part of the twentieth century explored new and increasingly complex musical concepts. Free jazz declared independence from most of the preconceived notions about jazz, allowing collective improvisation by the members of a jazz band. Fusion melds jazz and rock, and jazz musicians have found many ways to integrate foreign sounds into their music. Seemingly threatened with extinction for a time, as rock became ever more popular, jazz composition is now among the most important fields of American music.

Some late twentieth-century popular styles, including punk, new wave, and grunge, addressed social concerns with varying degrees of anger, humor, and resignation. New technologies continually alter the manner in which popular music is created, marketed, and consumed. Synthesizers and other electronic instruments increasingly have varied the sonorities of live and recorded performances.

Hip-hop culture, derived from Jamaican and African influences, evolved in the South Bronx and quickly spread across this country and around the world. Rap artists entertained with their steady stream of poetic patter while DJs became increasingly virtuosic with their turntable techniques. Old and new music, and new techniques such as sampling applied to old music, all have their place in today's pop scene.

PART

5

Music for Theater and Film

Music and Theater: Historical and Cultural Perspective

Music and drama seem meant for each other, each medium transforming and enhancing the other to form a perfect union immeasurably greater than the sum of its parts. In fact, a close relationship between the two arts dates back in Western history at least as far as the ancient Greeks, who claimed to have achieved the ideal mating of words and music in their magnificent theatrical choruses. Since that time, many have disagreed as to what the Greeks considered this ideal to be, and whether they found the music or the text the most important element in performances combining these arts. But the mutual attraction of music and drama remains as strong and as intriguing to most of the world's cultures today as it was in ancient times.

Musical Theater in America America's earliest professional musical performances (see pp. 63–64), mostly imported from England, proved highly popular in cities large enough and settled enough to indulge in extravagant entertainment. In the nineteenth century, Italian operas drew large and enthusiastic

290

**Alan Jay Lerner
(1918–1986), lyricist**
"We are not an aria
country. We are a song
country."

audiences in several southern cities and even in Boston—although the Bostonians' puritanical reservations caused nearly every theater there to be known as "Museum" or "Athenaeum." French light operas and—especially—the British Gilbert and Sullivan's hilarious operettas aroused tremendous enthusiasm among crowds of Americans, who returned again and again to see these shows.

Early American productions included some based on British ballad operas, incorporating popular songs into melodramatic stage presentations. The first notable American musical, *The Black Crook,* which appeared on Broadway right after the Civil War (1866), was a 5½-hour spectacle of song and ballet. Although so successful as to make its creator (Charles M. Barras) comfortable for life, the show spawned few imitations, and minstrel shows constituted the primary native contributions to the musical stage for the last half of the nineteenth century. The first American musical comedy is generally considered to be George M. Cohan's *Little Johnny Jones,* produced in 1904 (p. 299).

Broadway Musicals Much as art and literature reflect the mores and tastes of the era that produces them, Broadway musicals also review and

critique the standards of their time. The severe Protestant ethic instilled by the Puritans and practiced in much of American society through the nineteenth century appeared to be crumbling by the turn of the twentieth century, when a looser morality prevailed at least in the large cities. Increased knowledge of sexual hygiene lessened fears of infection; the automobile provided opportunities for courtship away from family observation; movies pictured situations previously unimaginable but highly attractive to the young and inexperienced. As we have seen, provocative Latin dances surpassed the sedate waltz in popularity. Women's dresses became shorter and their underwear less constrictive. And liquor prohibited was certainly more exciting than legal brew.

The Broadway musical stage reflected all of these and other characteristics of American life as well. George Gershwin's *Of Thee I Sing* (1931) was a sidesplitting musical satire on American politics, and his opera *Porgy and Bess* (written for the Broadway theater—not the opera house) offered a sympathetic view of Negro life in Charleston. Social commentary pervaded important shows, notably Jerome Kern's *Show Boat* (1927), and the revue *Pins and Needles* (1922).

Yet, though the Broadway musical today is the source of admiration and imitation in the very countries that inspired it, the medium is indeed grounded in foreign traditions, and the latter years of the twentieth century experienced a British invasion of the musical stage akin to, perhaps even surpassing, that of pop music in the 1960s and beyond. Thus perhaps it is not surprising that although the musical shows of a given period reflect certain styles and mores of their time, the American musical stage cannot be relied upon to provide a cultural snapshot of society. Broadway has been traditionally white and mainstream: jazz, rock, hip-hop, rap, and Latin music have made token appearances, but the overall picture is largely monochromatic.

For economic as well as cultural reasons, the strongest trend in recent years has been to stage revivals of safe (that is, formerly popular) shows: In the 1999–2000 season, only three new shows with an original book and score opened on Broadway, and no season since has been notably richer. The staggering expense of staging a new musical, and the perceived preference of the contemporary audience for nonchallenging entertainment, have had a profound effect upon the development of the Broadway musical.

Operas

Although the line between musical theater and opera used to be recognizable, if difficult to define, today's musicals and operas are almost interchangeable. Following the example of nineteenth-century European "realistic" (*verismo*) operas, such as Giacomo Puccini's *La Bohème* and *Madama Butterfly,* many American opera composers have based their works on stories of American life or legend (Douglas Moore's *The Ballad of Baby Doe*), or even, more recently, on relatively current events (John Adams's *Nixon in China,* for example). It remains to be seen whether these—as well as musicals based on popular Italian operas, such as *Rent* (by Jonathan Larson, based on *La Bohème*) and *Miss Saigon* (by Claude-Michel Schöberg and Alain Boublil, based on *Madama Butterfly*)—will attract the long-lasting devotion of their Italian forebears.

Today, in fact, musicals and operas have drawn so close as to render differences between them not only obscure but largely meaningless. For example, Broadway shows addressed to the children's market, including such mammoth Disney productions as *Beauty and the Beast* and *The Lion King,* are largely sung throughout, with little or no spoken dialogue, in the tradition of classical opera.

Films

When sound came to Hollywood films, music became indispensable to this new form of dramatic entertainment as well. Not only did music evoke emotional responses in movies of a dramatic nature; several outstanding Broadway composers took their talents to Hollywood and adapted old musicals or wrote new musicals for film.

Music continues to play a major role in the allure of movies, and we—the audience—readily succumb to its effects. Even movie musicals, out of favor with the filmgoing public for some time, seem to be making a strong comeback.

Despite the glut of alternative entertainment available on video, computers, television, and a multiplicity of home entertainment systems, audiences continue to fill theaters and movie houses and to buy albums of theater music. This part of our text explores the relationship between music and drama, the history of American musical theater, and the effects music achieves on screen, in the opera house, and on the Broadway stage. ♪

Musical Theater

V aried songs by European and American composers, including selections from popular English ballad operas and tuneful melodies from the Italian opera repertory, occasional art songs, sentimental ballads, and patriotic tunes, enriched early nineteenth-century theatrical performances in America. Although composers had begun to distinguish between music intended for professional performance and music to be sung and played at home, for the general public the differences between popular and classical, or formal and informal, music remained much less distinct than we find them today.

Variety Shows

As prosperity returned after the turbulent Civil War years, theater—especially musical theater—became increasingly popular in America. Then, as now, theater activity centered in New York City, and by the turn of the twentieth century several kinds of musical shows vied to appeal to the Broadway audience. Full-length musical performances imported from abroad became popular and received critical acclaim, but most American musical shows between the Civil War and World War I had a variety format with little, if any, plot.

Most popular by far of all the musical shows representative of the period leading up to and succeeding the Civil War were minstrel shows, but before the turn of the century *vaudeville* rivaled minstrelsy in popularity.

Vaudeville Tony (Antonio) Pastor (1837–1908), the acknowledged inventor of **vaudeville,** worked in minstrel shows, for the circus, and as a comic singer before forming his own theater and touring companies. His family-friendly variety shows, eventually known as vaudeville, quickly attracted the middle classes.

Vaudeville closely resembled minstrel shows and often included blackface acts; but whereas the members of a minstrel troupe remained onstage throughout a performance, each act of a vaudeville show involved different performers. Vaudeville also featured a much wider variety of entertainment than minstrelsy. Circus stunts, jugglers, dog acts, comedy teams, songs,

FIGURE 17.1

Edward Harrigan and
Tony Hart in a comic scene
from a vaudeville show.

dances—virtually anything conceived to amaze and delight an eager but unsophisticated audience occurred on the vaudeville stage.

Among the most popular performers of the post–Civil War period, or indeed
of any period, was the zany comedy and song team of Edward Harrigan and
Tony Hart. Depicting scenes of everyday American life, including "ethnic"
comedy sketches of Irish and German urban immigrants, Harrigan and Hart
(Figure 17.1) captured the devotion of New York City's vaudeville audiences,
who readily related to the topical humor of their shows. (In 1985, a musicaliza-
tion of the lives of Harrigan and Hart was highly *un*successful on Broadway.)

The musical *Chicago* (1975), with score by John Kander and lyrics by Fred
Ebb, gloriously, and hilariously, revived and celebrated the vaudeville tradition
in American musical comedy; in fact, its authors originally subtitled the show
A Musical Vaudeville. Quite unlike the distant, sentimental, and exotic worlds
of many shows of the 1950s and 1960s, *Chicago* brought peppy tunes, raunchy
lyrics, and brassy dances to the Broadway stage. The story—about a married
chorus girl who shoots her lover, is put on trial, learns how to capitalize on the
sentiment of the public, becomes a celebrity, goes free, and ends up as a popular performer—evoked the snap and crackle of Chicago in the 1920s but also
struck a familiar chord when revived in 1996 for an audience highly conscious
of media-savvy lawyers and of links between crime, celebrity, and money. Every
song and dance is staged as a kind of number performed on the vaudeville circuit
stage, and the audience members come to feel like the very public to whom the
girl plays, and pleads for her life. The film *Chicago* (2002) made the show available to anyone with access to a movie theater or a DVD player (though many
would argue that film cannot evoke the excitement of a live performance).

During the 2004–2005 season, a revival of old-time show business in New
York City, with echoes nationwide, further evidenced the lingering appeal of

vaudeville. New or postmodern vaudevillians are younger than were the original performers, their shows are often longer and more thoughtful, and ample
audience participation is a hallmark of their acts. Among the shows remaining
popular today, the Bindlestiff Family Cirkus on a given night might include
a ukulele duo, a yo-yo master, a trapeze artist, a whip act, and a sword swal-
lower, while Lazer Vaudeville shows mix juggling skits, daring acrobatics,
and laser light effects. (YouTube offers scenes from both of these vaudeville
teams.) The shows *Stomp* and *Blue Man Group* can also be seen as preservers
of the vaudeville tradition.

Burlesque

Burlesque, another kind of variety show popular in the last half
of the nineteenth century, is a form of satire that ridicules something important or, conversely, treats something inane or ridiculous with mock dignity for
humorous effect. Mid-nineteenth-century burlesque shows featured strings of
comic scenes of this type. Later, as striptease performances inserted between
the acts drew more applause than the comedy scenes themselves, burlesque
gradually degenerated from a rather risqué entertainment to a fairly crude—
although immensely popular—form of theater. But the true legacy of burlesque
is comedy. Although vaudevillians looked down on burlesque as an inferior
kind of entertainment, many vaudeville stars enhanced their incomes on the
burlesque stage, where they perfected their own style of comedy, heavily
weighted toward physical humor: pies in the face, seltzer in the pants, and so
on. Jackie Gleason, Bert Lahr, W. C. Fields, Red Skelton, Phil Silvers, and Bob
Hope, among many great comedians, learned their craft through burlesque.

By the 1920s, burlesque had largely degenerated to strip shows, and crack-
downs by law enforcers closed many burlesque houses. By the 1960s, with
hard-core pornography readily available, burlesque no longer held much interest. Yet the comic legacy remains strong. In 1979 *Sugar Babies,* a rollicking
remembrance of the best in burlesque, opened on Broadway starring Mickey
Rooney and Ann Miller, who sang and danced their way through an uproarious
evening of nonsense that delighted Broadway audiences for more than 1,000
performances and then toured until mid-1986.

Saturday Night Live and the *Jerry Springer Show* offer versions of burlesque on television—skewering politicians and titillating audiences to various
degrees. And big-screen spoofs such as *Young Frankenstein, Spaceballs,* and
the *Austin Powers* films—even *Shrek 3* (2007)—carry on the comic tradition of
burlesque. Today's burlesque performers often come from the world of modern
dance and use their dance background to give burlesque an experimental edge,
and sets and design are becoming as important to a burlesque show as inventive movement. Once a fading form, burlesque has reclaimed its place in the
varied world of music theater.

Revues

A common theme rather than a plot relates the scenes of a **revue,**
still another form of musical variety show. Songs by the same composer or
lyricist may be selected from several different shows, or each scene of a revue
may address the same topic—such as love through women's eyes, or relations

between the sexes, or married life—with music selected from various sources. In Irving Berlin's *As Thousands Cheer* (1933, successfully revived on Broadway in 1998), for example, each sketch or song was supposedly torn from a recent newspaper headline.

Lavishly staged revues of the early twentieth century featured lovely costumes, extravagant sets, and—especially—beautiful young women. Such spectacles, titled "Follies" or "Scandals" or "Vanities," staged every year from the early 1900s to the 1930s, provided generous job opportunities for composers, singers, dancers, stage and costume designers, and orchestra musicians.

Most popular of all revues were the **Ziegfeld Follies,** staged by **Florenz Ziegfeld** (1869–1932) nearly every year between 1907 and his death (with three more Ziegfeld Follies produced after that). With spectacular staging, extravagant costumes, and wonderful songs by Broadway's greatest songwriters, the Ziegfeld Follies glorified the American girl, to the delight of returning audiences year after year. (A musical biography of Florenz Ziegfeld, titled *Ziegfeld,* opened on Broadway in 1988 but was not very well received.)

During the Great Depression of the 1930s, when soaring budgets made the elaborate Ziegfeld-type spectacles too risky to produce, more intimate revues took over the popular theater. By then social and political commentary was accepted even in the format of a revue. Thus *Pins and Needles,* a very successful musical entertainment sponsored by the Garment Workers Union and created and performed by amateurs, was basically a propaganda forum for that union, but it included some great songs and became a hit on Broadway.

Since then revues have existed in all sizes and shapes, a glorious grab bag kind of theater, brainier than vaudeville or burlesque; consisting of sketches, songs, and dances; and often addressing a common theme with a humorously skeptical point of view. Many recent revues have been based on the music of one composer, such as *Side by Side by Sondheim* (1977); *Eubie!* (1978), a collection of the rag- and jazz-based songs of Eubie Blake; *Ain't Misbehavin'* (1978), with songs by Fats Waller; and *Sophisticated Ladies* (1981), a dance extravaganza based on the music of Duke Ellington. The all-black revue *Bubbling Brown Sugar* (1976) featured songs by several great African American writers, including Eubie Blake, Fats Waller, and Duke Ellington.

In recent years, Broadway occasionally has found revue revivals a refreshing format. *As Thousands Cheer,* with songs by Irving Berlin including "Easter Parade," was vibrantly revived on Broadway in 1998. A toe-tapping history of blues music, *It Ain't Nothin' but the Blues,* opened in New York in 1999. In 2007, the organization called Encores!, which presents musical revivals at New York's City Center, celebrated the centenary of the first Ziegfeld Follies by staging three musicals inspired or produced by Ziegfeld's grand old revues: Stephen Sondheim's *Follies;* a topical revue by the young Moss Hart and the veteran Irving Berlin called *Face the Music;* and an anthology of songs from the early years of the last century, including six by Berlin. The theme of the latter show is of social change in America from before the First World War to after the Second.

Operetta

Unlike variety shows, musical **book shows** have an integrated plot—a story told in song, in spoken dialogue, or in some combination of the two. One example of such a show, the European **operetta,** became immensely popular on Broadway before the turn of the twentieth century, providing a vital stimulus for the development of the American musical stage.

An operetta (sometimes called a **light opera**) is a musical play integrating the songs, dances, and instrumental pieces with a story. Although the music of the great operettas is of a quality and a level of difficulty suitable for trained singers, no special effort or experience is required of the audience, who may expect to be thoroughly entertained.

Gilbert and Sullivan

The delightful operettas of William S. Gilbert and Arthur Sullivan have been immensely popular in America from the time they first appeared in this country to today. Gilbert's **patter songs** ridiculed politics, manners, society—any subject was fair game—in rhyming multisyllabic words that delight audiences and stimulate imitation in every kind of humorous musical entertainment. Sullivan, poking musical fun at opera, religious music, virtuosic singing, and every other serious aspect of music, wrote delightful tunes with simple harmonies and attractive orchestration. Even today, **Gilbert and Sullivan operettas** provide virtually irresistible entertainment (Figure 17.2).

FIGURE 17.2

A scene from Gilbert and Sullivan's *H.M.S. Pinafore.*

American Operettas John Philip Sousa, his success as bandmaster and march king notwithstanding, hoped to become an American counterpart of Gilbert and Sullivan and in this quest composed fifteen operettas. The most famous, *El Capitan* (1896), a comic portrayal of the Spanish administration in colonial Peru, was highly successful in New York and then on a coast-to-coast tour. (The *El Capitan* march, based on two melodies from the operetta, appeared in arrangements for piano, banjo, guitar, mandolin, zither, and various combinations of each of these instruments and remains one of Sousa's best-known marches.) However, Sousa's lyrics were never as inspired as Gilbert's, and he never found a librettist who might have collaborated with him as successfully as Gilbert did with Sullivan. By the turn of the twentieth century, his theater works began to be eclipsed by European operettas and by a fledgling new form, musical comedy. Sousa's operettas are seldom performed today, but the New York City Opera produced his *Glass Blowers*—described by one reviewer as "a European-style operetta with a hard, bright American edge"—as recently as 2002.

In the early years of the twentieth century, several Viennese musicians recently arrived from Europe composed American operettas based on European traditions. Highly influential upon the development of American musical theater, these beautiful shows, more romantic than comical, featured exotic settings that lifted the audience from the everyday world to heights of delightful fantasy. The music, too, was romantic in style, with memorable melodies, rich harmonies, and attractive orchestration; and the complicated love stories, no matter how unlikely or contrived, nearly always ended happily.

Musical Comedies

Blessed with a wealth of European and American operettas as well as variety shows ranging from crude burlesques to extravagant revues, the early twentieth-century Broadway audience hardly felt the need for a new form of musical theater. Yet despite early resistance, an exciting new genre blending popular entertainment (as in vaudeville) with an integrated plot (as in operettas) emerged just after the turn of the century.

The earliest **musical comedies,** as the new musical shows were called, were gaudy, boisterous productions barely held together by a thin excuse for a story. Scenery was simply painted on backdrops, and there was little in the way of a stage set. As World War I lessened Americans' enthusiasm for European products, however, we developed a new confidence in our own artistic talents, and the zany entertainment provided by large and talented casts proved irresistible, if unsophisticated, fun.

The eventual great success of the fledgling form was largely ensured by the efforts of one brash Irish American who never gave up—George M. Cohan (Figure 17.3).

George M. Cohan (1878–1942) **George M. Cohan** was the
child of vaudeville performers and was virtually brought up on the vaudeville

FIGURE 17.3
George M. Cohan
(1878–1942).

stage. In fact, by the time he was in his teens, Cohan was providing most of the material for the family's acts. Completely self-taught, he made up the skits, composed the songs, wrote the lyrics, and promoted the shows, in which he acted, sang, and danced. (Remember Listening Example 31, "Rose," by Cohan.)

A zealous patriot, Cohan truly Americanized the Broadway theater. His shows, which always had an American theme, were filled with jaunty, flag-waving songs, such as "Give My Regards to Broadway" (Listening Example 59).

Listening Example 59

"Give My Regards to Broadway"
(from *Little Johnny Jones*)

This piece is from Cohan's first full-length show, *Little Johnny Jones* (1904), usually considered the first real musical comedy. It concerned a popular American jockey, of a jaunty character bearing unmistakable resemblance to Cohan, who goes to England to win the derby, is accused of throwing the race when he loses, but successfully restores his honor and wins his girl. (Johnny Jones is modeled on a real, but less fortunate, person named Tod Sloan.) Although the thin plot hardly holds together, the score is filled with tuneful, high-spirited songs, including besides this example "Yankee Doodle Boy." Cohan could not resist claiming, as in the latter song, that he was born on the Fourth of July, although his birth date was actually July 3.

CD 3
Track 2
2:39

—Continued

"Give My Regards to Broadway"
(from *Little Johnny Jones*)

(Note: Remember that the word *chorus* is applied both to a refrain and to a mixed vocal choir.)

Composer   George M. Cohan (1878–1942).

Genre   Musical comedy.

Timbre   Male vocalist (Al Jolson, 1888–1950), accompanied by theater orchestra and chorus.

Texture   Homophonic.

Form   Verse-chorus.

Meter   Duple.

Tempo   Brisk.

0:00   Orchestral introduction.

0:08   Chorus, or refrain: Sung by Jolson. Notice the manner in which his characteristic vocal "slides" add emotional effect to words such as "yearning."

    Give my regards to Broadway,
    Remember me to Herald Square. . . .

0:36   Verse 1: Sung by the chorus.

    Did you ever see two Yankees part
    Upon a foreign shore, . . .

1:06   Refrain: Sung by Jolson.

1:35   Refrain: Played by the orchestra.

2:05   Refrain: Sung by Jolson accompanied by the chorus humming and interspersing comments.

2:35   The orchestra finishes the piece with two chords, a kind of exclamation point (da-dah!).

Despite competition from highly popular, more sophisticated operettas, Cohan stormed Broadway with show after show that, although not always good, always had catchy tunes and featured American heroes—a reformed gambler, a baseball player, a senator—and rousing patriotic songs. Though to his great regret he was finally replaced in popularity by several more sophisticated composers, Cohan received the highest award our nation can bestow on civilians, the Congressional Medal of Honor, which President Franklin D. Roosevelt delivered to him in person in recognition of Cohan's contribution to national pride and morale during World War I.

James Cagney re-created Cohan's dramatic life in the movie *Yankee Doodle Dandy* (1942), and in 1968 a successful musical—*George M!*—brought the Cohan magic back to Broadway.

Black Musical Theater

Even as minstrel shows waned in popularity, African American musicians continued to be an important influence on Broadway, writing songs for white shows and also writing, directing, and performing in several all-black musicals in the first decade of the twentieth century. The earliest all-black musicals closely resembled minstrel shows, which had themselves become more black than white while still perpetuating the stereotypical African American characters.

The reference to minstrelsy is apparent in the title of a distinctive black show from 1898: *Clorindy, or the Origin of the Cake-Walk.* The composer, **Will Marion Cook** (1869–1944), was a concert violinist who had studied music at Oberlin College in Ohio, in Germany, and later with Dvořák at the National Conservatory of Music. Cook also wrote the music for several other black shows popular during 1900–1910, including *In Dahomey* (1903), the first all-black musical show to play in a major Broadway theater.

Although, as we have seen, the black influence on popular music was particularly strong in the early twentieth century, interest in black musical theater waned for about ten years (from just before until soon after the First World War), despite the generally flourishing state of the musical stage. Then in 1921 *Shuffle Along,* with music by Eubie Blake and words by **Noble Sissle** (1889–1975), became a Broadway hit. This was one of many shows lying somewhere between a revue and a musical comedy, its loosely integrated plot regularly interrupted by scenes of sheer entertainment. Whites laughed uproariously at the satire, much of which was directed at them, and enthusiastically applauded the stunning chorus line, tap dancing, and singing of the black performance troupe. The cast included **Josephine Baker** (1906–1975), who later became a star in Paris theaters; and the composer William Grant Still (see pp. 383–386) played oboe in the orchestra. One of the songs from the show, "I'm Just Wild about Harry," reappeared as a campaign song for Harry Truman years later.

The 1920s witnessed several other popular shows with all-black casts, although some, including two "Broadway operas" to be discussed in Chapter 19, were written by white composers and lyricists. And the landmark show of the decade, *Show Boat,* written by Jerome Kern (see pp. 142–143), addressed interracial relations with sympathy and sensitivity.

Jerome Kern's *Show Boat*

Jerome Kern (1885–1945), whose songs for Tin Pan Alley were discussed in Chapter 8, wrote a number of successful shows for Broadway, most notably in collaboration with the writers Guy Bolton and P. G. Wodehouse. All three artists were committed to creating shows with strong plots and fine songs, and their works are considered a cornerstone of musical theater.

In 1927 Kern wrote **Show Boat,** thereby making musical history in a number of ways. First, unlike earlier musical comedies, which were basically collections of songs and variety acts loosely held together by a thin plot, *Show Boat* had an integrated plot based on a novel by an established literary figure, Edna Ferber. Despite the success of *Show Boat,* however, it was a number of years before the revolutionary concept of a literature-based musical became the norm for many if not most musicals (American and other): *South Pacific* was based on a collection of short stories by James Michener; *Kiss Me Kate* and *West Side Story* on Shakespearean plays; *The King and I* on an autobiography; *Cats* on poems by T. S. Eliot; and *Phantom of the Opera* and *Les Misérables* on French novels, to name just a few.

Further, the story of *Show Boat,* and the song lyrics by Oscar Hammerstein II (see pp. 306–307) addressed highly sensitive social topics, expressing sympathy for the situation of black people in America and even including an interracial love story—astonishing at a time when audiences confidently expected only sheer entertainment from a musical show. This too was prophetic in the sense that serious social, political, and even religious messages have been included in many later musicals. After *Show Boat,* the term musical *comedy* would no longer be appropriate for all musical Broadway shows.

Most important of all, Kern wrote sophisticated music of the finest quality for his show. Melodies associated with particular characters recur throughout *Show Boat,* providing musical and dramatic unity, and his lovely melodies and interesting harmonies are as appealing today as they were over eighty years ago. Among them, the classic love song "Why Do I Love You?" the bluesy "Can't Help Lovin' Dat Man of Mine," and the moving "Ol' Man River" (Listening Example 60) seem likely to remain classics in the American song repertoire.

In yet one more way, *Show Boat* proved prophetic of the direction the Broadway musical would pursue. The quality of the music and the serious nature of the plot have caused some to refer to *Show Boat* as an operetta, and indeed the differences between musicals, operettas, and operas have become less distinct, and largely meaningless, in recent times.

Golden Age of Broadway Musicals (1930–1955)

Before the 1920s, many great songwriters made their living from songs that they created to be published by Tin Pan Alley and possibly included in a Broadway musical. Even Irving Berlin, who became involved with the Broadway musical stage while in his teens, was at his best writing individual songs, and his shows often seemed more like revues than like musical

"Ol' Man River" (from *Show Boat*)

CD 3
Track 3
3:31

Paul Robeson (1898–1976), whose beautiful voice we also heard in "Nobody Knows the Trouble I've Seen" (Listening Example 19), was a fine athlete, actor, singer, cultural scholar, author, and political activist who paid a heavy price for his radical social and political beliefs. In the 1940s, he attracted the unwelcome attention of Senator Joseph McCarthy and the House Un-American Activities Committee. Despite Robeson's courageous contributions as an entertainer of the troops in World War II and his outstanding accomplishments as an actor, singer, and civil rights advocate, the government deprived him of his passport. He thereby lost most of his income, which he earned performing abroad (where blacks found considerably more performance opportunities than the United States afforded them). When his passport was reinstated, in 1958, Robeson was ill and unable to perform as before, and so retired, tragically early, from public life. (Note: Singers including Robeson have altered the original words of this 1927 song to avoid racial terms commonly used in Kern's and Hammerstein's time that have become offensive to singers and listeners alike.)

Composer Jerome Kern (1885–1945).

Lyricist Oscar Hammerstein II (1895–1960).

Genre Broadway musical.

Timbre Bass voice (Robeson), accompanied by a string orchestra. Throughout the performance, the orchestra supports and enhances the voice part, filling in the ends of lines and greatly adding to the emotional impact of the song. The rich timbre of the bass voice and the dramatically deep tones at emotionally significant points also add to the drama of this moving song.

Texture Homophonic.

Form Verse-chorus. The four sections of the chorus occur in the order **a a' b a"**.

Meter Verse: Triple. Chorus: Quadruple.

Tempo Slow.

0:00   The orchestral introduction explores a phrase from the chorus.

0:15   Verse: The bass sings the verse, quietly accompanied by the orchestra. The minimal accompaniment and relaxed rhythmic structure emphasize and help to express the words.

There's an old man called the Mississippi. . . .

—Continued

> Listening Example 60—concluded

"Ol' Man River" (from *Show Boat*)

0:57 Chorus: After an emotional surge in the orchestra, Robeson begins the chorus. Perhaps you will notice the change in meter to quadruple, and certainly the more melodic nature of the music.

a (6 bars). *Ol' man river, that ol' man river, . . .*

1:34 **a'** (6 bars). *He don' plant 'taters, he don' plant cotton, . . .*

2:07 More agitated here, more dramatic, Robeson speaks, almost shouts, some of the words. Relish the slide to the gorgeous bass note, which Robeson beautifully sustains.

b (8 bars). *You an' me, we sweat an' strain, . . .*

2:41 Here Robeson returns to the resigned mood of the beginning. There is much to love here: the high tones, the little "roll" on "rollin'," and the emotionally intense ending supported by a big orchestral crescendo.

a" (6 bars). *Ah gits weary, an' sick of tryin'. . . .*

comedies. For example, Berlin's *Watch Your Step* (1914) became a hit despite its thin plot because of Berlin's great songs—and also because it featured the famous dance couple Irene and Vernon Castle performing the tango (Figure 17.4) and other popular dances of the day.

In the period just before World War I, the Castles helped spark a social dance craze, which in some sense changed American culture. More and more people participated in the new social exercise, often dancing to the music of

FIGURE 17.4

Irene and Vernon Castle dancing the tango.

urban black Americans. And Irene Castle, who remained prominent in public life after her husband's death in 1918, symbolized the newly independent American woman, unencumbered by Victorian restraints.

Like Irving Berlin, George Gershwin had a gift for creating delightful syncopated dance rhythms, and some of his shows included outstanding dance sequences. *Lady Be Good!* (1924) had the wonderful song "Fascinating Rhythm" and featured the famous dance team of Adele and Fred Astaire. These and many other early musicals provided vehicles for presenting great songs and dances with little pretense at dramatic unity or integrity.

But during the 1920s and especially the 1930s, after the economic crash of 1929, songwriters' income from sheet music sales drastically declined. Most people had radios in their homes by then and found it easier and cheaper to listen to the radio than to buy sheet music and pay for lessons to learn to read it. Yet somehow tickets to Broadway musicals continued to sell; so Kern, Berlin, Porter, Gershwin, and the other great songwriters turned their talents to the Broadway stage, producing an unprecedented quantity of sparkling popular music.

After 1929, sound movies gave further stimulus to songwriters' talents and another significant boost to their income. Several Broadway musicals were made into sound films that could be shown in any town with a movie house, and the great songs soon became familiar nationwide. Throughout the 1930s and 1940s, Broadway's amazingly gifted composers and lyricists continued to evolve artistically, producing many shows of lasting quality and beauty.

Rodgers and Hart

In a sense, **Richard Rodgers** (1902–1979) had two careers, both of them as a songwriter. Having worked with one lyricist for many years to produce a number of extremely successful musicals, he collaborated on several new shows with a different partner, whose style and character differed markedly from that of the first. Rodgers, who once remarked, "When the lyrics are right, it's easier for me to write a tune than to bend over and tie my shoelaces," effectively adapted the style of his music to suit the words his lyricists provided, thereby greatly furthering the transition from the loosely integrated shows of early musical comedy into unified musical theater.

The lyrics for Richard Rodgers's first outstanding shows were written by **Lorenz Hart** (1895–1943), one of the most talented lyricists Broadway has known. His rhymes—witty, sophisticated, clever, sometimes devilish, and often risqué—typically were unacceptable for the radio stations of his day (which would not play, for example, his famous "Bewitched, Bothered, and Bewildered" until one line was changed from "Couldn't sleep, and wouldn't sleep, 'til I could sleep where I shouldn't sleep" to " . . . 'til love came and told me I shouldn't sleep").

As the Broadway audience developed a strong fondness for classical ballet, this form of dance assumed an ever larger role in musical theater. The Rodgers and Hart musical *On Your Toes* (1936) was remarkable because the famous **choreographer** George Balanchine designed the dance steps to be integrated with the drama. One magnificent dance scene in particular, "Slaughter on Tenth Avenue," constituted an integral part of the story, advancing rather than interrupting the plot.

Rodgers and Hart's *Pal Joey* (1940), which also included a ballet scene, was remarkable in another way: the main character was an antihero—a two-timing gigolo who took advantage of the innocent to further his own selfish goals. For this reason, in spite of the wonderful music ("Bewitched, Bothered, and Bewildered" is probably the best-known song of the show), the critics hardly knew how to receive it, and the show was much more successful when it was revived twelve years later. (*Pal Joey*—its lyrics slightly laundered—was made into a film starring Frank Sinatra in 1957 and has enjoyed a number of Broadway revivals, the latest in 2008.)

Talented as he was, the erratic Lorenz Hart finally became impossible to work with, for Rodgers never knew when his lyricist would disappear on an alcoholic binge. Finally, Rodgers turned to **Oscar Hammerstein II** (1895–1960) to write the lyrics for his next show, *Oklahoma!*

Rodgers and Hammerstein The collaboration between Hammerstein and Richard Rodgers began as Broadway faced daunting challenges. The Great Depression had finally ended, and people wished to enjoy the theater and could afford to do so; but World War II caused a shortage of materials for sets and costumes, making new productions difficult to achieve. Therefore, it behooved the industry to fashion shows of sufficient quality to last for unprecedented numbers of performances; and so they did.

Still, it was widely assumed that *Oklahoma!* would fail, because it had no opening extravaganza, no chorus line, and no interpolation of songs for the sheer sake of entertainment—all considered requisite in a musical show in the 1940s. But Rodgers and his new lyricist, Hammerstein—already well known for his lyrics in several important shows, including *Show Boat*—believed that all music and dance should enhance rather than interrupt the plot and accomplished their ideal with magnificent success in *Oklahoma!* (1943).

Like *Show Boat, Oklahoma!* not only was a great success but also is considered a landmark in the history of the Broadway musical. The story was built upon believable characters and situations, and the choreography, by Agnes de Mille (a niece of the movie director Cecil B. de Mille), revealed her gift for the expressive story-dance. Every aspect of composition and production enhanced the narrative. As Rodgers himself said, "The orchestrations sound the way the costumes look." And unlike *Show Boat, Oklahoma!* changed the course of Broadway musicals, which never again could survive as loosely integrated songs held together by a shoestring of a plot. Most of all, the songs were simply irresistible. The carefree "Oh, What a Beautiful Mornin'," the romantic "Surrey with a Fringe on Top" and "People Will Say We're in Love," the comic "Everything's Up to Date in Kansas City" and "I Cain't Say No," and of course the rousing "Oklahoma!" were instant and lasting hits. Critics, audiences, and composers alike realized that *Oklahoma!* had ushered in a new kind of musical theater.

Rodgers responded to Hammerstein's words, more thoughtful and serious than Hart's, by writing a different kind of music, also more serious and profound than the simple lilting melodies of many Rodgers and Hart collaborations.

Carousel (1945), like *Oklahoma!* based on a play, had elements of tragedy and included a beautiful "message" song, "You'll Never Walk Alone." "Hello, Young Lovers" from *The King and I* (1951) is another example of a song more serious than any Rodgers and Hart would have produced. Like Jerome Kern's *Show Boat, South Pacific* (1949) addressed the sensitive subject of interracial marriage. Even *The Sound of Music* (1959), perhaps the frothiest of the Rodgers and Hammerstein shows, concerns real characters involved in difficult situations.

Expansion of the Broadway Musical

In a sense, the revolution Rodgers and Hammerstein implemented in the 1940s may be said to have finally overtaken them. As their success faded, other composers and lyricists came to the fore, reflecting in their own manner influences absorbed from the masters of the golden age. Classical and popular art again grew close together, as they were before the nineteenth century drew self-conscious distinctions between them, and this too affects current musical theater.

For example, **Frank Loesser** (1910–1969), a composer who previously had written such delightfully entertaining but traditional musicals as *Where's Charley?* and *Guys and Dolls,* produced in 1956 *Most Happy Fella,* which he referred to as "a musical with a lotta music" but which is often called a popular or Broadway opera. It was performed, in fact, by the New York City Opera in 1991, and many felt the show was more at home in the opera house than on the Broadway stage; for here Loesser demonstrated his heightened sense of *singing* in the Broadway musical. *Fella* requires highly trained voices and a full orchestra, and like Rodgers and Hammerstein's *Carousel* and Gershwin's *Porgy and Bess* (see pp. 340–343), it probes deeply the emotional lives of its characters. While providing plenty of entertainment and generous comic relief, *Fella* requires more of its performers and audience than did the conventional, earlier style of musical.

Lerner and Loewe The famous Broadway team of **Alan Jay Lerner** (1918–1986) and **Frederick Loewe** (1901–1988) wrote the wonderful shows *Brigadoon, Paint Your Wagon, Gigi, Camelot,* and *My Fair Lady*—the last closely based on George Bernard Shaw's *Pygmalion,* which Rodgers and Hammerstein had considered completely unsuitable for adaptation as a musical. Their particular contribution to the expansion of the musical, in fact, was a heightened sense of the *play,* whose spoken text they preserved as faithfully as its setting to music would allow.

The lyricist Lerner (whose family owned the Lerner women's wear shops) was an American, but the composer Loewe came to the United States from Vienna in 1924. His Viennese background is especially apparent in *Camelot* and *My Fair Lady,* which because of their period costumes, graceful and melodic scores, and magnificent sets are sometimes called modern-day operettas. "I Could Have Danced All Night," "On the Street Where You Live," "I've Grown Accustomed to Her Face," and "If Ever I Would Leave You" are among the great romantic songs from Lerner and Loewe's musicals.

FIGURE 17.5
Leonard Bernstein (1918–1990) conducting the New York Philharmonic, November 12, 1988.

Leonard Bernstein (1918–1990)

Leonard Bernstein (Figure 17.5) was a pianist, conductor, and composer primarily associated with concert music, although he made significant contributions as well to vernacular music and particularly to the Broadway musical stage. Bernstein adapted his early musical *On the Town* (1944) from a ballet he had written still earlier; and the ballet's famous choreographer, Jerome Robbins, participated in directing the new musical, in which the dances were an integral part of the show. Bernstein's *Wonderful Town* in 1953 and *Candide* in 1956 were also successful shows, and his Broadway masterpiece, *West Side Story* (1957), further demonstrated Bernstein's heightened sense of *dance* on the musical stage.

Robbins choreographed the wonderful dance scenes of *West Side Story*, effectively working them into the drama, which is a retelling of Shakespeare's *Romeo and Juliet*. The show is set in the streets of mid-twentieth-century uptown New York City, and although this Juliet (Maria in the show) does not die at the end, the aura of tragedy is palpable from the opening moments. The rough language, realistic characters, lyrical music, and stunning dance scenes had an overpowering effect on Broadway and have become familiar to untold numbers of people through the movie version of the show.

In one of the most effective kinds of music theater scenes, the **ensemble,** several characters present their own points of view, singly and then collectively, singing different words and music at the same time. The ensemble finale, or final scene, to Act I of *West Side Story* (Listening Example 61) vividly illustrates the musical and dramatic impact this affords.

"Tonight" (from *West Side Story*)

CD 3
Track 4
3:38

An old story (Shakespeare's *Romeo and Juliet*) set in modern times (New York City in the 1950s), *West Side Story* (1957) is timeless in its emotional and artistic appeal. Shakespeare's feuding families have become warring gangs, and Bernstein's Juliet (Maria) survives; but the plot and the stirring condemnation of unending feuds is basically unchanged. Bernstein's music suits the characters and their situations: jazz for a Jets scene; Latin-tinged music for some Puerto Rican scenes; love songs, humorous songs, and throughout, sophisticated dance music in many moods and styles. Not simply entertainment but tightly integrated into the plot, dance is an essential component of the fabric of the show. Beautifully filmed in 1961, *West Side Story* continues to be performed live around the country; and in 2008 a bilingual version was introduced in which the Puerto Rican Sharks sing in Spanish with the English translation running overhead.

Composer   Leonard Bernstein (1918–1990).

Lyricist   Stephen Sondheim (b. 1930).

Genre   Broadway musical.

Timbres   Vocal soloists, solo and choral ensembles, and orchestra.

Texture   Homophonic/polyphonic.

Form   Through composed. The piece is a quintet; for the American Jets, the Puerto Rican Sharks, Maria (Puerto Rican), her American lover Tony, and Anita (girlfriend of the Sharks' leader).

Meter   Changing. The sophisticated rhythms and changing meters lend to the excitement of the finale.

    The Jets have challenged a rival Puerto Rican gang, the Sharks, to a rumble (fight) "tonight." Tony, a reluctant Jet, tries unsuccessfully to stop the rumble. As the finale begins, the Jets and Sharks, each gang singing in unison, make excited threats to destroy the other. Their fast, highly rhythmic singing is punctuated by sharp accents in the orchestra.

0:00	Jets:	*The Jets are gonna have their day, tonight. . . .*
0:24	Sharks:	*We're gonna hand 'em a surprise, tonight. . . .*
0:44	Jets:	*We're gonna rock it tonight. . . .*
0:50	Sharks:	*They're gonna get it tonight. . . .*

—Continued

"Tonight" (from *West Side Story*)

1:08 Anita, girlfriend of the Sharks' leader, enters, singing of her plans with her gangleader boyfriend "tonight," to the same music, but with a sexy, sultry flavor.

Anita: *Anita's gonna get her kicks tonight. . . .*

1:25 Then Tony, the young Romeo of the show, has left the Jets but is later persuaded to join them in the rumble. His rapturous love song, "Tonight," expresses his fervent wish that the night and his time with his beloved Maria could last forever. Although the underlying pulse of Tony's song is the same as the rumble music sung by the gangs and Anita, his soaring melodic lines and emotional delivery provide a romantic contrast to the other music.

Tony: *Tonight, tonight, won't be just any night. . . .*

2:23 The gangs begin their threatening lines again, and as they continue, we hear Maria in the distance singing Tony's love song. Tony joins her, and finally Anita completes the ensemble, in which all the elements (the two gangs, Anita, and the lovers Tony and Maria) express independent and indeed conflicting plans for "tonight." The beautifully written, tightly integrated, and highly polyphonic ensemble achieves an almost unbearable level of dramatic tension.

We're countin' on you to be there tonight. . . .

2:40 As the gangs continue their threats, we hear Maria in the background singing Tony's love song, and then Anita, who doesn't know her boyfriend is about to be killed, continues making her romantic plans.

3:10 Jets and Sharks: *But they began it, they began it, . . .*

Stephen Sondheim (b. 1930)

One greatly gifted and prolific American composer, **Stephen Sondheim,** has continued to impress viewers and critics with imaginative, creative, often startling shows of endless variety. Having studied with avant-garde composer Milton Babbitt (see pp. 390–391), among others, Sondheim intended to become a composer of concert music; but like Jerome Kern, he was early and lastingly drawn to Broadway. His first experiences with musical theater involved writing song lyrics, a technique he studied diligently with Oscar Hammerstein II, his troubled family's neighbor, who became the boy's surrogate father. From Hammerstein, Sondheim learned the importance of emotional and verbal clarity and the necessity to seamlessly intertwine dialogue, melody, and lyrics to further a plot and give it dramatic force. Sondheim vividly demonstrated his own gifts in this area by writing the lyrics to Leonard

Bernstein's songs in *West Side Story,* and to *Gypsy* (1959), with music by Jules Styne. He then went on to become America's premier composer for the musical stage.

After his early collaboration with Leonard Bernstein, Sondheim wrote both the lyrics and the music for many important shows. *A Funny Thing Happened on the Way to the Forum* (1962) and *Follies* (1971) were traditional musicals that proved Sondheim could write within the conventions as well as anyone. *Follies,* however, masterfully reveals Sondheim's scorn for the old-time Broadway musical's inability—or unconcern—to deal with reality. Several songs in the show, which parodies the Ziegfeld Follies, brutally express the "folly" of trying to live in a rose-colored past, fantasize about a rose-colored future, or deny death—hardly the traditional happily-ever-after musical fare.

Critics admired the elegant *A Little Night Music* (1973), but audiences faulted the show for not having enough "good tunes," although it included the lovely "Send in the Clowns." The show, a musical version of Ingmar Bergman's film *Smiles of a Summer Night* and variously called a musical or an operetta, interweaves a series of bittersweet love stories that find more or less happy resolution in the end. "Every Day a Little Death" (Listening Example 62) is sung by two unhappy wives, Charlotte and Anne, whose husbands are both in love with the same woman, Desirée.

Listening Example 62

"Every Day a Little Death"
(from *A Little Night Music*)

"Every Day a Little Death" from 1973 is sung by Charlotte and Anne, whose husbands are both in love with a glamorous, though not young, actress, Desirée. Charlotte is perhaps middle-aged; Anne is the teenage wife of Fredrick, an older man. While she cannot love Fredrick as her husband, Anne is terribly jealous when her refusal to consummate their marriage drives him back to the arms of Desirée, with whom he had had a passionate affair years before. In the end, Fredrick's young son—who is actually a year older than his stepmother—and Anne have fallen blissfully in love, and Fredrick has decided he might be most content with Desirée after all. But this song precedes that happy conclusion.

CD 3
Track 5
2:26

Composer and Lyricist   Stephen Sondheim (b. 1930).

Timbre   Female vocal duet, accompanied by orchestra.

Genre   Musical/operetta.

Continued

Listening Example 62—concluded

"Every Day a Little Death"
(from *A Little Night Music*)

Texture   Homophonic.

Form   A B A.

Meter   Quadruple.

0:00   An unhappy little two-note phrase, delicately enhanced by the harp, introduces the poignant song.

0:08   **A:** Charlotte begins singing, her manner deceptively lighthearted but her words heartbreaking. The gently rocking orchestra lightly accompanies her crisply delivered words.

Every day a little death
In the parlor, in the bed . . .

0:38   **B:** The middle section is smoother, warmer, more intense than **A.** Here the strings become slightly more prominent, often doubling Charlotte's melody.

He smiles sweetly,
Strokes my hair, . . .

1:05   Anne: *So do I. So do I.*

1:09   Charlotte: *I'm before him on my knees,*
                    And he kisses me. . . .

1:34   Anne: *Oh, how true!*

       Charlotte: *Ah, well . . .*

1:41   **A:** Anne at first echoes Charlotte's thoughts, then adds her own, again in the light, crisp manner of the beginning. The women sing in unison at the end, symbolizing their like situation and sentiment.

       Charlotte: *Everyday a little death*

       Anne: *Everyday a little death . . .*

2:15   After the women's resigned close, the poignant little harp figure ends the piece.

The unlikely subject matter of *Sweeney Todd: The Demon Barber of Fleet Street* (1979), a grisly story of murder and cannibalism; and *Assassins* (1990), exploring the history of presidential assassination in the United States, shocked the public but won an audience and high critical praise. *Company* (1970) introduced the **concept musical,** a new kind of show—intellectually challenging and morally weighty—treating controversial subjects and intentionally leaving audiences wondering about the show's meaning and its resolution. *Company,* which raises questions and confronts issues it leaves unresolved, indicated important new directions that American musical theater would follow in the 1970s and 1980s. Another of Sondheim's concept musicals, *Pacific Overtures* (1976), succeeded several musicals by other American composers also reflecting a strong Asian influence, including *South Pacific* (1949), *The King and I* (1951), *Kismet* (1953), *Teahouse of the August Moon* (1953), *Flower Drum Song* (1958), and *The World of Suzie Wong* (1958). But *Pacific Overtures,* concerning Admiral Perry's opening of Japan to the West as seen from a Japanese perspective, was more serious than the other shows and followed Eastern techniques more literally than Broadway was prepared to receive. It also made the unwelcome suggestion, so soon after World War II, that Americans had erred by imposing Western ways upon the reluctant Japanese. The Asian cast, the Asian musical instruments, and the elements of stylized Japanese (*kabuki*) theater provided fascinating and provocative theater, but the show was not popular with audiences.

More Black Musicals

Little in the way of black musical theater appeared on Broadway after the opening in 1943 (and the revival in 1956) of Oscar Hammerstein II's jazzy adaptation of the French opera *Carmen,* which he called *Carmen Jones,* until several black musicals opened in the 1970s and 1980s. They included a black interpretation of *The Wizard of Oz* called *The Wiz,* an all-black version of *Guys and Dolls,* and the all-black revue *Bubbling Brown Sugar,* featuring fondly remembered melodies by "Fats" Waller, Duke Ellington, and Eubie Blake, among others, produced in 1976. *Me and Bessie* (1975), a two-woman show, narrated the tragic history of Bessie Smith and presented the songs she made famous. *Dreamgirls,* based on the experiences of the Supremes, had a successful run in 1981 (and in 2006 was made into an award-winning film).

The all-black show *Bring in 'da Noise, Bring in 'da Funk* (1996) tells the history—a version of the history—of African Americans more in dance than in song, with little if any connection between the scenes.

The Music of Musicals

Broadway has largely ignored jazz (*Jelly's Last Jam,* fashioned from Jelly Roll Morton's vintage jazz tunes being an exception), and it has not encouraged today's writers of hip-hop, rap, and Latin music to create new musicals. *The Capeman,* with music by Paul Simon, opened in 2000 and was billed as the first all-Latino musical, but it was poorly received.

Neither has country music generally been compatible with the musical stage, though a country-rock musical, *Pump Boys and Dinettes,* was nominated for best musical in 1982; and the delightful *Big River* (1985), with Roger Miller's appealing country music, had a modest success. Both shows continue to be revived in regional theaters, and *Big River* returned to Broadway in 2003. But the cultures of Nashville and Broadway spring from different, even conflicting roots: Commercial country music evolved from mountain music, with origins mostly traced to Scotland and Ireland, and its songs address hard-working, mostly churchgoing people. Broadway's roots go back to the make-believe world of Viennese operettas; lighthearted, giddy, Gilbert and Sullivan shows; and Yiddish theater based on magical themes and broad comedy. Even the realism that *Show Boat* and *Oklahoma!* introduced to the Broadway stage was highly colored with romance.

Nor does the stark simplicity of the blues lend itself easily to musical theater's expansive way with a story. Two small shows, *Blues in the Night* (1982) and *It Ain't Nothin' but the Blues* (1999), offered no new music but told their stories through the singing of classic blues songs. In 2002, *Thunder Knocking on the Door,* a book musical with an original score of guitar-driven blues and R&B-style ballads by Keb' Mo', drew mixed reviews. Keb' Mo' aptly described the incompatibility of blues and Broadway: "The blues is about being real. And a musical onstage is about being fake."

Even rock has had only limited effect on musical shows. Although several shows in the 1960s and 1970s were based on rock music, they do not seem to have established a discernible trend; in fact, with the advent of rock and roll, pop and show music diverged. *Hair* (1967), billed as a rock musical but more of a revue because it has no integrated plot, addressed concerns of the youth culture and counterculture of the 1960s—drugs, free love, racial prejudice, the Vietnam War, the burning of draft cards, and more. In one notorious seminude scene, "police" ran through the audience as if raiding the show, prophetic of the audience involvement that has become characteristic of many contemporary musicals. The spectacular staging of *Hair* indicated another important trend in modern musical theater. Although the show included the hit song "Aquarius" and unabashedly accompanied its many other compelling melodies with the chromatics, rhythms, and word patterns of rock, ultimately *Hair* attracted audiences more with its notorious "nude scene" than with its rock music. In 2009, a Broadway revival of *Hair* earned rave reviews.

At least two important shows of the 1960s and 1970s were based on religious themes, and one of them, *Jesus Christ Superstar,* became a wildly popular rock LP album before the show even went into rehearsal. This show's composer, Andrew Lloyd Webber, is British; but the other, nearly contemporary show based on religious themes was *Godspell,* with music by a New Yorker, Stephen Schwartz (b. 1948). In *Godspell,* more successful than *Jesus Christ Superstar* as a theater piece, a small cast interpreted the Gospel according to St. Matthew in a striking new way, singing Schwartz's simple, appealing contemporary revival songs, the best-known of which is "Day by Day."

Grease (1972), a rollicking hit about the rock and roll era, responded to a "nostalgia craze" of the time, as it does when the show is periodically revived. *Grease* attained renewed popularity in its film version as well, but seems to have been a show of a kind, not a precursor of things to come. In 1996,

Jonathan Larson offered the highly successful *Rent,* a retelling of the Italian opera *La Bohème* that intriguingly mixes and matches vernacular musics (reggae, gospel, rhythm and blues, hard rock, pop ballads) with classical forms. Of course rock has invigorated other shows as well, but in general rock has not been the music of Broadway.

A recent trend has been to recycle old rock hits in new shows, with great success on and off Broadway. *Mamma Mia!* (2001), which grafts twenty-two hit songs by the Swedish rock group Abba onto a superficial story, remains a hit throughout the Western world. *Hairspray* (2002), another Broadway hit (based on the 1988 movie), features an original score by Marc Shaiman, but the songs sound like rock and roll of the 1950s. One much-admired show, *Movin' Out* (2002), matches songs by Billy Joel, and some of his classical compositions as well, to the choreography of Twyla Tharp. One reviewer compared that show to a choreographed rock concert, which critics and audiences alike have found a joy. *Passing Strange* (2008) is also a quasi-rock concert, in which the alt-rocker Stew narrates his life story.

The highly original show *Spring Awakening,* which performed on Broadway from 2006 to January 2009, is the unlikely adaptation of a controversial 1891 German drama concerning traumas of the teenage years—sexual confusion, abuse, death—to the musical stage. Duncan Sheik's pulsating score, which the composer refers to as "contemporary alternative and indie rock," beautifully captures the youthful characters' inner lives and received enthusiastic reviews, as did the complete show.

In some ways, hip-hop seems better suited than rock music for the stage. One show based on hip-hop, *Def Poetry Jam,* earned critical acclaim on Broadway in 2003; but it was an evening of poetry, a spoken-word event, not a play in the conventional sense. *In the Heights* (2008) is a Latin- and hip-hop-flavored tribute to a Manhattan Hispanic neighborhood. New York City's Hip Hop Theater Festival is exploring feasible means of merging hip-hop and musical theater, perhaps by using elements of hip-hop, like rapping and DJs; perhaps by presenting conventionally written plays that deal with the concerns of urban youth—the hip-hop generation. (YouTube offers a sampler of the festival.)

Current Trends

New York's theater district, which had declined for some years into a sleazy and even dangerous area, has now revived and is again a vibrant, thrilling place to be. But economic pressures affect those on both sides of the footlights, causing ticket prices to soar and producers to cut the size of choruses and the lavishness of sets in an effort to control costs. (*The King and I* cost $360,000 to mount in 1951 and $5.5 million to revive in 1996—a fifteenfold increase.) In commercial theater, four out of five productions fail to pay back their initial investment. It is not surprising, therefore, that the 2004 fall season saw only one new musical open, the pop-rock show *Brooklyn.*

In 2009, Broadway addressed the economic downturn by discounting theater tickets and placing plays in theaters where more expensive musicals had closed. Yet—perhaps because some New Yorkers decided to stay home and enjoy theater in lieu of taking expensive vacations—Broadway theater remained vibrant despite severe economic stress.

As the expense of producing a new musical on Broadway increased beyond reason, audiences found more and more revivals of old shows opening there. Revivals—including *Cabaret* (1998), *Annie Get Your Gun* (1999), *Oklahoma!* (2002)—and imports, in fact, have kept Broadway alive in recent years. However, more recent Broadway revivals of *Gypsy, Man of La Mancha,* and *Wonderful Town* proved financial failures. The show *Contact* (1999), billed as a musical, won a Tony award without a note of original, or even live, music. It simply costs too much for many producers to take a chance on new material.

A further disappointment to musicians is the fact that revivals tend to use fewer musicians than the original productions did. For example, the original published score for *Pacific Overtures* lists twenty-four parts plus a conductor, but the revival in 2004 used only eight musicians, including the conductor. Most of today's Broadway orchestras range in size from one keyboard to thirty instruments; many rely on judicious use of a synthesizer to augment their sounds. Economic considerations involve more than musicians' salaries: The orchestrator who arranges the music they play, and the copyists who provide music sheets for each player, must also be paid. Space is an issue as well: Orchestra pits have sacrificed space for the addition of audience seats. Often the musicians are placed away from the stage, in separate rooms from one another, relying on a monitor to convey the conductor's image. Acoustic instruments are miked and then mixed by an engineer. The large, lush, string orchestra or pit band is only a sad memory today.

From Film to Broadway

In this challenging time for new talent, the Broadway musical has tapped one endlessly renewable source: movies. Thus, in a reverse of the tradition of transferring musicals to film, several films recently have become Broadway shows. Perhaps the first such happy turnabout, *La Cage aux Folles,* with music by Jerry Herman, opened in 1983. Since then, dozens of other films have been converted into musicals for the stage, on the assumption that a known quantity is likely to sell well.

Two of the biggest hits on Broadway, *The Producers* and *The Lion King,* were both based on movies, as were *The Full Monty, Forty-Second Street, Beauty and the Beast, Sweet Smell of Success, Thoroughly Modern Millie, The Rocky Horror Picture Show, The Graduate, Hairspray, Chitty Chitty Bang Bang,* and *A Man of No Importance.*

The year 2008 brought two stage adaptations of musical films to Broadway. *Billie Elliott,* ingeniously connecting psychodrama, social politics, and dance, scored a triumph with reviewers and audience alike. *Irving Berlin's White Christmas: The Musical* closely followed the 1954 film's story. The show, which opened on Broadway in the holiday season, had already played in theaters around the country and revealed how well the great Berlin songs—some dating back to 1915!—have stood the test of time. Happy or sad, funny or philosophical, Berlin's songs spanning the styles of ragtime, jazz, Tin Pan Alley, big band, Hollywood, and Broadway continue to work their special magic.

Effects Other than Music
Staging is a more important element of musical theater than ever before, as stage mechanics and scenic effects integrated into the story propel the action instead of providing background for it, and as visual impact has assumed more significance than the music in many musicals. Thus although questions of economy encourage the production of small or **chamber musicals,** the more widely popular shows feature large casts and sets extravagant in design and breathtaking in effect. Very few new shows offer memorable, singable songs destined to become standards comparable to the innumerable songs by Kern, Porter, Berlin, Gershwin, and Rodgers that we continue to sing in the shower and singers continue to record. (Webber's "Memory," from *Cats;* and Sondheim's "Send in the Clowns," from *A Little Night Music,* are notable exceptions to this rule.)

There is also today increasing interest in **multimedia shows** combining music, dance, drama, and sophisticated special effects. Audience involvement, complex lighting techniques, tape recordings, films, slides, and videos often are part of the modern music theater experience. Some relatively recent lavishly staged musicals on Broadway were foreign imports: Andrew Lloyd Webber's *Cats, Starlight Express,* and *Phantom of the Opera* feature elaborate staging and costumes, as do *Miss Saigon* and *Les Misérables* by the French composers Claude-Michel Schönberg and Alain Boublil. Roller skates race on ramps behind and over the heads of the audience in *Starlight Express,* a chandelier makes a spectacular fall over spectators at *Phantom of the Opera,* and a helicopter lands on the stage in *Miss Saigon.*

Dance is more important than ever in the Broadway musical. The loose plot of *A Chorus Line* (1975) concerns the way a choreographer selects dancers, and much of that delightful show's entertainment—in both its live and movie versions—is derived from its wonderful dance sequences. The movie *Saturday Night Fever* (1977) reflected in film the same sheer love of dance. The musical *Forty-Second Street* (1980) is an extravaganza of song and dance that continues to have successful runs around the country and abroad, and a revival of Rodgers and Hart's *On Your Toes* was very well received. In *Bring in 'da Noise, Bring in 'da Funk,* a dance show conceived by the dancer-choreographer Savion Glover, the music seems nearly incidental to the rhythmic patterning of feet to rap, tap, and funk.

Another phenomenon of the current Broadway musical scene is a concern to address children, an audience musicals rarely catered to in the past. *Cats,* introduced as a grown-ups' musical, turned out to have broad appeal for children; and since then *Beauty and the Beast, The Lion King* (Figure 17.6), *The Little Mermaid,* and *Mary Poppins* have drawn family audiences, happy to be lavishly entertained rather than challenged in Sondheim's way. However, *Seussical,* based on the books by Dr. Seuss (Theodor Geisel), did not prove a success.

FIGURE 17.6

The cast of *The Lion King* performs during the Tony Awards, June 15, 2008.

Several young composers and lyricists are making their mark in musical theater, though the significance of their contributions is yet to be determined. A show with the unlikely name *Urinetown* (2001), with music and lyrics by Mark Hollman and book and lyrics by Greg Kotis, was a smash success on Broadway and in regional theaters around the country. In 2003 Adam Guettel—a grandson of Richard Rodgers and son of Mary Rodgers, composer of the immensely successful Broadway musical *Once Upon a Mattress* (1959)—wrote the words and music to *The Light in the Piazza,* which received enthusiastic reviews. The music of some new musicals has achieved more success on CD than in the theater. Thus the young composer Michael John LaChiusa's *Wild Party* (2000) received poor reviews, but on CD the songs, which re-create— or better, reinvent—authentic period songs of the 1920s with a contemporary bite, make a strong effect. Another young composer, Andrew Lippa, wrote a different version of *Wild Party,* mixing everything from rhythm and blues to Latin to swing to produce a highly eclectic contemporary pop score that also works better, perhaps, as a recording than on the stage.

The Broadway musical has become an international phenomenon, with unprecedented creative and technological sophistication and an apparently limitless variety of styles. Certainly the talents of new choreographers, stage designers, and actors offer enormous hope for this indigenous American musical form. Today's Broadway audiences expect the ultimate mating of the arts that used to be considered the sole prerogative of opera, and many contemporary shows are entirely sung, using no spoken dialogue at all. Thus, Broadway has learned what opera lovers have always known—once caught up in the magic of musical theater, we readily allow reality to be superseded by art and enjoy the emotional and aesthetic rewards, which are grand.

Terms to Review

vaudeville	patter song	ensemble
burlesque	Gilbert and Sullivan operettas	concept musical
revue	musical comedy	chamber musical
Ziegfeld Follies	*Show Boat*	multimedia show
book shows	choreographer	
operetta (light opera)	*Oklahoma!*	

Key Figures

Florenz Ziegfeld	Jerome Kern	Alan Jay Lerner
George M. Cohan	Richard Rodgers	Frederick Loewe
Will Marion Cook	Lorenz Hart	Leonard Bernstein
Noble Sissle	Oscar Hammerstein II	Stephen Sondheim
Josephine Baker	Frank Loesser	

Critical Thinking

What changes do you think would be required to successfully transpose a film musical to Broadway? A Broadway musical to film?

The composer and singer Adam Guettel has said, "Melody is memorable." Compare the opening phrases of "Oh, What a Beautiful Mornin'" from *Oklahoma!* and "The Star Spangled Banner." Both songs are celebratory, both are in triple meter, and both feature wide leaps in the melodic line. Which melody do you find more memorable? Why?

When Jerome Kern's *Show Boat* was revived some years ago, many people refused to see the show, considering it racist. Do you think they showed moral rectitude in boycotting the show? Or do you think they should have seen the show before reaching conclusions about it? On the basis of what you have learned about the show, do you believe Kern's intentions were racist? Should terms originally used in Edna Ferber's 1926 novel and in Kern's 1927 musical, considered racist today, be altered in contemporary revivals of the show in the interest of political correctness?

Music for Films

Music was closely associated with and highly important to theatrical performances since well before the ancient Greeks staged their magnificent choral dramas. In modern times, it has been inextricably intertwined with film since the motion picture industry began, about 1895. In fact, as the famous American composer Aaron Copland (pp. 374–380) pointed out, a film score is simply a new form of dramatic music.

Whereas movie musicals, such as *West Side Story* or *A Chorus Line,* and film stories of great composers, such as *Rhapsody in Blue* (Gershwin) or *Amadeus* (Mozart), are best known and best remembered for their music, audiences seldom pay much attention to the music of documentaries, cartoons, and feature films having no inherent musical content. Yet for these, too, music serves as far more than accessory to the finished product, continually pushing our emotional buttons in subliminal fashion whether we "hear" it or not, while accomplishing a number of mundane technical chores as well. Imagine *Gone With the Wind* without "Tara's Theme," *Lawrence of Arabia* without Maurice Jarre's sweeping score, *The Third Man* without its prickly little zither theme—or the shower scene in *Psycho* (Listening Example 63) without Bernard Herrmann's shrill, stabbing strings.

Functions of Music in Film

Film music evokes moods, defines cultures, authenticates historical periods, and reveals personality traits more subtle but often more telling than spoken dialogue. Like any other work of art, the music for a movie, called the **film score,** is based on principles of variety and repetition. It builds a sense of continuity throughout the movie while filling holes or awkward pauses in action or dialogue. Music alters the pace of action by changes in tempo, and the sense of space by altering the level of volume, while decorating dull scenes and holding shaky ones together. Musically mimicking, or **Mickey Mousing,** a character's actions adds sub- or semiconscious humor to a scene, while suggestive melodic lines or harmonies effectively foretell or reinforce dramatic events. Sometimes music actually negates a visual image, in ironic denial of what appears or is said on the screen.

Having drawn the viewer from reality into the atmosphere of a film, music subtly identifies the movie's structural units, indicating the beginning and conclusion of significant scenes and bringing the film to an effective close. But while the show goes on, by lessening our defenses and increasing our susceptibility to suggestion, a good film score allows us to suspend disbelief and become gloriously immersed in the unreal—the superreal—world of cinema.

Source Versus Functional Music

Some film music emanates from a source, such as a radio, phonograph, or musical instrument, apparent to the characters and the audience alike. Such **source** or **diegetic music,** as it is called, often provides a thematic anchor for the images onscreen. In films featuring dance, for example, such as *Saturday Night Fever* (1977), *Fame* (1980), *Flashdance* (1983), *Footloose* (1984), *Dirty Dancing* (1987), and *The Mambo Kings* (1992), recorded music forms the natural accompaniment for the action. The rock and roll classics heard as source music in *American Graffiti* (1973) establish period authenticity, and the radio or jukebox songs in *The Last Picture Show* (1971) further suggest specific social values and moral attitudes—country-western music implying purity of character, timeworn tradition, and innocence, whereas Tin Pan Alley pop tunes suggest corrupting influences (money, greed, power) associated with urban life.

Movie convention also readily accepts **functional,** or **nondiegetic, music,** heard by the spectators but not by the characters in the film. When director Alfred Hitchcock expressed skepticism that viewers would accept music in his 1944 film *Lifeboat* (which takes place in the middle of the ocean), film composer David Raksin famously retorted, "Show me the source of the camera and I'll show you where the music comes from!"

Relationships between source and nonsource movie music are frequently complex, and the differences between them are easily blurred; but together they constitute an aural telling of the story parallel to the scenes viewed on the screen.

History of Music in Films

Even before movie theaters were wired for sound, music constituted an essential enhancement of the audience's pleasure, and thousands of musicians made their living in movie theater orchestras. Live musical shows performed before the film began, on a scale less lavish than but related to the concept of today's Radio City Music Hall extravaganzas, had much to do with attracting audiences; and a pianist, a theater organist, or even a chamber orchestra accompanying silent films not only heightened the dramatic tension but also disguised the noise of the projector.

Silent Films Knowing that familiar songs evoke associations with their text, time, and mood, accompanists made frequent references to songs familiar to the audience, thus subliminally adding the songs' unheard texts to the silent films' emotional and informative content. For smaller theaters relying on keyboard as opposed to orchestral accompaniment, musicians used stock musical phrases and harmonies to bring to viewers' minds the sounds and emotions associated with railroads, horse chases, love scenes, comic predicaments, and other formulaic situations. A book published in the 1920s titled *Motion Picture Moods* provided keyboard players with numerous pieces evoking images from gruesome to chaotic, humorous, sentimental, or impassioned. Of course this early movie music raised some questionable associations. Music often depicted women and African Americans unfavorably, and music associated in the public mind with the American Indian was then—as it remained in the lavish golden-era movie westerns and unfortunately often is today—highly stereotypical.

Early Sound Films

Although *The Jazz Singer* (1927), starring Al Jolson, was neither the first major motion picture to use sound nor the first to make notable use of music, its enormous popularity encouraged a succession of imitative efforts, many of which were greeted with resounding enthusiasm only to be almost immediately forgotten by the public. But by 1930, music accompanied film in radically varied ways, some films remaining "silents," some containing a sound track with music but no dialogue, some having intermittent dialogue and sparse music, and some constituting full "talkies" with or without musical accompaniment. (The **sound track** includes all of the dialogue, sound effects, and music of a film, whereas the term *film score* refers to the music only.) Soon most theaters were wired for sound, forcing movie-house musicians out of their jobs.

By 1934, major developments in recording technology made it possible to accompany dialogue with background music, immeasurably enhancing the emotional potency of a film without dominating or drowning out the spoken words. Hollywood hired classical composers to write the music, thus bringing the stirring sound of orchestral music to a new, highly appreciative, audience. Most of the classical composers working in Hollywood were Europeans, but two outstanding American composers, better known for their music written for the concert hall or opera house, also devoted serious attention to writing film scores. The first major American composer of concert music to write for films was Virgil Thomson (see pp. 339–340), who composed the scores for several government-sponsored documentary films, most notably *The Plow That Broke the Plains* (1936). Aaron Copland's film scores include *Quiet City* (1939), *Of Mice and Men* (1939), *Our Town* (1940), *The Red Pony* (1948), and *The Heiress* (1949), which brought him an Academy Award.

Movie musicals, too, became enormously popular, as Hollywood pounded out hundreds of adaptations of Broadway shows and musicals developed specifically for the movie screen. Sound films continued the tradition of sending programmatic messages through familiar tunes: In *Gone With the Wind* (1939), for example, "Dixie" is heard when war is declared and later as the anxious citizens of Atlanta review casualty lists; the defeated Confederates return home accompanied by "When Johnny Comes Marching Home"; "Marching Through Georgia" signifies Northern advances; strains of "Dixie," "Swanee River," and the somber bugle call "Taps" underscore the final shot of the tattered Confederate flag waving in the breeze; and competing phrases of "Dixie" and "The Battle Hymn of the Republic" suggest the military conflict pervading the period of the film.

Although familiar songs provide an audience with a comfortable frame of reference, the introduction of a pleasing new song often enhances sales not only of the movie sound track but also of tickets to the film itself. Several films made during the 1930s and 1940s brought Irving Berlin's music to great numbers of people far from Broadway but able to view feature films in their local movie houses. *Holiday Inn* (1942) introduced Berlin's "White Christmas," one of the most popular songs of the twentieth century; and in 1948 *Easter Parade* gave the title song, written by Berlin for a show in 1933, a new lease on life. These and innumerable other movie songs live a healthy and seemingly endless life quite independent of the films that launched or popularized them.

The Hollywood Sound
The Hollywood studio system, contracting thousands of actors and artisans, gave opportunities to vast numbers of composers, conductors, arrangers, and performers who from the 1930s through the 1950s produced film music of increasing complexity and increasing reliance upon nondiegetic scores. Using the lavishly varied sounds of orchestral instruments, composers drew upon a body of musical conventions to produce what became known as the **classical Hollywood film score.**

Unlike such well-known Broadway composer-songwriters as George Gershwin, Irving Berlin, Jerome Kern, and Richard Rodgers, whose scores supported numerous movie musicals—and unlike such concert music composers as Virgil Thomson, Aaron Copland, and Leonard Bernstein, who also wrote for films—the Hollywood triumvirate of **Alfred Newman** (1900–1970), **Max Steiner** (1888–1971), and **Erich Korngold** (1897–1957) are best remembered for the music they created for Hollywood films of the 1930s and 1940s. They applied the highly romantic European concert music techniques of lush orchestral scoring, rich harmonies, and sweeping melodies to achieve the grandeur characteristic of films of Hollywood's golden era. Largely ignored or taken for granted for years, their film scores now are recognized as dramatic music of a high level of composition and performance. There even seems to be some relenting of an entrenched prejudice among the serious concert public against the concert music of film composers who produced symphonic music unrelated to their film careers. The Viennese composer Erich Korngold, for instance, received lavish international praise for his choral, piano, opera, and orchestral music before he settled in Hollywood; but he died unforgiven by the establishment for the lush romantic music with which he had captivated the movie audience. Now, however, his symphonic music is receiving belated but respectful attention in recordings and live performances. Korngold's Symphony in F-sharp major and his rhapsodic Violin Concerto are among numerous compositions he wrote independent of any association with film music.

Two film composers—Bernard Herrmann and John Williams—largely retained the lush, classical Hollywood sound well beyond that period's dates.

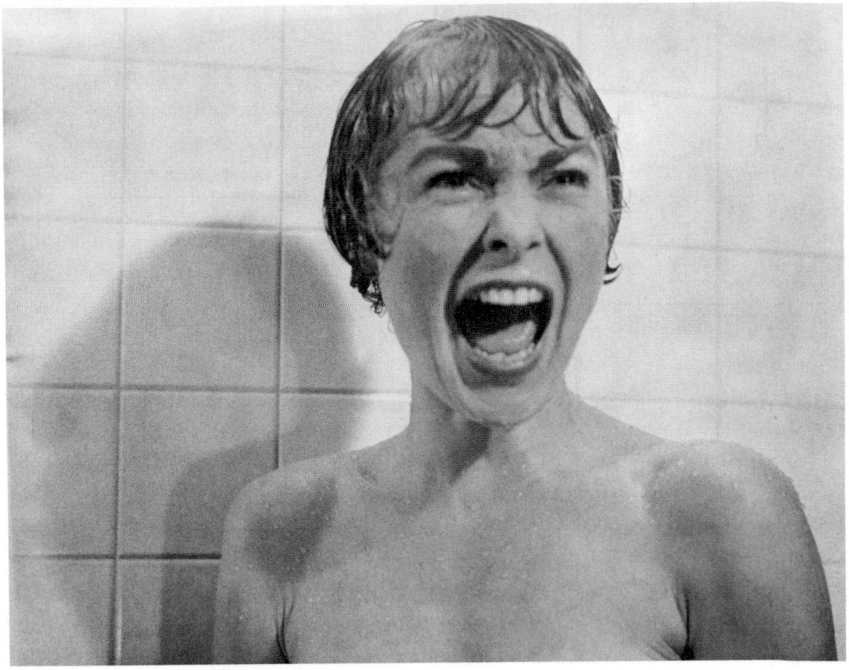

FIGURE 18.1

Janet Leigh in the murder scene from Hitchcock's *Psycho* (1960).

Bernard Herrmann (1911–1975)

Bernard Herrmann—a New Yorker who carried his classical music training to radio, where he worked as a composer and arranger, and then to film—established his reputation with his stunning score for Orson Welles's great film *Citizen Kane* (1941). His most memorable work, however, was for Alfred Hitchcock, for whom he composed a number of masterful film scores. Surely one of the most memorable scenes in all of movie history is the murder in Hitchcock's *Psycho* (Figure 18.1)—brought instantly back to vivid memory for anyone who has seen the film by Herrmann's unforgettable music (Listening Example 63).

Listening Example 63

"The Murder" (from *Psycho*)

One of the most truly terrifying scenes in movie history is made all the more frightening by the disturbingly effective music score. Imagine, if you will, which might be more unsettling: viewing the film in silence, or hearing the score without seeing anything on the screen. (Herrmann did arrange the score into a suite for strings, a highly effective concert piece.) Certainly either experience would be disquieting, but the "screaming strings" might

CD 3
Track 6
1:09

—Continued

Listening Example 63—concluded

"The Murder" (from *Psycho*)

raise your level of tension the most. Taken together, film and music achieve an overwhelming effect.

Composer Bernard Herrmann (1911–1975).

Genre Film music.

Timbre Orchestra, dominated by high-pitched strings as the players glide their fingers rapidly along the strings (a technique called *glissando*).

Melody Fragmentary phrases, repeated over and over. The very high level of pitch heightens the tension.

Texture Homophonic.

Form Programmatic—that is, the music describes (and enhances) the actions on the screen.

Rhythm Short, intense glissandos and harsh, accented bow strokes, recurring as relentlessly as the slashing strokes of the knife, set our nerves further on edge.

Tempo Rapid, to suit the desperate, frantic, scene.

0:00   In the film, for several moments we hear only the sound of the water as Janet Leigh enjoys her shower. We see the shadow of a figure stealthily approach the shower stall.

0:10   Suddenly Anthony Perkins snatches open the curtains and Leigh screams, the high-pitched strings echoing her terror and stabbing the air as Perkins's knife stabs Leigh again, and again.

0:35   Perkins hurries away as Leigh, mortally wounded, begins to slide down the shower wall, the strings correspondingly sliding downward in pitch.

1:08   The music stops as Leigh grabs for the curtain and finally falls, dragging the curtain down with her.

John Williams (b. 1932)

When in the 1950s science fiction spectaculars adopted the large-sounding effects of the full-blown orchestral score enhanced by increasingly sophisticated synthesized sound, the classical Hollywood score soared to new heights of popularity. Especially, **John Williams** (Figure 18.2) returned the romantic sound of the classical film score to popular

FIGURE 18.2
John Williams (b. 1932).

FIGURE 18.3
John Williams's two-note "shark" motif (da-da, da-da), probably the most famous motto in film music history, clearly warns of impending terror in *Jaws*.

favor, adapting the symphony orchestra for the modern recording studio in his stunning scores for the disaster films *The Poseidon Adventure* (1972), *The Towering Inferno* (1974), *Earthquake* (1977), and most notably *Jaws* (1975) (Figure 18.3), as well as *Star Wars* and *Close Encounters of the Third Kind* (both 1977), *Superman* (1978), and *Raiders of the Lost Ark* (1981). More than any others, the scores for the *Star Wars* films brought about a tidal wave of emotional film scoring that fully returned such overwhelming symphonic film scores to mainstream filmmaking.

The original *Star Wars* score, with its stirring, majestic opening and moments of mysterious quiet for young Luke (Listening Example 64), told the audience what to feel, while the visuals showed what was going on.

The maniacally mechanical Empire March of the second *Star Wars* movie, *The Empire Strikes Back,* was so compelling in its evil that it made viewers want to join the dark side. In *Return of the Jedi,* the third movie of the series, the musical themes of good and evil collided and resolved. The music in the fourth movie—Episode I of the series—perfectly enhances the spoken and visual melodrama of the film. John Williams's score for Episode II, *Attack of the Clones,* was widely praised, though the movie was not. In 2005 Episode III, *Revenge of the Sith,* completed this amazing series of films, which some have called space operas. In all the *Star Wars* movies, pyramiding brasses signal danger, trumpet fanfares on repeated notes signal battle, percussion points to something strange or illusory, and hymnlike writing indicates moments of public civil order or moments of private introspection.

Listening Example 64

Star Wars Main Title

This groundbreaking 1977 film, which lasts 121 minutes, includes 88 minutes of symphonic music, starting with the opening credits. As in many operas, melodic and rhythmic motives represent characters, ideas, and events, allowing the music to carry dramatic and even narrative responsibility. Thus motives for Luke, Princess Leia, Darth Vader, Yoda, and other characters recur in varied form, as their personalities and experiences evolve. Motives representing objects (such as the Death Star) and ideas or concepts (such as the love shared by Han Solo and Leia, or the Force) also are transformed throughout the film.

CD 3
Track 7
5:48

Composer John Williams (b. 1932).

Genre Film music.

Timbre Orchestra, dominated by brass and percussion rather than the usual strings.

Texture Predominantly homophonic.

Form The music is organized according to programmatic content.

Meter Quadruple.

—Continued

Star Wars Main Title

0:00　Following a brief but dramatic orchestral announcement, Luke's famous bold theme accompanies the opening shots, showing an Imperial star destroyer chasing a Rebel blockade runner. Brass instruments boldly state the martial theme, which has the form **aba.**

0:08　**a:** The brassy timbre and strong accents define one part of Luke's personality.

0:27　**b:** Strings play this section in sweeping melodic lines, adding a dashing, romantic dimension to Luke's motive.

0:49　**a** returns.

1:10　Transition.

1:29　A very brief reference to Princess Leia's quiet, more delicate theme.

1:35　Transition.

1:43　The brass defiantly play the Rebel spaceship fanfare (a brassy flourish) as the Rebel blockade runner appears on the screen.

2:22　**a:** Luke's theme returns.

2:40　**b.**

2:55　**a.**

3:19　Leia's lovely, wistful theme.

4:06　Luke, **a** and **b** only.

4:39　The Rebel attack theme.

5:02　Finally, Williams segues to music from the end of the End Title music, making this Main Title music the equivalent of an opera orchestral introduction, or *overture* (see p. 340).

Pop Scores　Around 1950, many composers began to accompany their films with pop music rather than the symphonic Hollywood film score. Soon movie songs were achieving unprecedented popularity. Although Anton Karas's zither theme for *The Third Man* (1949) became a pop instrumental hit, and adaptations of Scott Joplin's rags in *The Sting* (1973) stirred enthusiasm for ragtime among a new generation of listeners, songs are more likely than instrumental pieces to become hits. (By the summer of 1996, the album of songs from *Forrest Gump* had sold more than 6 million copies worldwide, whereas Alan Silvestri's score album had sold only about 100,000.) Sometimes words are even added to an instrumental movie theme for the purpose of popularizing both theme and film. Thus, noticing that audiences were enraptured by the lovely melody David Raksin composed as his theme for *Laura* (1944), studio executives commissioned Johnny Mercer to set lyrics to Raksin's music—whereupon "Laura" soared to the top of the Hit Parade, attracting new viewers for the film.

By the 1950s, many movie scores included or largely consisted of popular songs, such as "Do Not Forsake Me, Oh My Darlin'" (sung by Tex Ritter in *High Noon*) and the title songs from *Three Coins in the Fountain* (1954), *Love Is a Many-Splendored Thing* (1955), and *Around the World in Eighty Days* (1956). Also during the 1950s, jazz accompanied several important films, including *A Streetcar Named Desire* (Alex North, 1951), *The Man with the Golden Arm* (Elmer Bernstein, 1955), *Ascenseur pour l'échafaud* (*Elevator to the Gallows,* Miles Davis, 1957), and *Anatomy of a Murder* (Duke Ellington, 1959).

Pop scores achieved even more emphasis in the 1960s, attracting younger-than-ever audiences to films whose songs frequently outshone other features of the score and earned more money than the films that introduced them. (Few people today associate Henry Mancini's "Moon River," for example, with *Breakfast at Tiffany's,* the film that introduced it in 1962.) Burt Bacharach's scores epitomized film music of that decade and the next, beginning with *What's New Pussycat?* (1965), continuing with *Alfie* (1966), and attracting unprecedented attention with "Raindrops Keep Fallin' on My Head" in *Butch Cassidy and the Sundance Kid* (1969). Unlike movie songs that seem almost independent of the films that feature them, the pop songs providing the title sequence for James Bond films recur in instrumental as well as sung versions to underpin the drama throughout those movies. John Barry's title song for *Goldfinger* (1964), for example, is heard with lyrics also and is integrated into the instrumental score. Songs included in Paul Simon's score for *The Graduate*—"Sounds of Silence," "Mrs. Robinson," and the English folk song "Scarborough Fair"—subtly suggest and support mood changes and dramatic shifts in the narrative.

Randy Newman, whose uncles Lionel, Alfred, and Emil Newman composed some of the most famous movie scores of the 1930s, 1940s, and 1950s, produced several pop albums before establishing his own career as a film composer, which finally took off in the 1970s with *Cold Turkey,* and continued with numerous other well-received films, including *Toy Story 2* (1999), *Seabiscuit* (2003), and *Meet the Fockers* (2004). His beautifully orchestrated film scores typically incorporate echoes of Americana. Stephen Sondheim, apparently not interested in composing a full film score, wrote five songs for Warren Beatty's *Dick Tracy* (1990), effectively capturing in his music the period flavor of the film.

Sometimes the marriage of movie and music is less than ideal, of course, but the sound tracks of two hit films of the 1990s found commercial success while effectively expanding the vision of the filmmakers. The sound tracks for Quentin Tarantino's *Pulp Fiction* and Oliver Stone's *Natural Born Killers* used pop music to heighten the claustrophobic atmosphere of murder and chaos. Further, the sound track for *Pulp Fiction* sprawls from the crooning of the

1950s to the soul of the 1960s to the funk of the 1970s, enhancing the viewers' shifting sense of reality as we lurch from one decade to another.

But loose collections of pop songs, packaged by Hollywood for an audience shaped by MTV and Madison Avenue, increasingly displace integrated orchestral scores in motion pictures today. Electronic editing and other computer-driven techniques allow many young film composers never to develop the basic musical skills once essential in fashioning a score, to the detriment of the field according to some—to its enhancement, in the view of others.

Electronic Music

Today, of course, we take electronic effects for granted in movie music (and every other kind of music) but the eerie sounds of the **theremin,** the earliest electronic musical instrument (invented in 1920 by the Russian physicist Léon Thérémin), aroused unprecedented sensations of suspense. The theremin, a wooden cabinet on legs with antennas that respond to the slightest movement of the hands or body in the surrounding space, had prominent effect in *The Bride of Frankenstein* (1935), in Miklos Rozsa's score for Hitchcock's film *Spellbound* (1945), and in *The Thing from Another World* (1951)—an effect colored by the very unfamiliarity of the music's timbre. (*The Day the Earth Stood Still,* also 1951, was scored for two theremins, pianos, and a horn section.)

In the late 1960s, composers began to use analog techniques, although they were difficult to work with, hard to keep in tune, unreliable, and woefully inconsistent. Nevertheless, Giorgio Moroder's score for *Midnight Express* (1978) proved so effective it became the first electronic film score to win an Academy Award.

With the advent of digital systems in the early 1980s and sampling techniques developed later in that decade, exciting and almost limitless new possibilities appeared, and since then synthesized sounds have enlivened the sound tracks of numberless films. More flexible and less cumbersome than the early machines, the new technologies offered far more than new timbres suggesting otherworldly and futuristic effects. Whereas early keyboards allowed production of only one tone on one keyboard at a time, the new multiple-voice keyboards could be played like pianos or other keyboard instruments. And the new machines afforded extensive editing capabilities, enabling people with less experience as composers to create highly effective film scores. Further, a synthesized music track score, such as the nonacoustic score written by Maurice Jarre for *Fatal Attraction* (1987), needs no performing artist but may be accomplished by an "electronic ensemble" under the control of one individual.

Movie Musicals Revived

Movie musicals, popular during the 1930s and 1940s, lost favor in subsequent decades. However, during 2000 and 2001, at least three new Hollywood films—*Dancer in the Dark; O Brother, Where Art Thou?;* and *Moulin Rouge*—were billed as musicals, though none of them qualified as an original movie musical in the traditional sense: the first merely quotes numbers from *The Sound of Music,* the second uses music popular in the South during the Great Depression, and the third draws on the music of the Beatles, Madonna, and such contemporary musicians as Moby, Beck, U2, Massive Attack, and Fatboy Slim.

Moulin Rouge had a big impact on movie audiences, and the Oscar-winning film *Chicago,* in 2002, strengthened the perception that the movie musical had returned to favor. The musical biography of the songwriter Cole Porter, *De-Lovely* (2004), seemed to confirm this new, or renewed, enthusiasm. The musical biographies of Cole Porter (*De-Lovely*) and Ray Charles (*Ray*), both in 2004, were succeeded by the story of Johnny Cash (*Walk the Line,* 2005) and of the French popular singer Edith Piaf (*La Vie en Rose,* 2007). *Dreamgirls* (2006), based on the hit Broadway musical, was loosely patterned on the careers of the Supremes and Motown Records founder Berry Gordy.

Current Trends

Today all kinds of music, from classical to pop and from full-blown orchestral scores to synthesized sound tracks, accompany feature films. Some film scores raid the classics. The scores of two poignant films (*Elephant Man,* 1980; and *Platoon,* 1986), for example, quoted Samuel Barber's lovely *Adagio for Strings* (Listening Example 74) to accentuate the extreme pathos of those films. Audiences sometimes accept in films "ultramodern" music that they might reject in the concert hall, finding that dissonant harmonies, wide melodic leaps, instrumental timbres stretched beyond normal limits, and other extreme effects (discussed in Chapters 20 and 22) effectively raise their level of tension and emotional involvement. Henry Mancini used **quarter tones**—those lying halfway between the half steps of the major or minor scale—in *Wait Until Dark* (1967). John Williams's modernistic percussion effects in *Images* (1972) greatly strengthened the emotional effect of that score. And the *minimalist* techniques (pp. 402–404) used by Philip Glass in his Hopi-titled films *Koy-aanisqatsi* (*Life Out of Balance,* 1983) and *Powaqqatsi* (*Life in Transformation,* 1988) coordinated well with the visual effect of nonnarrative, time-lapse photography. In 1999 and 2000, the Academy Award for best film score went to classical composers: first John Corigliano for *The Red Violin,* then Tan Dun for *Crouching Tiger, Hidden Dragon.* And John Williams's score for *Minority Report* (2002) is interlaced with striking excerpts from masterworks by Bach, Haydn, Schubert, and Tchaikovsky.

Jazz continues to be a vital component of many movies today. Films featuring country-western, as either source or nondiegetic music, include *Nashville* (1975), *Honeysuckle Rose* (1980), *Coal Miner's Daughter* (1980), *Sweet Dreams* (1985), and *The Last Picture Show* (1971). In 1987, *The Big Easy* brought the exuberant sounds of Cajun music to a wide new audience. For the Civil War saga *Cold Mountain* (2003), the producer J. Bone Burnett effectively wove together original music, traditional folk songs, and standard music score fare.

Ethnic music often flavors film scores—to more or less legitimate effect. Although the adaptations of North American Indian music in *A Man Called Horse* (1970) and *Dances With Wolves* (1990), for example, pander to familiar, often inaccurate stereotypes, Barry Goldberg's score for *Powwow Highway* (1988) gives a more realistic portrayal of American Indian music. John Williams's score for the powerful Holocaust movie *Schindler's List* (1995) combines classical and folk-ethnic references: A winding, eastern European–flavored tune with a folk dance pulse evokes feelings of sad remembrance, and later thematic fragments accompanying harrowing scenes of genocide acutely express human anguish. Hispanic American and African American music enriches many films, recently including *Girlfight* (2000), accompanied with a distinctive blend of hip-hop, flamenco, and hand clapping. And Hans Zimmer's score for *The Lion King* (1994), which includes several songs by Elton John, combines Hollywood symphonics and African chant in an unlikely but highly effective representation of harmony among all peoples and species. Spike Lee's *Bamboozled* (2000) satirized racial stereotypes (white and black) in a modern take on minstrel shows.

By the 1980s composers had become highly skillful at integrating premarketed popular songs into a film score. The score of *When Harry Met Sally* (1989) consists entirely of songs, with no orchestral underscore whatsoever. Giorgio Moroder's songs in *Flashdance* (1983) genuinely support the film; and in *Philadelphia* (1995), songs by Bruce Springsteen and Neil Young replace the conventional orchestral scoring to profound effect. During the latter film's opening scene, as the camera roams over the slums of Philadelphia, Springsteen (as a homeless man staring at his reflection in a store window) sings to himself his melancholy and compelling ballad "Streets of Philadelphia": "Oh brother are you gonna leave me/Wastin' away/On the streets of Philadelphia?" And later in the film, toward the end of a poignant passage in which we view home movies of Tom Hanks (whose character now has AIDS) as a child, Neil Young sings in a small, cracked voice his moving ballad "Philadelphia," whose lyrics ("I won't be ashamed of love") refer obliquely to the gay lawyer who has been dismissed from his firm.

Rock has been used to accompany films since Bill Haley and his Comets performed "Rock Around the Clock" in *Blackboard Jungle* (1955). They were succeeded by Simon and Garfunkel's songs in *The Graduate* (1968), the Bee Gees's hits for *Saturday Night Fever* (1978), Pink Floyd's music in *The Wall* (1982), and songs by Prince for *Batman* (1989), to name just a few examples. The rock hits in *Forrest Gump* (1995), which surveys four decades of American life from the view of a rock fan of the 1960s, unify the film by identifying periods and styles: Creedence Clearwater Revival and Jimi Hendrix and the Doors bring to mind the Vietnam years; the Mamas and the Papas praise the hippies in "California Dreamin"; and "Running on Empty" and "On the Road Again" accompany Forrest on his run across America. The songs in *Pulp Fiction* (1994) also help identify periods (the 1950s and 1970s) and give insight into characters. Here the wail of surf music, normally associated with idyllic California beaches, ironically accompanies scenes of gangsters' carnage, the incongruity of this juxtaposition strongly heightening the horror.

Rock groups have produced scores varying in style from fusion to classical, and rock stars have taken more serious roles now than in earlier films—Sting in

Dune (1984) and the Byrds and Danny Elfman for Tim Burton's *Pee-wee's Big Adventure* (1985) and *Beetlejuice* (1988) come to mind. The soft rock phenomenon of the 1980s known as **new age** music, providing soothing, repetitious blocks of gentle, unassuming sounds produced by synthesizers or acoustic folk instruments, most notably affected Michael Convertino's score for *Children of a Lesser God* (1986).

Even opera has been welcomed into the broad realm of mainstream feature filmmaking. A number of movies produced during the 1980s and 1990s include entire scenes from famous operas that pack a potent emotional punch for unsuspecting listeners having little or no experience with this grandest form of music theater. *Fatal Attraction, Moonstruck, A Room with a View, The Witches of Eastwick, Someone to Watch Over Me, The Untouchables, Hannah and Her Sisters,* and *Prizzi's Honor* are only a few of the many films giving more than token attention to famous opera scenes. The powerful recording of Maria Callas singing "La Mamma Morta" (from *Andrea Chenier* by Umberto Giordano) heard as source music toward the end of *Philadelphia* nearly overwhelms the viewer as well as the film's afflicted star; the power and beauty of this serious music offer forceful contrast to Bruce Springsteen's and Neil Young's contemporary, relevant, and highly appealing ballads. To jump ahead, in 2007 Stephen Sondheim's unlikely and disturbing opera *Sweeney Todd: The Demon Barber of Fleet Street*—about an aggrieved barber who kills his victims and chops them up for meat pies—became a highly successful feature film.

The Composer's Perspective

Arnold Schoenberg (see p. 367) once was asked under what conditions he would work with a movie studio. "I will write music," Schoenberg replied, "and then you will make a motion picture to correspond with it."

Desirable as such an unlikely scenario might appear, composers of film music generally find themselves in the awkward position of writing music hardly intended to be heard. To this end, they read the script, listen to the **temp,** or temporary score (consisting of existing music prepared to demonstrate to the composer the type of music desired for the film) if one is provided, and perhaps scrutinize the film, laboriously determining when and how much music should occur and what sorts of music would serve the specific needs of each scene. Composers vary in their desire to view "dailies"—the detailed footage shot each day, which can be dull and tedious and so can inhibit the composer's emotional response to the action—and their preference to wait for the "rough cut," which tells the story from beginning to end with most of its elements in place. (The latter method allows composers to capitalize better on their first emotional reaction to the film, which is likely to mirror that of the eventual audience.) Some composers favor working from a script; some prefer talking with the director; some work from storyboards; some visit the set and talk with actors; some begin their composition and orchestration only when the film's final edit is complete.

Aaron Copland (1900–1990)
"Film music is like a small lamp that you place below the screen to warm it."

Techniques Film composers have developed a vast repertoire of methods, musical and technical, by which to accomplish their practical and aesthetic goals. They know, for example, that the harmonic system of *tonality* offers nearly unlimited means to create anxiety, expectation, or reassurance. Unresolved harmonies build suspense; unorthodox chord progressions effect surprise; and the change from major (often understood to suggest order or stability) to minor (more chromatic and therefore less stable) commonly darkens the mood. Similarly, tonal ambiguity or the use of foreign, artificial, or unfamiliar scales subconsciously affects listeners who are quite unaware of the intellectual reasons for their emotional response. As we know, listeners differ in their perception of *dissonance,* which some scholars believe in any case is a learned rather than innate phenomenon; but skillful composers use relationships between consonant and dissonant sounds to profound dramatic advantage. Extreme dissonance, suggesting disorder or instability, for example, may be relieved by consonant resolutions.

Timbre also has potent influence on our sensibilities: Orchestral strings tug our own emotional strings, and a trumpet's proud blare evokes within us ecstasies of patriotic pride. We can hardly imagine these instruments' roles reversed, whatever the melodic or rhythmic content of their music.

Thus, working at least from detailed charts of the length and description of scenes, with reference perhaps to a temp score as well, a film composer writes new music or adapts excerpts from existing classical or popular music to be heard as source music or skillfully woven into the fabric of the underscore. John Williams, who composes at a piano, has a projection room nearby where he views scenes from a film and compares them with cue sheets and with developing drafts of his musical conceptions.

Finally, the finished score is subjected to the indignities of being cut, mixed with dialogue and other sounds, and further altered by the director and assorted editors and sound engineers. Composers have been heard to lament that they scarcely recognize their own work in the finished product. Today's film composers also often complain of being asked to meet impossible deadlines, of having their music drowned out by deafening sound effects, or—worst of all—of having their scores rejected for entirely capricious reasons.

Film Score Performances and Recordings

Film music sometimes comes to attention independent of the film to which it belongs, through live or recorded performance. Discovering during the 1950s and 1960s the degree to which films sold music and vice versa, Hollywood's composers avidly entered the recording business, producing sound track or film score recordings including some, most, or all of the music of a film. Also, composers sometimes write a suite comprising significant sections of music from the complete score, such as Leonard Bernstein's suite of dances from *West Side Story* and his symphonic suite from *On the Waterfront.* From his sound track for Spike Lee's *Malcolm X,* which brilliantly documents the popular black music of the era, jazz composer and trumpeter Terence Blanchard excerpted *The Malcolm X Jazz Suite,* integrating the disparate moods of the movie score in eleven segments performed by a quintet of saxophone, piano, drums, bass, and trumpet in a highly effective independent composition.

Recently, movie music—suites, excerpts, or themes from popular films—has become a favorite focus of orchestral pops concerts, and such well-known pieces as John Barry's "Romance for Guitar and Orchestra" from the film *Deadfall* (1968) and Korngold's Cello Concerto from his score to *Deception* (1946) are among several movie compositions sometimes heard on the concert stage. The director of *The Red Violin,* released in 1999, commissioned John Corigliano to write an original score and then made the movie around it; and Corigliano fashioned a concert piece, *The Red Violin Chaconne,* from the movie music (for which he won an Oscar).

In 1999, Philip Glass achieved a sort of combination film-concert experience by composing an original score to accompany the classic horror film *Dracula* (1931). No musical score had ever been written for that early movie, which appeared just as silent films were giving way to talkies, when sound technology was in rudimentary stages of development. Glass's score is performed onstage by the well-known Kronos (string) Quartet while the film is projected on the screen.

Would we listen to the film score of a film we had never seen? Judging from sales of sound track and film score recordings, people do, in considerable numbers; sound track albums are selling at unprecedented rates and dominating sales charts more than ever before. Availability on popular recordings of the beautiful themes for *Chariots of Fire, Dances With Wolves,* and *Out of Africa* greatly enhanced ticket sales for those movies; and Elmer Bernstein's score for *The Magnificent Seven* (1960), which may be the most famous score ever written for a Hollywood western, became a classical crossover best-seller more than thirty years later when it was voted best sound track recording of 1994.

In the last two decades, sound track and film score collecting has accelerated among people who, although largely unaware of the music as they viewed a film, discover that the music allows them unlimited opportunity to "re-view" it. Although instrumental scores appear on best-seller lists infrequently, albums from *Apollo 13* and *Braveheart* have done very well; and the sound tracks for *Pulp Fiction* and *Natural Born Killers* (1994), which use pop music to heighten the claustrophobic atmosphere of murder and chaos, reached the Top 40 on *Billboard's* album chart. The number one album of 1998 was the sound track to the movie *City of Angels,* a film that made little impact in theaters, but whose sound track spawned two hit singles ("Uninvited" by Alanis Morissette and "Iris" by the Goo Goo Dolls) and stayed firmly lodged in the Top 40 for months. The number of sound tracks released in a single year has climbed steadily; however, some "sound track" albums, exemplified by *Godzilla,* actually have music "inspired by" the film, including songs not heard in the movie at all.

Studies of screen music came to the fore in the 1980s and 1990s with the improving quality and growing popularity of sound track recordings, and today movie music is recognized as a subject worthy of serious musicological consideration. Increasingly, movies are recognized as a source of concert music—a love scene, or a march, for example—equivalent to ballets and operas of the nineteenth century. Universities, libraries, and other institutions of higher learning are carefully preserving Hollywood film scores, and anthologies of articles, essays, score analyses, and memoirs about Hollywood film music attract favorable attention from scholars and film buffs alike.

Terms to Review

film score	**functional or nondiegetic**	**theremin**
Mickey Mousing	**music**	**quarter tones**
source or diegetic	**sound track**	**new age**
music	**classical Hollywood film score**	**temp**

Key Figures

Alfred Newman	Erich Korngold	John Williams
Max Steiner	Bernard Herrmann	

Critical Thinking

To what might you attribute the American public's apparent revived taste for movie musicals?

If you know the songs "Things Have Changed" (Bob Dylan, from *Wonder Boys,* 2000), "If I Didn't Have You" (Randy Newman, from *Monsters, Inc.,* 2001), and "Lose Yourself" (Eminem, Jeff Bass, and Luis Resto, from *8 Mile,* 2002), do you associate them with the films for which each won an Academy Award for best song?

The next time you view a film, notice as much as you can about the music. Who wrote it? Who performs it? What is the style of the music? How does it affect the movie? Is there both source and functional music in the film? Could the music stand alone as an album of the film score? Could it be arranged into a suite for orchestral performance?

American Opera

Almost since the first opera appeared in Italy, early in the seventeenth century, Italians have hummed their favorite opera tunes while strolling down the street. Other Europeans also have long delighted in the emotional intensity and high drama or comedy of wonderful operas in various languages and styles.

But many Americans until recently considered opera an elite and unlikely form of entertainment, and a characteristically American opera was almost inconceivable. The few nineteenth-century American composers involved with opera either intended their own works to sound Italian or sought to attract an American audience by translating Italian, French, or German operas into English. But neither ploy made the medium accessible or meaningful to most American listeners.

Yet opera, the grandest of all the arts, combines singing, acting, orchestral music, drama, staging, costuming, dance, and lighting effects in a form infinitely greater than the sum of its parts. Although opera took a long time to assume the vital role in American musical theater that it finally enjoys today, after World War II a significant number of American opera companies were formed, and performances in the major opera houses around the country today are regularly sold out.

During the 1980s, films of two Italian operas by Giuseppe Verdi (1813–1901)—*La Traviata* and *Otello*—achieved commercial success at popular American movie theaters, and many mainstream films have featured generous opera scenes: *Fatal Attraction, Moonstruck, A Room with a View, Philadelphia, Atonement,* and Woody Allen's *Match Point* are examples. Recently network television has been offering full-length live performances of great operas from many countries and periods. Saturday afternoon broadcasts of Metropolitan Opera performances began in 1931, and soon became the second most popular broadcast on daytime radio; they remain a part of many families' Saturday afternoon experience today. Further, the Metropolitan currently broadcasts a number of performances live from their stage into select movie theaters around the country. Metropolitan opera performances are available as well on satellite radio channels; and a new online subscription service offers high definition videos, historic TV performances, and numerous radio broadcasts delivered on demand. Thus opera lovers throughout the country have unprecedented access, at low or no cost, to performances of the highest quality.

Finally, then, Americans have discovered that there are as many kinds of opera as there are movies or books. Although the complexity of opera may require more preparation from the audience than other forms of art or entertainment, its combined visual and musical effects offer unparalleled rewards.

Opera

An **opera** is a drama that is sung instead of spoken. Like a play, it may be long or short, comic or serious, grand or modest—good or bad. Because ordinary conversation is normally not sung, the opera viewer must abandon or suspend rational thought to become immersed in the art—the magic—that is opera; but this is not as difficult as it sounds, for even skeptical viewers quickly become caught in a great opera's spell and forget to notice that the dialogue is being sung instead of spoken. As noted in Chapter 17, many modern musicals use this same technique, which Broadway audiences have come to expect. After all, it is the role of art to express human feelings at a level *beyond* the limits of ordinary communication. As our emotions become involved and the real world slips away (or gets out of the way), the most artificial aspects of art somehow seem more real than reality itself.

Solo and Ensemble Singing
In an opera, the exchange of dialogue occurs through **recitative** (from the same root as *recite*), a style of singing in which the words are expressed clearly and economically so as to move the drama along. The melody of a recitative often resembles the inflection of the words as they would be spoken; and the rhythm, free and flexible, also accommodates the text. As you might expect, recitative involves little repetition of phrases, because its purpose is to further, not delay, the action.

An **aria,** usually more melodic and often more expressive than a recitative, constitutes a dramatic soliloquy in song, with the emphasis upon the music rather than the text. Time is simply suspended as a character reflects upon and expresses deep emotions aroused by situations in the story. Arias fully display the beauty and range of a singer's voice, often allowing the performer to indulge in virtuosic singing, because here the words are less important than the expression of emotion. There also may be considerable repetition of text ("I love you, I *love* you . . .") to enhance the emotional impact. Unlike recitative, an aria has metered rhythm and is organized according to musical principles of design.

The orchestra often provides far more than simple support for an aria's vocal line, perhaps playing an introduction and concluding passage as well as interludes between sections or verses. Further, instruments may introduce or imitate the singer's melodic phrases throughout the piece or provide sound effects, such as birdcalls or thunder, independent of the singer's melodic line. Sometimes the orchestra even assumes a dramatic or psychological role, contradicting the singer's words by making musical reference to conflicting ideas, for example.

Ensemble scenes add excitement to opera as to all forms of musical theater. The members of an opera **chorus** (a large ensemble with several voices singing each line of music) generally represent characters in the drama, such as guests at a wedding or soldiers returning from battle. And again as in musicals, *solo ensembles*—duets, trios, quartets, quintets, or even larger groups of soloists—add thrilling drama as well as magnificent contrapuntal musical effect to the opera stage.

Opera in America

Before the twentieth century, the few American opera houses confined their repertoire almost entirely to foreign operas, because, as we know, little was available or would have been accepted of native work. During the first half of the twentieth century, several American composers sought to establish a national opera style by writing operas with American Indian settings; but the idea, although popular for a time, was short-lived.

The ragtime composer Scott Joplin wrote at least two operas, one of which, *Treemonisha,* was published in 1911 in what is called a "piano score"—that is, without orchestration. Joplin wrote the words as well as the music of *Treemonisha,* whose story illustrates his belief that blacks must acquire education in order to improve their social and economic situation. Joplin's opera includes some ragtime and other dance pieces, as well as more conventional operatic arias. In the very effective finale, the large, brightly costumed cast celebrates the happy ending by dancing a stately "slow drag" (an Online Listening Example).

The lack of interest during Joplin's lifetime in an opera by a black composer prevented him from ever achieving a proper performance of *Treemonisha.* However, in the early 1970s Gunther Schuller scored the opera for orchestral instruments, and it has been performed, with Schuller's or other orchestral accompaniments, numerous times since then, live and on public television.

Curiously, two operas by white composers, each with an all-black cast and both performed in Broadway theaters rather than in an opera house, first brought American opera to a broad and appreciative audience.

www.mhhe.com/ferrisaml6e

Virgil Thomson (1896–1989) Convinced by the time he graduated from Harvard University that concert music had become overly complex, **Virgil Thomson** imposed a refreshing simplicity upon his own compositions, often based on the folk songs, hymns, and Civil War songs he had heard as a child in Missouri. While continuing his music education in Paris with the extremely talented and influential teacher Nadia Boulanger (see p. 374), Thomson discovered that the French shared his appreciation for musical simplicity; they thought, as he did, the purpose of music is to amuse and entertain rather than to improve the listener. Thomson stayed in this congenial atmosphere for fifteen years but was eventually driven home by the impending catastrophe of World War II.

Among Thomson's most stimulating experiences abroad was his collaboration with **Gertrude Stein** (1874–1946), an American writer who spent most of her life in Paris. Stein used words for their sounds rather than their meanings, producing attractive, often funny combinations of syllables regardless of their sense or lack of it. Gertrude Stein wrote the words, or **libretto,** and Virgil Thomson wrote the music of *Four Saints in Three Acts,* the first American opera to appeal to the American public.

This stunning show, which actually concerns fifteen saints and has four acts, makes little if any sense but ravishes the eyes and ears with the most delightful entertainment. When the show opened in 1934 in New York City, its enchanting sets elegantly constructed of brightly colored cellophane—to the dismay of the city's fire department—provided a magnificent stage. Thomson's choice of an all-black cast seems curious, because the characters are (apparently) Spanish and have nothing to do with black culture, but simply reflect the daily blend of meditative creativity and ordinary socializing that Stein and Thomson experienced in Parisian life. (Thomson claimed that Stein patterned the opera's leading characters, St. Theresa and St. Ignatius, after herself and James Joyce.) In any case, although Thomson's declaration that he simply admired the appearance and voices of the black singers may seem racist in today's more sensitive environment, his intentions were artistic and aesthetic, and he would have been astonished to think his genuine esteem might be considered discriminatory.

Thomson set Stein's nonsensical but appealing libretto beautifully to music, although it had been thought that American speech did not lend itself to musical settings; this was, in fact, the first American libretto effectively and idiomatically set to an opera score. This, together with Thomson's folklike melodies, attractive hymn tunes, lovely choruses, colorful sets, and imaginative orchestration, won the appreciation of Broadway audiences accustomed to more frivolous entertainment.

Revived on Broadway in 1986, the show—on a Catholic theme, written by a Jew and a Protestant—seemed as fresh and bold as ever. Further, some reviewers recognized it as a direct antecedent of the nonnarrative, minimal music theater practiced now by Robert Wilson and Philip Glass (see pp. 346–347), David Byrne, Laurie Anderson, and John Adams.

George Gershwin's *Porgy and Bess*

The same year that *Four Saints* opened on Broadway, songwriter and symphonic jazz composer George Gershwin read a novel by DuBose Heyward based on the lives of real people who lived in a black tenement area in Charleston, South Carolina. Profoundly moved by the novel and by the play based on it, Gershwin decided to write an opera on the subject.

In preparation, this New Yorker spent a summer in the Charleston area, where he listened to people talk and sing. Then, having steeped himself in the sounds of the vegetable sellers' calls, the work songs of the men, the lullabies women sang to their babies, and the shouts and hymns performed at church on Sundays, he returned to New York to write *Porgy and Bess*. The new opera opened on Broadway a year after Thomson's opera—also with an all-black cast.

Porgy begins with an instrumental piece, usually called an **overture** but simply called an introduction by Gershwin, who intended his show for a Broadway audience. Like a conventional opera overture, Gershwin's introduction sets the appropriate mood for the show and includes some of its important themes.

Porgy, a poor man so crippled that he gets around only by goat cart, falls deeply in love with Bess, a "loose-living woman" from New York who gives up her "big city ways" to live and love with him. Their story, tender and moving,

FIGURE 19.1

A scene from Gershwin's
Porgy and Bess.

has flashes of wit and humor and plenty of tense drama. A number of the songs (Gershwin also avoided the term *aria*) became so popular that, finally, Americans were humming opera tunes in the streets!

The love duet in which Porgy and Bess eloquently express their devotion to one another is one of the most beautiful in the opera literature of the world (Figure 19.1 and Listening Example 65). The wide vocal range, difficult leaps,

Listening Example 65

"Bess, You Is My Woman Now"
(from *Porgy and Bess*)

In a moment when they are alone together, Porgy and Bess declare their love for each other in this moving duet, written in 1935. Notice the wide vocal range and the difficult leaps between tones, challenging for singers and more characteristic of opera than musicals. More subtle characteristics include unusual harmonic modulations, which enrich the quality of the piece even if we do not specifically identify them. In the traditional manner of opera, Porgy first declares his love, Bess responds, and then the two join in a rapturous duet

CD 3
Track 8
5:13

—Continued

"Bess, You Is My Woman Now"
(from *Porgy and Bess*)

transcending the problems their real lives present and transporting them, and us, to another, happier world. You will hear expressively inflected blue notes throughout, derived as we have seen from black performance practiced and associated with blues, jazz, and many styles of black music.

Composer George Gershwin (1898–1937).

Genre Opera.

Timbre Bass and soprano vocal soloists, with orchestral accompaniment.

Texture Basically homophonic; occasionally polyphonic during the duet.

Form Strophic.

Meter Quadruple.

Tempo Slow, relaxed.

0:00 Poignant falling figures in the strings introduce this beautiful duet, in which Porgy declares his love for Bess and insists that she must "laugh an' dance for two instead of one," because he is physically unable to get around.

0:12 The strings double Porgy's passionate melody, enhancing the emotional impact of the music. The verse has five lines of text, yet seems superbly balanced.

Bess, you is my woman now, you is, you is! . . .

1:05 Bess responds with her fervent declaration of love for Porgy, declaring she will go nowhere without him. At first her melody is the same as Porgy's, but soon she soars to rapturous high notes, as if overwhelmed with love and joy. Remember to listen for and enjoy the orchestra's important contributions to the music.

Porgy, I's your woman now, I is, I is! . . .

2:15 *Mornin' time an' evenin' time an' summer time an' winter time. . . .*

2:36 Porgy and Bess: Notice as they sing together that Bess (repeating the lyrics she has already sung) generally carries the melody whereas Porgy's comments add contrapuntal interest and harmony. Also notice the orchestra's contributions, including melodic support, harmony, and independent "commentary."

Bess, you is my woman now and forever. . . .

3:55 Bess: *Oh, my Porgy, my man, Porgy.*

Porgy: [*simultaneously*]: *My Bess, my Bess. . . .*

and unconventional harmonies distinguish the music from the usual Broadway fare of that period; yet the opera also features Tin Pan Alley-like songs and jazzy flavors providing a wealth of entertainment.

Gian-Carlo Menotti (1911–2007)

Gian-Carlo Menotti, another composer who has written operas well received by a Broadway audience, reversed the prevalent trend by coming from his native Italy to America to study music. A child prodigy who had written two operas by the time he was thirteen, Menotti arrived in 1928 at the Curtis Institute of Music in Philadelphia, Pennsylvania, where he became a close friend of another famous American composer, Samuel Barber (see pp. 380–383).

In 1947, Menotti wrote a two-act thriller, *The Medium,* which because of its modest resources—five singers, one dance-mime role, and an orchestra of only fourteen players—may be called a **chamber opera.** (It is also quite brief, Menotti intending it to be performed with another miniature opera of his, *The Telephone.*) Broadway audiences found *The Medium*'s eerie mood, memorable melodies, and dramatic libretto, which Menotti wrote himself, moving and exciting indeed.

Menotti's next major work, *The Consul,* opened on Broadway in 1950, had a long, successful run, and won the Pulitzer Prize and Drama Critics' Award. The story concerns the frustration and ultimate tragedy of a family desperately trying to escape from their country but confronted with bureaucratic nonsense in response to their urgent pleas for assistance. *The Consul,* written at the time of the Cold War, specifies neither country nor time, allowing us to relate the drama's events to our own knowledge, experience, or imagination. The moving aria "To This We've Come," eloquently expressing the rage and despair of a woman prevented by bizarre circumstances from saving her doomed family, is an Online Listening Example (and can be heard on YouTube).

www.mhhe.com/ferrisaml6e

The next year (1951), the National Broadcasting Company (NBC) commissioned Menotti to write the first opera conceived especially for television. Menotti based the resulting work, *Amahl and the Night Visitors* (Figure 19.2), on a painting formerly, but no longer, attributed to Hieronymus Bosch and on his own childhood memories. Amahl, whose simple, naive story and lovely music consistently appeal to children and, as Menotti says, to "those who like children" as well, has been performed at Christmastime every year since, often on television, and also by amateurs in church and community settings.

Menotti has written symphonic and choral works as well as several other operas, but he is primarily a man of the theater, whose gift for melody and drama seems to have been best expressed in his early operas written for Broadway or television audiences.

The Trend Toward Realism

Although traditionally operas have dealt with fiction, fantasy, myth, or ancient history, increasingly opera composers choose topics from recent history and even from everyday life. As early as 1937, Marc Blitzstein addressed the

FIGURE 19.2

A scene from Menotti's *Amahl and the Night Visitors.*

traumas of the Great Depression in a Broadway opera (sometimes called a musical play) about the struggle for labor rights: *The Cradle Will Rock.* Much of the music was popular in style, and the words—some of them spoken— reflected the ethnic speech of city streets. A movie, *Cradle Will Rock* (2000), dramatized the formation of the pro-union musical, the attempts to shut it down, and the fascinating manner in which the show finally was performed. Douglas S. Moore wrote about American pioneer life in *The Devil and Daniel Webster* (1939); and in 1958, he set another opera, *The Ballad of Baby Doe,* in the nineteenth century and included some of the musical styles popular then. Aaron Copland's *The Tender Land,* about a midwestern American farm family, also appeared during the 1950s. The opera *Frederick Douglass* (1983) by Ulysses Kay concerns the life of Frederick Douglass, a hero in African American history. Kirke Mechem's *John Brown* (2008), climaxing with the hanging of the famous abolitionist in 1859, took much of its libretto from Brown's actual speeches and writing, with the composer's expressed intention of helping a modern audience understand Brown's moral position.

Beginning in the 1980s, operas based on recent or even current social and political events began to appear, sometimes raising controversy among still-living participants in the events. Philip Glass's *Satyagraha* (1980) tells of the early struggles of Mahatma Gandhi; *X: The Life and Times of Malcolm X* by Anthony Davis (1986), concerns that black nationalist leader; John Adams's first opera, *Nixon in China* (1987), describes President Nixon's visits to and negotiations with that country (Figure 19.3); in 1990, an opera called *The Manson Family,* about the mass murderer Charles Manson, was written by John Moran; and in 1991,

FIGURE 19.3
A scene from John Adams's *Nixon in China*.

John Adams presented a new opera, *The Death of Klinghoffer,* which describes the highjacking of the ship *Achille Lauro* in 1985 and the murder of a wheelchair-bound Jewish American passenger. His 2005 opera *Doctor Atomic* concerns the physicist J. Robert Oppenheimer and the development of the atomic bomb.

Still another genre, science fiction opera, has recently been approached by some composers. There is even a talk-show opera, Mikel Rouse's *Dennis Cleveland* (1996), based on the life of a real talk-show host, in which cast members sprinkled throughout the audience suddenly stand up and sing; the music effectively incorporates rock and pop and digital samples from actual talk shows, bringing digital recording technology to (or behind) the opera stage. (Excerpts from most if not all of the works cited here can be heard at the composers' websites or on YouTube.)

Novels sometimes stimulate the creation of operas as well: Recent examples include *The Great Gatsby* (1999), *Dead Man Walking* (2000), and *Cold Sassy Tree* (2000). Another new American opera, *Margaret Garner* (2005), by Richard Danielpour, is based on the true story of a slave, a version of whose story Toni Morrison related in her novel *Beloved.* (Morrison wrote the libretto for the opera.) In 2007, audiences at the premiere performances of Ricky Ian Gordon's opera *The Grapes of Wrath,* based on John Steinbeck's novel set in the years of the Great Depression, seemed to find the subject matter timely and the characteristic American sounds—banjos, whistling, fiddlings, harmonica, swing—a congenial form of entertainment. And in 2008, *The Bonesetter's Daughter,* from the novel by Amy Tan, premiered at the San Francisco Opera. A cross-cultural project like the novel on which it is based, its cast includes acrobats, dancers, and traditional opera performers from China as well as singers from both China and the United States. Amy Tan wrote the libretto, Stewart Wallace (whose earlier operas include *Harvey Milk,* 1995) composed the music, and a Chinese director, Chen Shi-Zheng, directed.

It seems that American opera is re-establishing its links with popular theater. *Porgy and Bess, Four Saints in Three Acts,* and Menotti's operas were intended and performed for theater audiences, and many of our current opera composers (including Michael John LaChiusa, Jeanine Tesori, and Adam Guettel) come not from the concert world but from Broadway musical theater. Encouraging this trend, in 2006 the Metropolitan Opera and its neighbor, Lincoln Center Theater, jointly commissioned several works to be developed jointly and produced either at the theater or the opera house.

Einstein on the Beach (1976), a plotless opera written by **Philip Glass** (b. 1937) in collaboration with the playwright-director Robert Wilson, is based on a historical individual but is highly unusual in its organization—a series of stage pictures, dances, and narrations lasting about five hours—as well as its music. Three visual themes (Train, Trial, and Field), each with its corresponding music, are associated with Albert Einstein's thoughts and experiences. The visual themes, having three scenes each, are presented in four acts, sandwiched between five short connecting pieces called "Knee Plays" that allow time for changing sets and scenery. (Listening Example 66 is the last scene before the

Listening Example 66

"Spaceship" (excerpt)
(from *Einstein on the Beach*)

CD 3
Track 9
3:56

This 1976 opera is a true collaboration between Glass and the great American dramatist Robert Wilson, who shares Glass's concern for apparent motionlessness and seemingly endless durations during which significant things happen or are understood. The title, which refers to Nevil Shute's 1957 novel of nuclear holocaust, *On the Beach,* suggests that Einstein perhaps pondered the possible consequences of his own scientific discoveries. Beginning with a nineteenth-century train (a reference to toy trains Einstein played with as a child), the opera ends inside a twentieth-century spaceship—perhaps the symbol of potential liberation from worldly disaster. Throughout the work, harmonic and rhythmic structures are linked, integrating rhythm, harmony, and melody in a complex fashion that yet sounds simple and repetitious. Audiences having no idea of the complexities of Glass's conception have found the opera enchanting, almost hypnotic in its deceptively naive appeal. Rigorously intellectual in concept, the music achieves a calm, dreamlike, mystical effect. The electronic organ and the choral voices might even suggest a religious atmosphere, though this is never implied by Philip Glass.

Composer and Lyricist   Philip Glass (b. 1937).

Designer and Director   Robert Wilson (b. 1941).

—Continued

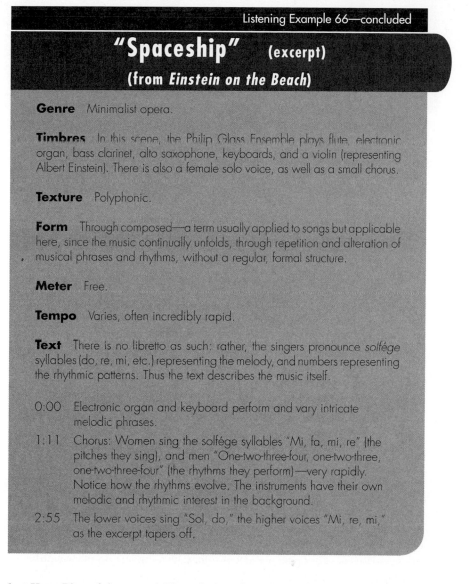

Listening Example 66—concluded

"Spaceship" (excerpt)
(from *Einstein on the Beach*)

Genre Minimalist opera.

Timbres In this scene, the Philip Glass Ensemble plays flute, electronic organ, bass clarinet, alto saxophone, keyboards, and a violin (representing Albert Einstein). There is also a female solo voice, as well as a small chorus.

Texture Polyphonic.

Form Through composed—a term usually applied to songs but applicable here, since the music continually unfolds, through repetition and alteration of musical phrases and rhythms, without a regular, formal structure.

Meter Free.

Tempo Varies, often incredibly rapid.

Text There is no libretto as such: rather, the singers pronounce *solfège* syllables (do, re, mi, etc.) representing the melody, and numbers representing the rhythmic patterns. Thus the text describes the music itself.

0:00   Electronic organ and keyboard perform and vary intricate melodic phrases.

1:11   Chorus: Women sing the solfège syllables "Mi, fa, mi, re" (the pitches they sing), and men "One-two-three-four, one-two-three, one-two-three-four" (the rhythms they perform)—very rapidly. Notice how the rhythms evolve. The instruments have their own melodic and rhythmic interest in the background.

2:55   The lower voices sing "Sol, do," the higher voices "Mi, re, mi," as the excerpt tapers off.

last Knee Play of the opera.) Though there is no intermission, audience members can come and go at will, as the music gradually unfolds lengthy repetitions and evolutions of small motives.

Opera or Musical: Which Is It?

Today many Broadway and London musicals are sung throughout, and operas by Philip Glass and John Adams, for example, often seem closer to Broadway productions than to opera in the traditional sense. How, then, to distinguish between these forms of musical theater? With difficulty, if at all! There are opera singers who sing musicals and musical theater performers who sing opera. The old definitions of a *musical* as a play with occasional music, an *opera* as a musical drama with no spoken drama, and an *operetta* as something between the two extremes are largely meaningless. Audiences both on Broadway and in the opera house have come to enjoy grand entertainment on a lavish scale and of unprecedented variety and scope.

Still, some suggest that a significant difference between operas and musicals lies not so much in the music, which has increasingly overlapped, but in the words. Whether one understands the language in which an opera is written or not, it is often difficult to understand the words as they are sung. Although many opera composers are famous for their music, the names of few opera librettists come readily to mind, and those who do are remembered more for their story than for the particular turns of phrase with which they delivered it. Broadway lyrics, on the other hand, full of puns and intricate rhymes, must be clearly understood to be appreciated and in fact assume a full share of importance together with the music. Great lyricists such as Lorenz Hart, Ira Gershwin, and Oscar Hammerstein II retain their reputations, and we admire the songs of Cole Porter and Stephen Sondheim as much for their words (written by the composers) as for their music.

Others propose the role of the orchestra as defining the critical difference between the two genres; that is, in opera the orchestra often plays a central role in the telling of the story, while in musicals the orchestra generally plays a supportive role. Advocates of this theory suggest that musicals in which the orchestra takes a more central and dramatic role, as in *West Side Story,* move toward opera, whereas the supportive role of Stephen Sondheim's orchestra relegates his works—for all their emotional power and dramatic subtleties—to the world of musicals. The fact that most opera composers orchestrate their works and most composers of musicals do not lends credence to this possible distinction. On the other hand, the orchestrator Jonathan Tunick refers to Stephen Sondheim's *Sweeney Todd* (made into a film in 2007) as neither opera nor musical but a successful American musical drama.

Stephen Sondheim himself suggests that the difference between Broadway and opera is in the expectations of the audience, going so far as to say that in his opinion, when Menotti's *The Medium* and *The Telephone* were performed on Broadway they were "sung-through" shows, and when they were performed in opera houses—for opera audiences—they were operas. In other words, for him the object changes in terms of how it is viewed.

Certainly there are significant differences between the vocal requirements for singing opera and singing musicals. Broadway theaters are usually about a third the size of an opera house, and even in the smaller theaters Broadway singers often rely on amplification, whereas opera singers are taught to project their voices, at soft or loud levels, for impressive distances over sustained periods of time.

Still another difference between the genres was recently voiced by an editor of musical scores, who described a musical as something made up by many people—designers, producers, directors, actors, orchestrators, choreographers, dancers, and maybe more, besides the composer and lyricist, all having creative input—whereas an opera normally is the product of one controlling consciousness.

American Opera Today

Although tightened budgets have put serious constraints upon the world of opera, whose complex presentations are exceedingly expensive to produce, Americans today are interested in all varieties of opera, old and new, domestic and foreign, funny and sad, short and long, simple and complex. Many American cities have an opera house and their own resident opera company, and virtually all Americans have access to live or taped performances on radio or television. Foreign operas often are performed in English translation, or, alternatively, English surtitles are projected above the stage to avoid interfering with the visual presentation. The American audience seems finally to have recognized opera as the marvelous form of entertainment it was always intended to be.

In 2004, however, a latent but smoldering issue came to the fore, when a famous and beloved American soprano, Deborah Voigt, was forced out of a production in London because the director deemed her too heavy to be suitable for the role she was to play. While vocal beauty has always mattered in opera, physical beauty is commanding ever more significance, as audiences require opera stars to look as well as sound their part. Opera singers, whose voices are never amplified, and who require extraordinary physical stamina to project their voices (even when singing pianissimo) to the back and the top of a theater, sometimes look as oversized as the melodramatic roles they portray; yet audiences increasingly require them to appear, as well as sound, beautiful. We will probably hear more of this debate concerning the significance of vocal versus physical beauty in the immediate future.

Terms to Review

opera	chorus	overture
recitative	*Treemonisha*	chamber opera
aria	libretto	

Key Figures

Virgil Thomson	Gian-Carlo Menotti	Philip Glass
Gertrude Stein		

Critical Thinking

Why do you think Americans have been slow to develop enthusiasm for opera? And why do you think operas (American and other) are increasingly popular here now?

Why do you think movies and television commercials often use famous opera themes to heighten emotion or to sell products? Do you think repeated hearing of an excerpt from opera in a radio or television commercial increases the popularity of the music or detracts from its appreciation?

Do you believe it is possible to "suspend disbelief" and forget that opera singers are singing rather than speaking their lines? Is this suspension of disbelief more likely to occur while you are viewing an opera or a musical (movie or live)? Why?

Where do you think opera directors should place their primary emphasis, when hiring singers: on acting? stage presence? singing? physical appearance? other?

PART 5
Summary

fter the Civil War, musical theater became increasingly popular in America, as the minstrel show waned in popularity but vaudeville and burlesque flourished. Revues, more elegant and sophisticated than the other variety shows, continue as a popular form of entertainment today.

European operettas, which have an integrated plot, soon stimulated composers to write operettas for an American audience. Gilbert and Sullivan's operettas provided hilarious entertainment; but most influential upon the American music stage was the Viennese operetta, with its romantic stories and make-believe settings.

Early musical comedies combined elements of operetta and variety shows. By writing several shows that had a story but included the song, dance, and comedy routines of vaudeville, George M. Cohan was most influential in accustoming the Broadway audience to the new style. Jerome Kern's *Show Boat* proved that a Broadway musical could be based on a literary work and could address serious subjects effectively. *Oklahoma!* by Rodgers and Hammerstein successfully integrated all the entertainment scenes with the drama. Each of these shows had a profound effect upon the development of the Broadway musical.

The 1920s and 1930s are considered the Golden Age of the Broadway musical because so many outstanding shows were produced. Since then, musical theater has become more complex and more sophisticated. Composers have revealed their heightened sense of singing (Frank Loesser's *Most Happy Fella*), the integrity of the play (Lerner and Loewe), and the importance of dance (Leonard Bernstein), and Bernstein and Stephen Sondheim are among several composers who have applied their classical and popular interests in various ways to the musical stage. Many of today's musicals are multimedia affairs combining technologically complex aural and visual effects.

From the earliest days of commercial films, live music introduced and accompanied a movie; and with the advent of sound films, the film score emerged as a new form of dramatic music. Film music, whether heard by the characters in the film (source or diegetic music) or by the viewing audience alone (functional or nondiegetic music), underpins the movie's emotional effects while serving innumerable practical functions as well.

Classical music, pop, jazz, rock, electronic music, and even opera effectively support feature films, setting a mood, establishing a time period, enhancing characterization, and bridging awkward gaps between scenes. Composers vary widely in their techniques of writing film scores, and all face the inevitability of having their music drastically altered by the director, various editors, and sound engineers. Some, however, compose orchestral suites from portions of their scores, allowing their music to be heard as they conceived it by a concert audience or on a recording.

Opera, too, is newly, but immensely, popular in America today. An opera is a grand combination of literary, visual, and musical arts. Although some composers include spoken words in their operas, traditionally opera dialogue was sung in recitative and emotional reactions were expressed in solo arias, duets, and large or small ensembles.

In the 1920s, several American operas were enthusiastically received. Both Virgil Thomson's *Four Saints in Three Acts* and George Gershwin's *Porgy and Bess* succeeded on Broadway, as did Gian-Carlo Menotti's operas nearly three decades later. Thomson sought an elegant simplicity in music, Gershwin spoke in the spirit of jazz, and Menotti represents the Italian tradition of lyrical melodies and good theater. Today's mainstream and progressive composers are producing a wealth of new American operas, and this form of entertainment is increasingly visible on Broadway, in the opera house, and on television and movie screens.

PART **6**

Tradition and Innovation in Concert Music

Music for the Concert Hall: Historical and Cultural Perspective

The twentieth century witnessed an unprecedented diversity of concert music styles, as new historical and cultural awareness broadened concepts of timbre, pitch, melody, harmony, and rhythm. The political and social turmoil of much of that century, and the many important new technological resources, all had strong cultural repercussions, as artists in every medium found their way along traditional paths or forged entirely new avenues of expression.

During the 1920s, several talented young Americans set out to make their living as composers of concert music, never before considered a viable profession in this country. Whereas earlier American composers had largely depended on income-producing careers as teachers or performing musicians, these young people intended to survive as successful professional composers. They meant to write music not radically different from the masterpieces of the European musical heritage, yet sounding distinctively American and of the twentieth century. We may consider that they took an *evolutionary* approach to furthering the history of music.

Other twentieth-century Americans took a *revolutionary* approach to the composition of music. With the energy, curiosity, and independence characteristic of the pioneering spirit, a number of Americans explored musical sound as never before, so extending the boundaries of the definition of the art as to constitute a veritable revolution in the concept of music.

Interaction Between the Arts

Throughout the twentieth century, visual and literary artists continued close interaction, sharing an expanded perception of their own disciplines and an interest in the interrelationships among them all. This close association among the arts—often enhanced by new technology—persists today, resulting sometimes in a kind of collision of artists exulting in their own independence and in the collage-like results of the interdependence they share. Some compare this congenial friction, if we can call it that, to the modern urban experience, in which widely disparate elements form a complex, somewhat fragmented whole.

The theater, requiring the services of painters, set designers, writers, musicians, dancers, choreographers, and actors, has always represented a collaborative form of art, and, as we have seen, nineteenth-century artists formed other, less traditional, liaisons as well. But today the visual, literary, and various performance arts influence and interact with music even more than in the past.

Dance, liberated from the expectation that it will tell a story, may or may not be accompanied by or set to music today; but although some dances are entirely independent of music or sound, most choreographers still consider music an inherent and vital dimension of dance. Jazz rhythms and electronically produced sounds as well as other popular and classical music dramatically widen the range of the dance experience.

Literature, too, is affected by the new intimacy among the arts. Several twentieth-century writers chose words for their sounds, rather than their meanings. For example, neither Gertrude Stein's libretto for Virgil Thomson's *Four Saints in Three Acts* (pp. 339–340) nor the stream-of-consciousness prose of William Faulkner, attempts to follow the rules of grammar or syntax. Further, poetry may have visual as well as intellectual values, as when *shaped poems* are placed on a page in a manner conceived to visually enhance the meaning of the words. Each of these literary concepts (or conceits) can be related to a painter's subjective choice of colors, regardless of their relation to real visual experience, and to a composer's choice of pitches for their timbre rather than for functional value.

Multimedia Performances.

The unprecedented degree of collaboration recently occurring among painters, dancers, poets, playwrights, and musicians has produced a wealth of interdisciplinary performances, awakening a healthy appreciation for the arts among audiences whose previous interest in and exposure to art were minimal. Some performances constitute "happenings" combining live or taped music with film, slides, speech, and lighting as well as dance, gestures, or movement of some kind, sometimes with audience participation. Painters and sculptors have combined shapes, colors, and sounds in large "environmental" works.

Because music for tape often requires visual or dramatic interest to sustain an audience's attention in the absence of live performers, some recent compositions involve a combination of live and taped music. Complex multimedia compositions simultaneously address two or more of the senses, and invite spectators to actively participate in their performance.

353

Relationships Between the Visual Arts and Music.

Shared interests and philosophies of art are not only revealed in such collaborative efforts but also individually expressed in each medium of art. Much in the way that *pointillist* painters treat spots of pure color as entities in themselves, for example, composers sometimes treat particular tones or timbres as isolated phenomena with independent, as opposed to interdependent, values. In the machines, advertisements, and commercial objects painted by Andy Warhol and other pop artists, we see the simplicity and repetition characteristic of musical *minimalism* (pp. 402–404), generally considered a part of the art or concert music experience, but of strong appeal to listeners more accustomed to popular than to so-called serious music. Visual artists often depict musical instruments or, more subjectively, the *experience* of listening to music.

Since the early twentieth century, texture has been a source of interest and experimentation throughout the arts. Painters such as Romare Bearden (pp. 125–126) often add a third dimension to their work by affixing pieces of fabric or other foreign objects to their surfaces. Other painters build up their surfaces by applying multiple thick layers of paint. Similarly, composers may vary musical texture by superimposing unrelated timbres or chords, or by combining complex layers of sound. Considering timbre, composers today find sounds of nature, of machinery, and of computer-generated effects to offer a virtually unlimited palette of musical sound, much as sculptors may replace traditional materials like marble and bronze with plastic or with various found materials.

The Value of Chance

Artists have long recognized the value of the unintended and the unexpected in the creative process. An ancient Roman treatise tells of an artist throwing a sponge at his canvas in a fit of rage and being delighted with the "effect of nature" resulting in his picture, and a ninth-century Chinese work describes an artist "who excelled in splattering ink to paint landscapes." Even Leonardo da Vinci advised aspiring landscape

Jackson Pollock, *Number 1*, 1948, oil on canvas. Pollock's Abstract Expressionist paintings, expressive of the energy and rapid tempo of American life in the 1940s, involve imaginative interaction between chance and the artist's creative intent.

painters to visualize landscapes when looking at a wall spotted with stains.

During the 1950s and 1960s, the concept of leaving significant details of their work to chance attracted many visual artists and musicians. *Op art*, like the chance music we shall consider in this part of the text, involves active rather than passive participation, as op artists combine lines and colors to create optical illusions that "activate" the eye instead of "acting upon it" in the traditional way. Jackson Pollock (1912–1956) led the Abstract Expressionist painters, who developed various means to achieve random effects: Pollock, for example, dripped or sprayed paint onto a large surface, carefully choosing the colors, direction, and density of his paints but allowing chance, or serendipity, to determine the result of his work. Like many artists intrigued with chance, Pollock considered the act of creating art a spiritual experience, more significant than the result. He did not create his work to be hung on museum walls but considered it to be as ephemeral—perhaps even as spiritual—as Navajo sand paintings.

Sculptors attracted to the idea of (literally) moving art experimented with motors, bands, and pulleys,

Untitled, a mobile by the American sculptor Alexander Calder, 1976. Aluminum and steel.

whereas Alexander Calder (1898–1976), finding such mobiles too predictable, created small, delicate sculptures to hang in space, subject to the whim of the lightest breeze. Just as one performance of chance music is never like another, Calder's small mobiles never appear exactly the same from one moment to the next.

Chance occurs in literature, too, when novels written in *hypertext* allow readers to choose on their computers which subplots they wish to follow, as through a maze, rendering a book's form and even its conclusion indeterminate.

American Concert Music

We cannot identify, either in Europe or in America, a unifying Western musical language such as prevailed in the several preceding centuries. Rather, the century we were born into gave us a rich multiplicity of musical tongues, which became ever more diverse as composers mixed the great Western tradition with the sounds of other cultures and other times. Experimental, often deliberately provocative music interested some twentieth-century American composers; others chose to follow more traditional paths.

In the early years of a new century, we can scarcely imagine what musical riches lie in store. Considering how significantly the music of each preceding era differed from the predominant styles it succeeded, we may expect the music of the twenty-first century to chart numerous new and adventurous courses. ♪

Experimental Music: Revolution

T hree musical pioneers initiated the **experimental** movement in America—one a Connecticut Yankee who explored the manifold characteristics of sound, the second a Californian who discovered new ways to use the piano, and the third a European, Edgard Varèse (see p. 384), who dreamed of new instruments that would create *new* sounds and lived to see his dream come true.

Charles Ives (1874–1954)

**Charles Ives
(1874–1954)**
"Music—that no one knows what it is—and the less he knows he knows what it is the nearer it is to music—probably."
(May 5, 1947)

Charles Ives derived his musical inventiveness from his father, George, an amateur musician who taught his son to play several instruments and (more significantly) to be ever curious about music and musical sound. George Ives continually conducted sound experiments in the family barn, to the annoyance of his neighbors and the fascination of his son. His father also taught Charles to value each piece of music for its own sake, and all his life the younger Ives valued Stephen Foster's music as highly as Bach's, and a good rag as much as a good symphony, viewing each piece according to its own particular merits and considering differentiation among genres of music in terms of quality a form of musical snobbery.

Ives studied music at Yale but considered his prestigious professor dogmatic and incapable of pursuing or appreciating new ideas. Convinced that his broad musical concepts exceeded those of his contemporaries, and declaring that he did not intend to let his family starve on his dissonances, Ives devoted his professional life to his own highly successful insurance business. (He is remembered in that industry as the father of estate planning and the author of a training manual, *The Amount to Carry,* still in use in the 1980s.) This left him free to write music only at night, on weekends, and during vacations.

Philosophy of Music An inveterate romantic, Ives had strong literary interests and expressed himself effectively in words as well as in music. He valued the substance, or character, of a piece over its manner, as he referred to music's superficial beauty, which to Ives was "like a drug that allows the ears to lie back in an easy chair." Ives believed that music should be strong and challenging, never "nice": He equated "niceness" with being weak or superficially polite, while he found dissonant sounds "clean and virile" and labeled people who feared them musical cowards.

Instrumental Compositions   Most of Ives's instrumental compositions are program pieces, many reflecting the New England environment he knew and loved. He dedicated his famous *Concord Sonata* to the transcendentalists, whom he admired and whose ideas he shared; each of the four movements of this substantial piano composition describes the ideas and character of one or more members of the famous group (Ralph Waldo Emerson, Nathaniel Hawthorne, Amos Bronson Alcott, Louisa May Alcott, and Henry David Thoreau). Ives prefaced this work with *Four Essays Before a Sonata,* explaining there in words the ideas expressed in the musical composition.

One of Ives's best-known programmatic pieces, "General Putnam's Camp" from *Three Places in New England* (Listening Example 67), depicts a small boy's fantasies as he enjoys a Fourth of July picnic held at a former Revolutionary War campsite.

Listening Example 67

"General Putnam's Camp"
(from *Three Places in New England*)

This brash and exuberant 1914 piece, which Ives apparently wrote over a long period of time, includes snatches of patriotic tunes that Ives altered in the most imaginative and sometimes amusing ways, a technique characteristic of much of his music. Whereas composers often quote familiar melodies in their own original compositions, Ives had a peculiar manner of distorting tunes and also combining them in layers of sound intriguing and sometimes puzzling to the listener's ear. Here he achieves a splendid confusion of timbres and tunes, with a raucous dissonance that perfectly suits the celebratory mood and childlike fantasies of the young boy.

CD 3
Track 10
5:38

Composer   Charles Ives (1874–1954).

Genre   Program music.

Timbre   Symphony orchestra.

Texture   Polyphonic. The texture is so dense that repeated hearings generally reveal tunes and fragments previously unnoticed or unrecognized. This is *linear polyphony,* in which each melodic line should be heard independently, and the resulting combination of tones, which may be quite dissonant, is not intended to be heard as chordal harmony.

Continued

"General Putnam's Camp"
(from *Three Places in New England*)

Form   The piece, one movement of a three-movement suite, is programmatic but follows a loose **ABA'** structure.

Meter   Quadruple.

0:00   The movement opens with a raucous blast (a sound dear to Ives's ears).

0:10   **A:** The main theme is a wonderfully virile and highly unorthodox march.

0:20   We begin to hear what sounds like *two* bands competing for attention. Snatches of John Philip Sousa's marches and patriotic American tunes emerge from the subsequent confusion.

1:06   "Yankee Doodle" is parodied in the trumpet, flute, and violins.

1:11   Softer, gentler violin music may represent the child's growing weariness and descent into fantasy.

1:55   The boy wanders off and falls asleep.

2:14   **B:** Dreaming of the hardship and suffering of the soldiers from long ago, the boy imagines that he hears the Continental Army General Israel Putnam (1718–1790) coming over the hill to save the troops. We hear an amazing juxtaposition of two bands (one for strings and woodwinds, the other for piano, drums, and trumpet) that approach and pass each other—as they might in a parade—playing different tunes, in different keys and in different meters. (Here the conductor must mark four beats to the measure at one tempo with one hand and three beats to the measure at a different tempo with the other.)

3:28   As the boy imagines the soldiers marching out of camp, the band plays a bit of "The British Grenadiers," a popular Revolutionary War tune. Other familiar tunes emerge among the confusion.

4:01   The gentle violin melody, perhaps representing the child's state between sleep and waking, returns.

4:20   **A':** The boy awakens, hears sounds of celebration, and rejoins his friends at the picnic. Snatches of "The British Grenadiers" (4:38) and the main march theme (4:58) catch our ears as the piece approaches its end, as satisfyingly raucous as the sound with which it began.

Songs Ives also wrote about 150 songs, covering many subjects, with settings that range from simple to complex. He frequently based his songs, like his instrumental pieces, on familiar tunes, quoting fragments, phrases, or complete melodies from American hymns, rags, marches, patriotic songs, Stephen Foster's melodies, and the music of Bach and other composers, altering and juxtaposing them into complex layers of sound.

More simply, "At the River" (Listening Example 68) turns a well-known tune into a new composition with its own Ivesian sound.

"At the River"

Ives borrowed the music and lyrics for this 1916 song from a well-known hymn titled "Beautiful River." (He had previously used the lovely melody for the final few bars of the third movement of his Sonata for Violin and Piano no. 4.) The melody closely follows the hymn tune, but the piano accompaniment is highly original, and the last line—a repetition of the initial question— adds a new dimension of ambiguous spiritual questing to the familiar song. The odd turns of phrase, together with the imaginative harmonics and unusual ending, make the music itself seem to pose the question.

CD 3
Track 11
1:19

Composer   Charles Ives (1874–1954).

Tune and Text   Robert Lowry (1826–1899).

Genre   Song.

Timbre   Bass voice, piano accompaniment.

Texture   Basically homophonic.

Form   Verse-chorus.

Meter   Quadruple. The rhythm is quite free and flexible, contributing to the "questioning" quality of the piece.

0:00   The piano introduction sets a tentative, questioning mood.

0:13   Verse: The piano accompanies the familiar hymn tune with richly dissonant chords, adding competing melodic interest toward the end of the verse. The contemplative repetition of the phrase "Gather at the river" is original with Ives.

Shall we gather at the river
Where bright angel feet have trod, ...

—Continued

Listening Example 68—concluded

"At the River"

0:41   Chorus: Again, the words and tune are borrowed, but the
       harmonies and unusual melodic inflections at the ends of some
       lines are Ives's.

       Yes, we'll gather at the river,
       The beautiful, the beautiful river, . . .

1:00   There is a brief piano interlude.

1:08   The tentative, questioning, ending adds poignancy to the simple song.

       Shall we gather?
       Shall we gather at the river?

Other Characteristics of Ives's Music Consistently delighted by the irregular and unconventional, Ives experimented with unusual tunings of musical instruments, sometimes deliberately achieving the intriguing effect of instruments being played slightly out of tune. Although generally respecting the concept of tonality, he considered allegiance to one key at a time confining and occasionally indulged in **bitonality** (two keys at once) and **polytonality** (multiple simultaneous keys). His use of all twelve tones of the chromatic scale in some pieces foreshadowed by some years the *atonal* music of other composers.

Ives also conceived extremely complex rhythmic relationships, frequently combining two or more rhythmic patterns into simultaneous **polyrhythms.** Recognizing the continuum of pitches lying between the half steps of a keyboard instrument, he availed himself of quarter tones and **microtones** in some of his music.

The qualities of sound were a further source of endless fascination for Ives, who made space and the manner in which sound traveled through it a significant element in some of his compositions. He also valued a degree of spontaneity in performance, anticipating what later became known as *chance music.* Both timbre and chance play more than the usual role in *The Unanswered Question* (Online Listening Example), a rather mystic, programmatic piece in which a solo trumpet poses "The Perennial Question of Existence." A group of woodwinds, positioned at a distance from the trumpet, attempts to find "The Invisible Answer," while a string ensemble, located offstage, plays slow, quiet, mysterious music, oblivious of the squabble taking place onstage. Six times the trumpet poses "The Question" and rejects the woodwinds' increasingly agitated replies. Finally, "The Question" is heard once more, to remain unanswered.

In his prefatory instructions for performing this piece, Ives indicated that "The Question" may be posed by any instrument that can play the trumpet's

www.mhhe.com/ferrisaml6e

pitches, and the woodwinds may either be all flutes or a combination of instruments from the woodwind family. He also suggested that "The Answers" need not begin at the points where he notated them in the score but could as well come a bit early or late. Thus, space (instruments widely separated from one another) and chance play a small but significant role in this fascinating piece, which has earned a distinguished place in the American repertoire. The moving sounds of *The Unanswered Question* have been heard in many media and contexts: The Moody Blues ended their long single "Knights in White Satin" ("But we decide which is right. / And which is an illusion") with a brief quotation of "The Question"; the piece was played with haunting significance at President John Kennedy's memorial service; and it is heard to poignant effect on the music track of *The Thin Red Line* (1999), a war film that hovers between layers of consciousness and leaves many disturbing questions unsolved.

Ives's Place in History Ill health prevented Ives from continuing his musical explorations after the 1920s, but it was twenty years after that before his music came to public attention and to high if belated recognition. His Third Symphony, written about 1904 but first performed in 1947, won a Pulitzer Prize; and other pieces by Ives have since received similarly prestigious awards. Although many of his innovations have become part of today's normal music experience, the spark of his invention, the verve, the very nerve of his style remain fresh and invigorating today.

Henry Cowell (1897–1965)

By the time of the birth of **Henry Cowell** (Figure 20.1), the American frontier had been pushed all the way to San Francisco, where Cowell was born, into an eclectic environment whose varied influences are reflected in

FIGURE 20.1
Henry Cowell (1897–1965).

his highly original compositions. Cowell based some programmatic pieces upon Irish folklore absorbed from his own Irish American family; and childhood friends introduced him to Chinese music, beginning a lifelong interest in the music of East Asia. Further musical experience was afforded by an organist friend who allowed the budding young composer to attend his practice sessions, where Cowell absorbed the modal sounds of Roman Catholic church music. Cowell also was attracted to early American hymn and fuging tunes, using some of them as inspiration for an attractive set of instrumental pieces.

Early Compositions

Having decided by the time he was eight years old to become a composer, Cowell taught himself to play the piano his own way, creating sounds he found interesting and eventually using those sounds for imaginative programmatic purposes in his highly original compositions. For example, while still in his teens Cowell wrote a piano piece, "The Tides of Mananaun" (Online Listening Example), in which the performer uses the flat of the hand or forearm to play large *clusters* of keys in the lower range of the piano, evoking the sounds of the rolling, roaring ocean tides. The extremely dissonant result effectively suggests the deep, unstable, ever-changing sounds he wished to achieve.

www.mhhe.com/ferrisaml6e

Cowell, who believed simply that dissonant combinations evoke strong emotions whereas consonance suggests simplicity, was astonished to learn later that some people tend to hear dissonance and consonance as "bad" or "good" sounds. He and others came to recognize dissonant **tone clusters** as a new kind of chord, built upon seconds rather than the thirds of conventional tonal harmony. Although they later became friends, Cowell and Ives did not know each other's music at the time they both began using clusters, and it was only later that both men discovered they had "invented" the same idea at about the same time.

Piano Experiments

Although Cowell wrote many kinds of music, the piano particularly interested him, probably because it was the most readily accessible musical instrument. Desiring to extend the range of sounds the piano could produce, for programmatic reasons or to achieve non-Western effects, he discovered he could do this by playing directly on the strings of the piano as on any other string instrument.

Cowell wrote several pieces in which the piano strings are to be stroked, strummed, plucked, or struck, each technique producing an entirely different effect. He achieved even further variety of sounds by having the pianist either depress some of the keys while manipulating the strings, or mute (stop) the strings with one hand while playing on the keyboard with the other. The techniques he applied to manipulating the piano strings in "The Banshee" (Listening Example 69) and other pieces are very similar to those indicated in the tablature notation used by Chinese and Japanese

Listening Example 69

"The Banshee" (excerpt)

According to Irish and Scottish folklore, a banshee is a fairy-woman who foretells death by materializing nearby one who is doomed to die and wailing her long, howling cry. To achieve this eerie effect, "The Banshee" (1925) requires two performers, one seated at the piano depressing the damper pedal, the other standing in the crook of the piano and manipulating the strings. The score indicates very little in terms of pitch—just a few notes, with wavy lines between them indicating direction (up or down), and various signs, noted in prefatory notes explaining how they should be read. The various techniques include sweeping the strings from the lowest note to a specified note with the flesh of the finger; sweeping the strings up and back; sweeping the length of one string with the flesh of a finger; plucking the strings; sweeping the strings with the back of a fingernail; and sweeping the strings with the flat of the hand.

CD 3
Track 12
1:41

Composer   Henry Cowell (1897–1965).

Genre   Experimental piano music.

Timbre   Piano, played mostly on the strings, the timbre altered by Cowell's experimental techniques.

Texture   Primarily monophonic.

Form   Through composed.

Meter   Free.

0:00   Hands slowly glide lengthwise on piano strings.
0:33   The strings are plucked.
0:46   Hands slide quickly, lengthwise, along the strings.
1:22   Hands slide more quickly, violently.
1:31   Fingernails slide slowly along the strings.
1:37   The strings are gently plucked.

players of various string instruments and flutes, indicating what their fingers should do in order to produce the required notes, rather than the notes themselves (Figure 20.2). These and other piano experiments proved particularly fruitful for other composers, suggesting the possibility of also

3. The Banshee

Henry Cowell
(1925)

FIGURE 20.2

For "The Banshee," Cowell modified traditional notation by the addition of circled letters, each identifying a specific technique for manipulating the piano strings.

The Banshee
Explanation of Symbols

FIGURE 20.2
(Concluded)

"The Banshee" is played on the open strings of the piano, the player standing at the crook. Another person must sit at the keyboard and hold down the damper pedal throughout the composition. The whole work should be played an octave lower than written.

R. H. stands for "right hand." L. H. stands for "left hand." Different ways of playing the strings are indicated by a letter over each tone, as follows:

(A) indicates a sweep with the flesh of the finger from the lowest string up to the note given.

(B) sweep lengthwise along the string of the note given with flesh of finger.

(C) sweep up and back from lowest A to highest B-flat given in this composition.

(D) pluck string with flesh of finger, where written, instead of octave lower.

(E) sweep along three notes together, in the same manner as (B).

(F) sweep in the manner of (B) but with the back of fingernail instead of flesh.

(G) when the finger is halfway along the string in the manner of (F), start a sweep along the same string with the flesh of the other finger, thus partly damping the sound.

(H) sweep back and forth in the manner of (C), but start at the same time from both above and below, crossing the sweep in the middle.

(I) sweep along five notes, in the manner of (B).

(J) same as (I) but with back of fingernails instead of flesh of finger.

(K) sweep along in manner of (J) with nails of both hands together, taking in all notes between the two outer limits given.

(L) sweep in manner of (C) with flat of hand instead of single finger.

producing effective new sounds by playing other traditional instruments in nontraditional ways.

Sources of Inspiration Cowell was among the first Americans to be fascinated with the music of central and eastern Asia and to be gifted in reflecting the sounds of Persia, Japan, and even Iceland in music that bore the distinction of his own style. The music of the East encouraged Cowell to explore elements he felt had been neglected by Western composers; that is, whereas they had concentrated primarily on melody and harmony, Cowell and soon many other American and European composers found that timbre and rhythm offered them many new and stimulating ideas.

Cowell divided rhythms by five, seven, or other numbers as well as by the conventional two, three, or four; and like Ives, he invented complex polyrhythms, difficult to notate and to perform. Cowell even devised a new rhythmic notation in order to write down his sophisticated concepts. In collaboration with Léon Thérémin (inventor of an early electronic instrument that bears his name; see p. 330), Cowell developed a machine called the *rhythmicon,* which made it possible to reproduce rhythms of a complexity beyond the capacity of human performance. Of course the rhythmicon has since been replaced by computers and electronic instruments, but in its time it allowed composers to greatly extend their rhythmic creativity.

Writings Like Ives, Cowell wrote about his ideas and ideals, beginning with a book called *New Musical Resources* while still a college student. Deploring the way conventional publishers ignored American experimentalists, he founded a quarterly journal, *New Music,* in which he published provocative works (and to which Ives apparently gave anonymous financial support). The term **new music,** in fact, came to mean music of an advanced or experimental nature. Cowell also edited a collection of essays by important contemporary composers, and he and his wife Sidney Cowell collaborated on a book about Charles Ives, with whom they became friends. Cowell was among the first to bring Ives's music to public attention.

Writer, teacher, lecturer, editor, inventor, theorist, and composer, Henry Cowell contributed immeasurably to the cause of experimentalism and opened many doors to the future of American music. He traveled extensively, seeking instruction from others and also sharing his own ideas. He played his compositions to appreciative audiences in Europe and was the first American to give concerts in what was then the Soviet Union (1928), thus arousing interest abroad in the new experimental American music.

Concrete Music

During the 1940s, a number of composers of different nationalities working in Paris experimented with recorded musical and nonmusical sounds, which they manipulated to form a new kind of music called **musique concrète,** or **concrete music.** Having altered the sounds electronically—a process made all the more versatile with the invention of magnetic tape after World War II— they used the products of their manipulations to create musical compositions, rendering the music *concrete* in the sense that it could not be performed or interpreted but existed only on tape.

Five processes are involved in the composition of concrete music:

1. *Selecting* the sounds to be taped. The sounds may include those of traditional instruments, such as piano or voice; sounds of nature, such as raindrops or birdcalls; or sounds of machinery, including a vacuum cleaner or jet plane. Any sound, in fact, may provide the raw material with which the composer works.
2. *Recording* the sounds. In order to alter the sounds and produce a work of art, the composer must have them on tape.
3. *Manipulating* the sounds. Sounds played backward, or faster or slower than normal, may become unrecognizable. Composers use these and other techniques to manipulate sounds as they please.

FIGURE 20.3
John Cage (1912–1992).

4. *Mixing* the sounds. This is the step in which the composer combines the sounds he or she has created, much as the traditional composer orchestrates a piece.
5. "Cutting and pasting" the tape—a process called *montage*—to achieve the form of the completed composition.

John Cage (1912–1992)

A true soul mate of Charles Ives's, **John Cage** (Figure 20.3) explored endlessly creative means of varying timbres and, in fact, the very concept of musical sound. For a time, Cage studied with an influential Viennese composer, Arnold Schoenberg, who lived and taught in the United States after World War II. Schoenberg devised a means of arranging all twelve tones of the scale into a series, or *row,* giving each tone equal significance and thus negating the concept of tonal relationships. Cage sampled both magnetic tape methods and Schoenberg's **twelve-tone** technique but soon rebelled against the technical, mathematical, and intellectual control these imposed on a musical composition.

The son of an inventor, Cage consistently addressed his musical problems with an inventor's ingenuity and creativity. Like Cowell, Cage was born on the West Coast and felt less tied to European traditions than did many German-trained composers in New England and New York. Profoundly interested in Asian philosophies, religions, and musical styles, he soon turned from traditional Western instruments to those producing an intriguing variety of sounds similar to the music of the East. Because he wished to use pitches not in the Western chromatic scale, such unusual "instruments" as cowbells, automobile brake drums, and anvils, combined with Japanese temple bells, Chinese gongs, and other exotic non-Western percussion instruments, attracted him and met his early purposes.

FIGURE 20.4

A Javanese gamelan.

Gamelan Music

Cage discovered that an elegant Indonesian percussion ensemble called a **gamelan** (GAH-meh-lahn) produced many of the sounds and pitches he desired. The gamelan is an orchestra, in the sense that it is a combination of instruments from various families; but unlike the Western string orchestra, the gamelan consists primarily of percussion instruments (Figure 20.4). These include *metallophones,* which are sets of metal keys suspended over a bronze or wooden frame and struck with a mallet; tuned gongs of various sizes, usually arranged in a semicircle; and drums. The gamelan ensemble also includes a few wind and string instruments that play sustained pitches and add color to the sound. Listening Example 70 gives a brief indication of the delicate and varied sounds of gamelan music.

Listening Example 70

Gamelan Gong Kebjar: "Hudjan Mas" ("Golden Rain")   (excerpt)

There are at least ten different kinds of gamelan in Bali today, of which the more traditional, glitteringly brilliant Gamelan Gong Kebjar from the early twentieth century is one of the two most popular (the other being the lighter-weight orchestra Gamelan Angklung). Gamelan Gong Kebjar was developed to accompany a brilliant Balinese dance but often accompanies other dances today and is sometimes played only for listening. This piece, for example, often serves as an instrumental interlude, or sometimes as a prelude to a larger dance composition.

**CD 3
Track 13
1:03**

Composer   Anonymous.

Genre   Gamelan music.

—Continued

Listening Example 70—concluded

Gamelan Gong Kebjar: "Hudjan Mas" ("Golden Rain") (excerpt)

Timbre A 25-piece orchestra of xylophone-like bronze-keyed instruments, tuned gongs, cymbals, drums, and flutes.

Texture Linear polyphony.

Form A series of simultaneous variations over relentlessly repeated ostinatos, which provide stability and seem to anchor the composition.

Meter Free.

0:00 The metallic sounds of gongs and metallophones dominating the beginning of the piece suggest the meaning of "kebjar"—to flash or flame, as in a burst of light. Our brief excerpt tapers off before the full gamelan accompanies the joyous peals of sound, but if you are intrigued with the sound, you will enjoy exploring the glorious range of gamelan music.

Prepared Piano Although Cage included a gamelan in some of his early compositions, the ensemble—visually as well as aurally stunning—is too expensive to be widely available (although gamelans are in fact becoming increasingly familiar in the West). Therefore, Cage invented a method of altering the grand piano in order to approximate many of a gamelan's sounds. In 1938, challenged by the dance company he was accompanying to extend the range of timbres in their performance music without exceeding the limits of their budget, Cage discovered that the grand piano could be altered or "prepared" so as to change the timbres and pitches it produced. By applying pieces of wood, metal, and rubber to the strings of the piano, he slowed the rate at which the strings vibrated, slightly changing the pitch as well as the quality of the sound. His new, or modified, instrument is called the **prepared piano.**

As most keys on a piano keyboard control three strings each, nuts, bolts, screws, bamboo strips, or other materials may be placed on one of the strings, between any two, or touching all three. A composer indicates for each composition precisely which strings of which keys are to be prepared, what foreign materials are to be used, and at what distance from the soundboard they are to be placed (Figure 20.5). When the hammers strike the prepared strings, timbres and tones similar to those of a gamelan or a Western percussion ensemble are sounded. A wide variety of sounds and pitches may be achieved in this way, all on a readily available instrument and at the control of an individual performer. Further, the pianist may also strike the wooden parts and metal braces of the instrument with the hand or an implement, producing even more varied sound effects.

FIGURE 20.5

The inside of a prepared piano.

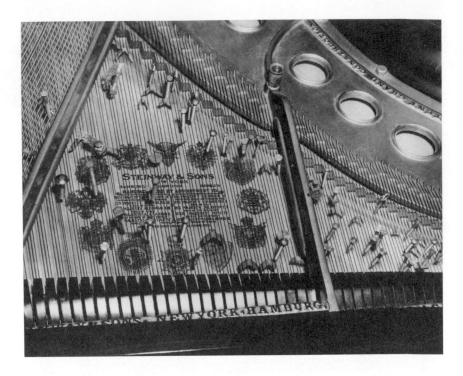

Many musicians were impressed with and influenced by Cage's several independent compositions for prepared piano, including *Sonatas and Interludes* (sixteen sonatas and four interludes), which called for altering forty-five of the piano's tones to produce percussive timbres and sometimes indeterminate pitches. (Sonata V from that fascinating work is Listening Example 71.) By the 1950s, John Cage had become the dominant figure of American experimental music, as we shall see in Chapter 23.

Listening Example 71

Sonata V (from *Sonatas and Interludes for Prepared Piano*)

CD 3
Track 14
1:22

This piece is from a set of twenty pieces that is considered Cage's masterwork for prepared piano, composed between 1946 and 1948. Having recently studied the Hindu perception that there are eight permanent emotions—four light moods (Heroic, Erotic, Wondrous, Comic) and four dark moods (Sorrow, Fear, Anger, Odious)—and that they share a common tendency toward tranquillity, Cage said he intended the *Sonatas and Interludes* to

—Continued

Sonata V (from *Sonatas and Interludes for Prepared Piano*)

represent this concept in music, though we do not know exactly how the pieces achieve that end. Cage would not mind our interpreting any or all of the pieces in this set as we find meaningful. Notice that in this piano piece, timbre and rhythm take precedence over melody and harmony as the elements of primary interest.

Composer   John Cage (1912–1992).

Genre   Music for prepared piano.

Timbre   The piano is prepared so as to produce wooden and metallic sounds somewhat similar to those of a gamelan.

Texture   Polyphonic, in the sense that each line is melodically independent; but this is linear polyphony, and we do not concentrate on resulting "harmonies."

Form   Binary (two-part): **aabb.**

Rhythm   The piece is organized according to rhythmically complex patterns, taxing our mathematical understanding but providing endlessly interesting patterns of sound. We can enjoy the piece for its musical and emotional appeal without recourse to a calculator or rigorous analytical effort.

Meter   Duple.

0:00   **a:** Both hands play ostinato figures, each within a narrow range of pitches. The left hand plays eighth-note patterns, in woodlike timbres; the right hand plays longer notes, in a more metallic timbre. Pause.

0:18   **a:** Repeat. Pause.

0:37   **b:** This section begins very quietly.

0:50   The dynamic level and activity increase.

0:53   The left hand rests as the right hand plays two tones simultaneously, sustaining one while the other fades. Pause.

1:00   **b:** Repeat.

Terms to Review

experimental music
bitonality
polytonality
polyrhythms
microtone

tone cluster
new music
musique concrète
   (concrete music)

twelve-tone
gamelan
prepared piano

Key Figures

Charles Ives   Henry Cowell   John Cage

Critical Thinking

Today we hear much talk about "high (classical) art" and "low (popular) art." How do you think Charles Ives would have addressed this subject? John Cage? Do you believe music and other art should be classified as high or low? What criteria might such a distinction be based on?

Do you consider Charles Ives's "At the River" an original piece? How does it differ from an arrangement of a piece by someone else?

How are Henry Cowell's and John Cage's piano experiments related? In what ways do they differ?

Can you conceive of ways in which musicians might continue to experiment with sound, other than by electronic manipulation?

Early Twentieth-Century Mainstream Concert Music: Evolution

nlike their experimentalist colleagues, many twentieth-century composers took an *evolutionary* approach to furthering the development of music. Some, notably William Schuman (1910–1992), found a source for their compositions in American subjects or tunes. Several American composers found useful material in jazz and other vernacular sources. Since folk and popular dances have long enlivened European concert music, it seems natural for contemporary classical musicians to draw ideas from popular musics, now more varied and sophisticated than ever; but in the 1920s and 1930s, many Americans found this a novel and intriguing concept. Although some musicologists now dispute the view, until recently it was generally acknowledged that Europeans preceded Americans in recognizing jazz as a source of inspiration and material for concert music. Almost from the start of jazz, such European composers as Darius Milhaud, Béla Bartók, and Maurice Ravel integrated the distinctive rhythms, timbres, and performance techniques of the new American vernacular music in their classical compositions.

George Gershwin's *Rhapsody in Blue* (1924; an Online Listening Example), originally conceived for jazz band and piano, though today it is more often performed by piano and orchestra, confused American critics, who were not sure on what grounds to attack it. They found the piece too jazzy for concert music, but unacceptable as jazz because it involved no improvisation. The public, by contrast, greeted *Rhapsody* with enthusiasm, and it remains among the best-known and best-loved symphonic compositions in the world. But Charles Ives's appreciation for good jazz, equal to his appreciation for good symphonic music, struck many as a veritable aberration.

In any case, evolutionary, often nationalistic, works constituted the mainstream of twentieth-century American concert music.

www.mhhe.com/ferrisaml6e

The Parisian Scene

Most of the eager young composers of the 1920s and 1930s traveled to Europe to study, as America did not yet offer comparably advanced music training. They turned not to Germany, however, as had the Second New England School composers, but to France, which became the world center of artistic creativity

FIGURE 21.1
Nadia Boulanger
(1887–1979).

FIGURE 21.1
Nadia Boulanger
(1887–1979).

after World War I. Not only musicians but also poets, writers, painters, dancers, and choreographers from all over the world met in Paris, where they shared ideas—disparate but fresh and invigorating—and stimulated one another to reach new heights of creativity.

The young American composers found their study in France a liberating experience indeed, for unlike the German masters who insisted on teaching the "correct" way to compose, the French encouraged them to develop their individuality and explore new ideas. A young French organist, composer, and highly gifted teacher, **Nadia Boulanger** (1887–1979; Figure 21.1), offered superb instruction to this generation and several successive generations of composers, brilliantly teaching skills and technique without inflicting style upon her students. Recognizing each young composer's distinctive talents, she defined the ways each might reach his or her best potential.

The first American to study with Boulanger was a young man destined to become known as the dean of American composers: Aaron Copland.

Aaron Copland (1900–1990)

Aaron Copland (Figure 21.2) was born in Brooklyn, New York, to a family not particularly interested in music. He decided while still in his teens to become a composer of serious music. To this end, Copland spent three years during his early twenties studying in Paris with Nadia Boulanger.

To his astonishment, Boulanger suggested that Copland borrow jazz techniques as one means of giving his music a distinctively American sound. In any case, several of Copland's early pieces, including a suite for small orchestra titled *Music for the Theater* (1925—the year after Gershwin's *Rhapsody in Blue*) and a concerto for piano and orchestra completed the next year, certainly reflect the rhythms, melodies, harmonies, and timbres of jazz.

Although appreciative of these fresh and nationalistic effects, Copland soon found jazz emotionally limited, and he sought inspiration in other American sounds, including cowboy songs and early American hymns. An avid proponent of American music from both north and south of the Mexican border,

FIGURE 21.2
Aaron Copland (1900–1990).

Copland also captured the flavors and spirit of Mexican folk and popular music. First performed in 1937 in Mexico City, his delightful *El Salón México,* a musical potpourri of his own versions and orchestrations of Mexican folk tunes, remains among the favorite Copland works today.

Depression and War Years
Determined to develop an American audience interested in hearing music by American composers, Copland and another prominent American composer, Roger Sessions (1896–1985), organized and supported a series of programs from 1928 to 1931 at which American concert music was performed, heard, and reviewed; thus important new American compositions received public and critical attention at a time before musicians could rely upon recorded music to reach a wide audience. The Copland-Sessions concerts had inestimable value in encouraging the development of American music.

The music Copland wrote just before and after the stock market crashed in 1929 is rather difficult, austere, and uncompromising, although beautifully written and stunning in effect when performed well. Many believe, in fact, that *Piano Variations* (1929) is his finest composition. But the Great Depression profoundly affected the development of an American repertoire, as it affected every phase of American life: People simply were not able to address new subjects and cultivate new tastes at a time when their energies were absorbed by private and public tragedies. Copland, deeply sympathetic to the conservative attitude of the shocked and saddened American people, urgently wished to communicate with them through his music, on which he deliberately imposed a new simplicity. Thus most of his works from the Depression period through the years of World War II are readily accessible and reflect Copland's great interest in all of America.

Intending his music to have a practical as well as an aesthetic purpose, Copland diligently provided scores for radio, films, schools, amateur musicians, and ballet companies. In 1942, he stirred the wartime audience's patriotic spirit with *Lincoln Portrait,* a musical composition that quotes fragments of Stephen Foster's songs and American folk tunes accompanied by the narration of some of Abraham Lincoln's well-known speeches. (After Copland was charged with having communist affiliations, a performance of his *Lincoln Portrait* was canceled just two weeks before its scheduled inclusion in a concert for the inauguration of President Dwight D. Eisenhower. Ultimately, Copland was vindicated of the charges against him.)

A festive **fanfare,** also written in 1942, has become one of Copland's most famous works. Although a fanfare usually celebrates a royal or state personage or occasion, Copland affirmed his respect and appreciation for the ordinary citizens of America by calling this wartime piece *Fanfare for the Common Man* (Listening Example 72). Further, Copland implied that the title, taken from a 1942 address by Vice President Henry Wallace, had radical left-wing significance, though he always declined to make his politics explicit. (Copland's "Simple Gifts" from *Appalachian Spring Suite* is an Online Listening Example.)

www.mhhe.com/ferrisaml6e

Listening Example 72

Fanfare for the Common Man

CD 3
Track 15
3:14

One of several fanfares written in response to a challenge issued by the conductors of the Cincinnati Symphony Orchestra, Copland's *Fanfare* from 1942 is often performed at occasions of patriotic significance and pride, such as the Olympic Games. The unusual title led to its premiere being performed in March, income tax time in that year. The piece has stirred pop and classical musicians alike—including Keith Emerson, who arranged a rock version; the Rolling Stones, who played their version as a concert opener on their American tour in 1975; and the rock group Queen, who incorporated some of the *Fanfare*'s features in their famous hit "We Will Rock You" (1977). Copland himself reused the *Fanfare* in the finale of his Symphony no. 3. In its original version, the dramatic theme, based on a rising motive introduced by trumpets, is stunningly presented by combinations of brass instruments, forcefully punctuated by percussion.

Composer   Aaron Copland (1900–1990).

Genre   Band music.

Timbres   Brass and percussion—characteristic of a fanfare, which is intended to make a dramatic and emphatic musical statement. The instruments include four horns, three trumpets, three trombones, tuba, timpani (tuned drums), bass drum, and a large gong called a tam-tam.

Key   Whereas most tonal music begins and ends in the same key, *Fanfare* begins in B major and moves through abrupt and startling key changes, keeping the piece harmonically interesting, to end in D major.

—Continued

Listening Example 72—concluded

Fanfare for the Common Man

Texture Homophonic.

Form Through composed.

Meter Quadruple.

Tempo "Very deliberate" (from the score).

0:00 The piece opens with a mighty pounding of the bass drum, dramatically punctuated by the tam-tam.

0:21 Trumpet theme. Bold ascending and descending leaps in the melody line lend strength and drama to the piece. Bass drum and timpani respond.

0:53 The horns join in the breathtaking trumpet theme. The tam-tam adds drama to the drum and timpani response.

1:37 Trombones and tuba begin the next statement, soon joined by trumpets and horns. The trombones drop out after two measures.

2:01 Trumpets, trombones, and tuba, *fortissimo*.

2:08 The horns add brilliance to the timbre, as well as an increase in the dynamic level.

2:18 Trumpets, trombones, and tuba begin the ascent, soon joined by horns.

2:25 (Marked *pesante*, "heavy.") Horns, trumpets, and trombones.

2:43 All the brass. Notice the startling major chord at 2:52.

2:56 The brass broaden their tempo to the thrilling conclusion, made more dramatic by the final flourish in timpani, bass drum, and tam-tam.

Music for Dance The interest Americans developed in stage ballets within the Broadway musical and modern dance during the 1930s and 1940s remained very strong; and Copland's best-known works include his dance compositions, usually called *ballets,* although in fact they represent *modern dance.*

Classical ballet is a formal, stylized dance form in which steps, gestures, and positions, together with mime, describe characters and dramatize a story. Particularly characteristic of classical ballet are the female dancers' positions *en pointe,* or on the points of their toes. (The language of ballet, which evolved in seventeenth-century France at the court of Louis XIV, remains French today.) The movements of the dancers (classical or other) are determined by a choreographer, who may set steps to existing music or to music composed especially for a particular dance. Choreography used to be handed down by tradition only, but methods of notation have been developed—some of them quite recently—that make it possible to preserve a choreographer's ideas accurately. Videotape provides another effective tool for this purpose.

Copland's "ballets," however, are examples of **modern dance** (Figure 21.3), a twentieth-century American contribution with steps and gestures more varied and less stylized than those of classical ballet. The costumes of modern dance also are simpler, and the dancers perform barefoot rather than in the rigid, tightly laced shoes that allow ballerinas to dance *en pointe*.

Copland's busy year, 1942, also produced (besides *Lincoln Portrait* and *Fanfare*) his famous ballet *Rodeo,* commissioned by the choreographer Agnes de Mille (who also choreographed *Oklahoma!*). The rollicking "Hoedown" from *Rodeo* (Listening Example 73) is familiar today through television commercials as well as frequent orchestral performances.

FIGURE 21.3

American modern dance.

Listening Example 73

"Hoedown" (from *Rodeo*)

The 1942 ballet relates the story of a cowgirl who dresses and acts like a man but wins the love of the head wrangler by appearing at a Saturday night dance wearing a dress, with a bow in her hair. Feminist critics have complained that the capitulation of the tomboy is politically incorrect; others suggest the cowgirl represents a closeted homosexual male, giving the story quite a different flavor. (Copland, though openly homosexual, never advertised the fact.) In any case, "Hoedown," reminiscent of old-fashioned barn dance or square dance music, retains its happy appeal.

CD 3
Track 16
3:29

Composer   Aaron Copland (1900–1990).

Genre   Modern dance music.

—Continued

Listening Example 73—concluded

"Hoedown" (from *Rodeo*)

Timbre Symphony orchestra.

Melody Based on two old-time fiddle-tunes—"Bonyparte" and "McLeod's Reel."

Texture Homophonic.

Form Three-part: **ABA.**

Meter Duple.

Tempo Fast.

0:00 Under the fanfare-like introductory music, we hear the fiddle "tuning up."

0:18 A simple rocking figure, repeated several times, introduces section A.

0:40 **Section A:** The music, a jiglike treatment of "Bonyparte," reflects the excitement of the cowgirl, who has put aside her cowpoke duds and reappeared as the prettiest girl in the room. Frequent repetition of the jolly phrase makes the music immediately familiar, and the buoyant rhythm almost compels a physical response. (Notice the wood blocks' contribution from the percussion section [0:56–1:04, 1:21–1:35]).

1:39 **Section B:** Initially lighter, less boisterous, this section treats the other old fiddle tune, "McLeod's Reel." Preserving the festive mood, this section becomes increasingly energetic as strings and brass call and respond to each other.

2:25 A brief interlude suggests that the music (and the dancers?) may be running down, but—

2:50 **Section A** returns, fully revived. The boisterous piece ends with three triumphant unison exclamations.

Later Works In the 1950s, Copland wrote two sets of *Old American Songs* and an opera with an American setting called *The Tender Land* (mentioned in Chapter 19). He also surprised many people by writing several works based on progressive principles, including twelve-tone technique. In fact, throughout his career, Copland demonstrated an unusual variety of tastes and talents, never remaining committed to a consistent trend or direction. Among his large body of works are choral pieces, film scores (including *Our Town*, 1940; *The Red Pony*,

1948; and *The Heiress,* 1949, for which he won an Academy Award), chamber music, large orchestral works, an opera, and other ballets or dance pieces. He also wrote several very readable books about music.

Samuel Barber (1910–1981)

Beginning in the 1920s, many American composers followed Copland to Paris to study with Nadia Boulanger. Most, like Copland, were basically **traditionalists,** who sought progress of an evolutionary kind. Many were at the same time **neoromantics** ("new romantics"), who organized their compositions according to programmatic rather than strictly intellectual concepts, emphasizing lyrical melodies and richly dissonant harmonies and imbuing their music with warm emotional expression.

www.mhhe.com/ferrisaml6e

Prominent among the latter was **Samuel Barber** (Figure 21.4), whose best-known works include several beautiful art songs. One, "Knoxville: Summer of 1915" for soprano and orchestra (Online Listening Example), is a setting of a beautiful text written by James Agee in 1938 (later placed by Agee's literary executors, after the author's death, as the Prologue to his Pulitzer Prize–winning novel *A Death in the Family*). So strongly was Barber attracted to song and the singing voice that even his instrumental pieces have lyrical, song-like melodies rendering them among the most accessible and appreciated compositions of this century.

In 1936, noticing that audiences particularly responded to the slow movement (*adagio*) of one of his string quartets, Barber arranged that movement to be played by a larger group of string instruments; and as an independent piece in this more sensuous guise, his *Adagio for Strings* (Listening Example 74) has become fondly familiar to the American public. This quietly solemn piece, acknowledging the reality of sadness but offering solace and rest, was played during the radio announcement of Franklin Delano Roosevelt's death in 1945 and has frequently been performed at solemn state occasions since. It was heard in its entirety at the

FIGURE 21.4

Samuel Barber (1910–1981).

Adagio for Strings

Some critics suggest that the long, asymmetrical, rhythmically relaxed melody of this emotionally expressive yet unpretentious piece, clearly unfettered by preconceived rules and measurements, characterizes the American spirit. Yet Barber was inspired to write the *Adagio*, in 1936, by a passionate poem of Virgil from the *Georgics;* and indeed, the wavelike motion of Barber's melody and the sensuous tension and release of the harmony seem closely linked to the subject of sexual abandon and fulfillment. As you listen to the music, consider the manner in which Barber causes and releases tension. And notice the overwhelming effect of the moment of silence succeeding the climax.

CD 3
Track 17
9:02

Composer   Samuel Barber (1910–1981).

Genre   Music for string ensemble.

Timbre   String orchestra: violins I and II, violas, cellos, double basses. (First and second violins are the same instrument, sometimes playing different lines of music.)

Melody   The lovely main theme winding gently throughout the piece is long and irregular, unbounded by conventional concepts of balance or symmetry.

Harmony   Tense dissonances alternate with soft, sensuous harmonic resolutions to raise and release the level of intensity.

Texture   Homophonic, polyphonic.

Form   Arch form. Gently rounded to end much as it begins, the *Adagio* forms an asymmetrical arch, building through most of the piece to its emotional climax and coming soon thereafter to a quiet close.

Meter   Quadruple (with occasional bars of five or six beats). The irregular measures, extremely slow tempo, and relaxed phrase endings lessen our metrical awareness and allow the music simply to flow.

Tempo   *Molto adagio* (very slow).

0:00   The first violins, accompanied by sustained chords in the other instruments, introduce the beautiful theme. Notice how the harmonies vary from gently dissonant (slightly tense) to consonant (relaxed, released) sounds.

—Continued

Adagio for Strings

1:05   The rising three-note pattern of the melody is repeated sequentially (at changing—in this case higher and higher—levels of pitch), to intense emotional effect.

1:28   The second violins imitate the upward leap in the melody.

1:40   The violas take the theme, as the first violins play a countermelody above them.

2:37   The violas retain the melody, slightly louder and gradually crescendoing, still accompanied by the violin countermelody and minimal support from the other instruments. Perhaps you will hear the slowly ascending line in the cellos.

2:57   The rich, low-pitched cellos echo—actually exaggerate—the violas' upward thrust.

3:08   The theme returns to the first violins, the violas adding their own melodic interest, also based on the theme.

3:50   The theme is in the cellos, the simple, soft, sustained chords in the other instruments allowing us to relish the deep cello tones.

4:40   As the cellos continue the theme, a slow but steady crescendo causes increasing intensity, enhanced by the rising pitches and upward melodic thrusts.

5:00   First violins take the theme, soaring to yet higher places.

5:24   Cellos respond, playing in their upper range.

5:35   Violins play a three-note motive as the violas assume the theme. The violins thrust ever higher, the violas doggedly climbing with them until at 6:06, the violins seem to *peak*. The violas, astonishingly, reach their own incredibly high pitches, and violins and violas sustain first consonant, then richly dissonant, then consonant chords, all at the highest levels of pitch and dynamics.

6:27   A long pause—a cessation of sound—further heightens the intensity.

6:31   The instruments return, softly, perhaps chastened, perhaps resigned, perhaps simply content. The accompaniment, alternately dissonant and consonant, seems to stretch and relax after the profoundly emotional experience.

7:00   The first violins and violas play the theme in unison, at its original tempo, gently accompanied by the other instruments. The levels of pitch, of dynamics, and of tension gradually lower.

8:00   Violins and violas, still in unison, begin the last phrase, which the first violins, playing in a very low range, carry away to the soft, soft, ending.

end of the poignant film *The Elephant Man* (1980) and was the musical theme of *Platoon* (which won the Academy Award for best picture in 1986).

Harlem Renaissance

The **Harlem Renaissance** was a movement of the 1920s in which African American painters, sculptors, poets, playwrights, musicians, novelists, and essayists broke from convention to "promote racial advancement through artistic creativity." Stimulated by poet Langston Hughes, writer Zora Neale Hurston, and many others, black artists in every field traveled to Harlem (in uptown New York City), seeking within the heady environment of this unprecedented concentration of African American talent to effect a true renaissance—a rebirth—of black "high art."

Although treated primarily as a literary movement, the Harlem Renaissance inspired visual artists as well to express modern urban life from the African American point of view. And the movement used and was supported and accompanied by music. Among the musicians it attracted to New York, Eubie Blake created *Shuffle Along* on Broadway, W. C. Handy ("father of the blues") established his music publishing house, Fletcher Henderson and especially Duke Ellington drew huge numbers of white people to Harlem to hear jazz, James P. Johnson and Thomas "Fats" Waller virtually created jazz piano, and Bessie Smith sang the blues. These were prominent among many others who introduced, developed, and promoted the black popular music and jazz of the Harlem Renaissance.

Primarily it was in the realm of concert music, however, that musicians of the Harlem Renaissance sought to develop folk materials from the black cultural heritage into artistic creations commanding the respect of white as well as black artists and intellectuals. Blacks who had begun to gain access to American and European conservatories and universities were eager to synthesize their own musical heritage with their new skills and perspectives, having as their primary goal the "elevation" of spirituals, blues, and jazz to symphonic form. Harry T. Burleigh and Robert Nathaniel Dett, for example, were among the most successful black composers basing classical compositions on familiar spirituals; and the singers Marian Anderson and Paul Robeson brought these eloquent songs to a large and appreciative concert audience. Although the Harlem Renaissance ended (with the onslaught of the Great Depression) before many composers could fully develop their skills, the accomplishments of these and countless others reveal the rich cultural milieu in which black intellectuals made high art in the Harlem Renaissance. Yet the subject remains controversial, many black musicians resenting the idea that mastery of classical techniques somehow advanced black music. Here we explore the sensitive issue from the point of view of those who were involved in a movement that at the time seemed meaningful and important to them.

Preeminent among the composers, William Grant Still became the first black composer to have a symphony played by a major symphony orchestra, the first to conduct a major symphony orchestra, and the first to have an opera produced by a major American company.

William Grant Still (1895–1978)

www.mhhe.com/ferrisaml6e

As a child, **William Grant Still** (Figure 21.5) showed both an interest in and a talent for music, studying violin and listening avidly to his stepfather's opera recordings. But as a young black living in the American South, he found it difficult to be taken seriously as a classical musician.

Nevertheless, Still won a scholarship to the prestigious Oberlin Conservatory of Music in Ohio, and after earning his degree continued his studies with the evolutionary composer George Chadwick (of the Second New England School) and a revolutionary European composer, Edgard Varèse (1883–1965), who considered all sounds, including those called noise, valid for use in a musical composition. For several years, Still played in dance bands and variety shows while working for a popular music publishing company, and before becoming definitively involved with concert music. Then, during a long and successful career, he wrote several operas and ballets, some film scores, and many songs and choral pieces.

Still, whose racial heritage was mixed, had a personal interest in American Indian and Spanish American music but identified primarily with black Americans, and it was their experience he wished to express. Declaring his purpose to "elevate Negro musical idioms to a position of dignity and effectiveness in the field of symphonic and operatic music," Still allied himself with the Harlem Renaissance during the pre-Depression years, producing his fine *Afro-American Symphony* in 1931 (Listening Example 75). (The first movement from this symphony is an Online Listening Example.)

Many American composers of the late twentieth century, including those discussed in Chapter 23, shared the ideals so eloquently expressed in the music of Copland, Barber, Still, and other early mainstream composers. Indeed, their accomplishments inspire much of today's American music.

Listening Example 75

Afro-American Symphony, third movement ("Humor")

True to his intention to "elevate" black music idioms to the level of symphonic music, Still incorporated the sounds of the blues, ragtime, and spirituals in this lively movement, titled "Humor," which he intended to reflect happier moments in the African American experience. Syncopated cross rhythms, rooted

CD 3
Track 18
3:23

—Continued

Afro-American Symphony, third movement ("Humor")

in African American dance, permeate the music, and the use of the tenor banjo—an instrument associated with country blues and New Orleans jazz—has much to do with the programmatic character of the music. Should you recognize what sounds like the tune to Gershwin's song "I Got Rhythm" (easily found on YouTube), it is interesting to know that the tune may have been improvised by Still while he was performing with the show *Shuffle Along* (see p. 301) and adapted later by Gershwin for his famous song.

Composer   William Grant Still (1895–1978).

Genre   Symphony movement.

Timbre   Symphony orchestra, with the unusual addition of a solo banjo.

Texture   Homophonic.

Form   Three-part: **aba.**

Meter   Quadruple.

Tempo   *Animato* (animated, rapid).

0:00   Following a cymbal crash, a brief introduction sets the carefree mood. Horns and bassoons make the first statement, lightly accompanied by the strings. The horns play a measure, answered by clarinet and lower strings, as the orchestra warms to the new movement.

0:14   **a:** The syncopated theme, with the feel of ragtime, enters in the strings, the banjo brightly marking the backbeat.

0:30   Strings soar to raptures of unalloyed pleasure.

0:45   The solo oboe returns to the theme, lightly, delicately, passing it to other instruments in the orchestra, which respond in call-and-response fashion.

1:03   Trombones and horns, soon reinforced by other instruments, take up the motive.

1:08   Strings, then woodwinds come to the fore. The first violins toss a four-note motive ("dum-te-dum-dum"), extracted from the lighthearted theme, sequentially higher and higher. The motive then passes through the ranges of the instruments.

—Continued

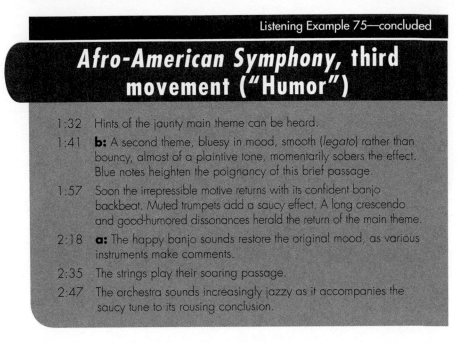

Listening Example 75—concluded

Afro-American Symphony, third movement ("Humor")

1:32   Hints of the jaunty main theme can be heard.

1:41   **b:** A second theme, bluesy in mood, smooth (*legato*) rather than bouncy, almost of a plaintive tone, momentarily sobers the effect. Blue notes heighten the poignancy of this brief passage.

1:57   Soon the irrepressible motive returns with its confident banjo backbeat. Muted trumpets add a saucy effect. A long crescendo and good-humored dissonances herald the return of the main theme.

2:18   **a:** The happy banjo sounds restore the original mood, as various instruments make comments.

2:35   The strings play their soaring passage.

2:47   The orchestra sounds increasingly jazzy as it accompanies the saucy tune to its rousing conclusion.

Terms to Review

fanfare   modern dance   neoromantic
classical ballet   traditionalist   Harlem Renaissance

Key Figures

Nadia Boulanger   Samuel Barber   William Grant Still
Aaron Copland

Critical Thinking

What images does Aaron Copland's "Hoedown" bring to your mind? What musical elements evoke those images?

If you have read the beginning of Virgil's poem that inspired Samuel Barber to write his famous *Adagio,* do you hear the music as primarily sensual, or elegiac? Tragic, or comforting?

What are your views on the Harlem Renaissance? Did its gifted black poets, writers, painters, and musicians choose the best route to secure economic, social, and cultural equality with white artists? What other recourse might they have had? Did efforts to raise spirituals and blues to "high art" enhance or detract from these forms? (To form and support your views, try to listen to recordings by Marian Anderson, Paul Robeson, and others.)

The Avant-Garde, Continued

Experimentalism, which romantically denies traditional boundaries, abandons established rules of composition, and explores new concepts of the very meaning of music, appeals strongly to Americans, a romantic people, creative, inventive, independent, and accustomed to freedom and space. It is not surprising, then, that Americans have often been in the forefront of the experimental movement in music.

Experimentalists both here and abroad have followed diverse paths, some choosing an intellectual, controlled approach to their music, and other avant-garde composers remaining detached from the compositions they produce, leaving important aspects to be decided by the performers, listeners, or simply chance. Some composers of new music include elements of both romantic and classical styles in their work.

Rhythm and Timbre

By the mid-twentieth century, rhythm and timbre had replaced melody and harmony as the elements of primary interest for many American composers. Experimentalists carried forward the work begun earlier in the century by Ives and Cowell, altering traditional instruments or playing them in new ways in order to produce unusual sounds. Today many composers use traditional instruments, including the human voice, to produce sounds—such as whispers, shouts, groans, or teeth clicks—that do not conform to the traditional concept of beauty. Instrumentalists may be directed to produce breathy, squeaky, or raucous sounds, sometimes but not always for programmatic effect. Several composers have found that the resonant timbres of mallet instruments, such as the marimba, xylophone, or glockenspiel, offer an attractive alternative to traditional orchestral or other Western sounds; and the precise rhythmic effects expert players can achieve on mallet instruments further enhance their appeal for many composers today.

Harry Partch (1901–1974) Some composers, of whom **Harry Partch** is best-known, invented entirely new musical instruments. Known as the hobo composer because during the Great Depression he actually did

FIGURE 22.1
Harry Partch's Quadrangularus
Reversum, 1972.

spend time on the rails, Partch designed and built an amazing array of exotically named instruments, including the kithara, crychord, marimba eroica, and spoils of war, among many others (Figure 22.1). He constructed his mazda marimba of lightbulbs, and he made an instrument of tuned beer and wine bottles reminiscent of Benjamin Franklin's glass harmonica.

Considering the division of the octave into twelve equal intervals both limiting and false, Partch divised a forty-three-tone scale, whose microtones more naturally reproduce the sounds of spoken, as well as sung, texts. Many of his inventions produce lovely, delicate tones, seemingly more suited to the world of nature than are traditional Western band and orchestral instruments. (Some of Partch's instruments can be seen and heard on YouTube.)

Tape Music and the Electronic Synthesizer

In the early 1950s some German musicians experimented with **tape music,** storing electronically generated sound materials on tape and then manipulating them, much as the French, a few years earlier, had manipulated prerecorded sounds to develop concrete music. Composers achieved the pitch they desired on the new **electronic synthesizer,** an instrument of seemingly unlimited capabilities, by plugging into electronic **oscillators.** (*Oscillation* is another word for "vibration.") A **fingerboard** allowed players to slide through a range of pitches, unlimited by frets or keys. By plugging into other outlets on the synthesizer, the player altered the shape of the sound waves, determining the timbre of the sounds to be produced. Electronic **filters** selected out high and

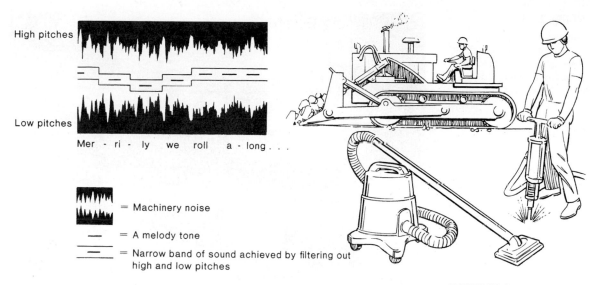

High pitches

Low pitches

Mer - ri - ly   we   roll   a - long . . .

= Machinery noise

= A melody tone

= Narrow band of sound achieved by filtering out
  high and low pitches

FIGURE 22.2

On an electronic synthesizer, high and low pitches can be filtered out of machinery noise to produce a narrow band of sound or a melodic line.

low ranges of a broadly spread sound, such as industrial or machinery noise, producing a narrow band of melody of an interesting but nontraditional timbre (Figure 22.2).

The first synthesizer in the United States, the RCA Mark II (sponsored in 1959 by Princeton and Columbia universities and located at Columbia, in New York City), filled most of a room and was driven by a strip of paper with holes punched in it; but huge and cumbersome as it sounds today, it offered a new world of sound and unprecedented accuracy of rhythm and pitch. Not only did synthesizers and other electronic means enable composers to achieve sounds never heard before, but composers could hear their compositions immediately, instead of waiting for a live performance, which was sometimes difficult to achieve. Further, composers could save the sounds they liked on tape. It was not necessary to rehearse a piece and rely on the abilities of (or pay a salary to) performers, because the composer might produce all the sounds of a piece, independent of human assistance. The new electronic techniques offered a thrilling range of experience to composers interested in creating new sounds and exercising total control over their performance.

Today computers aid composers in the process of notating music, rendering the procedure faster, more accurate, and more efficient than in the past. Computers also allow the use of tempos too fast and rhythmic combinations too complex for human accomplishment, as well as nontonal intervals very difficult for musicians to hear and reproduce with accuracy. In fact, computers often control every facet of electronic music-making today. For example, in the electronic music lab shown in Figure 22.3, an electronic keyboard and two computers generate the sounds indicated by a musical score; the sounds are fed into a computer that functions as the mixer; and another computer records the resulting composition. Synthesizers and further recording equipment are no longer necessary in the modern studio.

FIGURE 22.3

Electronic music workstation including sophisticated equipment with which to compose, perform, and record music.

FIGURE 22.4

Milton Babbitt (b. 1916) in 1965, with RCA Mark II Electronic Music Synthesizer.

Milton Babbitt (b. 1916)

While a student at New York University, **Milton Babbitt** (Figure 22.4) used the twelve-tone technique to achieve the mathematical precision he desired in his musical compositions; soon, he extended the orderly concept to other aspects of composition besides pitch. He arranged patterns of rhythms and durations, for example, into series that are systematically repeated throughout a composition. In some pieces composed according to this extension of the twelve-tone technique, called **total serialism, serialization,** or **serial technique,** the various series are mathematically related to each other; in other pieces, they are independent.

Babbitt also was one of the earliest enthusiasts and primary exponents of electronic music, codirecting the establishment of the RCA Mark II Synthesizer. It was several years later before synthesizers became available to composers in other parts of this country.

Babbitt, who finds rhythm and timbre more interesting to work with than melody and harmony, uses electronic techniques to achieve his exotic sounds and complex rhythms. A brilliant man who composes challenging music and deplores mistakes or misinterpretations by performers, Babbitt writes pieces that exist only on tape and for which there is no score, knowing that these will always be heard as he intended. Together with the resources of the electronic synthesizer, computers, and magnetic tape technique, total serialism allows Babbitt to achieve the highly ordered and logical music he prefers.

"Ensembles for Synthesizer" (Listening Example 76) is an early classic of this kind of electronic music.

Listening Example 76

"Ensembles for Synthesizer" (excerpt)

Babbitt composed this piece in 1967 to demonstrate the Mark II Synthesizer's capabilities to produce orchestrations of varying colors, gestures, and phrasings. This is, of course, concrete music, which cannot be "interpreted" by a performer but must be heard as Babbitt composed it. Because the music is conceived and constructed so differently from traditional compositions, it must also be approached differently by the listener. Here we listen not for melodies and harmonies; rather, concentration on and appreciation of the highly sensuous timbres and the fascinating rhythmic techniques yield intense listening pleasure.

**CD 3
Track 19
2:01**

Composer Milton Babbitt (b. 1916).

Genre Electronic synthesizer music.

Timbres Babbitt programmed the synthesizer to produce various metallic, wooden, and mysterious airy sounds, with occasional references to the sound of an electronic organ.

Texture Polyphonic (contrapuntal).

Form Through composed. The piece is a mosaic of tiny fragments (ensembles), each distinguished by a characteristic timbre, range of pitch, rhythmic pattern, dynamic level, and texture.

Pitches All twelve tones are used, although not according to Schoenberg's row technique. The ranges of pitch level are extreme.

Meter The meter is free, or constantly changing. The rhythmic patterns, varied and complex, are sometimes played at extremely rapid tempos, requiring electronic performance techniques.

John Cage and Chance Music

Some musicians turned away from the taut control provided by twelve-tone and tape techniques, preferring to leave certain aspects of the performance of their music to *chance.* Their counterparts in the visual arts were by the Abstract Expressionist painters, led by Jackson Pollock; and the moving sculptures of Alexander Calder, among many others. Free jazz musicians brought chance to the world of vernacular music, and John Cage the leading experimentalist of the 1950s and 1960s, led the movement toward chance, or indeterminacy, in the concert world.

Cage, whom we met in Chapter 20 as the inventor of the prepared piano and a composer who experimented with twelve-tone and concrete music, soon turned away from those two techniques, disturbed by their lack of spontaneity—which he, indeed, carried to new extremes. For many years his primary interest was **chance** or **aleatory music,** in which the composer leaves significant aspects of each performance to chance. His commitment to Zen Buddhism, which he found less judgmental and dogmatic than Western philosophies and religions, inclined him to resist hierarchical determinations as to what in music is proper and desirable. Like Partch, Cage resisted the ancient Greeks' determination that division of the octave into seven tones constituted the most satisfactory system of scales. Cage proposed that the octave might as well be divided by ten, twenty, or any other number of intervals.

Improvisation is one form of such **indeterminate music** (as chance or aleatory music is also called), requiring performers to make certain decisions concerning melody, rhythm, and harmony; but aleatory music encompasses much more than this. *Aleatory* comes from the Latin word for dice, and throwing dice is among the ways of determining various aspects of an aleatory piece—for example, melodic or metric patterns, or the number of repetitions of a phrase or section. Other imaginative techniques used by composers of chance music include graphic notation that may be interpreted in many different ways; performance decisions based on the Chinese *Book of Chance,* called *I Ching* (pronounced "E Jing"); scores that may be read backward, forward, or upside down; and circular scores that may be read clockwise or counterclockwise.

The degree of possible indeterminacy ranges from minimal, as in Ives's *The Unanswered Question,* to **random** music, in which almost all of the composition changes from one performance to another. Thus Cage scored *Imaginary Landscape No. 4* (1951) for twelve radios, indicating specific positions on the radio dials, dynamic levels, durations, and even the degree of abruptness with which each sound begins and ends; but of course different material will be broadcast at each "performance."

As we reexamine the meaning of music in our time, respected opinions on the subject of what constitutes music and musical sound vary. Some people argue that Cage's *Imaginary Landscape No. 4* is random sound as opposed to music, whereas others believe that the piece is clearly "organized sound" and therefore meets that broad definition of music. Still others insist that the quality of the sounds determines whether a composition is music or simply a listening experience. Certainly Cage was a disciplined artist, who clearly defined the freedoms he introduced into his compositions. "Freedom is one thing," he said, "but liberty is, so to speak, going too far." (Cage's aleatory *Aria* and his complex collage of taped sounds titled *Fontana Mix,* often performed as a pair, are Online Listening Examples.)

www.mhhe.com/ferrisaml6e

Silence We have seen that composers notate rests, or periods of silence, as carefully as they notate pitches (see Table 1, p. 2). But Cage discovered that although specific sounds may cease, there are always other sounds that continue; thus true silence is never part of the human experience. Traditionalists call the continuing sounds "noise" as opposed to "music," but Cage considered all sounds worthy of attention and encouraged us to be aware and appreciative of them. In fact, he flatly stated that "silence" is an absurd concept and simply does not exist.

To demonstrate the nonexistence of silence, Cage placed himself in a soundproof chamber, as silent as technicians could make it—in which his own bloodstream and nervous system produced clearly audible sounds. Next he wrote a book titled *Silence* (1961) and composed the notorious "4'33"" ("Four Minutes Thirty-Three Seconds") for "any instrument or combination of instruments," the score indicating three movements, each marked *tacet*—the term musicians use to mean "be silent." According to Cage, although the instruments make no sound at all, the audience has "a profound listening experience" throughout the duration of this noncomposition.

John Cage became the most controversial and influential American composer of the twentieth century. When he died, the American Society of Composers, Authors, and Publishers (ASCAP) expressed profound respect and regret with the full-page black-bordered announcement shown in Figure 22.5.

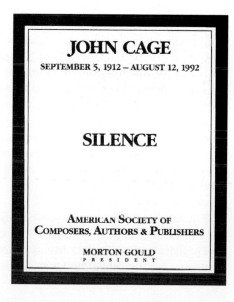

FIGURE 22.5

This full page appearing in the Sunday issue of the *New York Times* the week of Cage's death gave poignant tribute to this influential composer.

Other Composers of Chance Music

During the 1950s, three composers based in New York City became closely associated with John Cage while developing related ideas of their own. Like him, they intended to achieve objectivity in their music by refusing to specify details in the traditional way: in other words, they allowed their music to "come into its own."

Morton Feldman (1926–1987) sometimes used graphic notation to indicate his general intentions, leaving specific pitches and their durations to be determined by the performers. In one piece, he indicated the notes but left rhythms unspecified, allowing them to evolve within a general tempo established by the conductor at the beginning of each performance. Feldman is among those experimentalists whose imaginative scores sometimes also constitute works of visual art. Feldman's *Projection 2,* for example, is a series of rectangles indicating periods of time, small triangles placed within the rectangles suggesting when to play and how long tones should endure, and the vertical placement of the triangles giving a general idea of approximate levels of pitch.

Earle Brown (1926–2002), another associate of Cage, reflected in his music the mobility of Alexander Calder's sculptures and the spontaneity of Jackson Pollock's paintings, claiming to have composed some pieces so rapidly and spontaneously that they represented "performances" rather than "compositions." Brown, too, developed intriguing and attractive graphic notations for his scores, such as *December 1952* (Figure 22.6), written on one page as a series of vertical and horizontal lines that indicate only in a general way the direction, dynamic level, duration, and pitch of the sounds. A decade later Brown further demonstrated the affinity between music and visual art by composing *Calder Piece 1963–1966,* for which Alexander Calder made a large mobile sculpture expressly for use as an instrument in the work.

The third New Yorker who was an associate of John Cage, Christian Wolff (b. 1934), like Feldman wished to "set sounds free," and like Cage was interested in silence as well as sound. His tones sometimes seem suspended in air, surrounded by space that lets them "breathe." Wolff has written some chamber pieces for which neither the instrumentation nor the duration of the tones (which *are* notated) is specified. The score for *1, 2, or 3 People* is a good example of the artistic nature of Wolff's original notation.

The ever-adventurous Henry Cowell wrote at least one piece of genuine chance music, *26 Simultaneous Mosaics* (1963), for clarinet, violin, violoncello, piano, and percussion. These brief pieces, written for each of the instruments individually, may be played in any order chosen by the players, who also, according to Cowell's instructions, may start and stop playing as they please.

Indeterminacy continues to be significant in today's concert music among so-called mainstream as well as new music composers. Many who desire a degree of indeterminacy in their largely structured music have devised ingenious techniques for indicating the limits within which performers are to interpret their compositions.

FIGURE 22.6

Excerpt from the score for *December 1952* from *FOLIO* by Earle Brown.

Notation

Chance musicians such as Morton Feldman, Earle Brown, and John Cage are not the only composers who have created original means of notating their music. **Theater scores,** for example, require performing musicians to act as well as sing and play musical instruments, and such scores often require original methods of notation as well. **Laurie Anderson** (b. 1947), one of today's best-known performance artists, uses a variety of media, including film, electronic and acoustic music, slides, costumes, and other effects in her live performances, which defy traditional means of notation. Anderson's albums, too, demonstrate her technical wizardry and avant-garde vision.

Other characteristics of new music necessitating new kinds of notation include unusual techniques of playing on traditional instruments, passages to be sounded so rapidly that composers notate only their start and finish, clusters showing the number and range of tones but not the actual pitches, extremely complex divisions of beats, and extremely long durations better expressed in seconds of time than in quarter, half, and whole notes.

Graphs serve some composers as a means of notating the bounds within which pitches, rhythms, durations, and metric patterns are to be determined. Several composers have devised different means of notation to accommodate

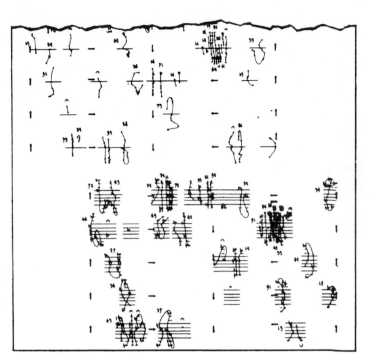

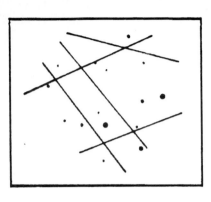

FIGURE 22.7

Nontraditional notation by
John Cage.

the specific demands of each new piece. And visual interest and appeal continue to attract many of them (Figure 22.7).

Since about 1950, in fact, music notated as art has become quite usual. And as music looks more like visual art, art is looking more like performance—many museum pieces, for example, requiring movement or interaction between the artist or viewers and the visual work.

Pauline Oliveros (b. 1932)

Pauline Oliveros began composing music in a traditional manner but soon became fascinated with the qualities of all sounds, including those produced by nature (raindrops, wind) and by machinery. She avoids the meter and pulse characteristic of Western music in favor of rhythms that shift, expand, and contract more or less systematically, and her heightened sensitivity to timbre has led her to explore and experiment extensively with vocal and instrumental colors, often to stunning effect.

Oliveros is among the composers who have chosen to give up the idea of individual control over their music. She prefers to guide a group—often of music amateurs—through a shared creative experience. For example, she once asked the members of a large audience each to sing a pitch of their choice, sustaining it for the length of one breath. Coming to the end of that breath, they were to listen to someone as far away as possible and respond to his or her pitch. For the next fifteen minutes, extraordinary waves of harmony washed over the room, thrilling "composer" and performers alike.

Like John Cage, Pauline Oliveros clearly structures even her pieces that rely heavily on free improvisation. Her conceptual score for *Portrait of the Quintet of the Americas,* for example, consists of circles and spokes all mapped out with the look of computer graphics, and each of the five performers has a set of assigned pitches based on his or her astrological chart. No two performances will be the same, but the performers' options are limited by restrictions imposed by the composer. Using tape and other electronic techniques, Oliveros creates distinctive pieces of sound imagery, haunting in their seductive sonic beauty.

In *Sound Patterns* (Listening Example 77) Oliveros dispensed with words in favor of a variety of meaningless syllables and mouth sounds, and indicated pitch only approximately, creating sound clusters rather than pure tones.

Sound Patterns

Finding that conventional musical scores bore less and less relevance to the sounds she wanted to make, Oliveros devised her own systems for notating the sounds she required. For example, the score to *Sound Patterns*, a choral work from 1961 with no text, indicates very precise and quite difficult rhythms to be realized by singers improvising pitches within specified ranges. The singers also must produce various sounds, including tongue clicks, whispers, shouts, lip-pops, and finger snaps. The abstract sounds the voices produce are as unrelated to traditional concepts of melody and harmony as are abstract paintings to the shapes and colors of representational art. The effect, although entirely the result of human performance, suggests electronic enhancement and is somehow, unaccountably, whimsically, humorous.

CD 3
Track 20
4:03

Composer   Pauline Oliveros (b. 1932).

Genre   Experimental choral music.

Timbre   Mixed chorus (soprano, alto, tenor, bass), a cappella.

Meter   Changing. Meters are indicated in the score in traditional fashion, but the performance technique renders them obscure.

The sopranos begin the piece with "shi—ee—ih—sh." The other voices enter in turn with similar hushed sounds. Conceived and notated in nontraditional ways, the piece is difficult to analyze according to formula; but listen for tongue clicks, popped lips, fluttered lips, operatic articulations, snapped fingers, nasal sounds—and more. Understand that the performers, while following a score, yet have much more effect upon the sound—the "sound patterns"—than performers of a traditional piece of music. And relish the intense listening experience, the sheer enjoyment of sound, which is what Oliveros intends.

Technology, of course, offers experimentalists possibilities dreamed of but unrealized by Ives, Cowell, and their cohort. On the simplest level, microphones placed inside a musical instrument amplify and alter or distort its sounds and may produce echo effects. Quarter-note flutes can play twice as many notes as a conventional model, and a device exists to give pianos "fluid tuning," releasing them from confinement to the eighty-eight tones created by their keys. A Hypercello and a Hyperviolin use electronic enhancement to expand what musicians can do with those instruments.

Our final chapter concerns other, more conservative, composers who also, in more traditional ways, have profoundly enriched America's musical landscape.

Terms to Review

tape music
electronic synthesizer
oscillators
fingerboard

filters
total serialism, serialism, or
    serial technique

aleatory music, chance music,
    indeterminate music, or
    random music
theater score

Key Figures

Harry Partch   Milton Babbitt   John Cage   Pauline Oliveros

Critical Thinking

John Cage said that fear in life is the fear of change. Do you agree? Can change be avoided? Should art (of any kind) be a fixed idea?

What do you think John Cage meant when he said that freedom is one thing, but liberty is going too far? The Latin root of *liberty* suggests release from bondage (separation), and *freedom* shares northern European origins with *friend* (connection). Do you think these concepts are relevant to Cage's remark?

In classical music, there has been a change in emphasis from melody and harmony to rhythm and timbre. Can you relate this to changing tastes in pop music? Do you consider the modern urban experience relevant, or irrelevant, to changes in artistic preferences?

Given a choice between attending a concert of traditional orchestral music and a concert involving new (experimental) instruments, which would you choose? Why?

The Recent Mainstream

By the 1950s, Americans enjoyed unprecedented access to a broad range of concert music. They could purchase long-playing records (LPs), listen to many hours of concert music a week on radio stations, and watch live performances on television. Centers for performing arts were being built at many places around the country, and important conservatories in several American cities offered music training of the highest quality. All this activity stimulated large numbers of American composers to write music intended for concert performance.

Many of these composers, choosing to write music rooted in the past, entered the modern American mainstream rather than joining the avant-garde. They may be seen as traditionalists, desiring to continue the evolution of music in a logical and orderly, rather than a revolutionary, manner. Yet their music, like that of their revolutionary colleagues, also reveals modern trends.

The Elements of Music

While the elements of music remain the fundamental materials with which composers work, today even mainstream composers often approach the elements in new ways. Harmony in recent music, for example, is often entirely dissonant, never resolving to or even alternating with traditionally consonant sounds. And while some composers retain a firm preference for lyricism, others have been accused of writing music with no melody at all. A contemporary piece rarely has "no melody"; but modern melodies often have a more angular contour than the songlike melodies of the nineteenth century, making them difficult to recognize. A few composers continue to base their melodies on twelve-tone and serial techniques, no longer considered avant-garde; and some choose melody tones far distant from each other, perhaps including microtones unfamiliar to Western ears. The fact that such techniques make it challenging to follow a melodic line, however, is not to say that no such line is present.

Still, modern traditionalists, like experimentalists, often focus on rhythm and timbre, rather than on melody and harmony, as the elements of primary interest and potential development.

399

New Concepts of Form

Some contemporary composers adapt the symphony, concerto, and other traditional forms to meet their personal creative needs. Others, however, consider such forms too tied to earlier concepts of symmetry and tonal relationships to stimulate their own creativity. Modern concepts of form are more likely to be based on principles of repetition with variation, as exemplified by *minimalist* music (see pp. 402–404), than on the complex development of motivic ideas characteristic of music in the classic style. Some composers actually invent a new form for each piece they write, allowing characteristics of the particular piece to determine its organizing principles.

The many significant twentieth-century American mainstream composers include the New Yorker William Schuman.

William Schuman (1910–1992)

William Schuman, a rather conservative composer with a strong interest in musical nationalism, reigned as one of the giants of twentieth-century American music. He began composing while in high school, when he also formed a jazz ensemble (in which he played violin and banjo) and played in the school orchestra. After years of writing popular songs (many with the famous lyricist Frank Loesser, none of them a hit), he finally realized that his real gift lay in the composition of orchestral and other concert literature—often flavored, however, with jazz and with the sounds of American folk traditions. Schuman also had strong executive talents, serving as an officer of several organizations: he was, for example, president of Juilliard, first president of Lincoln Center for the Performing Arts, and chairman of the MacDowell Colony.

Schuman's orchestral music is mostly for a large orchestra, featuring distinct blocks—as opposed to delicate lines—of color. His long melodies soar over strong rhythmic foundations, giving much of his music an aura of majesty. Among his compositions based on American tunes, the three-movement *New England Triptych* includes sections on two tunes we have studied: William Billings's "When Jesus Wept" and "Chester" (Listening Example 78).

Listening Example 78

New England Triptych, third movement ("Chester")

In a preface to his score for this three-movement composition from 1956, Schuman claimed to feel a sense of identity with Billings, whose works he said "capture the spirit of sinewy ruggedness, deep religiosity, and patriotic fervor that we associate with the Revolutionary period in American history." Schuman

CD 3
Track 21
2:50

—Continued

Listening Example 78—concluded

New England Triptych, third movement ("Chester")

intended his own composition to fuse the styles of the eighteenth-century composer's music with his own.

Composer   William Schuman (1910–1992).

Genre   Symphonic movement.

Timbre   Orchestra.

Texture   Homophonic.

Form   Rather free, a fantasy based on Billings's famous tune.

Meter   Quadruple.

0:00   The movement begins slowly and quietly (the score is marked "Religioso") as the woodwinds play a relatively straightforward version of "Chester," the flutes carrying the melody.

0:35   The last phrase of the tune, begun by a solo bassoon, is picked up by a bass clarinet and tapers off.

0:49   After a suspenseful pause, brass and strings abruptly introduce a fiery new section (allegro in tempo and percussive in effect).

0:55   The meter changes to duple as the woodwinds play the theme in unison, punctuated by short (staccato) chords in brass and strings.

1:07   Rapid figures swirl throughout the woodwinds.

1:23   The strings begin a rapid new pattern, accompanied by a drone in the bass instruments (tuba, cello, and double bass).

1:35   The horns sound a fragment of the theme, answered by the trombones and tuba.

1:43   Other brasses and woodwinds sound a celebratory fanfare.

1:54   Trumpets take the melody, as snare drums lend a military flavor. A long crescendo leads to the exciting final section.

2:14   Dissonant trombones and horns presage the finale, as all the instruments join in to bring the movement to a rousing, resounding conclusion.

www.mhhe.com/ferrisaml6e

Minimalism

Minimalist art, which strips objects to their elemental geometric shape and makes no attempt to symbolize or represent any real object or experience, often takes the form of sculpture or installations, such as Robert Smithson's *Spiral Jetty* (Figure 23.1). During the 1960s, some composers carried **minimalism** to music, writing simple, restful sonorities that changed very slowly over a drone. Just as visual minimalists restricted colors, values, shapes, lines, and textures, composers used minimal changes in melody, harmony, and rhythm, allowing the structure of a composition simply to evolve as the music quietly continued. (The Online Listening Example *Drumming,* by Steve Reich, is a well-known composition in minimalist style.) Terry Riley is considered to have introduced this musical style, and Philip Glass has been closely associated with it.

Terry Riley (b. 1935) The composer and pianist **Terry Riley** pioneered minimalist music in the mid-1960s, writing music reflective of the rhythmic subtleties of the classical music of India, where Riley studied for a time, and also revealing the improvisatory characteristics of jazz. He experimented with tape loops (varying the synchronization of repeated patterns by altering the length of tape, for example). Then, influenced by his experiences with non-Western music, and by the work of another American composer, La Monte Young, he composed a number of pieces in what has come to be called minimalist style.

Riley's composition *In C* (1964) in a sense reinvented the whole process of listening to music. *In C* consists of fifty-three brief motives, each consisting of tones chosen mostly from the octave beginning on middle C. The number or kind of instruments required to perform the piece is not specified, although usually a piano is included in the ensemble. While someone—usually the pianist—marks a pulse by repeatedly playing two very high C's at the same time, the other musicians each play each of the motives, starting together with the first motive and proceeding to the next motives, in order, as they individually choose. Each musician may repeat a motive any number of times (or not), moving to the next motive when ready, regardless of where the other players are in the piece. Each musician chooses how to phrase each motive, where to put the downbeats, and how long to rest between motives, with the piece ending when all musicians finally reach Motive 53. The sound of the music, which has an almost hypnotic effect, has been described as a highly appealing, continually evolving tonal tapestry; and certainly it constitutes a kind of chance music. (An excellent performance of *In C* [Part I] can be heard on YouTube.)

Terry Riley remains an active, creative musician involved in a vast array of projects around the world, including music for theater and for films. For NASA, he composed *Sun Rings for String Quartet* (2002), incorporating sounds of the planets recorded by the *Voyager* mission on its journey to deep space. His projected scores for 2004 included *The Cusp of Magic* for string quartet and pipa (a Chinese string instrument) and *Melodious Junkyard* for prepared piano.

Philip Glass (b. 1937)

Philip Glass (Figure 23.2) has been among the leading exponents of minimalism. Having studied traditional composition techniques with Nadia Boulanger and others, he developed a strong interest in sonority, leading him to linger on interesting sounds for such long periods that all sense of pulse became obscured. Impressed by the sophisticated rhythms of the music of Africa and India and thinking he might somehow adapt them to

FIGURE 23.2

Philip Glass (b. 1937).

his needs, Glass studied with Ravi Shankar, a famous Indian sitar player, who interpreted various complex and subtle Indian rhythmic techniques in a manner Glass might apply to his own compositions.

From Indian practice, Glass derived a rhythmic system unlike the Western metric system, which divides measured units (see Table 1, p. 2). Glass's is an additive procedure, starting with a simple rhythmic pattern, repeating it for some time, and then altering it very gradually by systematically adding or removing units.

Glass, like so many contemporary musicians, finds affinities with colleagues in the visual arts. For example, he says that the work of certain sculptors, who stripped their art of all superfluous lines to produce figures of extreme simplicity, inspired him to vary the slowly evolving sounds in his minimalist music by occasional abrupt shifts of timbre or harmony.

More interested in the sound than in the form of a piece, Philip Glass often requires performers of his music to have creative as well as interpretive skills beyond those of the usual ensemble player. Therefore, he formed his own Philip Glass Ensemble, consisting of players—for whom some of his music is specifically conceived—who are able and willing to perform in this new and challenging way. The ensemble, which Glass himself directs, consists of two electric organs, four woodwind players who double on several amplified wind instruments, and a female singer who uses her voice as another, wordless "instrument." Glass often leaves the choice of instrumentation of a piece to the ensemble members, so that the sound of a particular composition is actually determined at the time of each performance and may differ considerably from one concert to the next.

Although some listeners consider Glass's music monotonous, it has attracted many enthusiasts who find it soothing, easy to follow, and stimulating in a new, even a spiritual, way. Its cosmic sense of ongoing time addresses an increased interest in various non-Western concepts and techniques, including meditation and an unhurried, relaxed, less organized approach to life. The music is controlled but not intellectual, and its simple, naive effect has been compared to that of popular music. A visit to Glass's website indicates his continuing prolific contribution to American music: For example, in 2002 he wrote the stunning score for the feature film *The Hours;* his ninety-minute work *Orion* premiered as part of Cultural Olympiad 2004 in Greece; and the National Symphony Orchestra commissioned his Symphony No. 7 to celebrate the sixtieth birthday, in 2005, of the conductor Leonard Slatkin. Glass's recent film scores include *Notes on a Scandal* (2006) and in 2007, *No Reservations, Cassandra's Dream,* and the wildlife documentary *Animals in Love.*

Gwyneth Walker (b. 1947)

No longer routinely denied educational and professional opportunities in music, women are earning prestigious reputations on a par with their male colleagues as composers, conductors, and performers. Indeed, a composer's

FIGURE 23.3
Gwyneth Walker (b. 1947).

gender becomes of increasingly, and refreshingly, less significance with every year.

Gwyneth Walker (Figure 23.3), a resident of Vermont, retired from her position on the faculty of Oberlin College Conservatory in 1982 to become a full-time composer and since then has created a large catalogue of works for orchestra, chamber ensembles, choral ensembles, and solo voice. "Maggie and Millie and Molly and May" (Listening Example 79) is the fourth in a set, or *cycle,* of five art songs with words by the American poet e. e. cummings (famous for using no capital letters) and by Gwyneth Walker. (An **art song** is a concert setting of a poem, usually by a well-known poet, to music.) The poems in the cycle include many references to fingers and to the number five; and Walker says she made subconscious decisions to set five songs, use five words in the title, and use quintuplet figures in the music of some songs (not this one).

"Maggie and Millie and Molly and May" (from *Though Love Be a Day*)

CD 3
Track 22
1:10

This song cycle composed in 1979 takes its title from a line in the first song: "Do not fear, though love be a day, we will go a-maying." The lighthearted, lively, and whimsical music is beautifully responsive to e. e. cummings's thought-provoking text. The piano, for example, anticipates, accompanies, or echoes their feelings throughout the piece. Notice, too, the wide leaps in the melodic line—challenging to sing but expressive of the motions of the skipping girls. You will want to read the poem—readily available online by entering the song's title—as you hear the song.

Composer   Gwyneth Walker (b. 1947).

Poet   e. e. cummings (1894–1962).

Genre   Art song.

Timbre   Soprano and piano (Walker wrote the song for a "high voice"—soprano or tenor).

Texture   Homophonic.

Form   Through composed.

Meter   Duple.

A Promise of New Sounds

Compared with music in the first half of the twentieth century, music in recent decades has remained relatively stable. Largely because of prevailing economic conditions, for example, the symphony orchestra has changed relatively little in recent years. Traditional pieces, which make up the bulk of orchestral programming, call for traditional instrumentation; and orchestras struggling to fill seats are reluctant to challenge audiences with the unfamiliar.

In fact, orchestras around the country are trying to make new listeners comfortable by developing programs to help them understand the language of classical music. One concert hall offers electronic devices that allow audience members to read commentary on pieces in "real time," like program notes cued to particular parts of a piece. Another has tried oversize television screens to bring members of the orchestra to the audience in close-up. The New York Philharmonic tried an experimental personal digital assistant (PDA) providing live visuals of the orchestra and descriptive listening guides.

Thus for economic reasons as well as their own personal reasons, contemporary mainstream composers have reached out to audiences with modest, accessible works. Yet it seems inevitable that, to transform themselves into twenty-first-century media, orchestras must come to terms with electronics and amplification, and many mainstream as well as avant-garde composers today are seeking ways to combine electronic and acoustic sounds effectively. To their considerable advantage is the fact that performance standards have improved significantly in the last quarter century, as performers have become familiar with new instruments and with new techniques applied to conventional instruments. And much to the advantage of audiences is the new musical polylingualism, as composers mix the great Western tradition with music of other cultures and times. New timbres and new levels of amplification may well require new performance spaces, suggesting that concertgoing may soon acquire a new character and new dimensions.

Scientific discoveries and the capabilities of recent technology have dramatically altered our perceptions, not just of music, but of the meaning and goals of human life and the role art plays in it. Laws of relativity, for example, replacing comfortably established laws of science and nature, have weakened our sense of stability while expanding the range of our imagination. We have come, in fact, to *expect* the unpredictable, for we know that in life (and certainly in art) things are not always as they seem. But we know that the human experience will continue to be explored and reflected in our visual, literary, and performing arts.

We also know that all the arts will continue to explore and reflect the human experience and the wonders of our changing sensibility, to our lasting benefit and joy.

Terms to Review

minimalism   art song

Key Figures

William Schuman   Philip Glass   Gwyneth Walker
Terry Riley

Critical Thinking

Do you share Charles Ives's scorn for "music that sounds pretty"?

The performance artist Laurie Anderson has said, "Writing about music is like dancing about architecture." How do you interpret her thought?

The art critic for the *New York Times,* Hilton Kramer, said, "The more minimal the art, the more maximum the explanation." What do you think he meant, and do you agree?

Do you imagine that women entering such traditionally male professions as orchestral conductor face obstacles their male colleagues do not experience? If so, what might these obstacles be? How might they be addressed (by women, and by men)? Research the experience of Marin Alsop, appointed Music Director of the Baltimore Symphony Orchestra in 2005.

PART 6
Summary

Like pioneers defying geographic boundaries, some early-twentieth-century Americans extended the horizons of music, breaking ground for succeeding generations of experimentalists by exploring and widening the concept of musical sound. Charles Ives, curious about the properties of sound, equated dissonance with strength and composed in a bold, complex, independent style. Scoffing at the musically timid and encouraging adventurous listening, Ives greatly expanded the sounds and the meaning of music.

By directly manipulating piano strings, Henry Cowell proved that conventional musical instruments could produce new timbres. Cowell, who was among the first Western composers to draw inspiration from cultures to the East rather than from Europe, also extended the range of rhythmic complexity and actively supported New Music. Harry Partch, also interested in Asian music, invented many new instruments of his own.

Both revolutionary and evolutionary modern composers have often shown more interest in rhythm and timbre than in melody and harmony. Those preferring music that is highly organized, such as Milton Babbitt, may use the twelve-tone or total serial technique or render their music "concrete" by electric manipulations recorded on tape. John Cage and other composers of aleatory music moved in the opposite direction, requiring performers not only to interpret their music but also to share in its creation.

Although the mainstream of modern American music remains varied and changing, its new modes of expression are derived from the past. Most of America's first professional composers studied in Paris with Nadia Boulanger. The first of them, Aaron Copland, based some of his early music on jazz and later used other means (folk, religious, and cowboy music, for example) to give his music a nationalistic stamp. Seeking to please his audience during the trying years of the Great Depression, Copland wrote orchestral, vocal, and dance compositions with tuneful melodies and catchy rhythms. Some of his more challenging later works have yet to become part of the familiar American repertoire. Other mainstream composers include Samuel Barber, whose music is melodically lyrical and warmly expressive; William Grant Still, who addresses the experience of black Americans; and William Schuman, whose interest in American folk traditions and in jazz flavors much of his music. Minimalism, of particular interest to Terry Riley and Philip Glass, among others, has disappointed some critics while at the same time attracting new listeners to the concert hall.

Whereas the symphony orchestra has remained relatively stable in recent years, the meaning and concepts of music and art have changed more significantly in the last half century than during the previous 300 years. As the visual arts, dance, literature, and music offer an unprecedented variety of individual and multimedia experiences, we enjoy increasingly ready access to them, thanks to advances in technology and increased opportunity for travel by creators, performers, and audience members alike. More than ever, the arts play a vital role in everyday American life.

The Charge

ou are now well prepared to enjoy all kinds of American music. You know about the music of the Yankee pioneers, conceived for utility but considered art today. You have learned about our vernacular musics— from Stephen Foster's songs and Sousa's marches through ragtime, jazz, rock, and musicals. You have followed the development of American concert music and have seen how Americans became leaders in experimentalism. You understand that American music, rooted like the American experience itself in the cultures of Europe, Africa, Asia, and Latin America, stands now, brave and free, a monument to *our* culture and a source of infinite pleasure and stimulation.

The new and unfamiliar will not intimidate the initiated listener: Of course it is safe to listen to a work long acknowledged as a masterpiece, but it is exhilarating to hear the first performance of a potential masterpiece of our own culture and day. To condemn a piece for having "no melody" may be as absurd as to condemn a doughnut for having no center, a piece by Mozart for having no electronic synthesizer, or an African dance for not being accompanied by a symphony orchestra.

And so, armed with the experience you have gathered through this course, with a sense of adventure, and in a spirit of curiosity and happy expectation, may you venture forth to join the ranks of adventurous, prepared, receptive, creative listeners absorbing the many musics of today. Enjoy!

Glossary

A

a cappella   Unaccompanied choral music.

acoustic   A natural, as opposed to electric, instrument.

alabado   A religious song of praise, belonging to Spanish and Mexican folk traditions.

aleatory music   Sometimes referred to as **chance** or **indeterminate music,** aleatory is music in which the composer has left significant decisions to the performer or to chance. An extreme example is called **random music.**

alternative country   A term encompassing progressive or non-traditional approaches to country music.

alto or contralto   The low female voice.

American Society of Composers, Authors, and Publishers (ASCAP)   Performance right licensing agency formed in 1914 to protect the rights of music creators.

aria   A songlike setting, musically expressive, accompanied by the orchestra.

armonica or glass harmonica   A musical instrument invented by Benjamin Franklin, consisting of tuned, wet glasses that were rubbed to produce sound.

arrangement   In jazz, a written musical score that includes most or all of the notes to be played.

art rock   A blend of rock and symphonic or concert styles.

art song   Concert setting of a poem, usually by a well-known poet, to music.

atonality   With no tonic note or tonal relationships.

augmentation   A rhythmic variation in which note values are doubled, making a theme twice as slow as it was originally.

B

backbeat   Heavy accent on normally weak second and fourth beats of a measure in quadruple meter.

ballad   A folk song, strophic in form, that tells a story.

banjo   A string instrument derived from the African *banjar.*

barbershop style   Unaccompanied (traditionally male) voices singing popular songs in close harmony.

bass   The low male voice.

Bay Psalm Book   The first book printed in America, a psalter that first appeared in 1640.

bebop   A complex, highly improvised jazz style, largely developed by Charlie Parker and Dizzy Gillespie.

big bands   Popular dance ensembles of the 1930s and 1940s, consisting of twelve to eighteen players. The bands had brass, reed, and rhythm sections.

bitonality   Two keys at the same time.

blue notes   Flexible tones derived from African scales.

bluegrass   A commercial instrumental style derived from mountain music.

blues   A black vocal folk music.

bomba   Puerto Rican couple dance derived from Africa.

bones   A folk percussion instrument consisting of a pair of casta-nets tied together and held in one hand.

boogie-woogie or piano blues   A popular piano style with the form and harmony of the blues, but a faster tempo and a dance beat.

book shows   Musicals with an integrated plot.

bossa nova   Brazilian rhythm, slower, more subtle than Cuban dances, reflecting the influence of cool and progressive jazz.

break   A dramatic, unstable, strongly rhythmic section, as in a march.

Broadcast Music, Inc. (BMI)   Performance right licensing agency formed in 1940 to protect the rights of music creators.

broadside   A written ballad, printed on a large sheet or in a set of sheets called a *songster*.

burlesque   A variety show featuring satirical humor; later associated with striptease acts.

C

Cajun music   A country music of the Cajuns (Acadians), vibrant, lighthearted, often with a strong dance beat.

cakewalk   A plantation dance with syncopated melodies, including the *short-LONG-short* figure that became characteristic of ragtime.

call-and-response   A solo voice alternating with a chorus of singers. The effect may be applied to instrumental music as well.

calypso   Caribbean song style with humorously satirical topical texts.

canon   A polyphonic composition in which all of the voices perform the same melody, beginning at different times.

chachacha   A slower version of the mambo, with a double beat added between the last and first beats of each measure.

chamber musical   Musical for a small cast and economical resources.

chamber opera   An opera for a small number of performers.

chamber orchestra   A small orchestra with a few instruments per line of music.

chance music   See **aleatory music.**

changing meters   A different number of beats to the measure within a piece or section.

chantey   Folk song about sailors and the sea.

character piece   A relatively short piano piece, often in ternary form, in a characteristic style or mood.

chord   A meaningful combination of three or more tones.

chordal texture   The texture in which a melodic line is accompanied by chordal harmony. Also called **homophonic texture.**

choreographer   Person who designs the steps and movements of dancers.

chorus   A large ensemble, with several voices on each part.

chromaticism   Use of tones not belonging in a particular major or minor scale.

classical   A restrained, objective style of art. Spelled with a capital letter, refers to music of the eighteenth-century Classical period.

classical ballet   A formal, stylized dance form that evolved in seventeenth-century France.

classical Hollywood film score   Lush orchestral score particularly associated with films of the 1930s, 1940s, and 1950s.

classic blues   Professional, stylized blues, conceived for performance in theater and clubs and on commercial recordings.

clef   A sign placed on the staff that fixes the pitch of each line and space.

coda   Closing section.

collective improvisation   Simultaneous improvisation by some or all members of a combo.

combo   A small jazz ensemble.

compound meter   Each beat in a measure is divided by three.

concept musical   A musical show presenting ideas subject to the audience's interpretation and leaving situations unresolved at the end.

concert band   An instrumental ensemble including brass, woodwind, and percussion instruments.

concertina   A kind of accordion or portable reed instrument. Melody and chords are achieved by depressing buttons or keys, and the wind is supplied by a folding bellows.

concerto   A multimovement (usually three-movement) work for orchestra plus solo instrument or instruments.

conga   Cuban carnival dance-march, performed in a chain, with a heavy kick marking every fourth beat.

conjunto   Ensemble accompanying dance and song in norteño music, north and south of the Mexico-Texas border.

conservatory   A professional music school.

consonance   Musical sounds that seem to be passive or at rest.

contrapuntal   Another term for **polyphonic.**

cool jazz   A style introduced about 1950 for large bands that included some symphonic instruments.

Copland-Sessions concerts   A series of concerts sponsored by Aaron Copland and Roger Sessions from 1928 to 1931 for the purpose of promoting music by American composers.

corrido   Storytelling song (ballad), with roots in Mexico and the southwestern and western United States.

countermelody   A melody performed together with another melody.

country-western   Western music with a country flavor, including western swing, honky-tonk, and cowboy songs.

cover, cover recording   A re-recording by a different performer of a popular record, sometimes intended to appeal to a broader audience than the original recording addressed.

Creole   In nineteenth-century New Orleans, a person born in America of a family native to another country. Later the term was used for people of mixed racial heritage.

crossover   Music that appeals to more than one kind of audience.

cu-bop   Dizzy Gillespie's fusion of Latin rhythms with bebop.

D

diminution   A rhythmic variation in which note values are halved, making a theme twice as fast as it was originally.

disco   Commercial dance music popular in the 1970s.

dissonance   Musical sounds that imply tension, drive, or activity.

Dixieland   A white imitation of New Orleans jazz, introduced in Chicago; faster, more intense than New Orleans jazz.

Dobro   A wood-body guitar with a metal resonator and an aluminum cone for amplification.

dominant   The fifth tone of the major or minor scale, the tone most closely related to tonic. Often represented by the Roman numeral V.

doo-wop   The name given to background vocal ensembles that accompanied Motown singers, often by singing neutral or nonsense syllables.

drone   A single tone, sounded continuously or repeated.

dynamic level   The level of volume (loudness or softness) of a musical sound.

E

eight-to-the-bar   Ostinato that accompanies a boogie. Each of the four counts in a measure is divided into a long and short beat.

electro, nu-wave, house, techno   Machine-like sounds, revived from the 1980s.

electronic synthesizer   An electronic sound generator capable of producing, imitating, and altering sounds.

elements of music   The basic materials of which music is composed.

ensemble   In music theater, a group of solo singers, performing their own words and music at the same time.

experimental music   Music challenging traditional concepts of musical sound.

exposition   The first section of a fugue.

F

falsetto   The singing voice above the normal (full or chest voice) range.

fanfare   A brief, dramatic phrase or piece for brass and perhaps percussion instruments, with the character of an announcement or celebration.

field holler   An emotional vocal phase, sung as a long, loud call, developed by blacks as a kind of communication with fellow workers.

fife and drum corps   An early band, consisting of fifes and drums, which performed for military and later for entertainment purposes.

film score   All the music accompanying a film.

filters   Devices to select out high and low pitches electronically from a wide band of sound to produce a narrow band of melody.

finale   In music theater, the final scene of an act or of the show.

fingerboard   A board on the synthesizer that is uninterrupted by keys or frets, allowing a player to slide through a continuum of pitches.

First New England School   America's first composers. Also known as Yankee pioneers and singing school masters, they lived in New England in the late eighteenth century and wrote music for practical purposes.

folk hymn   Another name for a white spiritual.

folk music   Usually music of unknown origin, transmitted orally and enjoyed by the general population.

folk rock   The addition of light rock effects to urban folk music.

form   The organization or formal design of a musical composition.

forte   Loud.

free jazz   A style of free improvisation introduced by Ornette Coleman in 1960.

fret   A strip of material attached to the fingerboard of a string instrument, allowing players to stop the strings at specific pitches.

fuging tune   A song in two sections, the first homophonic and the second polyphonic in texture.

fugue   A polyphonic composition, originally for keyboard instruments, in which the imitative entrances of the voices alternate between tonic and dominant.

functional or nondiegetic music   Film music heard by the audience only.

funk   Rock music rooted in soul but with lyrics that express interracial concerns.

G

gamelan   An Indonesian percussion ensemble.

genre   Category of music.

Gilbert and Sullivan operettas   Comic English musicals (words by Gilbert, music by Sullivan).

glee   A part-song with three or more lines of music, in chordal or homophonic texture, with the melody usually in the top voice.

glissando   An expressive slide between pitches.

gospel   Folklike religious songs. White gospel includes camp-meeting spirituals; black gospel has had far more influence on popular music.

Grand Ole Opry   The world's longest-running radio show, which continues to present country music's top performers.

grunge   The Seattle sound, a hybrid of pop, heavy metal, and punk.

H

habanera   Cuban dance, whose rhythm is the basis of the tango.

half step   The smallest interval on a keyboard, and the closest interval in traditional Western music.

hard bop   Simple tunes accompanied by repetitive rhythms.

Harlem   A black neighborhood in uptown New York City that became an important center for jazz.

Harlem Renaissance   A cultural movement centering in Harlem in the 1920s in which African American artists in every field achieved high art.

harmony   The meaningful combination of two or more different tones.

heavy metal   Loud, heavily electronic music, often with distorted sound.

heterophony   The simultaneous sounding of two or more different versions of the same melody.

hillbilly music   A term applied to early country music.

hip-hop   African American–based culture derived from Jamaica, developed in the 1970s South Bronx, comprising breakdancing, graffiti writing, DJing, and rap.

homophony   The texture in which a melodic line is accompanied by chordal harmony. Also called **chordal texture.**

honky-tonk   A Texan vocal style with harsh, honest lyrics.

house   Machine-like sounds, revived from the 1980s.

hymn   A religious verse set to music suitable for congregational singing.

I

improvisation   The simultaneous invention and performance of music.

indeterminate music   See **aleatory music.**

interval   The distance between two tones.

iPod   Portable digital audio player.

irregular meters   Meters other than duple, triple, or quadruple (usually five or seven to the bar).

J

jam   To improvise together informally.

jazz   A means of performing music. There are many moods and styles, but improvisation is an inherent characteristic of jazz.

jazz-rock, fusion, or jazz-rock-fusion   Rock instrumentation blended with the improvisation and flexible rhythms of jazz.

K

Kansas City jazz   A light, spacious, relaxed style based on melodic riffs.

key   The name of the tonic upon which a tonal piece is based; also called **tonality.**

L

legato   Smooth, uninterrupted.

libretto   The words of an opera or another dramatic vocal work.

lining out   Practice whereby each line of text is sung by a leader and echoed by the congregation.

M

MacDowell Colony   An artists' colony established on the estate of Edward MacDowell in Peterborough, New Hampshire.

major, minor scales   The tonal scales.

mambo   Afro-Cuban form of big band dance music.

mariachis   Mexican strolling groups of musicians, including strings and often led by one or more trumpets.

melody   A meaningful succession of pitches.

meter The organization of rhythm into patterns of strong and weak beats.

Mickey Mousing Musically mimicking or accenting an action.

microtone Any interval smaller than a half step.

minimalism A style of music based upon many repetitions of simple melodic and rhythmic patterns.

minstrel show An entertainment in which (originally) white men performed music and comedy in imitation of stereotypical African Americans.

modern dance A contemporary American dance form, less stylized than classical ballet.

modes Seven-note scales within the range of an octave, including but not limited to the scale patterns we call major and minor.

modulate To change key systematically, usually by using one or more tones common to each key as pivotal.

monophony The musical texture consisting of one melodic line.

motive A short melodic phrase, subject to development.

Motown A highly successful black company that recorded, published, and sponsored black popular music.

movement A section of a complete work that has its own formal design and a degree of independence but is conceived as a part of the whole; usually separated from other movements by a pause.

multimedia show Performance including some combination of music, dance, film, slides, tape recordings, and other sound and visual techniques.

musical comedy A play with music, in which the elements of entertainment are connected by a plot.

musique concrète or concrete music Music that has been created by manipulating taped sounds. Any sounds may be selected for this purpose.

N

Nashville sound Country music's commercial response to rock and roll, with country themes, pop instrumentation, and cultivated singing voices.

nationalism A nineteenth-century movement in which artists of many nationalities sought to express the particular characteristics of their own cultures.

neoclassicism The preference of some twentieth-century composers for the small performing ensembles, emotional restraint, and formal designs of the Baroque and Classical periods.

neoromantic A twentieth-century composer whose music has nineteenth-century melodic, harmonic, and expressive characteristics.

new age A soft rock style providing soothing, repetitious blocks of gentle, unassuming sounds produced by synthesizers or acoustic folk instruments.

new grass A bluegrass style fusing elements of jazz, rock, and blues.

new music The term used for music of an experimental nature.

New Orleans jazz Virtuosic improvisation by members of a jazz combo on a given melody.

new wave A term encompassing several styles, all conceived within the context of modern studio and electronic techniques.

norteño Texas Mexican-American style of music.

notes The symbols with which music is written down.

nu-wave, electro Machine-like sounds, revived from the 1980s.

O

octave The interval of an eighth.

octave displacement The choice of a note of the same name from a distant octave.

Oklahoma! Landmark musical, by Rodgers and Hammerstein, integrating all elements of entertainment into the drama.

opera A drama that is sung, usually with orchestral accompaniment.

operetta or light opera A form of music theater in which the music and dancing are closely integrated with the plot.

oscillators The means by which pitch is determined on the electronic synthesizer.

ostinato A repeated melodic or rhythmic pattern.

overture In musical theater, an introductory instrumental piece.

P

patter song A feature of Gilbert and Sullivan operettas (and other forms of music theater) in which humorous words are sung very rapidly, with comic effect.

payola The acceptance by disc jockeys of money and gifts in return for plugging recordings.

pentatonic scale A five-note scale within the range of an octave.

piano   Soft. Also, the pianoforte, a keyboard instrument.

piano roll   Perforated paper roll on which pianists recorded their performances.

pitch   The highness or lowness of a sound.

player piano   Instrument for playing piano rolls by pumping pedals, forcing air through the holes in a piano roll as it wound over a tracker bar.

polymeters   Two or more meters performed simultaneously.

polyphony texture   The musical texture in which two or more melodic lines are simultaneously combined.

polyrhythms   Two or more simultaneous rhythmic patterns.

polytonality   Multiple simultaneous keys.

powwow   A contemporary pan-Indian gathering for singing, dancing, rodeo, carnival, and other celebrations.

prepared piano   A grand piano on which some or all of the strings have been "prepared" by placing foreign materials on them to alter pitch, timbre, and dynamic level.

process music   Steve Reich's term for music whose form can be heard to evolve from the repetition of patterns slightly out of synchronization with each other.

program, programmatic music   Instrumental music that describes a story, scene, idea, or event.

progressive jazz   A symphonic approach to jazz, introduced by Stan Kenton.

psalm tunes   Tuneful settings of the psalms in versions suitable for congregational singing.

psalms   One hundred fifty inspirational verses found in the Old Testament of the Bible.

psalter   A collection of the psalms in metered and rhymed verse, suitable for setting to simple tunes.

psychedelic rock   Music that attempts to evoke the sensations experienced by a person under the influence of LSD.

punk   A British reaction to flagrantly commercial rock and roll.

Q

quarter tone   The interval halfway between half steps.

R

race records   The term used before 1949 by the popular music industry for recordings intended for an African American audience. (Later called *rhythm and blues*.)

ragtime   A written piano music, duple in meter and moderate in tempo. The left hand generally marks the beat and the right hand plays a syncopated melody.

random music   See **aleatory music.**

rap   Rapid spoken patter accompanied by funk-style rhythms; derived from reggae performance practices.

recitative   A declamatory setting of a text, with rhythms and inflections related to those of speech. Used in opera and other dramatic vocal works.

reed organ (parlor organ, cabinet organ, cottage organ, melodeon)   A keyboard instrument, popular in the nineteenth-century for its relatively small size and price, the variety of sound produced by adjusting stops, and

the small amount of maintenance it required.

reeds   Wind instruments in which the player causes small, flexible pieces of material called reeds to vibrate. Clarinets and saxophones are single-reed instruments. Oboes and bassoons have double reeds.

refrain   A section of melody and text that recurs at the end of each verse of a strophic song.

reggae   A blend of rock and Afro-Jamaican styles.

rests   Symbols indicating the cessation of musical sound.

revue   Originally, a show with lavish staging and costumes but no integrated plot. Later, a series of scenes united by a theme but without a plot.

rhythm   The arrangement of time in music.

rhythm and blues (R&B)   Broadly, black popular music of the 1950s. More specifically, a black popular style in quadruple meter, with strong backbeats and a danceable tempo.

riff   A repeated melodic or rhythmic pattern that provides unity in a jazz composition.

rock   A collective term encompassing many styles of popular music that evolved from and succeeded rock and roll.

rock and roll   A popular music of the mid-1950s to mid-1960s that combined characteristics of rhythm and blues and country-western music.

rockabilly   A close amalgamation of country music and rock and roll.

romanticism   Emotional, subjective approach to art. So romantic was the period from about 1825 to 1900 it is referred to as the Romantic period of music.

rondo   A musical form in which various episodes alternate with the opening material: **A B A C A.**

round   A circular canon, which may be repeated indefinitely.

row   The term for the arrangement of pitches on which a twelve-tone composition is based.

rubato   Flexible rhythm and tempo. The word means "robbing" and refers to stealing from the tempo at some points and roughly repaying the lost time at others.

rumba   Group of Afro-Cuban musical and dance forms, with many variants.

rural (country) blues   Folklike vocal blues.

S

The Sacred Harp   A popular nineteenth-century collection of hymns and spiritual songs.

salsa   Popular Cuban dance band music with rhythms derived from African American dances.

samba   Most famous Brazilian song-dance; duple meter.

scale   A stepwise rising or ascending pattern of pitches within the range of an octave.

scatting, scat singing   Improvising on nonsense or neutral syllables.

Second New England School The first American composers to write significant works in all of the large concert forms; some-times referred to as the *Boston classicists.*

sequence   The repetition of a melodic figure at different levels of pitch.

shape-note notation   A method that assigns a shape to the notated pitches of *fa, sol, la,* and *mi,*

placing them on the staff in normal position.

shout, ring shout   A lively dance, performed at religious services with shuffling but vigorous steps by dancers in a ring, accompanied by the singing of a religious song.

Show Boat   Landmark musical by Jerome Kern, based on a literary work and addressing sensitive social issues.

simple meter   Each beat in a measure is divided in half.

singing school masters   America's first composers. See **First New England School.**

singing school movement   An effort by music amateurs to teach New Englanders to read music and to sing. The movement began in the early eighteenth century.

slack key guitar   Hawaiian guitar with loosened strings, having a characteristic resonant sound.

sonata   A multimovement form for one or more solo instruments.

song plugger   A music store employee who played popular songs on the piano to demonstrate them for customers.

soprano   The high female voice.

soul   A fervent, emotional black style rooted in gospel and the blues.

sound track   All the dialogue, sound effects, and music of a film.

sound wave   Longitudinal pres-sure waves. As the shape of the sound wave is altered, the timbre of the sound changes.

source or diegetic music   Music heard by characters in a film as well as by the audience.

spiritual   A folklike religious song with a simple tune.

staccato   Short, detached tones.

staff   Five lines and four spaces upon which music is notated.

steel drum, pan   Percussion in-strument made by pounding the bot-tom of an oil drum into a concave shape and hammering grooves for the notes.

steel guitar   Guitar with metal strings, held on the lap, played by sliding a metal bar along the strings with the left hand while plucking the strings with the right hand.

stops   Levers or buttons that allow the player to adjust the tim-bres produced by certain keyboard instruments.

strain   A melodic section in a rag, march, or other vernacular form of music.

stride piano   A jazz piano style in which the left hand alternates low bass notes (on *one* and *three*) with midrange chords (on *two* and *four*).

strophic form   The most common song form. Two or more stanzas are set to the same melody.

style   A characteristic manner of composition or performance.

subdominant   The fourth tone of the major or minor scale, repre-sented as IV.

subject   The principal melodic theme of a fugue.

suite   An instrumental work com-posed of several dances or other semi-independent pieces. A suite from a film includes several sections of music from the film score.

surfing songs   Songs by the Beach Boys and other groups reflecting the easy California lifestyle.

sweet jazz   Music with the sound and flavor of jazz, but arranged so that playing it requires little improvisation.

swing   A term with many meanings, including a mood of lilting spontaneity and a danceable music played by the big bands in the 1930s and 1940s.

symphonic jazz   Concert music that has some of the sounds of jazz.

syncopation   The occurrence of accents in unexpected places.

T

tambourine   A small drum with metal disks that jingle when the instrument is struck or shaken.

tango   Graceful, sensuous Argentinean dance, the first of the Latin rhythms to become popular in the United States.

tape music   Electronically generated sounds that have been recorded on tape and manipulated to create a music composition.

techno   Futuristic electronic music featuring hard, driving sounds and rhythms.

tejano   Music of Mexican Americans born and living in South Texas.

temp   Temporary film score, composed of existing music, offered to demonstrate to a film's composer the type of music desired for the film.

tempo   The rate of speed at which music is performed.

tenor   The high male voice.

texture   The manner in which melodic lines are used.

theater score   Concert pieces that include visual and dramatic elements as well as music.

theme and variations   An instrumental form in which a theme or melody recurs to provide unity, but in altered guises for variety.

theremin   The earliest electronic musical instrument.

third stream   Term coined by Gunther Schuller, referring to the combination, but not the blending, of jazz and classical music. The term is loosely used today to refer to avant-garde jazz styles.

through composed   A song form containing new music throughout, as opposed to setting new text to the repetition of music as in strophic form.

timbre   The characteristic quality of the sound of a voice or instrument.

Tin Pan Alley   The popular music publishing industry from the late nineteenth through the·first half of the twentieth centuries. Also, the neighborhood in New York where the publishing houses were then located.

toasting   A technique developed by Jamaican disc jockeys of rapid patter-talking over the sound of spinning records.

tonality, tonal system   The system of harmony that has governed Western music for nearly four centuries.

tone   A sound with a specific pitch.

tone cluster   A chord, usually of several tones, built upon seconds. Clusters are often played with the flat of the hand, the arm, or a board cut to a particular length.

tonic   The first and most important note of a tonal scale, often indicated by the Roman numeral I.

total serialism, serialization, or serial technique   Application of the twelve-tone technique to other aspects of a composition, which may also be arranged into series and repeated systematically.

traditionalist   A composer who makes no radical departures from the styles and conceptions of earlier music.

transcription   An arrangement of a piece originally composed for a particular instrument or ensemble so that it can be played by a different instrument or combination of instruments.

treble clef (𝄞)   Symbol often used to notate higher pitches.

Treemonisha   An opera by Scott Joplin.

triad   The most basic chord in the tonal system, consisting of three alternate pitches or two superimposed thirds.

trio   A strain that is lighter in texture, softer in dynamic level, and more melodic than the others in a march or rag.

tune   A melody that is easily recognized, memorized, and sung.

twelve-bar blues   The classic form of the blues, consisting of three-line stanzas with four bars or measures in each line.

twelve-tone   A technique of organizing music in which all twelve tones of the octave are of equal significance.

two-step or fox-trot   An American dance derived from ragtime. The meter is duple, the rhythm syncopated, the tempo moderate.

U

ukulele   Small Hawaiian guitar-like instrument with four strings.

unison   The same pitch at the same octave or different octaves.

urban blues   Blues pieces written for publication and professional performance.

urban folk music Socially conscious movement popular in the 1960s, relating country music and mainstream pop.

V

vaudeville A show with various acts including blackface scenes, dogs, circus stunts, songs, and dance.

vernacular The common language. In music, refers to popular music.

verse-chorus form Common song form in which the *verses* relate the story and a tuneful *chorus,* or refrain, is repeated after each verse.

vibrato A slight variation in pitch that adds warmth and intensity to vocal or instrumental sounds.

virtuoso A performer who possesses dazzling technical brilliance.

vocables Neutral syllables, sometimes called consonant-vowel clusters.

W

walkaround A lively plantation song-and-dance routine often forming the finale of a minstrel show.

walking bass A steadily moving pattern in the plucked string bass that has melodic as well as rhythmic implications.

waltz A ballroom dance in triple meter.

western swing The Texas swing band style, influenced by Mexican and Hawaiian sounds and by jazz.

whole step An interval equal to two half steps.

work song Song sung to relieve tension and to regulate the movements of people working alone or in unison with others.

Y

yodel A singing technique that involves changing rapidly back and forth between the normal and falsetto voices.

Z

Ziegfeld Follies Elegant revues produced by Florenz Ziegfeld nearly every year from 1907 to 1932.

zydeco A rock-flavored black Cajun style of country music.

Credits

176: Ray Avery/CTSImages.com;
182: Shooting Star.

Chapter 11
Page 186: Jerry Howard/Stock Boston;
194: Cheryl Higgins/Decisive Moment, Inc.; **198:** Hulton Archive/Getty Images; **200:** Michael Ochs Archives/Getty Images; **203:** Ross Andersen/Getty Images.

Chapter 12
Page 210 (top): Mark Andersen, Getty Images; **210 (bottom):** The Kobal Collection/Picture Desk; **218:** Hulton Archive/Getty Images; **219:** Photo © by Susan Titelma, Courtesy Brazos Films, 10341 San Pablo Ave, El Cerrito, CA 94530. From the film: *Chulas Fronteras;* **220:** Corbis.

Part 4
Page 224: © 2009 Andy Warhol Foundation for the Visual Arts/Artists Rights Society (ARS), New York.

Chapter 13
Page 229: AP Images; **230, 234:** Corbis; **239:** Robyn Beck/AFP/Getty Images; **241:** Hulton Archive/Getty Images; **243 (top):** AP Images; **243 (bottom):** Photograph by Joseph Sia, © wolfgangsvault.com.

Chapter 14
Page 248: Hulton Archive/Getty Images; **250:** Corbis; **251:** AP Images; **255:** Lisa Blumenfeld/Getty Images.

Chapter 15
Page 257: © 2009 The Pollock-Krasner Foundation/Artists Rights Society

(ARS), New York; **258:** Historical Pictures Service/Stock Montage; **260:** Courtesy of Atlantic Records; **263:** Reuters; **267:** AP Images.

Chapter 16
Pages 274, 275: Hulton Archive/Getty Images; **280:** Al Pereira/WireImage/Getty Images; **282:** The McGraw-Hill Companies, Inc./Christopher Kerrigan, photographer; **284:** Corbis.

Part 5
Pages 290, 291: Photofest.

Chapter 17
Page 294: Corbis; **297:** Courtesy of Opera News; **299:** Culver Pictures; **304:** Hulton Archive/Getty Images; **308:** AP Images; **318:** Andrew H. Walker/Getty Images.

Chapter 18
Page 324: Bettmann/Corbis; **326 (top):** Michael Caulfield/WireImage/Getty Images; **326 (bottom):** The Kobal Collection/Picture Desk; **333:** Photofest.

Chapter 19
Page 341: Courtesy of Opera News; **344:** Corbis; **345:** Andrew Popper.

Part 6
Page 352: Courtesy of David Adickes; **354:** © 2009 The Pollock-Krasner Foundation/Artists Rights Society (ARS), New York; **355:** *Untitled,* Gift of the Collectors Committee, © 2009 Board of Trustees, National Gallery of Art, Washington, D.C.

Chapter 20
Page 356: AP Images; **361:** Corbis; **364–365:** Copyright © 1930 by W. A. Quincke & Company, Los Angeles, CA. Copyright renewed 1958 by Henry Cowell. Copyright Assigned 1959 to Associated Music Publishers, Inc. (BMI) International Copyright Secured. All Rights Reserved. Reprinted by Permission; **367:** Steve Kagan/Photo Researchers; **368:** George Holton/Photo Researchers; **370:** John Cage Prepared Piano Courtesy of the John Cage Trust.

Chapter 21
Page 374: Courtesy of Milton Babbitt; **375:** League of American Orchestras; **378, 380:** Corbis; **384:** Hulton Archive/Getty Images.

Chapter 22
Page 388: Mitchell Danlee/Harry Partch Foundation; **390 (top):** Solus-Veer/Corbis; **390 (bottom):** Corbis; **393:** Courtesy of American Society of Composers, Authors & Publishers; **395:** Copyright © 1953 (renewed) Associated Music Publishers, Inc. International Copyright secured. All Rights Reserved. Reprinted by Permission.

Chapter 23
Page 402: Estate of Robert Smithson. Courtesy James Cohan Gallery, New York. Art © Copyright Estate of Robert Smithson/Licensed by VAGA, New York, NY; **403:** AP Images; **405:** Christian Wideawake.

Index

The letter f following a page number denotes a figure. Guides for Online Listening Examples, identified by the letters OLE, may be found at the Online Learning Center.